A PASTOR'S
Sketches

5/24/08

Zach,

Thank you for being my best man and even more than that thank you for being a close friend over the years. May this book encourage and strengthen your faith. Thanks again.

In Christ,

[illegible signature]

A PASTOR'S *Sketches*

Conversations with Anxious Souls Concerning the Way of Salvation

ICHABOD SPENCER

SOLID GROUND CHRISTIAN BOOKS

SOLID GROUND CHRISTIAN BOOKS
PO Box 660132, Vestavia Hills, AL 35266
205-443-0311
solid-ground-books@juno.com
http://www.solid-ground-books.com

A Pastor's Sketches
Ichabod Spencer (1798-1854)

Published by Solid Ground Christian Books

First printing June 2001
Second printing October 2002

New Double-Volume Edition July 2006

ISBN: 1-59925-085-3

Cover design by Borgo Design.

Introduction to Spencer and his Sketches

Solid Ground Christian Books is deeply honored to be able to introduce Dr. Spencer and his remarkable book, *A Pastor's Sketches,* to a new generation. No one living in the northeastern part of the United States in the middle 1800's would have believed that Spencer or his *Sketches* would ever be forgotten. Sadly and tragically this book and its author have been forgotten, and it has not been without consequences. Those who take the time to read this book will immediately recognize the poverty of modern methods of evangelism and pastoral ministry when compared to this man's work. It is with much pleasure that we introduce a servant of God who willingly poured himself out for the sake of immortal souls.

Ichabod Smith Spencer was born in 1798 in Rupert, Vermont. He was unconverted until just after he turned eighteen years old. The previous year his beloved father died. This left him utterly devastated. "It is highly probable that his father's death so deeply felt, and so great a trial, was sanctified to his soul, and overruled to lead his mind and heart, so dark and trembling, to the only *true* 'Rock of hope and support.' It was more than a year, however, after this event occurred, before the grace of God changed his heart, and turned his feet into the way of life."

Spencer was converted in Granville, New York and was educated in the upstate NY region. He became a school teacher, and his fame as a teacher and administrator grew to the place that he was soon in great demand. In fact, in 1830 he was called to be the President of the University of Alabama, and in 1832 the President of Hamilton College of NY. He refused both positions because by this time the Lord had called him to preach to immortal souls. He was called to serve as colleague-pastor of the Congregational Church in Northampton, Massachusetts in 1828. This was the very church made famous by Jonathan Edwards in the 1700's.

Spencer's ministry at Northampton from 1828-1832 was remarkably blessed with genuine conversions. More than 250 in those few years came to Christ under his ministry, and he wore himself out in the work. For health reasons he was forced to resign that demanding and large ministry in 1832. The people of that city and congregation wept and mourned the loss of this precious servant of God, and they never forgot him, nor he them. They always delighted to receive reports of the work to which the Lord called him, and he rejoiced to hear how the hand of the Lord was extended to the brethren in his first parish.

Spencer refused a call to Park Street Church in Boston, MA at this time, the largest and most influential in New England, because of his tender health. Later in 1832 he accepted the call to the Second Presbyterian Church of Brooklyn, NY. This was a church planting effort with no building and about 40 people. He remained at this post the rest of his life, thus spending 22 years at this church. By the time of his death the church had grown to be one of the largest and most influential in all of NY State. His biographer states that he was one of the greatest preachers the American Pulpit produced during that era. At the same time, his greatest gift and legacy was in the pastoral ministry. He was a true shepherd.

Spencer placed upon himself the demand that he would have a home visit for every member of his church every year, which he did for all 22 years. These visits were not for social but spiritual purposes, and were rarely spent in vain. It is said that he averaged over 800 appointments with souls every year for the 25 years of pastoral labor. Perhaps the most remarkable thing is that he recorded each of these in careful fashion and had a dozen huge volumes containing detailed information on each of these visits. His *Pastor's Sketches* contain material drawn from these volumes. The two volumes of *Sketches* contain but 77 specimens taken from over 20,000 available to him. It is no wonder that he came to be referred to as *The Bunyan of Brooklyn.*

He was a man fully committed to the doctrines of grace, and he constantly preached upon the themes of total depravity, sovereign grace, free justification by faith in Christ alone, the certainty of the judgement to come, the greatness of the mercy and love of God. He preached these themes both publicly and from house to house. As great and gifted a preacher as he was, and as effective as his sermons were to awaken sinners, it was his personal ministry that was most mightily blessed by God as he dealt with anxious inquirers.

Spencer would likely have never published this priceless book had it not been for the constant prodding of his ministerial friends and congregation. After many years of such prodding he finally acquiesced and released the first series of *Sketches.* The response was so overwhelming that he soon was pressed to put out a second series, which he did more than two years later, the year before he died. We are told that the first volume "at once received no little attention. It was noticed with universal favor in the religious, and even the secular press. It has already (by 1856) run through many editions; having had a larger sale than almost any other strictly religious book which has ever been issued in this country."

"No one familiar with *A Pastor's Sketches*, wonders at their popularity. They combine the graphic and the pathetic interest of the productions of the best class of novelists, with the instruction of a great mind and of extensive experience on the highest and most solemn of all themes. None but a genius of the first order, a wisdom imbibed at the feet of the Great Teacher, a thorough knowledge of the human heart in its most subtle forms of deception and in all its casuistries and varied developments, and a personal observation of singular scope on this field of labor, could have produced such deeply interesting and life-speaking sketches."

One of the results of the publication of these volumes was the spread of his fame as a healer of souls. Soon he was receiving letters from all over the country from sin-sick souls seeking relief. He answered every one with care. Along with preaching four to five carefully prepared sermons each week, and ministering to his growing congregation, he now had to stretch himself even further. Sadly, within a year his health broke down and he never recovered. He suffered greatly his last months. One of his dearest friends, Gardiner Spring, was with him as he drew near to the grave, and the Lord gave Spencer wonderful peace to the end. He fell asleep in his Lord on Nov. 23, 1854.

The privilege of preaching Dr. Spencer's funeral sermon fell to Gardiner Spring, and he preached a passionate sermon entitled "Triumph in Suffering," from Romans 8:18, *"For I reckon that the sufferings of this present time are not worthy to be compared with the glory which shall be revealed in us."* The large Church was crowded to its utmost capacity, and thousands more stood outside in deep mourning, so universal was the respect felt for his memory, and so great the anxiety to mingle in the melancholy scenes of his burial. An eyewitness described the scene: "My eye has never rested on a more sublime spectacle than was presented by that house of God, clothed in its gloomy drapery, and crowded with that sea of faces; now turned upward to listen to the venerable preacher, as he expatiated on the glories of that land where these is no sickness, nor crying, neither any more pain; and now bowed down to weep when reminded that the body of him who had so long been the light of that sanctuary, was coffined before its altars." It is not often that so many pious tears consecrate the burial-service of the dead. The death of this saint was *precious* not only *in the sight of the Lord,* but in the sight of his whole Church, and of the city in which his light had shone so long and so conspicuously.

This book is not only for pastors or missionaries. In fact, the intention of the author was that it be used for troubled and anxious souls, as well as for ministers of the gospel. It is most appropriate that this introduction conclude with the words of the author taken from his Preface to the second series of *Sketches* which was written in March 1853. It expresses his desire for both volumes: "If this humble volume, by the blessing of God, shall be the means of aiding sinners in the way of salvation, and of any little assistance to the younger ministers of the Gospel, in directing the anxious, and guiding the perplexed, and comforting the broken in heart, the author's hopes will be realized." And also those of this publisher.

SOLID GROUND CHRISTIAN BOOKS
MAY 2001

We are delighted with the reception that has been given to *Pastor's Sketches* all over the world, and we are honored to release a double-volume edition in July 2006. May the Lord continue to use this work to the glory of His name and the good of His people to the end of the age.

Author's Original Preface

This is a book of truth. These Sketches are taken from real life. They are facts, not fancies. They are the experiences of some whom the Author has known in the course of his ministry. He has not given to them an item of coloring. The only thing about them, from which any erroneous impression can possibly arise, is to be found in the fact, that they are *only* sketches, not containing all that could be given, in respect to the individuals here mentioned. But they are believed to contain a fair and sufficiently full representation of each case.

The Author has made this selection from the materials in his possession, on the principle of avoiding useless repetitions as much as possible, and on the principle of meeting some of the strange difficulties, which sometimes trouble inquirers after salvation.

If this humble volume shall fall into the hands of any, who recognize their own portrait among the sketches here drawn; the Author would affectionately suggest to them the propriety of permitting that fact to remain unknown. He solicits this as a special favor to himself; while he assures them, he would deem it an injustice and a breach of confidence, to disclose to other people the particular feelings of individuals, made known to him in the sacredness of religious intimacy. He has been careful not to write anything here, which can injure the feelings of any living person. It must be by the person's own act, not the Author's, if any one of the portraits here sketched is ever known to the public, as that of any particular individual.

The most of the instances here mentioned occurred in revivals of religion; but the Author would be sorry to have it thought, that he has any preference for the piety commencing at such a time, before that which commences at other seasons. He would also be sorry to be at all instrumental in leading any soul to think, that salvation is not as certainly and as easily attainable at any other time, as during a revival, if the soul will as diligently seek it. It would still more grieve him, to do anything towards fostering those spurious excitements, so often *called* revivals, which have done so much to distract the churches and corrupt the religion of this country. He has no fear of any excitements, which divine truth will produce; and he believes, that, if the *truth has* produced them, they will be ready and willing to be *controlled* by the truth, come from what lips it may; and will not, therefore, induce the people to rely upon some particular *men*, "Revival Preachers," as they are sometimes called. He would not undervalue revivals of religion, because abuses have sometimes crept into the churches under that name; nor would he dare to think of choosing the mode, in which the Holy Spirit shall do his own blessed work.

The particular religious experiences of individuals are not guides for other people. They are only illustrations of divine truth, by its application. *The Sacred Scriptures are the only just guide*. Still, religious history and religious biography, though often abused, by an over-trusting, and by a misguided taste, have some distinct advantages, and, fitly used, may be of peculiar benefit. It should be carefully remembered, that such biographies are written for the very reason, that they are supposed to contain something uncommon; and therefore cannot be applicable, as examples, to believers, or inquirers in every case. Nobody would ever think of publishing the religious experience of every believer in a church or city.

But the Author has hoped, that these Sketches might be useful, not on the ground of their marvelousness, so much as on the ground of their applicability, as they refer to common experiences and common difficulties, which have occurred under the ordinary ministration of a very humble individual; and are, therefore, likely to occur again. He has hoped, that they might be instructive, by showing the application of divine truth to human hearts—by leading some anxious inquirers after salvation to see what it is that hinders them from peace with God—and by leading private Christians and young Ministers of the gospel to study more carefully what they shall say to those, who inquire what they shall do to be saved. Twenty years ago, he would have valued a book like this, above all price. And if this, by the divine blessing, shall be of any assistance to young Ministers, on a very delicate and important part of their duty, or of any assistance to inquirers after salvation, its purpose will be accomplished.

Dr. Ichabod S. Spencer
Brooklyn, NY
August, 1850

A PASTOR'S SKETCHES.

First Series.

Contents.

I. THE YOUNG IRISHMAN, ... 11
II. FAITH EVERYTHING, ... 52
III. SIMPLICITY OF FAITH, ... 57
IV. WAITING FOR THE HOLY SPIRIT, ... 66
V. BUSINESS HINDRANCE, ... 67
VI. WAITING FOR CONVICTION, ... 69
VII. NOT DISCOURAGED, ... 78
VIII. RELIANCE ON MAN, ... 81
IX. BAD ADVICE, ... 84
X. THE WHOLE HEART, ... 87
XI. THE WELSH WOMAN AND HER TENANT, ... 89
XII. THE HOLY SPIRIT RESISTED, ... 104
XIII. THE HEART PROMISED, ... 107
XIV. FIXED DESPAIR, ... 110
XV. TOTAL DEPRAVITY, ... 116
XVI. IGNORANCE OF SELF, ... 123
XVII. SUPERFICIAL CONVICTION, ... 125
XVIII. EXCITEMENT, ... 128
XIX. ASHAMED OF CHRIST, ... 131
XX. THE LAST STEP, ... 139
XXI. THE PERSECUTED WIFE, ... 143

XXII. THE ARROW DRIVEN DEEPER, ... 152
XXIII. DIVIDED MIND, ... 155
XXIV. HUMAN RESOLVES, ... 157
XXV. I CAN'T REPENT, ... 158
XXVI. A STRANGE SNARE, ... 167
XXVII. FANATICISM, ... 174
XXVIII. A MOTHER'S PRAYER, ... 176
XXIX. EASY TO BE A CHRISTIAN, ... 180
XXX. PROSELYTING, ... 182
XXXI. THE OBSTINATE GIRL, ... 184
XXXII. CONVICTION RESISTED, ... 192
XXXIII. DETERMINATION, ... 202
XXXIV. THE MISERABLE HEART; OR, DELUSION AND INFIDELITY, ... 206
XXXV. UNCONDITIONAL SUBMISSION, ... 220
XXXVI. THE UNPARDONABLE SIN, ... 225
XXXVII. ELECTION, ... 230
XXXVIII. THE BROWN JUG, ... 256
XXXIX. THE HARVEST PAST; OR, THE DYING UNIVERSALIST, 264
XL. DOCTRINES AND DEATH, ... 278

A PASTOR'S SKETCHES.

I.

The Young Irishman.

ON a very hot day in July, a boy called at my house with a gentleman's card, saying that a lady had sent him to request me to visit a young man, who was sick. Both the lady and the young man were strangers to me. I had never heard of either of them. They resided more than three miles from me, in another city; and, as I understood, the lady was an attendant upon the ministry of another clergyman, who was absent from home. I could not learn from the boy why she should have sent for *me*. I was very much occupied, the day was intensely hot, the place was distant, many other clergymen were more convenient to it; and I felt disposed, for these reasons, to excuse myself from going. As I was considering the matter, the boy, as if reading my thoughts, spoke out earnestly, "She said you *must* come."

I went, though I felt it to be a hardship. Finding the street and the number of the house, by the card which was sent to me, I rang the bell, and inquired for the young man, whose name was on the card. I was shown to his room. He was seated in an easy-chair, with a book in his hand, and appeared somewhat pale and feeble, but not very sick. He rose to receive me. I told him who I was, and that the boy who brought me his card said he was sick, and would be glad to see me. He made no reply, except to offer me his hand and ask me to be seated. We had some general conversation, in which he took the lead. But he said nothing about his sending for me. Aside from his paleness and an occasional cough, I saw nothing in him to indicate the presence of any disease. He told me something of his history. He was a young Irishman, about twenty-six years of age; had been educated in one of the European colleges; had studied law in Ireland; and, designing to enter the legal profession in this country, had been engaged in its studies here about two years. He was a man of dignified appearance, of very handsome address, fluent in conversation, perfectly easy in his manners, and evidently of a vivid mind. He had seen much of the world, and told me he was fond of society. But for the last six months, since his health began to decline, he had been very much secluded, according to the advice of his physician. Said he, "I have been obliged to exchange the society of living men for the society of dead men, and was just amusing myself with reading Tacitus's 'De Moribus Germanorum' when you came in." He manifested no disposition to advert to the subject of my visit. On the contrary, he seemed to avoid it. He so often changed the subject of conversation, when I attempted to introduce it, that I was compelled to ask him plainly if he desired to see me for any particular reason. He was silent for a moment, apparently lost in thought, and then replied,—

"It would certainly *seem* very unpolite in me to say I did *not* wish to see you, since you have taken pains to come so far through the dust and heat; but I think it would be *really* unpolite in me, not to tell you exactly the truth. I have an old aunt, who is a very religious woman; and she has been urging me to send for you, almost ever since I have been secluded here. She thinks I am not to live long, and has talked to me often on the subject of religion. But as she and I could not think alike, she insisted that I ought to converse with some minister of the gospel, and finally became so urgent, that I reluctantly consented. But you will allow me to say, that I should have had no reluctance at all, at all, if I had supposed she was going to lead me to form so agreeable an acquaintance."

"I am happy to know you," said I, "and am glad it was in my power to obey your call."

"It was *she* that *called*," said he. "When I consented to see a clergyman, I left the selection and all the preliminaries entirely to her, and she selected yourself. I told her the selection lay in her line, as she was religious and I was not; and that I should judge of religion very much by the specimen of a minister she sent to me."

I answered, "I must take care, then, how I demean myself, if you are going to rest your opinion of religion on that ground. And I suppose, in equity, you will allow *me* to judge of the science of law in the same manner."

"Ah!" said he, "I shall be obliged to fling in a demurrer on that point. I should be sorry to have you form your opinion of the law by such a specimen of the legal profession as myself."

"Your demurrer certainly cannot avail anything in your favour," said I. "If it can come in at all, it will be easy to turn it against you. For, since religion is a much higher matter than law, it is not to be demanded that a *man* should be as good a representative of it, as a man should be of law; and if you demur to my forming an opinion of law by the impression I have about one of its disciples, *much more* may I demur to your forming an opinion of religion on that ground."

"Well, indeed," said he, "I cannot respond to that. You have floored me the first onset. But are you not a lawyer? Your pleading indicates as much."

"Not at all. I am only a very ordinary minister. But since your aunt has done me the honour to send for me, I should be happy to form her acquaintance. Does she reside here?"

"No. She lives a little distance off. I must tell you, she is very retiring, and lives very much secluded, though she spends much of her time with me; and I doubt whether she will allow you to see her at all. She is not so young as she used to be. She has been a beautiful woman—an elegant woman; and I tell her that her *pride* keeps her away from society now, because she is not so handsome as she was once. But she seems to think that idea a reflection upon her religion; and wonders that I can think of such a thing, and cannot have sense and sobriety enough to rise above such trifling thoughts."

"Wherein do she and you differ on the subject of religion?"

"Really, sir, I can scarcely answer that question. We *never* differ, only in a friendly way. But though she is a woman of very fine mind, in my opinion, yet her notions are too rigid for me."

"Perhaps she has examined the subject of religion more than you have."

"I have no doubt," said he, "that she has spent more *time* over it. But *my* mind is not so formed as to take things upon *trust*. I want *knowledge*. I am not prepared to yield to assumption and dogmatism."

"I am very glad to hear you say that," said I; "but perhaps you and I should not agree, in respect to your aunt's yielding to assumption and dogmatism. We are not accustomed to do that in religion. I venture to affirm that your aunt is not guilty of it. And I do this, because *I know*, that we who espouse the cause of religion are not credulous, assuming, or dogmatic; and on the contrary, the rejecters of religion are themselves the *most* credulous, assuming, and dogmatic people amongst us."

"Well, indeed," said he; "you have fairly flung down the gauntlet to me."

"Not at all. *You* flung it down at the name of your aunt; and I, as her champion, take it up. I am prepared for the contest, the very moment you will name any definite matter of disagreement betwixt yourself and her."

"I must give you the credit for no small gallantry," said he.

"Your chivalry is of high bearing indeed, if you will so readily espouse the part of a lady entirely a stranger to you, and are prepared to defend her opinions, when you do not even know them."

"I risk nothing, however," said I. "And I am prepared to contest the point you named, or any other point. You mentioned her taking things upon trust—her yielding to dogmatism and assumption."

"Yes, I did. But I did not mean her in particular. I meant religionists in general."

"So I supposed. And I now ask you what it is that we take upon trust, or assume, or wherein we dogmatize, any more than you lawyers dogmatize."

"Well, to tell you the truth, I had reference to what my aunt is constantly saying about God. She seems to me to assume his existence, and character, and government over us. I tell her that *I want knowledge.*"

"Very well," said I; "that is a definite point. Let us get it fixed clearly in mind, and then bring it before the bar of our reason. The question is this: Is the existence, is the character, is the government of God *known* to us? are these things matters of *knowledge?* I affirm, in your aunt's behalf, they are. You deny it."

"Right," said he. "That is the question. And as you are the plaintiff you must open the case. Yours is the affirmative. Bring on your witnesses. I have only to deny, and to show that your proofs are insufficient."

"Very well," said I; "we are agreed so far. I commence the argument. The matter before us regards *knowledge.* I have, therefore, a preliminary question to settle first; and I think it may be settled amicably betwixt us, without any debate. I now put the question to you, *What is knowledge?*"

"You have taken me by surprise," said he, a little confused and hesitating.

"Certainly," said I, "the question is a fair one; and it belongs to *you* to answer it. It is *you* who complain of your aunt, that she has not *knowledge* on a particular subject, to which she urges you to attend. We are to examine the question; and, therefore, we ought to know what we are talking about, so as to understand one another. You say you 'want knowledge;' and I ask, what do you mean by knowledge? I only give you a fair opportunity to explain your own word."

"Why, sir," said he with a forced smile, "I venture to say, that you and I employ that very common word in the same sense."

"I beg pardon," said I. "In our profession we do not allow any *assumptions;* we take nothing *upon trust;* we never *dogmatize.*"

He laughed quite heartily at this; and replied, "I believe I have been away from court too long. My wit is not keen enough for this contest just now. You have floored me again."

"Oh," said I, "your wit is not at fault, but your *assumption*, your taking things *upon trust*, your *dogmatism.*"

"Well," said he, "since I own upon this point, you will do me the favour to answer the question yourself. I will assent to the answer, if I can without injuring my cause.

"Most willingly," said I. "But this is a serious and momentous subject. It is the *most* momentous of anything on this side of death. Let us, then, deal with it in a careful and candid manner."

"I will," said he, "most certainly."

Said I, "Knowledge is founded on certainty. Something must be certain, or it cannot be known. Knowledge is the cognizance which the mind has of realities, of facts, of some certainty or truth. It exists in the mind. The realities may exist outside of the mind, or inside of it. But they exist *first;* and when the mind makes an ascertainment of them, it gains *knowledge.* That ascertainment is made by what we call proofs or evidences. And these evidences will vary as the subjects of knowledge or the certainties vary. There is one sort of proofs for mathematical knowledge, and another sort for legal knowledge, and another for historic knowledge; but each is good in its place, and sufficient. You would not expect me to prove a truth in morals or history by mathematical demonstration; or a truth about the soul by the evidences of eyes which cannot see it; or a truth about the invisible God by the authority of a law-book, such as Blackstone, or Starkie, or Vattel. But whatever evidences or proofs do, fitly, justly, convince a reasonable understanding, furnish that understanding with knowledge; because they enable it to ascertain a reality, a certainty, so that the conviction of the mind accords with the fact. That is what I call knowledge. Do you assent to the explanation?"

He replied, "I have no fault to find with it. And if the whole of religion were as clear and certain as that, I should not reject it."

"The whole of it *is* as clear and certain as that, whatever you may think about it."

"But," said he, "how do you apply your explanation to the existence of God? What are the evidences of his existence?"

"There are numerous evidences, sir, and fit ones. Your own existence is one of them, and not a minor one. You are an effect. There is a cause somewhere, adequate to the production of such an effect. That cause, whatever it be, is God. You did not make yourself. Your parents, your ancestors, however far back you trace them, were not self-created. Your own mind assigns a cause somewhere, an original cause, and that cause is God. And you are just as certain that there is such a God, as you are that you are yourself an effect. You *know* it just as well,—not in the same way, but yet just as certainly. And you know you are an effect of an intelligent cause. Your common sense will not allow you to believe that you and all your ancestors sprang from accident, from chance. You do not find chance operating in such a way. You do not fling dust in the air, and find it come down a man or a monkey. If you should find anywhere a machine, a living or dead one, which had in it a tenth part as many manifestations of intention, and power, and skill, as your own mortal body, you could not avoid believing that some mind had contrived it, and some power beyond itself had brought it into existence. You would know it as well as you know anything. The perfect proof is before you. And your own living body and thinking mind are perfect proofs of the existence, power, and wisdom of God. There is no assumption or dogmatism in this. It is only cool and certain reasoning, which conducts to an inevitable conclusion, and the conclusion is knowledge.

"On the same principle, the whole universe and its living inhabitants, rational and irrational,—its suns and comets, its whales and butterflies, its motes and mountains,—are proofs of the existence and power of God. And every change, every motion in the universe is an evidence which speaks for him. Our reason tells us they are not uncaused. The cause is God."

To all this the young man listened with the most fixed attention. He seemed to drink in every word. I thought his attention had fatigued him; but he said, Not at all, he loved to think. "But," said he, "you have led me into a new world of thinking. Your positions are very bold; and before I come to any conclusion, I must review the matter in my own mind."

"Shall I call on you to-morrow?" said I.

He answered, "I can scarcely ask it or expect it of you; but if it is not too much trouble, I should like to see you again. You need not be afraid of wearying me. I can study or talk all day."

The next day I called again. He appeared glad to see me, and immediately began to speak of our interview the day before. Said he, "Your bold position yesterday startled me. I have been thinking of your argument ever since. I cannot overthrow it. That idea about a change or a motion being an effect, and the human mind assigning a cause to it, and our having knowledge on that ground, was new to me. But I find much that men call knowledge rests precisely on that ground. And yet, I am not fully satisfied. I have been accustomed to think that the existence of God was at least doubtful, that the proofs of it were very obscure, and when you brought up my own existence as a proof, it startled me. I have often said to my aunt, that we know very little about spirit,—that we can understand matter, but spirit lies very much beyond our knowledge; it is all a mystery to us. And now, though I dare not assail your position or your arguments, still, it does seem to me that I have a degree of knowledge and certainty about *bodies* that I cannot have about *spirit;* and I should like to hear what you can say on that point.

"I say that it is a mere impression," said I; "a common one, indeed, but an erroneous one. There may be some faint apology for it. The most, if not all, of our primary ideas reach our mind through the inlet of the senses; and therefore, when such an idea as that of spirit is presented to us,—spirit, a thing which we cannot see, cannot hear, cannot touch, cannot bring within the immediate cognizance of any of our bodily senses,—the idea appears to lie beyond the grasp of the mind, hung round with a deep, and misty, and mysterious obscurity. If eyes could see it, or hands could handle it, men would have none of this seeming uncertainty and doubt. But since they cannot, and since the idea of spirit must come to them through some other channel,—for example, by comparison, by reasoning, by tracing effect to cause, or some such device,—the whole doctrine of spirit assumes to them a kind of dim and misty significance, too much like an airy fancy or unsubstantial dream. That is just the state of your mind at the present moment. The seeming uncertainty is not a real uncertainty, it is only an impression; and that is the reason why you dare not assail my argument of yesterday. Your *reason* perceives its truth, but your impression and your prejudice are against it.

"And since I am on this point now, I will pursue it, if you please, a little further. From the necessity of our nature, while here in the body, the most of us are more conversant with sensible objects than spiritual ones. We employ, from morning till night, our sensitive organism in our ordinary occupation. We gain most of our knowledge itself in that mode; and hence, when we turn to ideas of immateriality, we come into a new field, where we are almost strangers, and cannot, therefore, feel as if we were among the familiar and well-known realities and certainties of home."

He replied to this, "Do you mean to affirm, then, that human knowledge in respect to spirit is as clear and certain as in respect to material things?"

"Certainly, sir; I mean to affirm just that; and I maintain, that the idea of the imperfection of our knowledge about spirit is all a mere impression and mere prejudice. The mind has taken an untenable position, and has espoused a falsehood, when men declare, 'We know little about spirit; we can understand what matter is, but spirit is beyond our comprehension.'"

"Have you been talking with my aunt?" says he.

"No, sir; I have not seen her; though I should like to, very much."

"I thought you had," says he; "for I have made that affirmation, which you just condemned, to her a thousand times; and I thought she had told you."

"I cannot help it," said I. "My position is taken, and I cannot retract. Unless you will retract your affirmation, I shall be compelled to show its falsity."

"I am not prepared to retract it at all," said he; "and if you have boldness enough to attempt to show its falsity, I am sure you do not lack courage; and if I am not asking too much of you, I assure you I should be greatly pleased to hear what you have to say."

"Well, then," said I, "we are at issue, and I have much to say,—perhaps more than you have strength to hear."

Said he, "I am not wearied at all. You need have no fear. I told you I love to think, and you delight me by setting me to thinking."

"Then," said I, "I will enter upon the matter. And, in the outset, I admit that our knowledge about matter comes in such a *mode*, that that knowledge has a vividness, and often an impressiveness, which belongs to no knowledge gained in another way. We have a sensible organism, which brings us into contact with matter. Our nerves are affected by it. And through that machinery, sensitive as it is inexplicable, we have impressions as well as knowledge, and have an instant certainty, which requires no slow and cool processes of reflection, or examination of evidences. We see the sun; and that is enough: the moment we have the sight we have the knowledge. We hear the thunder; and that is enough: the moment we hear, that moment we have the knowledge. We need not any other examination.

"Now, this sensitive machinery, and the instant rapidity and suddenness with which it acts, give to the knowledge which we gain in this way a vividness, an impressiveness, and force. But is not that all? Have we any greater certainty about things seen, and things heard, and things handled, than we have about things reasoned and demonstrated? How is this? Can we trust the mechanism of our nerves any better than we can trust the multiplication table, or the mathematical processes of astronomy and the counting-house,—any easier than we can trust the deep philosophy of law? Indeed, is it not *more* probable, that some derangement should come in among the mechanism of the senses, and make us see wrong, or hear wrong, or taste wrong, than that the sure processes of mathematical calculation should deceive us? In our knowledge derived through the senses, we can employ only our own processes; nobody else can use our nerves of sight, or hearing, or taste. But in our knowledge derived through mathematics, and in some other modes, we employ the same processes which others have employed before us, and are employing all around us; and we can, therefore, fortify our own conclusions by theirs, and substantiate our certainty in knowledge, if need be, by a comparison of calculations. *Their* processes, by which they obtained their knowledge, their certainty, we can make *our* processes; but we cannot use another man's eyes or ears, or the nervous mechanism by which they act. All we can do, is to take the testimony of the men who do use them; and then our knowledge rests only on testimony, not on the senses. And because we are confined to our own machinery of sense, and cannot employ another man's machine, we have *not*, herein, one of the advantages for certainty which attend knowledge in mathematics, and all other matters of reasoning. We can employ for our assurance another man's reasoning powers, but his eyes are his own, and we cannot use them. We can add the *testimony* of one man to that of another man, and then add another, and make them all auxiliary to our own, for heightening our assurance and certainty in knowledge; but we can do nothing of this in the knowledge derived from the senses—we cannot borrow another man's nerves. And it follows from all this surely, that, instead of there being *more* ground of certainty in knowledge derived directly through the senses, there is *less* certainty than in knowledge that comes in some other modes."

"Why," said he, interrupting me, "you do not intend to say that our knowledge is *doubtful*, when we see and hear?"

"Not exactly that," said I. "But I am comparing different grounds of knowledge. And I admit, that sensible knowledge is the more *impressive*, by reason, first, of its nervous machinery, and, second, of its instant suddenness. It comes to the mind at once. It makes its impression at a dash. We have no time to get cool, or keep cool, as we have in the slower business of reasoning out our knowledge. But if this superior impressiveness is not all—if it is thought that there is really any superior *certainty* attending what is known by the senses, let any man attempt to tell what that certainty is, or where it lies. He cannot tell. He can tell nothing about it. Indeed, he can *conceive* nothing about it. The thing defies conjecture. I can tell why I believe my eyes sooner than I believe the testimony of an unknown witness before me. I have known men testify falsely, oftener than I have known my eyes testify falsely; and, therefore, I have the more certainty about my eyes. And I would *not* have the more certainty, if I could not tell why. And if my neighbour cannot tell why his knowledge derived through the senses has more *certainty* about it than knowledge coming in some other way, though he believes it has, then I must beg leave to think him a very imperfect man;

and though I might trust his eyes, I would not trust his powers of reasoning. The truth is, it is a mere prejudice, when men think that they can know by the senses any more certainly than in other ways. There is a vividness and impressiveness in knowledge gained through the senses, and this freshness and strength are mistaken for an additional degree of certainty. The idea, then, so common among men, that the senses are the surest means of *certainty*, is all false. We can be equally certain on other grounds. It is not true, that while we have clear knowledge of matter, we have only doubtful knowledge of spirit, because spirit does not come within the cognizance of the senses. That notion has just mistaken vividness of impression for strength of proof; and '*assumes*' what is not true, that other kinds of evidence are not equal to the evidence of the senses—that we cannot *know*, because we have not seen."

"Why," said he, "if my aunt were here now she would rejoice over me. I have silenced her many a time by saying to her, 'If I could *see* God I would believe in him.'"

"You are not alone in that," I answered. "Many have said it. But if it means anything, it is only a miserable *assumption*, a pitiful *dogmatism*. It *assumes* that there is a just suspicion resting upon all evidence, except that of sense. It assumes too much. How far does this doubt about spirit intend to go? what is precisely its ground? If its ground is at all definable it is this, namely, that a degree of uncertainty attaches to all matters not evinced to us by our own senses. This is implied in the very language which men employ. They say, 'If my eyes could see it, if my hands could handle it, I should know. But I cannot see or touch spirit.' Well, now, if we can *know* nothing but sensible objects, our knowledge will be extremely limited. Does this man *know* that he has got a soul? He never saw it—he never handled it—he cannot taste it. Does he know that he has reason, or the power of reasoning, or any mind at all? He cannot *see* his mind, or touch it. How, then, on his own principles, can he certainly know that he has got any? Where will his doubting end? He is bound to doubt whether he has a soul,—whether he has an imagination, a memory, a faculty of reason. Indeed, he is bound to doubt whether he has the power of doubting; because he never saw it, or touched it, tasted it, or heard it speak. So that his principle of doubting about spirit, if he will only be self-consistent, will cut him off from all that he calls certain knowledge, except merely on the field of matter, and indeed that *part* of the field which lies within the reach of his fingers, his ears, or his eyes. On his own principles, he cannot certainly know anything more. Just in this absurdity lies every man who exclaims, 'We cannot know much about spirit; we are certain about matter, because our senses can reach it.'"

My young friend appeared to be surprised. Said he, "You seem to be fond of turning the tables upon me. You make out that the sin of assumption is more mine than my aunt's."

"So it is," said I.

"Well," said he, very thoughtfully and gravely, "I believe it is, after all. I think I shall have to go to her to confession."

"I hope you will confess to God also," said I; "for your sin of assumption was more odious to him than to her.

"But I have not done with the charge. There is another item in this count. There is another false assumption in the notion which I am combating. Your notion is, that we can have a certainty of knowledge about matter, such as we cannot have about spirit, because our senses furnish evidence of matter, but not of spirit. This is a mere assumption, and a falsehood. Have you *no sensible evidences* of spirit? When you move your tongue and utter your arguments, are not the motion and the arguments any evidences of an unseen mind? They are *sensible evidences* of something to me, for I see the motion and I hear the arguments. And will you tell me that the *matter* of the tongue, the mere material of it, moves of its own accord, and weaves the arguments by its own power? If not, then the motion I see and the arguments I hear are sensible evidences of the existence of an unseen spirit, which prompts the motion and weaves the arguments. Though my senses do not *directly* reach the spirit itself, yet they do reach the effects of that spirit (the motion of the tongue and the audible arguments), which come from the unseen mind. And thus my very senses do furnish me with an evidence of the existence of that mind, as clear and certain as if my eyes could behold it. They do behold the effects of it, the traces of it, the signals of it, as clearly as they behold anything. The signals, the traces, the effects, cannot come from any other quarter. They must come from mind. A reasonable argument must be a production of reason. And just as certainly as I hear it coming from human lips, just so certainly I have the evidence of two of my senses that a mind exists somewhere—a spirit which has moved the lips and contrived the argument. It is, therefore, an *assumption* and a falsehood when one says he has no sensible evidences of spirit, and hence cannot know much about it."

The attention of my Irish friend was intently fixed on every word I had uttered. And when I paused, he remained silent for some minutes. At length he said to me,—

"You have convinced me of one thing, at least. I perceive that I have often taken false ground. And yet, though I am not prepared to controvert your position, and it seems to me that your argument is unassailable, still, the manner in which you reason from effect to cause may have some error in it. At least, it is so new to me, that I am at a loss, though it all seems perfectly clear. Are we certain, after all, about causes and effects?"

"Yes; just as certain as we are of anything. There may be unfathomable mysteries somewhere in the subject, just as there are in every other subject; but I have had nothing to do with *them.* I have only employed the plain principle of common sense —that effects, changes, motions, must have some cause. Did your question mean to inquire whether that principle is certain?"

He sat in silence for a long time. I did not think it best to interfere with his thoughts. I took up one of his books, and retired to the window, to await the result of his cogitations. He paced the floor, back and forth, for a full half hour, manifestly in profound meditation. Finally, stopping before me, he said,—

"What *is* a cause?"

"That which produces the effect," said I; "an antecedent, without which the effect would not exist."

"Is it *certain*," said he, "that there is a fixed connection betwixt the two?"

"Yes; *you* are certain of it, or you would not ask that question, or any other. You speak to me to produce an effect; and speaking, you know you are the *designing* cause. You employ this principle in every action of your life. You *cannot* act without it. You never did, and you never will. You cannot utter a word or make a motion on any other principle if you try."

He made another long pause; and as he walked the room I went on reading my book. But finally, I laid aside the book, and took my hat to depart, saying to him that I would not have made my visit so long, if his residence had been more convenient for me to reach.

"I *must* see you again," said he. "Can you give your company an hour or two to-morrow?"

"Not to-morrow," said I; "but I will see you the next day, if you please.

"Well, now, do not disappoint me," said he. "I am sorry to trouble you, and I feel more grateful to you than I can express; but I cannot rest our subject here, and I am afraid I could not manage it alone. I have been a sceptic on religion for eight years; and if left alone, I am afraid my old sceptical notions would return upon me."

As I called upon him two days after, he immediately told me that there were two points which he wanted cleared up. He had been studying the subject ever since I left him, and acknowledged that his mind was convinced as far as I had gone. He "believed all my positions were impregnable."

"But," said he, "your affair of cause and effect, which you

brought to bear upon me like a battery—wherein does the efficient *power* of the *cause* lie?"

"In the will that wields it, sir."

"What! in *the will?*"

"Yes, sir, just in the will."

"I am confounded! What will come next?"

"Your own conviction of truth, sir, will come very soon, and the entire abandonment of your sceptical infidelity."

"*I believe it,*" said he, very solemnly. "But you surprise me by saying that power lies in will."

"Just in will, sir," said I; "nowhere else. This presides over the whole field of causes and effects. It belongs to the very nature of the human mind to attribute *any change* which we behold to *something.* That something we denominate the cause. It may not be itself the cause, only instrumentally, unless it is the will; and when it is *not* the will, then we must trace our way back through the instruments, till we reach the real seat of power; and we shall always find that to be the will. My motions, my speech, my walking, are changes, and no sane man supposes them to be *un*caused. Everybody supposes them, knows them, to proceed from some cause adequate to the production of the changes. This is common sense, and on this principle every language on earth is formed. The principle is interwoven with the structure of the Greek, the Latin, the French, the Chinese, with every tongue. No man's mind rejects this principle. If anybody thinks changes to be uncaused, he is a madman or a fool. Common sense always knows that changes are the *effects* of some *cause* which holds power over them. That cause, in respect to my motions, is my spirit. My motions are *an effect;* my spirit is the cause. The cause of all the changes in the universe is God. All these changes are effects coming from something, and that something, whatever it be, is God. He is the great *first* Cause of all things. But he has delegated to me a little power, for a time, over a few particles of matter, which I call my body; and by the exercise of that power I can move. My agency is only a subordinate agency, limited, and not lasting. It may last till I die, but no longer; and then I must account for my stewardship. It extends only to my own flesh. I cannot make a stone or a clod of earth move, by my willing it, as I can move my material frame. And, dependent creature that I am, I cannot move my material frame, except by the mysterious power of my spirit which *wills* it—a power not my own, in the sense of independency, but only in the sense of subordination. But in this subordinate sense, *I* am the cause of my own actions, and accountable for them—sometimes to men, and always to God.

"Now, just on this ground of common sense, my motions are all evidences of the existence of my spirit, which has power over them; and the great motions of the universe are all evidences of an unseen Spirit, which has power over them. That unseen Spirit is God. These changes of the universe are visible. Our senses take note of them; and therefore our senses, though they cannot directly reach the Divine Being, *can* reach, and reach *everywhere*, those changes which are his effects, and demonstrations of his existence and mighty power. This argument is rock. There is no getting away from it. These changes of the universe *are* effects, by the common consent of all mankind. Being so, they must have a cause; they demonstrate the existence of a cause. And whatever that cause be, it is God. Our senses come in contact with the effects. And now, who shall maintain that we have not as good evidences about God as if our eyes could behold him? It may be less sudden, less startling, and hence less impressive evidence; but is it not as good? May I not be as *certain* as if I saw him? Do not I *know* that a cause of visible changes is operating, just as well as I know the effects which I behold? If there is any uncertainty about my knowledge of God in this way of knowing, let any man attempt to tell where it lies. He cannot tell. The changes? My eyes see them. I therefore know them by evidences of sense. They are effects. I know this by my common sense, and the common sense of every man around me. And the *cause* of these effects you must either allow to be the Deity, or you must maintain that dumb matter, mere dirt and rock, has reason, and will, and power of motion of its own. And coming in contact with these effects constantly, as I do, I certainly am unable to perceive why I do not positively know there is a God, as well as I know there is a sun that moves or a drop of rain that falls. My knowledge may not be impressive and startling; but is it not real, certain, founded on good and legitimate evidences?

"And now, what *is* power? or, where does it lie? or, what wields it? Where is its seat—its home? Where *does* power originate? There is something which men call power—something which is capable of effecting some change; and the question you put to me is, What is it? or, Where is the seat of it? And the answer is, *Power lies in the spirit—not in matter, but in spirit.* The power by which all changes in matter are effected, resides immediately in spirit, in mind. The power by which I move a muscle does not belong to the muscle itself. The muscle is only an instrument which obeys that act of my spirit, which I call my *will.* My will is that mysterious thing with which my Maker has invested me, and by which I can move. The will is the power. We cannot move a single atom of matter in the universe without it. It has a *direct* power over our bodies in health, and till we die; and an indirect power over a little other matter. Acting indirectly, our will can bring our bodies, or some portion of our material frame, into contact with other matter; and thus we can effect some changes in that other. The stones we lift, the mountains we level, the ships we build, are all lifted, and levelled, and built, by the power of our will. Power resides nowhere but in spirit. You speak of the mechanical powers, and I am not going to find fault with your language. But let not the imperfection of language mislead your understanding,—as it certainly does, if you suppose these mechanical powers have an item of power of their own. They have none. The power exists only in your will. You use them. You bring your hands, or feet, or some other portion of your body into contact with some other matter, the lever, the screw, the pulley; and thus you *willingly* employ these contrivances to do what you could not do without them. But the lever, the screw, the wedge, the pulley, have not an item of power in themselves. Nobody ever saw them doing anything alone. It is will, it is spirit, which employs them. The will first formed the contrivances themselves; and could not form them so as to invest them with power to work alone. And the will, in every instance of their operation since they are formed, must come along with its continued power, or they will do nothing,—*can* do nothing. They have no power, because they have no will. You have, then, this great universal lesson, *Power resides only in mind: all power exists in spirit, and in spirit only.*

"God's will is his power. He employs his power directly or indirectly, as he pleases. He can use instruments, or do without them. He has no need of them, as you have. The direct power of your own spirit is limited—it is limited, as I said, to the few particles of matter which make up your mortal body; and if you would move or change anything beyond that, you must contrive some mode to bring your material body into contact or some connection with it. But God, the unseen, eternal Spirit, is able to bring the power of his will to bear directly upon all things,—*as* directly as the power of your will bears upon the body it moves. He has only to will it, and any conceivable change will instantly take place. The power all lies in the Infinite Spirit. God is spirit. His will is the effect. Nothing intervenes between his volition and the change which follows it, to give any power to the volition itself. The mere volition is all his power. Awful God! Tremendous Deity! On his simple volition hangs this mighty universe of being! Earth, heaven, hell depend upon it! If he should will it, there would not be an angel in heaven, or a devil in hell! existence would cease! this universe would become a blank! and nothing would *be*, except 'that high and lofty One, who inhabiteth eternity!' Oh! who would not have this God for his friend? Oh! who could endure to have him his enemy?

Enemy? sooner come annihilation! Let me perish — let my spirit die—let all these thinking faculties, my soul, go out in eternal night, sooner than have this awful God against me! It need not be. That God who 'spake and it was done,' who 'commanded and it stood fast,' who said, 'Let there be light,' and there was light,—this God is love. I hear a voice coming from resurrection lips, 'All power in heaven and earth is given unto me; go ye into all the world, and preach the gospel to every creature, and, lo, I am with you alway, even unto the end of the world. He that believeth shall be saved—though he were dead, yet he shall live again.' Blessed words! blessed Saviour! Open your heart, sir, to this message. Take this offer. Poor sinner as you are—weak mortal—being of a day, and soon to lie in the dust,—cast your immortal soul upon the power of this Christ, to save you from eternal death, and give you life evermore!"

As I uttered this exhortation with all the force I could give to it, my young friend sunk back upon his chair with his eyes fixed immovably upon me, and held his breath in a sort of agony of attention. He turned more pale than I had ever seen him. And when I stopped, he drew a long breath, his eyelids dropped over his eyeballs, and he looked like a corpse.

"I beg your pardon," said I. "I have talked too long. I have wearied your strength."

"Not at all," said he; "but you have conquered me. I see I have been wrong. But I must think of this more."

I replied, "I hope you will. And I will see you again in a few days."

As he had not fixed any time for another visit, and as I wished to leave him some time for reflection, I did not call on him again for two days. As I then entered his room, he said to me,

"I am glad to see you. And I am glad you have come so early in the morning. You will be able to make me a long visit, I hope. I should have sent for you, but I know I am taking up too much of your time."

"Oh, no; not at all," said I. "But have you not gained the victory over your doubts?"

"Partly. I will tell you how it is with me. You recollect I told you about my difficulty. I thought that nothing about spirit was really certain as we are certain about material things. And still, some of the same difficulty occurs to me, and often tempts me and troubles me, though I believe all you have said about God's existence and will, and about cause and effect. When I attempt to pray, the idea will come up to me, that I have not such a certain knowledge about God, and about my own spirit, as I have about objects of sense. My knowledge about spirit seems to me to be inferior. Can you relieve me from this trouble?"

"Probably not," said I. "This matter is not a truth, but what you have just called it, a temptation; and I cannot chain the devil, or check the evil suggestions of your own heart. What I have already said to you I did suppose to be sufficient on that point, so far as the mind is concerned. If you are *tempted*, your hope lies in prayer."

"But yet," said he, "I do think that material objects assail the mind, as mental or spiritual ideas do not; and I think that we have a more *extensive* knowledge of matter than we can have of spirit. And hence, I feel that I am not on *as sure ground* in the abstract and spiritual matters of religion as I wish to be."

"We are at issue again," said I, "if that is the case."

He replied, "I know that very well. And I half know that I am wrong. But I cannot get my mind clear on these points."

"I think you can," said I. "And at the risk of some little repetition, which indeed seems to be needful to you, I join issue with you again.

"You speak of knowledge; and you want to be *as sure* in religious knowledge as you feel that you are in other matters; and you want your knowledge to be as *extensive*. You affirm that there is, after all, a deficiency on these points. I affirm there is not."

"Exactly that," he replied.

"Then," said I, "let us attempt to examine these questions.

"What is it *to know?* Where does knowledge lie? What is that kind of operation, exercise, or experience, which men call knowledge? We want no school metaphysics on this point. Metaphysical fog is not equal to the noon-day clearness of common sense.

"Knowledge is the ascertainment which the mind has of some certainty or reality. It does not make the certainty. That exists before. It is only a recognition of it. That recognition, or sure perception of mind, call it what you will, is knowledge. Knowledge, then, exists in the mind; not in matter, but in mind; not in the matter of your bones, or blood, or muscles, of your eyes that see, or your ears that hear. Knowledge exists only in mind. The mind has a sure perception of some reality, and that is knowledge."

"*Yes*," said he, emphatically.

"This perception," I continued, "comes, indeed, in different ways. I perceive some truths by my eyes,—as when I behold the sun, or admire a rosebud. I perceive other truths by my ears,—as when I leap at the sound of music, or tremble at the thunder. I perceive other truths by my reason,—as when I know that the half of any substance is not as much as the whole, or that two men are stronger than one, if all three are equals. But in all cases, the perception is in the mind; the ascertainment of the certainty, *the knowledge*, exists in the mind, and nowhere else."

"*Yes*," said he.

"Now, therefore, if any man knows he has knowledge, he knows he has *mind*. And he knows another thing about it,—he knows it is a *knowing* mind, a spirit capable of knowing, of perceiving truth. And what, then, does the man mean, when he pretends he knows little about mind, about spirit? He cannot know anything about matter, *without* knowing something about spirit. It is his spirit only that *knows.* He does not know with his hands, or his feet, or his eyes. He knows only with his mind. And if he knows that rock is hard, or night dark, or water fluid, he *equally* knows that he himself possesses a perceiving, knowing mind—a reasonable spirit within him, capable of being affected by a reality."

"*Yes,*" said he, as if he would fix it in mind.

"But he is certain of these things. He says he is. He feels the hard rock—he sees water run—his eyes tell him it is dark in the night. But where lies his certainty? Why, he is just certain of his own *mind*—that is all. He is just certain that he has got a mind *to be* certain—that he has a perceiving spirit within him, capable of knowing things without him,—knowing that rock is hard, and water fluid, and night dark. He is, therefore, reduced just to this: *he cannot be certain of anything at all without being certain of mind,*—certain that he possesses a spirit capable of perceiving and knowing."

"*That is true,*" said he, most emphatically.

"Does he not, then, learn to know spirit as fast as he learns to know matter? Can he stretch out his fingers anywhere upon a tangible universe, and take a lesson upon it, and not *therewith* take a lesson upon the spirit, which *alone* perceives its tangibility? Can he open his eyes, amid the flowers of his beautiful garden, and admire the sweet pencillings which delight him, and not, at the same moment, just as well know that he himself has a spirit capable of admiration and delight, as he knows the hues of beauty which are blending into one another? Can he listen to the wild-bird's song, and the forest-echo which repeats it, and not just as well know that he himself has a spirit within him susceptible of the sweets of music and the soothing of its melting echoes, as he knows that his feathered friend upon the wing has a mellow throat and an exultant song? This man, this very man, who deplores his uncertainty about spirit, *cannot himself take a single step in the knowledge of matter, without, at the same moment, taking a step in the knowledge of spirit.* Every new lesson he learns about material things which affect his senses, is a new lesson about the immaterial spirit which *learns* it. He cannot know a single quality in matter without knowing a quality in spirit; for mind only has knowledge. He knows *with* his spirit. And if he is sure of anything, he must be sure of the spirit which has the surety."

"*Yes*," said he. I now admit all that. I confess that I cannot have any certainty about matter, unattended by an equal certainty about mind. But here is my trouble: the surety in reference to matter comes into the mind through the channel of the senses. The organic structure is affected—the nerves of seeing, hearing, feeling, tasting, or smelling. And, therefore, is not the knowledge about spirit inferior to this, because it is a kind of knowledge that does not affect this organic structure?"

"How *can* it be inferior?" said I. "Knowledge exists in mind. Is it any matter how it got there? If it is there, and is knowledge, what matter is it whether it got in by one channel or another? If our houses are light, is not the light which comes through the open doors as trustworthy a reality as that which is transmitted through the glass of the windows? Knowledge is knowledge, no matter how it comes. Certainty is certainty. If it comes through our sensitive organism it is knowledge. If it comes by consciousness or reason, it is knowledge. And the idea, that all knowledge which comes through our sensitive organism is genuine and sure, while all other must lie under a suspicion of being counterfeit or unsafe, is an idea which would overthrow more than half the science, and more than half the jurisprudence of all mankind. Nobody acts upon it. Nobody ever did, or ever will, except simply in the matter of religion, when depraved men wish to cast off its obligations. There is not a human being to be found who ever resorts to this idea of the inferiority of all but sensible knowledge, except when error suits his heart better than truth—when he is blinded by the love of sin—when he dislikes the duties of the gospel, such as prayer and preparation for a future life.

"But more. You spoke of the organic structure, and the nerves, and the channel of the senses, as if one could be more sure when his material body is affected, and he learns anything in that way."

Said he, "That is the very point. Speak to that."

"Then think a little further," said I. "Two of our most important senses seem very much like an exception, usually. In our seeing and in our hearing, the organ that sees and the organ that hears are seldom touched so rudely, as to make us sensible at all that anything has touched them. And yet, this seeing and this hearing, the very senses which come nearest to spirituality, the very senses whose organism is seldom sensible to matter at all—these are the very senses in which every man has most confidence, and most employs. Every man seems himself to be assured *most*, when in his bodily organs sensibility of impression is *least*.

"But beyond this, and beyond the fact that it is the mind which sees and feels, and not the mere organs, which can do nothing alone, it is not true that matter alone can affect our material organism, and thus give us *more surety* about itself. Thought, pure thought, affects it also. You may find a merchant, whose mere contemplation of his embarrassed affairs makes him tremble like an aspen leaf. His mind affects his material body, and his mind alone. He is not in jail. The sheriff has not seized him. He is not turned out of his house. His eyes have not seen his ships sink, or his goods burn. But he trembles, and turns pale, and loses his appetite, and grows lean; and all this, from the mere knowledge he has that he is an irretrievable bankrupt. And what will you say to him? Will you bring him your sweet doctrine of uncertainties to comfort him? and cheeringly assure him that he may be altogether mistaken, that he cannot be *quite sure*, because he has not *seen* his gold sink, or his goods burn, or his debtors run away? You may find a culprit whose crimes are known only to himself,—you lawyers know nothing about them, —and yet, under a sense of his guilt, he is shaken as a reed in the wind. His knowledge affects his nerves. 'A dreadful sound is in his ears.' He turns pale, and trembles. 'The sound of the shaken leaf shall chase him.' And what will you say of such examples? This knowledge—a knowledge apart from the senses—a knowledge existing only in mind, by reflection and consciousness, as really and powerfully affects the material body itself as any sensible knowledge can do. Yea, more so. 'The spirit of a man sustaineth his infirmity; but a wounded spirit, who can bear?' And what will you say now about the uncertainty of knowledge which does not come by what you called 'the channel of the senses,' when these men find their nerves shattered, their muscles trembling, the circulation of their blood deranged, and their whole material frame under the dreadful sway of a thought within them—just a thought? If you cannot believe in the reality and sureness of knowledge which does not come *by* matter, you must at least believe in the reality of a knowledge which makes the whole matter of a man's frame tremble, as if it would shake to pieces. Look at him, and answer; have you certainty only about matter? have you not equal certainty about mind? Do you not know that it possesses a dreadful power? that it has capabilities of thought, of apprehension, of agony and torture inconceivable? Do you *not* know that these are the realities, the certainties, compared with which, all the certainties about matter are a mere dream?"

"*Yes*," said he, springing upon his feet like a well man, "I *do* know it. I shall never call *that* in question again."

With a contemplative air he walked a few times across the floor, and then turning suddenly to me, exclaimed very earnestly:—

"But the *extent* of knowledge, sir, the *extent* of knowledge! Our knowledge of spirit is *limited!* We know many things about matter, and only a few about spirit! The *essence* of spirit is unknown to us! We cannot tell what spirit *is*, sir!"

"I venture to affirm you *can* tell what spirit is, just as well as you can tell what matter is. You know just as much about the essence of the one as you do about the essence of the other. Be so good as to make a little comparison. Take any example you will. Here is a rock. It is matter, not spirit. Well, what do you know about it? You know it is hard and heavy, and has figure or shape, and has some kind of colour, and, it may be, some sort of odour. But what of all that? We are asking about the *essence* of matter, and take the rock for an example. What *is* the essence of it? It has weight. Is its weight the essence? It has shape. Is its shape the essence? It has colour. Is its colour the essence? It has hardness. Is its hardness the essence of matter? Everybody says, *No, no!* Then, what is its essence? what is that *something*, that substratum, that real existence, in which all these qualities of colour, and figure, and weight, and solidity exist? *No man can tell!*

"Turn, then, to a spirit. Here, for example, is your own soul—the thing which now attends to my ideas. What is the essence of it? It is spirit—no *matter* at all about it. Well, what do you know of it? You know it perceives, it thinks, it remembers, it reasons, it imagines, it fears, it hopes, it resents, it has joy sometimes, and sometimes sorrow. But is joy its essence? or sorrow? or hope? or memory? or hate? or love? or judgment? or thinking? Everybody says, *No, no!* Then, what is its essence? what is that something, that substratum, that real existence, in which all these qualities of thought and feeling exist? No *man can tell!*

"Sum up the whole rock, then, and the whole soul, and *just confess*, sir, that you know as much about the essence of the one as you do about the essence of the other. Your knowledge about the essence of matter is just equal to your knowledge about the essence of mind. What do you mean, then, when you say you know something *surely* about matter, but you know little about spirit? You know, indeed, some qualities of both; and beyond that your knowledge does not extend."

My young friend had become by this time exceedingly excited. His excitement, which seemed to have been growing upon him for half an hour, had risen, as it seemed, to the highest pitch. His cheek was flushed, his eye sparkled, his frame rose erect, and he paced the room, more with the firm tread of a soldier than the feeble step of a sick man. Fearing his excitement might do him an injury, I proposed to leave him, and allow him to rest.

"*No, sir!*" said he, with an accent as if he had been angry,—"*no, sir;* you are not to leave me yet! You have asked me to confess! And I *do* confess! I yield this point! Your argument is unanswerable! But, sir, the victory has been all on one side, ever since we commenced these conversations, and I am chagrined; I am deeply mortified at my defeat! My blood boils in my veins, and all the life there is left in me is aroused, when I perceive you are pushing me further and further into the position of a sinner against God, with all my eternity to cry out against me! Do not mistake me, sir. My excitement is not against *you;* it is against *myself!* And I have an inch or two of ground left yet. I say that you have not answered *all* my objections. I affirmed that we have a more sure knowledge of material things than we have of our spirits, or any spirit, because we have a more *extensive* knowledge. Our knowledge of spirit is limited. What do you say to that?"

"I say that our knowledge of matter is limited also, and the more limited of the two. I say that we have *more extensive* knowledge of spirit than we have of matter."

"Is it possible!" said he. "Go on, then. Show it to be so. I will sit down and listen."

"Another time, perhaps, you—"

"Do not *mention* another time," said he, interrupting me. "I may be a dead man before I see you again! Tell me *now!* Take away, if you can, the last inch of ground I have left, and show me to be without excuse in the sight of that God in whom you have compelled me to believe, and before whom I must soon stand! I am a dying man. I have no time to lose."

"Since you desire it," said I, "let me prove to you that we know *more things* about spirit than we do about matter. We know a few qualities in each. Compare them with one another. Make two chapters—one for the known properties of matter, the other for the known properties of spirit; and then compare the chapters, and see of which your knowledge is the more extensive, matter or spirit :—

"*First* chapter: On Matter. You know it has the following qualities, to wit: weight, colour (sometimes), figure, inactivity, hardness, smell (sometimes), and it is movable. This is about all you know. All else you can say of it is included in these properties, or results from them.

"*Second* chapter: On Spirit. You know it has the following properties, to wit: it perceives, it compares, it judges, it reasons, it remembers, it wills, it fancies, it has conscience, it has imagination, it has consciousness or perception of its own acts, it is capable of pain and pleasure. That is enough. You need go no further. Cut the chapter short. You have *more* knowledge about spirit than you have about matter—more *extensive* knowledge. You can tell of more properties of spirit than of matter. Your spirit chapter is longer than your matter chapter. In one word, you do positively know a great deal more about spirit than you do about matter. Your knowledge of matter is confined to just a few qualities; but your knowledge of spirit is far *more* extensive, embracing all kinds of operation, all kinds of thought, all kinds of emotions and passions."

"*All true!*" said he. "I confess it. But spirit may have other faculties or properties which we know nothing about."

"So may matter," said I,—"so may matter. But that is an idea addressed to our *ignorance*. We are talking about knowledge. What we do *not* know about spirit or about matter has nothing to do with our subject or with our duty. We want *knowledge* to act upon and to die upon. A mere *perhaps*, about something else, does not weigh a feather against known truth. A *perhaps* is bad foot-hold for a dying man. You would be ashamed of this kind of suggestion in court. Matter and spirit both may have a thousand qualities which we know nothing about. But we act like fools, if we will not breathe the air because it may have some unknown properties; and we act just as much like fools if we will not repent and believe in Christ because our immortal soul may have some unknown properties. Religion asks us to act upon knowledge, upon certainty. Infidelity must always act upon ignorance, if it acts at all. And for that reason, I affirmed to you, the first time I saw you, that infidels are the most credulous, assuming, and dogmatic men in the world."

"*That is true*," said he, rising suddenly from his seat,—"that is all true. I have done. I have no more to say. I have been *a fool*, and have groped in the dark all my days! I have spent my life in conjecturing what *might* be, and neglecting what *is*, and what I now *know* is."

Being quite certain that he was exhausting his strength too much, I entreated him to rest, proposing to call on him again at any time he should choose.

"Have you seen my aunt to-day?" said he, suddenly.

"No; I have not had that pleasure; but I begin to think I have a kind of *right* to see her."

"I thought you had seen her. You talk just as she does about my exhausting my strength; and I thought she might have given you a little blarney, to have me receive it second-hand, since I refused it from her."

"No, I have never seen her."

"She *ought* to see you. She is a noble woman. You would like her. Her beauty has bidden her good-night, long, long ago, but her heart is as green as a shamrock. I love her. My heart will warm towards *her*, after its blood shall be too stiff to move at anything but the thought of her. She has a true Irish heart. There is no English blood in her."

"Perhaps," said I, "some of her excellences which you admire may be owing quite as much to Palestine as to Ireland. I can very honestly assure you of my high admiration of the Irish character. When I once heard one of the judges of the Supreme Court warmly affirm, 'The most noble living creature in the world is a well-educated Irishman,' my whole heart accorded with the declaration of that great man, with no other reserve than the idea, that religion is the crowning excellence of men, after all.

But I suppose he had no reference to religion, and I therefore adopted the sentiment as my own. But now, I wish to ask you to discriminate a little betwixt your aunt's qualities as an Irish woman, which I have no doubt are great, and her qualities as a Christian woman. In my opinion, her Christian excellences you call Irish excellences, and what in her helps to bind your heart to the Emerald Isle ought to bind it also to the Saviour she adores. Indeed, I have no hesitation in expressing the opinion, that however admirable she may be as an Irish woman, she is far more admirable as a Christian woman. You ought to do justice to her religion, and feel the force of her character and example. I will venture to affirm for her, that she herself, much as she loves Ireland, will tell you that she is indebted to the Rose of Sharon more than to the green of the shamrock. Love Ireland, sir, as much as you will. I have no quarrel with you on that ground. But do justice, in your estimations, to a heavenly religion, and to what lies nearest to your aunt's own heart. She, I venture to affirm, will lay down all the honours you can heap upon her at the foot of the cross. It will grieve her to have you honour her country, and *not* honour her Christ."

Springing suddenly upon his feet, with a look of astonishment and indignation, he stood before me, bending almost over me:—

"You *have seen her!*" said he, with an accent of resentment.

"I have *not*," said I, firmly.

"Do you speak *true?*" said he.

"Sir," said I, "my *word* must not be called in question anywhere."

Said he, "I beg your pardon. Excuse me; I was wrong. But it suddenly occurred to me that you and my aunt were playing a game with me. I thought she had been telling you all about me."

"What gave you such a suspicion?"

"Because you employed one of her own thoughts,—that I honoured her country and her blood, when I ought to have given the honour to her Redeemer. She has said it to me this day, sir, and often in past time. But do not look so sternly upon me. I thought she had been telling you. I take back what I said. I beg your pardon. I am incapable of offering you an insult."

"Let that pass," said I; "I play no games upon anybody. I only desire your good."

"I know it; and I thank you for every word you have said to me. I could have no claim upon you for so much kindness. You have given me much of your time. Your patience has not been worn out with me. You have done what few men could do; you have seen the heart of me rightly, and have indulged me in having my own strange way in talking about religion, as I believe few ministers would have done. And if there is a God in heaven he will reward you,—I know he will reward you."

The tears gushed from his eyes; and pulling his handkerchief from his pocket, he turned away from me, to the window, and wept convulsively. After a moment, turning suddenly to me, with a manifest effort to conceal his emotions, he said:—

"I am too apt to lead you off from our subject. I am sorry for it. But you have prevailed by yielding to me. I want you to stay a little longer to-day, if you can. I have not long to live. This cough and these night-sweats will soon wear me out. I should be an idiot to hope to get well. I have no company now, except yours and my aunt's. Conversation does not hurt me; and it would be no matter, you know, if it did. I am soon to go. Earth has done with me. The grave lifts up her voice to claim me. I am preparing to say, Yes, I come. But one thing troubles me. My heart is, to tell you that difficulty. It is not easy for me to keep clear from my old infidel thoughts, and I want to tell you how I was led on to be an infidel."

"I should like to hear that very much," said I. "And as to your amount of strength, I leave you to judge of it. I will go or stay, just as you desire, only tell me frankly what your desire is."

"I thank you," said he, his eyes filling with tears, "I am unable to tell you how much my very heart thanks you. I know there is little value in the thanks of a dying man; but they are all I have to give, and my heart forces them to my tongue."

"I ought to thank *you*," said I, "for these interviews. They gratify me much, and I assure you they profit me too."

After a short pause, and subduing his emotions, he continued:—

"For some time I have been astonished at myself. My thoughts are full of evil. The old follies will come over me. They torment my mind; and I know they offend God. My infidelity had become interwoven with my strongest feelings. Though I have been led to know its deceptions, its old lies still haunt me, as if a host of infernal spirits were sent to thrust them back into my heart. This troubles me. I am vexed with myself, because I have not vigour of mind to stand to the truth, since I have been convinced of it. My wickedness within is too mighty for me. Satan tempts me with his lies. It *is* Satan. He comes to me suddenly. He comes at midnight sometimes, when I would pray, if I could; and the horrible idea darts like an arrow, into my mind, 'Religion is all a delusion.' I have said that to my aunt very often; and now Satan says it to me. I know it is a lie; but the thought torments my very soul."

"You need not be troubled about it," said I. "If you *hunted up* the idea yourself, or if you *welcomed* it when it comes, you would have some cause for trouble and alarm. It is not *temptation* that can injure us or prove our insincerity. The *treatment* we give to temptation is the thing to be looked at. Since the temptation comes to you without your bidding, and since you do not welcome it, but reject it, and aim to dismiss it *as* a temptation, the treatment you give it accords with the will of God, and shows that you desire and intend to obey him."

"So I do, sir; but my wicked heart is overflowing with evil. I wanted to tell you how my unbelief became blended with my blood. I am an Irishman. Early in life my country's wrongs lay on my heart like a burden. My blood burns at this moment to think of the oppressions of England! Before the suns of a dozen summers had shone upon me, I had learned to say, 'The English are tyrants and hypocrites. They profess to be a Christian people; but they wrong my country.' As I grew older I read history. I read the court trials which grew out of what they called 'the Irish rebellion of ninety-eight.' I read of Emmet, and other men like him, led to a disgraceful execution, when they deserved the plaudits of all mankind! I read Curran's Speeches. I read of the infamous informers hired by the government to swear to *anything*, in order to get the blood of an Irishman! The English have oppressed us, sir! They have ruined Ireland by the most cruel and heartless injustice—by their tyranny and taxation; and then, to crown their barbarity, they call us low, and stupid, and incapable of improvement, sir! and all this, though their victories have been bought with Irish blood, and no small part of the eloquence of their Parliament itself was the eloquence of Irishmen!"

He was becoming so much excited, that I thought it best to interpose, for the purpose of quieting his feelings, and leading his thoughts into another channel. I said to him,—

"The things you complain of were acts of the *government*, not of the *people*. Many of the people did not approve of them. None of the *Christian* people approved of any injustice. It was not religion, but irreligion, which led to any oppression; and you ought not to lay down at the door of Christianity the blame which belongs to her enemies. You attribute to religion what you ought to attribute to the want of it. If all the people and the government had been controlled by the principles of Christianity, there would have been none of those wrongs which so much excite you."

"I know it, sir; I am sure of it," said he. "But I was telling you how I was made an infidel. The English boast of their magnanimity. They talk loftily of 'English honour' and of their 'religion.' And only a few days since—let me see, it was this day eight days—as I was reading an old paper, I came upon the place where one of your own statesmen calls England 'the bulwark of our holy religion.' It is too much, sir. Oppression, heartless and unrelenting oppression carried on through ages, cannot be justified! There is no apology for it. And after all this, for the English to speak of their Christianity, and call themselves 'the most religious nation on earth,' and make other people believe it! Sir, there never was any impudence equal to this! Look at India, sir! The English have made her red with the blood of her innocent children! They have made themselves rich with the gold of which they have robbed her! They have butchered the half-civilized people by the thousands and hundreds of thousands, with no decent argument of justice, and for no other reason than to gratify their own lordly pride, and get riches by the right of their cannon! And when the news of a new victory over the feeble reaches '*brave England*,' they call themselves a religious people, and give thanks to God in their churches for success on another field of butchery! This completes the farce, till the very next year brings round a like occasion. All this is true, sir. You cannot dispute it. It is history. And when I began in early life to learn such transactions, I could not respect a religion that would allow them. I disbelieved in such a religion. I became an infidel. The true history of England is enough to make a world full of infidels! Ireland and India tell tales of blood about the religion of England. I can respect Mohammedanism—it acts according to its principles; I can respect Popery and her Inquisition, for the same reason;—but Protestant England, as she calls herself, I despise for her mean hypocrisy! Her religion is described in three words—*pride*, *avarice*, and *oppression*. All this became stamped into my heart as I was growing up towards manhood. I knew that the Established Church of England was nothing but a part of her governmental hypocrisy; I knew that her Protestantism was only a political pretence. I felt for my country's wrongs, and I rejected religion because of the example that I studied so constantly. The example never appeared more base to me than it does this moment. And I am troubled now because my old system of thought will come back upon me like a torrent, and tempt me tc disbelieve in Christianity as often as I think of the wrongs of my country."

Said I, "In my opinion you can easily get over all that difficulty. You have only to think of that which you know to be true, that is, that Christianity never sanctioned any of the pride, avarice, and oppression you complain of, but that it was abusively made a cloak to cover such sins. In that nation it became linked with the government (which union I dislike as much as you do), and because of that union it became corrupted. As you took the government and its actions for an example of the influence of religion, or for a test of its truth, you looked in the wrong direction. You should rather have looked at the pious in private life. You should have looked where there *was* some influence of Christianity, not where there was none. You should have looked at the Bible Society, the Missionary Society, the Sunday Schools and Orphan Asylums, and attempts to relieve the oppressed and down-trodden. *There* was religion in fact, not in mere name. And now, when you perceive that you erred, in taking what men *falsely called* religion as an example of it, surely you need not be troubled with your old infidelity."

"So it seems to me," said he; "but Satan tempts me, as if I was now embracing a religion which has crushed my country."

"It never crushed your country; you know it never did. It was a spirit directly the *opposite* of Christianity which perpetrated the sins you complain of. Christianity would have saved your country; and you ought to welcome it to your heart, for your eternal salvation, more eagerly than you would ever have welcomed a deliverer to your native land."

"So I do," said he; "so I will. I believe in Christianity. I know I need it. I believe Jesus Christ came to save sinners. I trust him to save me. I rely on the Holy Spirit to aid me against the temptations of Satan and the sinfulness of my own heart. You spoke of examples of religion in private life. Let me tell you, the example of my old aunt has been a *demonstration* to me. Satan cannot shake it."

I again proposed to leave him for the present, and call at another time, lest so long a conversation should injure him.

"*Another time!*" said he,—"another *time!* You astonish me, sir! I am a dying man! I stand on the verge of time now! I feel that the grave-digger is at the side of me! *You* may talk of time. With your health and prospects, it is not unnatural. But if I should be talking of time, Death would laugh at me, and call me fool and liar!" And then, turning to me, and fixing his keen eyes upon my face as he stood before me—"Tell me what to do to be ready to die."

Said I, "You believe in God, the Infinite, Eternal Spirit."

"*I do,*" said he.

"Then pray to him," said I.

"I *have*, and I *will*," said he.

"You believe you are a sinner?" said I.

"*I know I am,*" said he.

"Then repent, and trust in Christ for pardon."

"Will repentance save me?"

"No," said I; "Christ Jesus saves sinners. You must not trust to your repentance and faith to save you. That would be self-righteousness. Trust only in the crucified Son of God, your proposed Surety." After a pause—

"What must be done first, *before* I trust in him?"

"Nothing—just nothing."

"How? Is there no preparation to make?"

"No; none at all."

"But, holiness—" said he.

"Results from faith in Christ," said I.

"And the Holy Spirit—" said he.

"Is your only hope," said I. "Without his aid you will neither repent nor believe. It is his office to take of the things of Christ, and show them unto us."

"Will you pray with me?" said he.

We fell on our knees. I offered a short prayer, and left him. I never saw him afterwards.

I called to see him the next day, but his friends would not allow it, because he was so much exhausted. I understood from his nurse that immediately after I left him the day before, he sent for his aunt, told her that he renounced all his infidelity, that he had not a doubt the Bible was from God, and that the atonement of Jesus Christ was all-sufficient for a dying sinner. He continued his conversation and prayer with her till he fainted; and she was obliged to call for aid, to lift him from the floor and lay him upon his bed.

I made another attempt to see him, but his aunt sent word to me at the door that she was very grateful for my attentions to him, and thanked me much; but she begged me not to come in, for he was not able to see me. He had not strength to utter a sentence.

Just at this time I left home, and on my return, after an absence of three weeks, I learned that he was buried the week before my return. I could not find his aunt. I have never seen her, and know not the reason why she sent for me, only, as I understood from the lady at whose house he died, that she had at some time heard me preach. This same lady told me that "the young man died in peace, with praises for the atonement of Jesus Christ on his lips."

I have never had my feelings more deeply interested than they were in this young Irishman. He was a man of uncommon talents. He was frank and candid. He was full of enthusiasm. It is impossible to convey in writing any just idea of the ardour and eloquence with which he spoke, when he became excited. There was a sort of romance, too, in the mystery in which his aunt so constantly shrouded herself. He was an avowed infidel; and what, in my opinion, is a very uncommon thing, he was an honest infidel. The arguments by which he attempted to sustain his infidelity were peculiar. He was evidently in the last stages of life, the subject of a hasty consumption, of which nobody could be more sensible than himself. He was open to conviction; and it was very evident that he entertained a most profound respect for his pious aunt, who had induced him to send for me.

I think it likely that that woman was the real means of his conversion and salvation. She was an example of practical piety which his infidelity could not refute, and which his conscience could not but honour. He evidently did not say to me all that he felt on that subject. Whenever he alluded to her, after a few words, he would seem to check himself, and soon change the subject. But occasionally, when he became excited, some expression would come out which showed how powerful her influence had been over him. I can never forget the ardour and depth of emotion with which he uttered the expression: "You spoke of examples of religion in private life. Let me tell you, the example of my old aunt has been a *demonstration* to me. Satan cannot shake it."

It is true that infidelity cannot withstand the force of reason and argument; but true godly example can come nearer the life-spot of religion. It knocks at the door of the heart. If the truths of Christianity were seconded by the devoted and pious lives of all her professed disciples, the unbelief of the world would soon cease. *Private example of godliness* is what the world most needs.

All men will not think alike in reference to the mode in which this young Irishman was led into infidelity. Perhaps he too much blamed the government of England. Perhaps also, his feelings towards the people were governed by a very natural prejudice. But it is much to be deplored, that the governments of nations professing to be Christian, have been so unjust, so ready for war and conquest; and that the Christian people of such nations have so often sunk their principles amid the waves of some exciting popularity, and have shouted over a victory in war, when they ought to have shed tears of bitterness over its injustice and cruelty. They little reflect how much their conformity to the world hinders the triumphs of religion. War and conquest, too, may sometimes be inevitable, perhaps. The general injustice of mankind may sometimes make deadly conflict necessary for the defence of the good against the wicked. But *Chris-*

tians and Christian nations have much to answer for, on account of such things as this young Irishman complained of. Too much of our religion is stained with the pride, and politics, and avarice of the world. "Come out of her, my people."

I have some reason to believe that no small blame was imputed to me for remaining so long at a time with a sick man, and hastening, as they said, his death, by my exhausting conversation. But *he* never blamed me. I venture to affirm his aunt never blamed me. They were quite as good judges of propriety as those who were half-strangers to him in a boarding-house. Moreover, it would have been heartless to leave him, and would have tended to make him call in question my sense of the importance and reality of the religion I urged upon him, when he used such language as I have here recorded: "No, sir; you are *not* to leave me yet. Conversation does not hurt me; and it would be no matter, you know, if it did. I am a dying man. I stand on the verge of time now. I feel that the grave-digger is at the side of me. Another time! sir; another time! You astonish me! *You* may talk of time. But if I should be talking of time, death would laugh at me, and call me fool and liar. Earth has done with me. The grave lifts up her voice to claim me. I am preparing to say, Yes, I come." Some men, perhaps, might have left a man who talked thus. I could not. I am sure, if any wise man had been in my place, and known him as I did, he would have done as I did.

II.

Faith Everything.

AMONG a large number of young people, who, at one time, were in the habit of meeting me every week, for the purpose of personal conversation on the subject of religion, there was a very quiet, contemplative young woman, whose candour and simplicity of heart interested me very much. She did not appear to me to be susceptible of much impulsive emotion, but to be very much a child of thought. Her convictions of sin, which appeared to me to be deep and clear, were uniformly expressed more in the language of reason, than of emotion; so that I sometimes feared that she had only an ordinary and intellectual conviction, without much real discovery of her character as a sinner against God. In addition to all the conversation I could have with her in the presence of others, I often visited her at her own home; and because of her apparent destitution of any deep emotions, and my consequent fear that her convictions were more speculative than real, I laboured to unfold to her the character of God, his law, the nature of sin, the state of her own heart, and aimed to impress truths of this kind upon her feelings and conscience. She assented to it all. I urged upon her the necessity of immediate repentance, her lost condition as a sinner, and her indispensable necessity of the atoning blood and righteousness of Jesus Christ, to save her from merited condemnation. She assented to all this. I explained to her, again and again, the whole way of salvation for sinners, the grace of God, and the willingness of Christ to save her. She said she believed it all. I cautioned her against resisting the Holy Spirit by unbelief, by prayerlessness, by delaying her repentance and her fleeing to Christ; and in every mode that my thoughts could devise I tried to lead her to the gospel salvation. But it all seemed to be ineffectual. She remained, apparently, in the same state of mind. Thus she continued for several weeks. She gained nothing, and lost nothing. Studious of her Bible, prayerful, attentive to all the means of grace, she was still without peace, and still manifested no additional anxiety, and no disposition to discontinue her attempts to attain salvation. For a time there had been with her manifestly an increasing solemnity and depth of seriousness; but this time had gone by; and she remained, to all appearance, fixed in the same unchanging state of mind.

Such was her condition when I visited her again, without much expectation of any good to result from anything I could say. After many inquiries, and trying all my skill to ascertain, if possible, whether there was any vital religious truth which she did not understand, or any sin which she was not willing to abandon, I said to her plainly, "Mary, I can do you no good; I have said to you everything appropriate to your state that I can think of. I would aid you most willingly if I could; but I can do you no good."

"I do not think you can," said she calmly; "but I hope you will still come to see me."

"Yes, I will," said I. "But all I can say to you is, *I know* there is salvation for you; but you must repent, you must flee to Christ."

We went from her house directly to the evening lecture. I commenced the service, by reading the hymn of Dr. Watts:—

"There is a voice of sovereign grace,
Sounds from the sacred word;
'Ho! ye despairing sinners come
And trust upon the Lord.'

My soul obeys the Almighty call,
And runs to this relief;
I would believe thy promise, Lord.
Oh! help my unbelief.

To the dear fountain of thy blood,
  Incarnate God, I fly;
Here let me wash my spotted soul
  From crimes of deepest dye.

Stretch out thine arm, victorious King,
  My reigning sins subdue;
Drive the old dragon from his seat,
  With his apostate crew.

A guilty, weak, and helpless worm,
  On thy kind arms I fall;
Be thou my strength and righteousness,
  My Jesus and my all!"

This hymn was sung, and the service conducted in the usual manner. I forgot all about Mary, as an individual, and preached as appropriately as I was able to the congregation before me.

The next day she came to me to tell me, that she "had made a new discovery."

"Well," said I, "what is it that you have discovered?"

"Why, sir," said she; "the way of salvation all seems to me now perfectly plain. My darkness is all gone. I see now what I never saw before."

"Do you see that you have given up *sin* and the world; and given your whole heart to Christ?"

"I do not think that I am a Christian; but I have never been *so happy* before. All is light to me now. I see my way clear; and I am not burdened and troubled as I was."

"And how is this? what has brought you to this state of mind?"

"I do not know *how* it is, or what has brought me to it. But when you were reading that hymn last night, I saw the whole way of salvation for sinners perfectly plain, and wondered that I had never seen it before. I saw that I had nothing to do but to *trust* in Christ:—

"A guilty, weak, and helpless worm,
On thy kind arms I fall."

I sat all the evening just looking at that hymn. I did not hear your prayer. I did not hear a word of your sermon. I do not know your text. I thought of nothing but that hymn; and I have been thinking of it ever since. It is so light and makes me so contented. Why, sir," said she, in the perfect simplicity of her heart, never thinking that she was repeating what had been told her a thousand times, "*don't you think that the reason why we do not get out of darkness sooner*, is that we don't *believe?*"

"Just that, Mary; precisely that. Faith in Jesus Christ to save is the way to heaven."

The idea had not yet occurred to her mind that she was a Christian. She had only *discovered the way.* I did not think it wise for me to suggest the idea to her at all, but leave her to the direction of the Holy Spirit and the truth of the hymn. If the Holy Spirit had given her a new heart, I trusted he would lead her to hope, as soon as he wanted her to hope. The hymn which had opened her eyes was the best truth for her to meditate at present.

I conversed with her for some time. She had no more troubles, no darkness, no difficulties. All was clear to her mind, and she rejoiced in the unexpected discovery she had made. "I now *know what to do,*" said she, "I must trust in Jesus Christ, and I believe God will enable me to do so."

It was not till after the lapse of some days that she began to hope that she had really become reconciled to God. But she finally came to the conclusion that her religion commenced when she sat that evening pondering that hymn, and wondering she "had never discovered before that sinners must *believe.*"

She afterwards became a communicant in the church; and to the day of her death, so far as I have been able to ascertain, she lived as a *believer.*

This case has suggested to my mind the inquiry, whether, as ministers, after all our preaching upon faith, we do not fail to insist directly upon it as we ought, and tell inquirers, as Mary told me, "We have nothing to do but to trust." I deem it not improbable, that by the extensive and laboured explanations we give, the minds of inquirers are often confused; and the very way we take to make religion plain, is the very means of making it obscure; and that Mary's simplicity of faith would be a far better sermon for many such persons. All the matter of a soul's closing with Christ may be wrapped up in a very little space, may be a very simple thing. And what that thing is the Holy Spirit seems to have taught Mary, "We have nothing to do but to trust."

III.

Simplicity of Faith.

THE simplicity of faith was once illustrated to me in another and a very different manner.

I was preaching my ordinary weekly lecture in the evening, when I was sent for in great haste to visit a woman who was said to be dying, and who very much desired to see me. I closed the service as soon as I could, and went immediately to her house. She was a member of my church, whom I had known very well for years; with whom I had been acquainted ever since her first serious impressions, before she became a communicant. As I entered the room where she lay, I found it filled with her friends, who had gathered around her to see her die. Making my way through the midst of them, I reached the side of her bed, and found her apparently in the last agonies of death. She was bolstered up in her bed, gasping for breath, almost suffocated by the asthma; and the whole bed shook by a palpitation of her heart, which seemed to be shaking her to pieces. It appeared to me that she could not live the quarter of an hour. I said to her,—

"Mrs. M——, you seem to be very sick?"

"Yes," said she, "I am dying."

"And are you ready to die?"

She lifted her eyes upon me with a solemn and fixed gaze, and speaking with great difficulty, she replied:—

"Sir, God knows—I have taken him—at his word—and—I am not afraid—to die."

It was a new definition of faith. "I have taken him at his word." It struck me in an instant as a triumph of faith. "God knows I have taken him at his word, and I am not afraid to die." It was just the thing for her to say. I have often tried to think what else she could have said, that would have expressed so much in such few words.

I prayed some four minutes by her bed-side, recited to her some passages of God's word, and was about to leave her for a moment to her friends, whom she seemed anxious to address. She held me by the hand, and uttering a word at a time, as she gasped for breath, she said to me:—

"I wanted to tell you—that I can—trust—in God—while—I am dying. You have—often told me—he would not—forsake me. And now—I find—it true. I am—at peace. I die—willingly—and happy."

In a few minutes I left her, uttering to her such promises of the Saviour as I deemed most appropriate. However, she did not die. She still lives. But that expression of her faith has been of great benefit to me. It has aided me in preaching, and in conversation with inquiring sinners very often. It gave me a more simple idea of faith than I ever had before. It put aside all the mist of metaphysics, speculation, and philosphizing. It made the whole nature of faith plain. Everybody could understand it: "God knows, I have taken him at his word."

If I am not mistaken, many of the speculations about faith have no tendency to *invite* faith. Rather the contrary. The speculations tend to throw over the exercises of faith an obscurity—tend to give them a dimness and distance, which make them too uncertain and too far off, for either clearness or comfort. We cannot afford to take such long journeys, and through such intricate windings. The Bible never asks us to do it. "The word is nigh thee, even in thy mouth and in thy heart, that is, the word of faith which we preach, that if thou shalt confess with thy mouth the Lord Jesus, and shalt believe in thy heart that God hath raised him from the dead, thou shalt be saved." This is all clear; "nigh thee." It is God's word. Speculations cannot improve it. Explanations cannot make it invite faith, only as they make its simplicity understood.

Many of the published dissertations on the nature and philosophy of the atonement may be deep, but they are dark. We cannot afford to travel along such weary distances, and through snch twilight paths, in order to get at the fact—at what it *is*, that we are to believe and trust in. The Bible puts it directly before us, "Slain for us: the just for the unjust, that he might bring us to God." We are asked to receive it, just on God's testimony; not by the aids of philosophy, but on the declaration of the fact. We "make God a liar," if we do not believe the testimony which he hath given us of his Son." We must take it *on God's declaration.* That is faith. The speculations may be useful to silence scepticism, but they never soften hearts. They may make us scholars, but they never make us children, or lead us home. The atonement satisfies God. He says so. That is enough. Leave it there. Men may try; but they will try in vain, when they attempt to convert the weapons for defending against infidelity, into bread to feed God's hungry children. We must "take God at his word." The philosophy of religion is just faith, nothing more.

Many of our treatises on the subjects of faith, having a kind of Germanizing about them—a kind of crazy philosophizing, are so filled up with explanations, and laboured justifications, and attempted analogies, that they have more tendency to awaken doubt than call forth faith. They have just the effect to make the reader believe that the authors are not themselves quite certain of *the thing*, since they take so much pains to demonstrate, explain, and *justify* it. They appear to go back of God's word, and invite other people to go along with them, as if God's word needed the props of their philosophy. This is no aid to faith. Let us "take God at his word." No philosophy can prop up a divine promise, or build a scaffolding to reach it. Some of our theologians, having a kind of German baptism, are more likely to make infidels than make Christians. The same thing may be said of a great deal of modern religious literature—filled with philosophy "falsely so called."

IV.

Waiting for the Holy Spirit.

NEARLY twenty years have now passed away since I became acquainted with the individual of whom I am now to speak. I was called upon to preach, in connection with other ministers of the gospel, in a large village, and during the continuance of what was denominated a "protracted meeting." These meetings had this designation from the fact, that they were continued from day to day, for several successive days. The exercises usually consisted, in that part of the country, of preaching in the morning, afternoon, and evening, with meetings for prayer and religious inquiry, before or after sermon. The sermons were usually preached by those ministers settled in his vicinity, whom the minister of the church where the meeting was held had invited for that purpose. At one of these meetings I preached a sermon on the influences of the Holy Spirit. It was a time of revival in the Church; and the truths of the gospel, preached at such a time, when the Spirit of God was poured out, and when people were peculiarly attentive and solemn, were not likely to be entirely forgotten, even by those who were mere hearers of the word.

Some months after this, as I entered the same village again on my way from a similar meeting in an adjoining parish, I beheld a crowd of people entering the Town Hall. I inquired the reason, and was told there was a "religious meeting there that evening, probably a prayer meeting." I gave my horse into the charge of the hostler at the tavern, and without waiting for tea, mingled with the crowd and entered the hall. Having already preached three times that day, and conversed with numbers who were seeking the Lord, I was too much wearied to think of doing anything more, and therefore endeavoured to keep out of the sight of the clergyman, by taking a back seat and leaning down my head. My attempt was in vain. He discovered me, and requested me to come forward to the desk. I preached a short sermon, the people dispersed, and I went with the clergyman to his home.

We were not seated in the parlour before a servant entered, and said a lady in the hall wished to see me. I immediately stepped into the hall, and a very genteel woman, about forty years of age, addressed me with evident agitation:—

"I beg your pardon for troubling you to-night, sir, but I cannot help it. I have longed to see you ever since you preached here in August. I have often felt that I would give *anything* to see you, for even five minutes. I have prayed for that privilege. And when I saw you in the Town Hall to-night, I was so rejoiced that I could hardly remain in my seat; and I determined to follow you when you went out, till I got a chance to speak with you."

"I am very glad to see you, madam; but I suspect you have taken all this trouble in vain."

"Why, sir, cannot you talk with me one minute? cannot you answer me one question?" said she, her eyes overflowing with tears.

"Certainly, certainly, madam; I can talk with you as long as you please to favour me with your company, and will answer any questions you choose to ask, as well as I can; but I suspect you need an aid which I cannot give you."

"Sir, I want only one thing of you. I want you to tell me how I shall procure the Holy Spirit. I have wanted to ask you this question for months. If you will only tell me, I will not intrude myself upon you any longer."

Entirely overcome with her emotions, she wept like a child.

"*Intrude!* my dear lady. This is no intrusion. I am glad to see you. I thank you, with all my heart, for coming to me. I beg you to do me the justice to believe it, and feel yourself perfectly at ease. Ask me anything, or tell me anything you will, with entire freedom. I will not abuse your confidence.

She stood before me, trembling and weeping, as if her heart would break. And as she aimed to repress her emotions, and removed her handkerchief from her eyes, the light of the hall-lamp shone full upon her face, and I was surprised at the deep solemnity and determination, which appeared in one of the most intelligent and beautiful countenances that I ever beheld.

At this instant the lady of the house, perceiving the nature of our conversation, invited us into a private room. My new acquaintance told me who she was, and repeated the cause of her calling upon me. I asked her some questions, and conversed with her for some minutes, for the purpose of ascertaining more exactly the state of her mind, and adapting my words accordingly. Her intelligence and the elegance of her language surprised me. She was in middle life, a married woman, having a husband still living, and two small children. Her husband was not a pious man; and her thoughts about her own salvation had led her to think much of his, and of the duty she owed to her children. Her first serious impressions arose from the thought, that, not being a member of the Church, she could not dedicate her children to God in the ordinance of baptism; and this led her to think, that in her unbelief she could not fitly train them up in the nurture and admonition of the Lord.

"O sir!" said she, the tears streaming from her eyes, and her sensations almost choking utterance, "I would give all the world to be a Christian! I know I am a sinner, an undone sinner! I have a vile and wicked heart. I have sinned all my life! I wonder God has spared me so long!"

"But he *has* spared you, madam, when you did not deserve it. And what has he spared you for, but that you should repent of sin and flee to Christ for pardon?"

"I would repent if I could. I want to be a Christian. But my hard, wicked heart is stronger than I! For years I have read my Bible, and struggled, and prayed; and it has done me no good! I am afraid I shall be cast off for ever! God has not given me his Spirit!"

"I too am afraid you will be cast off for ever! Probably your danger is greater than you think! But there is mercy in Christ for the chief of sinners. His blood cleanseth from—"

"I know it, sir; I know all that, from my Bible. I have read it a thousand times. But I cannot *come* to Christ without the Holy Spirit."

"Madam, the text is plain, 'If ye, being evil, know how to give good gifts to your children, how much more will your heavenly Father give the Holy Spirit to—'"

"But I am *not* one of his children, sir."

"The text does not say, *to his children*, my dear madam; it says, '*to them that ask him*.' 'Ask and ye shall receive.'"

"Oh! I *have* prayed—I *do* pray."

"Allow me to ask you, madam, how long you have been in this state of mind?"

"About three years. I was first brought to think of my salvation soon after the birth of my first child, when my duty to my family led me to feel the need of religion. I could not have it baptized, for I was not a member of the church; and what troubled me more, I could not do my duty to it, for I was not a child of God."

"And have you been accustomed, for so long a time, to read your Bible carefully!"

"Oh! I have read it all, again and again! I read it daily. I have prayed and wept over this subject, for long *years!* and have waited for the Holy Spirit to renew my heart."

"And have you been waiting for the Holy Spirit for three years, in this state of mind?"

"Indeed, sir, I have."

"Then, for *three years you have been waiting* for what God *gave you three years ago.* It was the Holy Spirit which first led you to feel you were a sinner and needed Christ. The Holy Spirit has been striving with you all along, and you did not know it. He led you to the Bible. He led you to prayer. He sent you here to-night. He strives with you *now*, to lead you to Christ for forgiveness and peace."

"Do you think *so?*" said she with astonishment.

"I *know* so," said I. "God has been better to you than you have thought. He has done what you have never given him credit for. He has called, and you have refused. He has invited, and you have held back. You thought you must not come, and could not. You may, on the spot. The Holy Spirit has not left you yet. I wonder that he has not; but you have another call to-night. And now, madam, accept his invitation; repent; take Christ as your Saviour. Go home and give your heart to God, just as it is. You cannot make it better. The Holy Spirit is with you. Do not resist him any longer. You have stayed away from Christ, because you supposed you must. You wanted the Holy Spirit *first*, and thought you must not come to Christ till your heart was better. The dispensation of the Spirit is in his hands. Go to the fountain. The Bible nowhere tells you to *wait* for the Holy Spirit; but, fleeing to Christ, to depend on his aid *now*."

"Pardon me, sir; I must ask you again if you really think the Holy Spirit is striving with me?"

"Yes, my dear friend, I *know* he is. He has been for years. He offers you his aid. He calls you to Christ now. Go to Christ. Repent to-night. Accept and rest on Christ now. The Holy Ghost saith, 'To-day, if ye will hear his voice, harden not your heart.'"

"And is that all you have to say to me about the Holy Spirit?"

"Yes, that is *all*. The Holy Spirit this moment strives with you. God is willing to save you. Nothing but your own unbelief and impenitence can ruin you."

"Has the Spirit been striving with me?—and I did not know it?" said she, in the manner of meditation, the tears streaming from her eyes. She left me and returned to her home.

Early the next morning, before the sun rose, as I looked from my window, I beheld her coming through the thick dew which lay upon the grass, with hasty steps ascending the hill, on which the house where I lodged was situated. She asked for me at the door, and I immediately met her in the parlour.

"I thank you, my dear friend,—I thank you a thousand times for telling me that," said she, the moment she saw me, her eyes streaming with tears and her countenance beaming with joy. "It was all true. I have found it true. I can rejoice in Christ now. I am happy, sir, oh, I am happy. I thought I *must* come and thank you. I am afraid you will think me rude in calling upon you at such an hour. But I was afraid you would be gone if I delayed; and I could not let you leave town without telling you how happy I am, and how much I thank you. After I heard you preach, three months since, I thought you could tell me something about obtaining the gift of the Holy Spirit, and when I asked you about it last night I was very much disappointed by what you said. I was amazed and confounded. You did not say what I expected. But I *believed* you. I spent the night over this subject. Happy night for me! And now, I *know* you told me the truth. You read my heart rightly. I bless God for what I have found. Pardon me, sir; I *must* ask you to *tell other sinners that Christ is waiting for them.* They do not know it, I am sure, any more than I did, or they would go to him. The Holy Spirit calls us to do so. With all my glad heart, I yield to him. I do not wait any longer. I bless you for telling me, I need not wait."

Weeping for joy, she continued to talk to me in this manner for some minutes.

I have not seen her since. But I have learned that she publicly professed her faith, and has lived for years as a reputable and happy believer.

Probably the influences of the Holy Spirit are more common with impenitent sinners than they suppose. Such persons greatly err, when, instead of fleeing at once to Christ, they wait, and think they *must* wait, for some attainment first. Their waiting for it is but a deceptive excuse; and if they suppose they have gained any attainment, and on that ground Christ has accepted them, their religion is only self-righteousness and delusion. A broken heart is invited to the balm of Gilead. "Tell other sinners that Christ is waiting for them."

The subtlety of the adversary is wonderful. The want of the Holy Spirit was this woman's obstacle. The devil had led her to believe that she was forsaken of the Spirit; and if she was, she knew from the Bible that there was no other help for her. Instead of going to Christ, therefore, in faith, she miserably supposed that she must wait. She did not know that the very urgency and influence of the Holy Spirit consist in bringing sinners to embrace Jesus Christ, as he is offered to us in the gospel. The very thing that God wanted her to do, was the very thing that she supposed she must *not* do, and thus she was compelled to wait in darkness and fear, by a subtle device of the adversary. It is important for convicted sinners to know, that the cause of their irreligion is *not*, that Christ is not willing to receive them, but that they are not willing to trust in him.

V.

Business Hindrance.

A MEMBER of my congregation, a young man who was an apprentice, became attentive to the subject of religion; and, finally, his convictions became very distressing. I had many conversations with him. It all appeared to be in vain. He continued in his distress, without hope, and almost in despair.

One day he said to me, that he believed he never should obtain religion, if he did not quit work and devote his whole time and thought to the subject of his salvation. I told him that that would do him no good—that his duty was to work—that if he would not work he ought not to eat—that neglecting an earthly duty would not lead him to the discharge of a spiritual one. I argued the case with him strenuously on the ground of the Scriptures, "Six days shalt thou labour." I insisted upon it, that the Bible gave no such directions about work as he was inclined to follow—that if he expected to do his duty to God, he must not omit doing his duty to the world—that, at most, he ought not to do without working, any longer than he could do without eating,—for, "if any would not work, neither should he eat".—and that this want of time was only an excuse of a deceitful heart, to keep him from an instant duty, that is, fleeing to Christ in faith.

But I could not convince him. He said his mind was drawn off from religion by his daily employment; and in his opinion, if he had nothing to do, but to seek God, to read and pray, he should soon find salvation. I told him he would be more likely to find a delusion, and *call* it salvation. But I could not shake him from his purpose.

He did quit work. He went away over the river, beyond the reach of his companions, got a room alone in an obscure house, and shut himself up with his Bible. He remained there a week. At the end of that time he called himself to an account, examining his heart, whether he had made any progress. It seemed to him that he had made none at all. He then determined to be more diligent in the study of his Bible, more anxious in prayer, and to compel his obstinate heart to yield. He often attended our religious meetings in the evenings, and then would return to his solitude. He remained there three weeks; and, to his utter astonishment, he found his religious impressions almost entirely gone. He abandoned his retirement and came back to his work in self-defence. "I found," said he, "my own heart was the worst companion I could have. If I cannot come to repentance in the work-shop, I am sure I never can *alone*. If I had stayed there much longer, I should have cared nothing about religion."

He went to work. His seriousness returned; and in about four weeks he entertained a hope in Christ. He united with the Church, and I knew him for years afterwards. He appeared to be a decided and happy Christian.

The human heart will weave an excuse for impenitence out of anything. This want of time is a very common excuse. But it is a falsehood. The advice given to anxious inquirers so frequently in times of revival, to shut themselves up alone till they have found salvation, just misleads them. It makes them think they lack *time* for religion, while, in fact, they only lack *heart*. Let us obey the Bible.

VI.

Waiting for Conviction.

THERE was a young woman in my congregation at one time, about whom I felt no little interest, and had for a long time sought an opportunity to speak with her alone, on the subject of religion. I had spoken to her more than once, sometimes in the presence of her mother, and sometimes before some other member of the family. But she was very reserved. She seemed entirely disinclined to any conversation on the subject. Her taciturnity was so constant, that I could only ask questions, and she answered only in monosyllables, or not at all. I had some acquaintance with her, as a neighbour and friend, but little as a minister. She appeared to me to possess more than an ordinary share of intellect and amiability. I had often noticed that she gave strict attention to my sermons. But, though many others, some among her acquaintance, and some in her own family, had then recently become, as we hoped, the children of God, yet she never manifested any special concern. When I thought of her good sense, her candour, her kindness of feeling, and her sobriety, I was surprised that she did not seek God. She was now passing by the first years of her youth, and it pained me to think that they were gone, and that she was now entering the years of her womanhood, a stranger to Christ. I resolved to see her in private, and aim to overcome that obstinate taciturnity, which I despaired of overcoming in the presence of any other person, and which, as I supposed, hindered me from perceiving the real state of her mind, and knowing what to say to her.

I called at her house and asked for her. But as she and her

mother, both at the same time, entered the room where I was, I was obliged to say to her mother that I desired to see her daughter alone, if she would be so kind as to grant me that privilege. "Oh, *certainly*," said she, and left the room manifestly disconcerted, if not displeased.

I immediately said to the daughter, "I am always happy to see your mother, but I called this morning on purpose to see you alone."

"I knew you asked for *me*," said she; "but mother would come in; she always *will*, when you ask for me. I don't know why it is, but she always seems to be unwilling to have you see me alone."

"And did you wish to see me alone?"

"Not *particularly;* but mother and I are such great *talkers*, that you will find one of us at a time quite enough."

"Do you call yourself a great talker?" said I.

"Oh yes, they say I am; and I suppose it is true."

"Well, will you talk with *me?* I have called on purpose to talk with you on the subject of your religion, if you will allow me that privilege."

She was mute. She cast her eyes downwards, and seemed confused.

"I hope you will not consider me intrusive," said I, "or impertinent; but I have long felt a deep interest in you, and have desired an opportunity to converse with you freely and confidentially about your religious duty."

"I did not know that you ever thought of me."

"Then certainly I have need to beg your pardon," said I. "I must have treated you very impolitely if you did not know that I ever thought of you."

"Oh *no*, sir; you have never treated me impolitely."

"And certainly I never *will*. But permit me to ask you, are you willing to converse with me about your own religion?"

"I have got no religion," said she, with a downcast and solemn look.

"And do you mean always to live without it? and die without it?"

She made no answer. I paused for an answer, as long as I thought I could, without embarrassing her feelings; but no answer came. I continued:—

"You say you have got no religion. Would it not be wise and well for you to attend to that subject, and aim to attain a religion that will secure to you the favour of God and everlasting life?"

She made me no answer. After another pause, I said, "You think of this subject I suppose, sometimes?"

She made no reply.

"Are you unwilling to think of it?"

No answer.

"Are you unwilling to have me speak to you about it?"

No answer.

"Perhaps this *time* is not agreeable to you. Would you prefer to have me call at some other time?"

No answer.

"My dear girl," said I earnestly, "I did not come here to embarrass you, or annoy you in any manner. I love you, and wish to do you good. But if you prefer it, I will leave you at once. I will not intrude myself upon you, or intrude upon your attention a subject to which you do not wish to lend your mind."

"Why sir," said she, "I am glad to see you."

"Why, then, will you not talk with me?"

"Indeed, sir, I do not know what to say."

"Pardon me, my dear girl, I do not wish to embarrass you, or blame you; but certainly you *could* answer me some of the questions I have asked. And, now allow me to ask you again, do you think much on the subject of religion? or have you any concern about it?"

She made me no answer. After a painful, but brief pause, I continued,—

"I beg you to speak to me. Say anything you think or feel. I assure you I have no feelings towards you but those of kindness and respect. I *will* treat you politely and kindly. But, my child, your silence embarrasses me. I am afraid to say another word lest I should hurt your feelings. You might deem another question an impertinence."

"You may *ask* me," said she, with a forced smile.

"Then," said I, "are you giving any serious or prayerful attention to religion?"

"No, sir, not at present."

"I thank you for the answer. But let me ask, do you not think that you *ought* to attend to it earnestly, and prayerfully, and without delay?"

She did not answer, but appeared quite confused. The blood mounted to her cheeks. I pitied her.

"Believe me," said I, "I do not mean to confuse you; but why do you not speak to me, and tell me your feelings plainly and freely? And I will hold all that you say as confidential as you please to make it."

"Well, sir, *I will*. But I know you will not like it."

"No matter for that," said I.

"I do not wish to oppose *you;* but *I* do not think it would do any good for me to attend to religion, with my present feelings."

"Pray, what do you mean? I do not understand you."

"I mean," said she, "that I have no particular anxiety about religion; and I do not believe it would do any good for me to attend to religion, till I have some greater anxiety about it."

"And are you *waiting* for such an anxiety?"

"Certainly I am."

"Do you expect to get it by *waiting?* Do you think it will ever *come* to you?"

"I do not know, indeed," said she, very sadly. "I used to hope so; but I have waited for it a long time."

"Does the Bible tell you to wait for it?"

"I do not know as it *tells* me to wait. But it speaks of conviction, of broken and contrite hearts; and Christian people speak of awakenings, alarms, and distresses of mind, and influences of the Holy Spirit, with those who are led to religion. And you preach such things, as if these were the beginning. And if I have none of these, how *can* I begin to seek God?"

"Did you ever hear me preach that one should *wait* for these?"

"Yes."

"No, *never!* my child."

"Yes I have, I am sure."

"*Never, never!* I preach nothing like it."

"I remember your *text*, sir; and you always preach the text: On thee do I wait all the day.'"

"Yes; and in that sermon I told you that waiting *on* God was one thing, and waiting *for* God was quite another. The first was right, and the last was wrong. We wait *on* him by such things as prayer. Did I not tell you so?"

"Yes, sir; you did."

"And do you pray?"

"No."

"Then you do not obey my sermon and wait *on* God."

"How can I, with no conviction?"

"How do you expect to get conviction?"

"I do not know."

"Do you know and feel that you are a sinner against God, and not reconciled to him?"

"Yes, I do."

"Do you know that you cannot save yourself, and need Jesus Christ to save you?"

"Yes, I *know* it," said she, with a very significant accent upon the word know.

"Then you have *some* conviction."

"You may call it conviction, if you will; but I have no deep impressions."

"And are you just waiting for such impressions, before you will do anything; and when they come you mean to seek God?"

"Yes, sir."

"Then *you may wait for ever!*"

"Oh! I hope not!"

"Probably you will! Such deeper impressions seldom come by waiting for them. How long have you been waiting for them already?"

"About five years, sir."

"And have you *gained* anything in those five years,—any deeper impressions?"

"I do not know as I have."

"Will you gain anything by waiting five years more?"

"I am afraid not," said she, sadly.

"And *I* am afraid not," said I. "You may wait on till you have just waited into the grave, and your *waiting will do you no good!*"

"What *shall* I do?"

"'Seek ye the Lord while he may be found. Call ye upon him while he is near.'"

"What! with my present impressions."

"Yes; with just your present impressions."

"I do not believe it will do any good."

"Perhaps not. But five years' *waiting* has done you no good; and you have no reason to think that five more would do you any. You have tried *waiting;* and now I want you to try seeking, as the Bible bids you."

"I would seek the Lord, if I thought it was possible with my present feelings."

"It *is* possible. I am confident you would not seek in vain. I *know* you are deceived. I know you are acting contrary to the commands of the gospel. I know you are putting your own wisdom in the place of God's wisdom, which calls you to seek the Lord now, to-day. But you are waiting for conviction. Now, I beg you to hear me, and treasure up what I say. I have several things to say to you. Will you hear me?"

"Most willingly, sir."

Then, 1. Remember that God never tells you to *wait* for convictions, or anything else. He tells you, 'Behold now is the accepted time, behold now is the day of salvation.'

"2. You have *no occasion* to wait for any deeper impressions. In my opinion you do not need them. You have impressions deep enough. How deep impressions does a sinner need? What does he need to know and feel, in order to be prepared to come to Christ? I will tell you: he needs to know that he is a sinner—that he cannot save himself—that he needs Christ to save him. That is all, and you have all that already.

"3. Deeper impressions *never yet came* by waiting for them without prayer and without attempting to flee to Christ, and they never *will.*

"4. Your *duty* is to turn from sin and the world to Christ, at once, to-day.

"5. If, after all, you do need any deeper impressions, I will tell you *how* you may get them, and you will get them in no other way. You will get them *just when* you aim to do as God bids you, to repent, to flee to Christ, to give God your heart. At present you are excusing yourself from all this, by the false notion that you have not impressions enough to be able to do so. You do not, this moment, feel condemned for neglecting the great salvation, because you think you cannot attain it till you have deeper convictions. This is your excuse; and it is all a deception, in my opinion. But if you do need deeper convictions, you will get them when you aim to come to Christ. Then you will find you have no *heart* to do it, no *will* to do it, no readiness to deny yourself, and renounce the world, and then you will begin to see what an undone and helpless sinner you are, and how much you have need to pray for God's help, as you are *not* doing now. This is the way to gain deeper impressions if you need them,—and the *only* way. Five years more of waiting, or fifty years, will not give them to you. This is all I have to say."

I left her. About three days after this I called on her again, and found her in a very solemn and sad state of mind. She said that on thinking of what I had told her, she believed every word of it, and tried, with all her might, to do as I had exhorted her. She read her Bible, and prayed, and the more she tried to give up the world, and give God her heart, the more she found that her heart would not yield. She said she "could do nothing with it, —she did not believe there was ever such a heart, so opposed to God,—she never knew before what a sinner she was,—she did not believe there was any possibility of her ever turning to God."

"Jesus Christ," said I, "is able to save you."

She replied, "I suppose he is; but I do not think he ever will!" As she said this she appeared deeply solemn, and was overcome with her emotions, which choked her utterance.

"Jesus Christ," said I, "is *more* than able to save you; he is willing."

She lifted her eyes upon me with a despairing look; "I wish I *knew* that he is willing."

"You *do* know it," said I. "His word tells you so. 'Come unto me all ye that labour and are heavy laden, and I will give you rest. Take my yoke upon you and learn of me, and ye shall find rest for your souls'—'If any man thirst, let him come unto me and drink'—'Whosoever will, let him take the water of life freely'—'Ho! every one that thirsteth, come ye to the waters' —'Let the wicked forsake his way, and the unrighteous man his thoughts, and let him return unto the Lord, and he will have mercy upon him; and to our God, for he will abundantly pardon.'"

"Oh!" said she, "I will try to seek God."

I instantly left her.

Not long after (a few days) I called upon her, and found she was calm and happy in hope. She said that all her trust was in Christ, and that the forbearance and love of God appeared to her most wonderful. She thanked me for what I had said to her. "You opened my eyes," said she. "When you came here that morning I did not intend to talk with you; and when you began to ask me, I was resolved not to tell you how I felt. And if you had not *made* me tell, and had not almost forced me to attend to religion now, I should have waited for deeper convictions all my life. But, sir, I think you were wrong when you told me I did not need any deeper convictions. At that time I knew almost nothing of my heart. I never found out how much it was opposed to God and his demands, till some time afterwards, when I resolved that I would become a Christian that very day."

"And did your resolve bring you to Christ?"

"Oh, no! not at all. It did me no good. My heart would not yield. I was opposed to God, and found I was such a sinner that I could do nothing for myself. My resolutions did me no good, and I gave up all and just cried for mercy. A while after that I began to be at peace. I do not know *how* it is, but *I* have done nothing for myself. Indeed, when I cried so for mercy, I had *given up trying* to do anything. It seems to me that when I gave up trying, and cried to God, he did everything for me."

Some months after this she united with the Church, and has lived in its communion ever since, a useful and decided Christian.

There are multitudes in our congregations, who are just *waiting*, while they ought to be *acting;* who have a sort of indefinite hope about the aids of the Holy Spirit yet to be experienced, while they are pursuing the very course to fail of attaining any such aids. They think they *must* wait. They think wrong. They must work, if they would have God work in them. There can be no religion without obedience. And there is not likely to be, with any sinner, a just sense of his dependence, till he earnestly intends and attempts to *obey the gospel.* Religion is practical. Much of its light comes by practical attempts. "If ye will do the works, ye shall know of the doctrine whether it be of God."

Probably this young woman would have been led to her Saviour five years before, had it not been for her error about waiting for deeper impressions.

VII.

Not Discouraged.

A YOUNG woman of very yielding and amiable disposition, who belonged to my congregation, became alarmed about her condition as a sinner, and set herself to seek the Lord. I visited her, and conversed with her repeatedly. Her seriousness became deeper and deeper. I left her one day, with a very strong expectation upon my mind that the next time I should see her she would be at peace with God. I thought so, because she seemed to realize that God's law justly condemned her as a sinner, that she was dependent upon sovereign grace, and that she ought to repent and flee to Christ. I thought so also, because she appeared to me just as others, with whom I was conversing every day, *had* appeared immediately before their hopeful conversion to Christ. She seemed to me to know and feel the truths of the gospel which are addressed to unconverted sinners, and, therefore, I believed the Holy Spirit was with her to lead her to salvation. I left her with the urgency of the text, "Behold, now is the accepted time," pressed upon her conscience and her heart with all the emphasis my words could give it.

The next time I saw her—a day or two afterwards—her whole appearance was altered. Her solemnity was gone. Her anxieties were evidently diminished. She met me with a smile that surprised and pained me. And, directly the contrary to her former habit, she began to speak of some common matter. Said I—

"Have you given Christ your heart, Mary?"

"Oh no, not yet," said she; "but I don't feel so bad as I did."

"Why not?" said I. "What reason have you to feel any better?"

"I don't know as you would think I have any reason, but I hope I shall be a Christian by-and-by. I don't feel in so much haste as I did, and I am not so much afraid God will cast me off; and the sinfulness of my heart does not trouble me so much."

"My dear Mary!" said I, with astonishment and pain, "how is this? I expected different things! Evidently your seriousness is diminished! You care less for salvation than you did! What has altered your feelings since I saw you?"

"Why, when you left me the last time you were here, and told me to repent that day, I was dreadfully troubled. I felt that my heart was opposing God, and I was afraid to think of living without Christ another hour. Your last words, '*To-day*, *to-day*,' rung in my ears! I could not get rid of them. But pretty soon, Miss S—— S—— came in, about an hour after you went away, and I told her how I felt. But she told me not to be discouraged, only to keep on seeking the Lord. *She* said I was doing very well, and I ought not to feel so; and if I did not get discouraged, I should soon find religion."

"And you believed her?" said I.

"Yes, I believed her; and I have felt better ever since—a great deal better."

"Felt better! Mary! You are resting on a lie! You are miserably deceived! Doing well? How can you be doing well, while an impenitent sinner, rejecting Christ, and exposed every moment to the wrath of God for ever? Your friend, as you call her, has been doing the work of the great deceiver! She did not talk to you as the Bible does, '*To-day*, *to-day*, if ye will hear his voice!'"

I aimed to arouse her, but it was all in vain. Her anxieties departed! She ceased to pray! and in a few days more she was as careless and worldly as ever.

It is not true that a convicted and praying sinner is *doing well* while without faith in Christ. Something more is needed. He must repent and believe. And certainly, if prayerless, he is doing ill.

This young woman who misled the yielding and affectionate Mary, was a professor of religion, and one of those who are very apt to be busy in times of revival. Doubtless she meant well; but her influence was very unhappy. No one is ever safe in giving any counsel to impenitent sinners, unless he is careful to talk just as the Bible talks to them. Blind guides do mischief.

VIII.

Reliance on Man.

AS I was leaving the place of a morning prayer-meeting, which was attended, in a time of revival, very early in the morning, a young man about sixteen years of age came to me, and asked permission to accompany me home, for "he wanted to talk with me."

"What do you wish to say to me?" said I.

"Why, I want you to tell me what to do."

"I *have* told you again and again. I can tell you nothing different, nothing new. You must repent, if you would be saved. You must give up your self-righteousness and flee to Christ. The law condemns you. The sovereign grace of God only can save you. You must give up your miserable and long-continued attempts to save yourself. You must give God your heart, as he requires, and as I have explained to you already many times."

"Yes, I know that, but I am so distressed! I cannot live so! I want you to tell me something else."

"*I* cannot relieve your distress. Christ alone can give you rest. I have nothing else to tell you. I have told you all the truth—all you need to know."

"I thought," said he, "perhaps you could say something that would help me, if I went to your house."

"So you have said to me more than once, and I have told you better. God only can help you. You must rely on him."

"But I should like to talk with you again about my feelings, in your study."

"It would do you no good. You have nothing to say that you have not said before, and I have nothing new to say to you."

"Well, may I go home with you?"

"No. Go home. Man cannot help you. The whole matter lies betwixt yourself and God."

He turned away, the most downcast creature I ever saw. It seemed as if his last prop was gone. He walked as if his limbs could scarcely carry him.

I had not been at home an hour before he came to tell me that his burden was gone. He said that after I "had cast him off," all hope forsook him, and he "had nowhere else to go but to God." Before he reached his home, about a mile, he had given all into the hands of God, and he felt so much relieved of his burden of sin and fear, that he thought he "would turn right about, and come right back and tell me." "But," said he, "I do not believe I should have gone to God if *you* had not cast me off."

Anxious sinners are often kept from Christ by their reliances on men. A great amount of religious conversation often diminishes their impressions. It tends to blunt the edge of truth. It keeps the heart in a kind of reliance on men. Conversation with judicious Christians and judicious ministers is vastly important for inquiring sinners, but there is a point where it should cease. All that men can do is contained in two things—to make sinners understand God's truth, and make its impression upon their hearts and consciences as deep as possible. If they aim at anything more, they are just trying to do the work of the Holy Spirit. Visiting among inquirers one morning, I called on five different individuals, one after another, in the course of a single hour, and in each case was sorry I had called at all; for in each case, after a very few minutes of conversation, I was fully persuaded that God's truth was deeply felt, and that anything which I could say would tend to diminish the impressions which the Holy Spirit was making on their hearts. I aimed to say just enough not to have them think I did not care for them; and got away as soon as I could, for fear of doing an injury. Every one of these individuals afterwards dated her religious hope from the same day. No *man* can preach so powerfully as the Holy Spirit. It is vastly important to *know when to stop*. The divine writers understood this. They are perfect examples. Their *silence* is to be imitated, as well as their utterance.

IX.

Bad Advice.

A FEW weeks after this I had a similar request from another young man, whom also I had often seen, and with whom I had many times conversed about his salvation. We were leaving the church at the close of the evening service when he met me at the door, and said to me that if I was willing he would go home with me. He seemed to be under just and deep conviction as a sinner; and more so, when I had conversed with him on the former part of the same day, than I had ever seen him before. I knew it was not in my power to teach him any important truth which I had not already taught him, and I feared that anything which I could say to him would diminish instead of increasing the impressions which the Holy Spirit was making upon his mind. I wished him to realize that his help must come from God. I recollected the case of the other young man. He appeared just like him when he made the same request. I have never known two persons more alike. Consequently I refused his request. He entreated; but I would not yield. I wished to treat him affectionately, but as he said he had no question to ask me and nothing new to tell me, I refused to allow his accompanying me home, and bade him good night. As he turned away he seemed ready to sink, and I could not but hope that he was about to give up all his attempts to save himself, and flee to the Saviour of sinners.

A few evenings afterwards he came to the meeting appointed for conversation with a very altered look. I asked him,—

"Do you think you have made any progress, since I saw you, in seeking the Lord?"

"No, I do not think I have."

"Do you think you ever will?"

"Oh yes, I believe I shall."

"When?"

"I don't know *when;* but I am not discouraged. I mean to keep on."

"Keep on in what?"

"In seeking religion."

"Then you are keeping on *now* without religion."

"I suppose so."

"Is that a good way to keep on? keeping on in impenitence, in enmity against God, in 'trampling under foot the blood of Christ, and doing despite to the Spirit of all grace?' It seems to me that you would do well to stop and turn about, instead of *keeping on* towards perdition any longer!"

"Why," said he, "ought I to be discouraged?"

"Certainly; the sooner you are discouraged from 'keeping on' towards ruin the better."

"I am not much troubled about that."

"So I perceive. But you *were* troubled when I parted with you a few evenings since."

"Yes, I was *then* very much."

"And what has altered your feelings? Is there not quite as much reason for your being troubled now?"

"I do not know but there may be as much *reason*, but just after I left you and was going home, I met Mr. —— and told him how I felt, just as I had told you; and *he* told me not to be discouraged, but to keep on, read the Bible and pray, and I should find peace of mind by-and-by."

"He *told you wrong*. He ought to have told you to turn from sin to God instantly, embracing Christ in faith, not to keep on in your wicked rebellion, 'according to your hard and impenitent heart, treasuring up wrath against the day of wrath.' 'To-day,' the word of God says,—'to-day, if ye will hear his voice, harden not your heart.' A sinner is *always* hardening when he is intentionally delaying, because he is sinning by disobedience, and sin always hardens. Your mind was relieved by what he told you?"

"Very much. I have felt more at peace since."

"The peace of the wicked! peace in sin! peace without Christ! peace, while there is no peace! peace, while exposed to eternal perdition!"

He smiled at this, though I spoke with the utmost solemnity, and I left him. I saw him many times afterwards, but he seemed to have turned his face towards the world. His attention to religion continued for a little while; but it was not long before all appearances of seriousness had left him. He soon became one of the most stupid and indifferent sinners I have ever seen, and continued to be so as long as I knew him. I have not a doubt that his interview with that man, who was an excellent member of my church, helped to dissipate his serious impressions. His heart seized upon an idea presented to him, and misinterpreted it, and wrought it into an excuse. The idea presented to him, beyond all question, was the idea that he ought not to despair in God, but keep on 'striving to enter in at the strait gate,'—not to keep on in his impenitence. But he took it as a sedative to his conscience. The directions of God's word are the only safe directions for inquiring sinners. The more accurately we see their hearts the more appropriately we may bring Scripture truths to bear upon them. In this perception of their state and this application of divine truth consists the skill of any one who would guide them to Christ. There is no reason to believe that the Holy Spirit ever leaves awakened sinners,—only as *they* leave the truth of God for some error or some sin. Truth is the Spirit's instrumentality. "Sanctify them through thy truth; thy word is truth." We never should cease to cry to a sinner, *Flee*, *flee;* till, safe within the city of refuge, he cannot be reached by the sword of the avenger of blood.

X.

The Whole Heart.

IN the early part of my ministry I was requested by a clergyman to attend a meeting for religious inquiry, and converse with the young men who were there. I spoke to each one separately. Nothing occurred to impress the circumstance particularly on my memory. Twenty years afterwards I met with a clergyman who called up my recollection of that meeting. Said he, "I was there, and you spoke to me. Do you remember what you said?" I had no recollection of the particulars. "Well, I have," said he, "and I will tell you how it was. I have long wanted to tell you. You asked me if I was seeking the Lord; and I told you that I was trying to. You asked me if my trying had done me any good; and I answered that I did not know that it had. You told me then that you could tell me the reason why it had *not;* the reason was, that I had sought with only a part of my heart. You went on to say to me, You must search with all your heart, not half of it; 'Ye shall seek me and ye shall find me, when ye shall search for me with all your heart.' I wondered you said *that.* I thought I *was* seeking with all my heart. But this idea, 'with all your heart,' remained with me. I could not get rid of it; and finally I found out that this was exactly my difficulty. I had been seeking for months, but with a part of my heart only. Your words, '*All your heart, all your heart,*' led me into the knowledge of my character and into the right way. I have often thought of that meeting, and wondered that you should know me so well. That circumstance has since been of great use to me in conversing with anxious inquirers."

Ministers must sometimes draw their bow at a venture. But it is better to take aim. There are *some* Scripture arrows which we should always have in our quiver, because they are sure to hit. They will at least ring upon the harness if they do not penetrate the joints. They will alarm if they do not kill. After we have "toiled all night and taken nothing," if we cast our net on the right side of the ship it will not come in empty. There is but one way to Christ. Faith saves; the faith of the whole heart. Jesus, save me, or I die!

XL

The Welsh Woman and her Tenant.

A MAN, who was entirely a stranger to me, and whose appearance convinced me he was poor, and whose address showed that he was not very familiar with the subject of religion, called upon me one morning, and with some agitation desired me to go to a distant street to see his wife, who was sick. On making some inquiries I learned that his wife had consumption, was not expected to live many days, had not expressed any desire to see me, but that he had come for me at the request of an aged Welsh woman who lived in the same house. I immediately went to the place he described. I found the woman apparently in the last stage of her fatal malady. She was an interesting young woman of about twenty years of age, and had been married a little more than a year. All the appearance of her room was indicative of poverty, though everything manifested the most perfect neatness. She was bolstered up upon her bed, her face pale, with a bright red spot in the centre of each cheek. She appeared exceedingly weak, while her frequent cough seemed to be tearing her to pieces. Her condition affected me. Manifestly, her youth and beauty were destined to an early grave. She must soon leave the world; and how tender and terrible the thought that she might still be unprepared for a happier one!

As I told her who I was, and why I had come there, she offered me her hand with a ready and easy politeness; and yet, with a manifest embarrassment of feeling, which she evidently struggled to conceal.

I have seldom seen a more perfectly beautiful woman. Her frame was delicate, her complexion clear and white, her countenance indicative of a more than ordinary degree of intelligence and amiability; and as she lifted her languid eyes upon me, I could not but feel in an instant that I was in the presence of an uncommon woman.

I felt her feverish pulse, which was rapidly beating, and expressing my sorrow at finding her so ill, she said to me, speaking with some difficulty:—

"You find me—in very humble circumstances—sir."

"Yes," said I, "you seem very sick."

"We have not—always been—so straitened as we are now," said she. "We lived—very comfortably—before—I was sick. But I am not able—to do anything now. And I am ashamed—to have you find me—with my room, and all things—in such a state," casting a look about the room. "Once—I could have seen you in a more inviting place. But, sir—we are now—very poor—and cannot live—as we used to. My situation—is—very humble—indeed."

"You have no occasion to be ashamed," said I. "Your room is very neat; and if you are in want of anything, it will give me pleasure to aid you to whatever you need."

"O sir, I am not—in want—of anything now. I am too sick to need anything—more than the old lady—can do for me; and she is—very kind."

"And who is the old lady?" I asked.

"Mrs. Williams," said she, "in whose house—we have lived since ours—was sold;—the woman that—wanted me to have you—come and see me. She has been—talking—to me about religion (she is a Welsh—woman),—and she has read—to me—in the Bible, but—I cannot—understand it."

"And did you *wish* to have me come and see you?"

"No—yes—I am willing—to see you; but—I am—in such—a place here—my room—"

"My dear friend," said I, "do not *think* of such things at all.

You have something of more moment to think of. You are very sick. Do you expect ever to get well?"

"No, sir; they—tell me—I shall not."

"And do you feel prepared to die?"

"I do not know—what that—preparation—means. And it is too late now for me to do anything—about it. I am too far—gone."

"*No,* madam, *you are not.* God is infinitely merciful, and you may be saved. Have you been praying to him to save you?"

"I never—prayed. Indeed, sir,—I never thought—of religion till I was—sick, and the old lady talked—to me. But I cannot—understand her. I have never—read the Bible. I never was inside—of a church—in my life. Nobody—ever asked me—to go, or told me—I ought to. I did not think—of religion. I just lived to enjoy—myself—as well—as I could. My aunt—who took me—when my mother—died, never went—to church, and never said anything—to me about religion. So I lived—as she—allowed me to, from the time I was three years old. I had property—enough for everything—I wanted—then; and after I left—school—about four years ago,—I had nothing—to do—but to go to parties—and dances—and attend to—my dress, and read—till—I was married. Since that—we have had trouble. My husband—I suppose—did not understand things—in our country—very well. He mortgaged—my house, and in a little while—it was sold—and we were—obliged—to leave it, and come here."

"What did you read?" said I.

"Oh, I read novels the most of the time—sometimes—I read other books; but—not much, except—some history, and biography."

"Did you never read the Bible?"

"No, sir."

"Have you got a Bible?"

"No, sir. The old lady—has got one—which she brings to me; but I am too weak—to read it. It is a large book; and I—shall not live—long enough to read it."

"You need *not* read it," said I. "But now suffer me to talk to you plainly. You are very sick. You may not live long. *Will* you give your attention to religion, as well as you can, in your weak state, and aim to get ready to die?"

"I would sir—if I had time. But I do not—know anything—at all—about religion—and it would do me—no good—to try now, when I have—so little time—left."

"You have *time enough* left."

"Do you—think so—sir?"

"I *know* you have, madam."

She turned her eyes upon me, imploringly, and yet despondingly; and with a voice trembling with emotion, she said to me, speaking slowly and with difficulty,—

"Sir, I cannot—believe that. I have never *begun*—to learn religion. I lived only for my—present enjoyment—till I was married; and since that, after—my husband—failed—all I have thought of—was to save—some little—of my property—if I could; so as not to—be a burden—to other people. And now,—there cannot—be time—enough left—for me—to begin with religion—and go—all the way through."

"*There is time enough*," said I.

Perceiving that she was already exhausted by her efforts to speak, I told her to rest for a few minutes, and I would see her again. I went into another room to see "the old lady," as she called her, whom I found to be a pious Welsh woman, who had rented a part of her house to the sick woman's husband some months before, and who now devoted herself to take care of the poor sufferer. The tenant had squandered all his wife's property; and now during her sickness continued his dissipation, paying little attention to his dying wife. If he ever *had* a heart, rum had destroyed it.

"She is a good creature," said the Welsh woman, "all but religion. When she was well, she was very kind to me. Though she was *a lady*, and had fine clothes, she was not ashamed to come and sit with me an hour at a time, and talk to me, and try to make me happy; for I am a poor, lone widow, seventy years old, and all my children are dead. And when I told her how it was with me, that I had nothing to live upon but the rent I got for the rooms of my house; and she found out (*I* did not tell her of it) that her husband did not pay the rent any longer, she sold her rings and some of her clothes, and brought me the money, poor thing, and told me to take it. I did not know, at first, that she sold her rings and her clothes to get it; and when I asked her how she got it, and she told me, I said to her I would not have it, it would burn my fingers if I took it, and the rust of it would eat my flesh, as it were fire, and be a canker in my heart, and be a swift witness against me in the day of the great God our Saviour. So I gave it back to her. But she would not take it; she laid it down there," pointing to it with her finger, "on the mantlepiece; it is five weeks yesterday, and there it has been ever since. I cannot touch it. I *never will* touch it, unless I am forced to take it to buy her a coffin. Christ Jesus would not have taken the price of a lady's rings and clothes in such a case; and it is not for the like of me to do it. Poor thing! she will soon die, and then she will want rings and clothes no longer! O sir! if I could only think she would wear robes of glory in heaven I would not weep so. But I am afraid it is all too late for her now! Religion is a hard business for a poor, sick sinner! And her husband would not go for you the week before last, nor last week. He *never* went till this morning, when I told him, as I was a living woman, he never should enter the house to-night—he should sleep in the street, if he did not bring you here before the clock struck twelve. I want you to pray for her. There is no telling what God may do. Maybe he will send suddenly. But *I* cannot tell her the way. I have tried. I tried hard; but, poor thing, she said she could not understand me. And then I could do nothing but come to my room and weep for her, and go to prayer, and then weep again. I am glad you have come. And now *don't leave her*, till you have prayed and got a *blessing*, if it is not too late."

I have seldom heard eloquence surpassing that of "the old lady." Some of her expressions were singular, but they seemed to have in them the majesty and tenderness of both nature and religion.

I borrowed the "old lady's" Bible, and returned to the sick woman's room. Seating myself by the side of her bed, I told her I did not wish her to talk, for it wearied her. But I wanted she should listen to me, without saying a word, only if she did not understand me, she might say so, and I would explain myself.

"*Can* I understand?" said she, with a look of mingled earnestness and despair.

"Certainly you can. Religion is all simple and easy, if one desires to know it; and if you do *not* understand me, it is *my* fault, not *yours*. And now, my dear child, listen to me a little while. I will not be long. But first allow me to pray with you for a single minute."

After prayer, I took the Bible, and told her it was God's word, given to us to teach us the way to eternal life and happiness beyond the grave; that it taught all I knew, or needed to know about salvation; that though it was a large book and contained many things which might be profitable to her under other circumstances, yet all that she needed to think of just now was embraced in a few ideas, which were easy to be understood; and I wanted her to listen to them, and try to understand them.

"I will—sir," said she, "as well—as I can."

"Hear what God says, then," said I.

"The first thing is—that *we are sinners*." I explained sin. I explained the law which it transgressed, how it is holy, just, and good; and we have broken it, because we have not loved the Lord our God with all our heart, and our neighbour as ourselves.

"No, I have—never loved—him," said she.

I dwelt upon our sin, as guilt and alienation from God; explained how sinners are worldly, proud, selfish; and read the texts as proofs and explanations,—"By the deeds of the law shall no flesh be justified"—"The carnal mind is enmity against

God, for it is not subject to the law of God." In short, that man is, in himself, a lost sinner; God is angry with him, and he has a wicked heart.

Said she, "That seems—strange—to me; I wish—I had known it—before."

"The *second* thing is—that just such sinners may be saved, because Jesus Christ came to seek and to save the lost." I read from the Bible, "'God so loved the world that he gave his own Son, that whosoever believeth in him should not perish, but have everlasting life'—'The blood of Jesus Christ his Son cleanseth us from all sin'—'He was wounded for our transgressions, he was bruised for our iniquities; the chastisement of our peace was upon him. The Lord hath laid upon him the iniquity of us all.' You see, therefore, that sinners can be saved. Christ died for them."

"Will he—save *me?*" said she.

"I hope he will—but listen to me. The *third* thing is, that lost sinners will be saved by Christ, if they repent of sin and believe in him." I continued to select texts and read them to her. "God now commandeth all men everywhere to repent"—"Except ye repent, ye shall all likewise perish"—"As many as received him, to them gave he power to become the sons of God, even to them that believe in his name"—"Christ is the end of the law for righteousness to every one that believeth"—"Though your sins be as scarlet, they shall be as white as snow; though they be red like crimson, they shall be as wool."

As I read such passages, turning over the leaves of the book, as I stood by her bedside, her eyes followed the turning leaves, and she gazed upon the book in astonishment. At times, when repeating a peculiar text, my eyes rested on her face instead of the book, and then she would ask, "Is that in God's word?" I found it best, therefore, just to look on the book, and read slowly and deliberately.

"The *fourth* thing is, that we need the aid of the Holy Spirit to renew our hearts, and bring us to faith and repentance. 'Except a man be born again he cannot see the kingdom of God'—'That which is born of the flesh is flesh; that which is born of the Spirit is spirit'—'No man can come unto me, except the Father which sent me draw him'—'In me is thy help'—'Let him take hold on my strength, that he may make peace with me, and he shall make peace with me.' Man is *helpless* without the Holy Spirit.

"The last thing is, that all this salvation is freely offered to us *now,—to-day;* and it is our duty and interest to accept it on the spot, and just as we are, undone sinners. 'Hear and your soul shall live'—'Seek ye the Lord while he may be found; call ye upon him while he is near. Let the wicked forsake his way, and the unrighteous man his thoughts, and let him return unto the Lord, and he will have mercy upon him, and to our God for he will abundantly pardon'—'If ye, being evil, know how to give good gifts unto your children, how much more will your heavenly Father give the Holy Spirit to them that ask him'—'Behold, now is the accepted time; behold, now is the day of salvation'—'Come unto me, all ye that labour and are heavy laden, and I will give you rest'—'The Spirit and the bride say, Come; and let him that is athirst come; and let him that heareth say, Come; and whosoever will, let him take of the water of life freely.'

"Now, my dear child, this is all; only these five things. I will now leave you for an hour to rest, and then I will be back to see you."

In an hour I returned, determined to go over the same things, and explain them, if needful, more fully. As I entered the room she looked at me with a gladsome smile, and yet with an intense earnestness, which for an instant I feared was insanity. Said she, "I am so glad you have come;—I have been—thinking—of what you read—to me. These things—must be true; but—I don't know—that I should—believe them, if they were not—in the word—of God. I understand some—of them. I know I am—a sinner—I feel it. I never knew it—so before. I have not—

loved God. I have been—wicked and foolish. I am—undone. And now—when I know it, my heart—is so bad, that instead of —loving God—it shrinks from—him,—and I am afraid—it is too —late—for me!"

"Yes," said I; "your heart is worse than you think. You can make it no better. Give it to God. Trust Christ to pardon all. He died for just such lost sinners."

"Yes, sir,—I remember—that; but—what is it—to believe? I do not—understand *that—thing*. You said I must repent of sin,—and must *believe*—in Jesus Christ. I think that I understand one—of these things. To repent is to be sorry for my sin, —and to leave it. But—what is it—to *believe?* I cannot—understand that. What is believing—in Jesus Christ?"

"It is trusting him to save you. It is receiving him, as your own offered Saviour, and giving yourself to him, as a helpless sinner, to be saved by his mercy. He died to atone for sinners."

"I believe that,—for God's word—says so. Is this—all the faith—that I must have?"

"No; not at all. You must have more. You must *trust* him. You must receive him as *your own* Saviour, and give yourself to him. You may remember the passage I read to you. Here it is in God's word: 'As many as received him to them gave he power to become the sons of God, even to them that believe on his name.' You see that here 'believing' and 'receiving' express the same thing. You are to take Christ as God offers him to you, and you are to rely on him to save you. That is faith."

"Sir—I am afraid—I can never—understand it," said she, the tears coursing over her pale cheek.

"Yes, you *can*. It is very simple. There are only two things about it. Take Christ for your own, and give yourself to him to be his. Sometimes these two things are put together in the Bible, as when a happy believer says, 'My beloved is mine, and I am his.' It is union with Christ, as if he were your husband, and you were his bride."

"Oh! sir,--it is all dark to me! Faith—I cannot—understand it!"

"See here, my dear child. If you were here on this island, and it were going to sink, you would be in a sad condition if you could not get off. There would be no hope for you if you had no help. You would sink with the island. You could not save yourself. You might get down by the shore, and know and feel the necessity of being over on the other side, quickly, before the island should go down. But you could not get there alone. There is a wide river betwixt you and the place of safety, where you wish to go. It is so deep that you could not wade it. It is so wide and rapid that you could not swim it. Your case would be hopeless if there were no help for you. You would be lost! But there is a boat there. You see it going back and forth, carrying people over where they want to go. People tell you it is safe, and you have only to go on it. It seems safe to you as you behold it in motion. You believe it is safe. Now, what do you do in such a case? You just *step on board the boat.* You do not merely *believe* it would save you, if you were on it, but *you go* on it. You commit yourself to it. When you get on you do not work, or walk, or run, or ride. You do *nothing but one. You take care not to fall off.* That is all. You just trust to the boat to hold you up from sinking, and to carry you over where you want to go. Just so, trust yourself to Jesus Christ to save you. He will carry you to heaven. Venture on him now. He waits to take you."

"But—*will* he save—such--a wicked—undone creature—as I am?"

"*Yes, he will.* He *says* he will. He came from heaven to do it—'to seek and to save that which was lost.' He invites you to come to him. I read it to you in his word; 'Come unto me, all ye that labour and are heavy laden, and I will give you rest.'"

"May *I* go?" said she, her countenance indicating the most intense thought; and her eyes, suffused with tears of gladness and doubt, fixing upon me, as if she would read her doom from my lips.

"Yes, you may go to Christ. Come and welcome. Come now. Come just such a sinner as you are. Christ loves to save such sinners."

She raised herself upon her couch, and leaning upon her elbow, with her dark locks falling over the snowy whiteness of her neck, her brow knit, her lips compressed, her fine eyes fixed upon me, and her bosom heaving with emotion,—she paused for a moment,—said she,—

"I do want—to come to Christ."

"He wants you to come," said I.

"Will he—*take—me?*" said she.

"Yes, he will; he *says* he will," said I.

"I am wicked—and do not—deserve it," said she.

"He knows that, and died to save you," said I.

"Oh, I think—I would come, if God,—if the Holy Spirit—would help—me. But—my heart—is *afraid.* I thought,—just now, if I only knew—the way, I *would* do it. But now, when—you have told me, I cannot believe it. I cannot—trust Christ. I never—knew before; what—a distant heart I have!"

"The Holy Spirit does help you. At this moment, in your heart, he urges you to come, to trust Christ. The Bible tells you to come. 'The Spirit and the bride say, Come.' God lengthens the hours of your life, that you may come; while he says to you, 'Behold, now is the accepted time, now is the day of salvation.'"

I paused for a little time; and as I watched her countenance, she appeared to be absorbed in the most intense thought. Her brow was slightly knit—her lips quivered—her fine eyes roamed from side to side, and often upwards; and then closed for a moment. And seeming utterly forgetful of my presence, she slowly pronounced the words, with a pause almost at every syllable:—"Lost sinner—anger—God—Christ—blood—love—pardon—heaven—help—Bible—now—come." And then, turning her eyes upon me, she said,—

"I do want—to come—to Christ—and rest on him. If my God—will accept—such—a vile sinner—I give myself—to him—for ever!—oh!—he will—accept me—by Christ—who died! Lord—save me—I lie on thee—to save me."

She sunk back upon her bed, with her eyes lifted to heaven, and her hands raised in the attitude of prayer, while her countenance indicated amazement.

I knelt by her bed, uttered a short prayer, and left her, to return at sunset.

As I returned, the old Welsh woman met me at the door, her eyes bathed in tears, and her hands lifted to the heavens. I supposed she was going to tell me that the sick woman was dead; but, with uplifted hands, she exclaimed, "Blessed be God! blessed be God! The poor thing is happy now; she is so happy! Thank God she is so happy! She looks like an angel now! She has seen Christ, her Lord; and she will be an angel soon! Now I can let her die! I can't stop weeping! She has been a dear creature to me! But it makes my heart weep for joy now, when I see what God has done for her, and how happy she is."

She conducted me to her sick friend's room. As I entered, the dying woman lifted her eyes upon me, with a smile:—

"The Lord—has made me happy! I am—very happy. I was afraid—my wicked heart—never would—love God. But he has—led me to it. Christ—is very dear—to me. I can—lean on him now. I—can die—in peace."

I conversed with her for some minutes, the "old lady" standing at my elbow, in tears. She was calm and full of peace. She said, "All you told me—was true; my heart finds it true. How good—is Jesus, to save such sinners! I was afraid—to fall upon him; but I know now—that believing is all. My heart—is different. I do love God. Jesus Christ is very dear—to me."

She appeared to be fast sinking. I prayed with her, and left her. The next day she died. I visited her before her death. She was at peace. She could say but little; but some of her expressions were remarkable. She desired to be bolstered up in her bed, that she might "be able to speak once more." She seemed to rally her strength; and speaking with the utmost difficulty, the death-gurgle in her throat, and the tears coursing down her pale and still beautiful cheek, she said,—

"I *wonder*—at God. Never was there such love. He is all goodness. I want—to praise—him. My soul—loves him. I delight—to be his. He—has forgiven me—a poor sinner—and now—his love exhausts me. The Holy Spirit—helped me—or my heart—would have held—to its own—goodness—in its unbelief. God has—heard me. He has come—to me,—and now—I live—on prayer. Pardon me—sir,—I forgot—to thank you—I was—so carried off—in thinking—of my God. He will—reward you—for coming—to see me. I am going—to him—soon—I hope. Dying will be sweet—to me—for Christ—is with me."

I said a few words to her, prayed with her, and left her. As I took her hand, at that last farewell, she cast upon me a beseeching look, full of tenderness and delight, saying to me: "May I hope—you—will always—go to see—dying sinners?" It was impossible for me to answer audibly; she answered for me: "I know—you will—farewell."

She continued to enjoy entire composure of mind till the last moment. Almost her last words to the "old lady" were, "My delight is—that God—is king—over all, and saves sinners—by Jesus Christ."

I called at the house after she was dead, and proposed to the "old lady" that I would procure a sexton, and be at the expense of her funeral; lifting both her hands towards the heavens, she exclaimed, "*No, sir!* indeed; *no, sir!* You wrong my heart to think of it! God sent you here at my call; and the poor thing has died in peace. My old *heart* would turn against me, if I should allow *you* to bury her! the midnight thought would torment me! She has been a dear creature to me, and died such a sweet death. I shall make her shroud with my own hands; I shall take her ring-money to buy her coffin; I shall pay for her grave; and then, as I believe her dear spirit has become a ministering angel, I shall hope she will come to me in the nights."

She had it all in her own way; and we buried her with a tenderness of grief, which I am sure has seldom been equalled.

If this was a conversion at all, it was a death-bed conversion. A suspicion or fear may justly attach to such instances, perhaps; and persons wiser than myself have doubted the propriety of publishing them to the world. But the instance of the thief on the cross is published to us; and if the grace of God does sometimes reach an impenitent sinner on the bed of death, why should we greatly fear the influence of its true history? The wicked may indeed abuse it, as they abuse everything that is good and true; but it must be an amazingly foolish abuse, if on account of a few such instances, they are induced to neglect religion, till they come to die. It is very rare that a death-bed is like this.

I deemed it very important to convince her it was not too late to seek the Lord; and I found it a very difficult thing. The truth, that it was not too late, came into conflict with the unbelief and deceitfulness of her heart. It seems to me, that we ought not to limit the Holy One of Israel, leading sinners to believe that even a death-bed lies beyond hope. Truth is always safe; error, never. And if there is good evidence of a death-bed conversion, why should it be kept out of sight?

And yet it is no wonder that careful minds are led to distrust sick-bed repentance. It seldom holds out. Manifestly, it is commonly nothing but deception. Health brings back the former impiety, or that which is worse.

It does not appear that the dying thief knew anything about the Saviour till he *was* dying; and this woman seems to have been like him. And what a lesson of reproof to Christians, that this woman, living for twenty years among them, and in the sight of five or six Christian churches, should "never have been inside of a church in her life," and that "nobody asked her to go." Year after year she was in habits of intimacy with those who belonged to Christian families; she associated with the children of Christian parents; and yet she never had a Bible—she never read the Bible—she never was exhorted to seek the Lord! And probably she would have died as she had lived; had not divine Providence sent her, in her poverty, to be the tenant of the "old lady," who loved her so well. Oh, how many are likely to die soon, with no "old lady" to bring them the Bible, and pray for them in faith and love!

XII.

The Holy Spirit Resisted.

AS I was riding through a village, in which I was almost a stranger, I saw a number of young people entering a school-house. The clergyman of the place was standing by the door. He beckoned to me to stop. He told me he had appointed a meeting for inquiry, and was surprised to find so many assembling. He wished me to go in, and have some conversation with those who were there. I asked to be excused, as I was on my way to fulfil an engagement, where I *must be* punctually at the time. He would not excuse me, I *must* stop, if it were "only for five minutes."

He conducted me into a room, where were fifteen young women. "Say *something*," said he, "to every one of them." I did, though I was not in the room ten minutes. At the same time, he was conversing with some young men in another apartment.

As I passed from one to another, in this rapid conversation, I came to a young lady about twenty years of age, whose countenance indicated great agitation of feeling. Said I, "Do you feel that you are a sinner, unreconciled to God?"

"Yes, I do; I am a *lost sinner!*"

"Can you save *yourself?*"

"None but Christ can save *me!*"

"Why, then, don't you come to him? He is willing to save you; he *loves* to save sinners like you."

"Indeed I do not know! My heart is hard and wicked; and I am afraid I never shall be saved!" She burst into tears, which she had seemed anxious to suppress, and buried her face in her handkerchief.

"How long have you been in such deep trouble of mind?"

"For three weeks," said she, sobbing aloud.

"Then, *for three weeks you have done nothing but resist the Holy Spirit!*"

I left her and passed to the next individual. In a few minutes I left the room, and went on my way.

The next week, as I was riding in a carriage alone, a few miles from the same village, I saw before me a young gentleman and a young lady in a carriage, riding in an opposite direction, and I was just meeting them. She appeared to be trying to induce him to stop, and he did not seem to understand what she wanted. She finally took hold of the reins herself, stopped the horse, and motioning to me, I reined up also; and we sat in our carriages, face to face, and close together.

"That was true—that was true, sir," said she.

"What was true?" said I. For I did not know who she was, though I recognised her face as one that I had seen.

"What you told me at the inquiry meeting that morning,—that I had done nothing for three weeks but resist the Holy Spirit. That expression pierced my very heart. I did not believe it. I thought I was *yielding* to the Holy Spirit, because I was anxious and had begun to seek the Lord; and I thought you was *most cruel* to speak to me so. I did not believe you, but I could not get the idea out of my mind. It clung to me night and day, 'For three weeks you have done nothing but resist the Holy Spirit.' That expression opened my eyes. And I could not let you pass us here, without stopping to tell you how much I thank you for it."

She said this very rapidly, her eyes swimming with tears, and her countenance beaming with joy. Her whole heart seemed to be embarked in what she was saying.

By this time I fully recognised her, and recollected my former hurried interview with her. For a few minutes I conversed with her, as we sat in our carriages. She hoped that God had given her a new heart. She was at peace not only, but full of joy. "Oh, I am happy," said she, "I am so happy. You opened my eyes. You told me just the truth. I thought you was a cruel man. I wanted you to explain yourself, but you would not stop to hear me. As I reflected on what you said, I hated you with all my heart. But the words would come up, 'For three weeks you have done nothing but resist the Holy Spirit.' It seems to me now, that if you had said anything else, or made any explanation as I wanted you to, I should not have been led to Christ. I can never thank you enough for the words which showed me my very heart."

I have not seen her since. I learned that a few weeks afterwards she made a public profession of religion. Her pastor told me that he esteemed her highly, as one of the most intelligent and accomplished of his flock. She belonged to a very excellent family, She possessed a discriminating mind; and did she err in thinking that for three weeks she had done nothing but resist the Holy Spirit?

XIII.

The Heart Promised.

ONE of the most perplexing and, to me, distressing instances of continued and ineffectual seriousness that I have ever known, was that of a young woman who seemed to me to be as near perfection as any person that I have ever known. She was about twenty years old, of good mind and more than ordinary intelligence. Everybody that knew her loved her. She had been religiously educated, and was of a very sober and thoughtful disposition, though uniformly cheerful. She became interested on the subject of religion, and attended the meeting for religious inquiry week after week. In personal conversation with her at her house I aimed repeatedly to remove all her difficulties of mind, and explain to her the way of salvation. She appeared to understand and believe all that was said to her. Her convictions of sin seemed to be clear and deep. That she could be justified only through faith in Christ she had no doubt. Of his power and readiness to save her, if she would come to him, she had not a doubt. She deeply felt that she needed the aids of the Holy Spirit, and seemed to realize with peculiar solemnity that the Holy Spirit was striving with her. Her seriousness continued for weeks; and while others around her were led to rejoicing in the Lord, her mind remained without peace or hope. I exercised all my skill to ascertain her hindrances, to show her the state she was in, and lead her to Christ. It was all in vain. There she stood, left almost alone. Her condition distressed me. I had said everything to her that I could think of which I supposed adapted to her state of mind. I had referred her to numerous passages in the Bible, and explained them to her most carefully. She had no objections to make. She heard all I said to her with apparent docility and manifest thankfulness, and yet she said she was as far from the kingdom of heaven as ever, her heart was unmoved, and at enmity against God.

Just at this period I accidentally met her one morning in the street. I was sorry to meet her, for I thought I must say something to her; I had said all, and I knew not what to say. Offering her my hand, I asked, "Sarah, have you given your heart to God?"

"No sir," said she, tremulously.

"Don't you think you ought to?"

"I *know* I *ought* to."

"Do you *mean* to do so?"

"Yes, sir, I do."

"Don't you think you ought to do it *to-day?*"

"Yes, I do."

"Then *will you?*"

"Yes, *I will*," said she, emphatically.

"Good-bye," said I, and instantly left her.

A day or two afterwards I saw her, and she had wanted very much to see me; she wanted to tell me how she felt and how she had been affected. She said that she had never felt so before,—that her mind was at rest—that she now loved God—that his character and law appeared to her most excellent, worthy of all admiration and love—that she could now trust in the blood of Christ, and wondered she had never done it before. She partly hoped, though she scarcely dared to hope, that her heart was renewed by the Holy Spirit. "But," said she, "after I made you that promise I would have given all the world if I had not made it. I hunted after you to take back my promise, but I could not find you. The thought of it haunted me. It distressed me beyond measure. I wondered at myself for being so rash as to make it; but I dared not break it. I had a dreadful struggle with myself to give up all into the hands of God; but I am glad of it now."

"Then you think," said I, "that you have done something very acceptable to him?"

"Oh no! not *I!* *I* have done nothing. But I hope God has done something for me. All *I* could do was to tell him I could do nothing, and pray him to help me."

She united with the Church, and yet honours her profession.

This is the only case in which I have ever led any person to make such a promise. I doubt the propriety of doing it. I did not really intend it in this instance. I was led into it at the time by the nature of our conversation and the solicitude I felt for one to whom I knew not what to say.

The resolutions of an unconverted sinner are one thing, and the operations of the Holy Spirit are quite another. They may coincide, indeed, and if such resolutions are made in the spirit of a humble reliance on God, they may be beneficial; "I will arise and go to my father" was no improper purpose. But if such resolutions are made in self-reliance, they are rash, and will seldom be redeemed. Sarah seems to have found herself insufficient for keeping her promise. "All I could do was to tell him I could do nothing, and pray him to help me."

If any one thinks that he has turned to God without the special aids of the Holy Spirit, it is probable that he has never turned to God at all. Certainly he cannot sing, "He sent from above: he took me, he drew me out of many waters; he delivered me from my strong enemy."

XIV.

Fixed Despair.

THERE was in my congregation, at one time, a woman about forty years of age, who was a subject of wonder to me. She was one of the most intelligent and well educated of the people; she had been brought up from her childhood in the family of a clergyman as his daughter; she was very attentive to the observance of the Sabbath; she was never absent from her seat in the church. As the mother of a family she had few equals. Everybody respected her. But she was not a member of the Church. And whenever I had endeavoured to call her attention to the subject of religion, she was so reserved that I could not even conjecture what was her particular state of mind. I was told that she never spoke to any one in respect to her religious feelings.

My ignorance of her views and feelings led me to be in doubt what to say to her. I felt that I was groping in the dark every time I attempted to converse with her. Sometimes I suspected that she secretly indulged a hope in Christ, though she told me to the contrary. At other times I suspected that she was relying upon her perfectly moral life for salvation, though she denied this also.

I could not persuade her to seek the Lord, nor could I ascertain what was her hindrance. And I was the more surprised at this on account of the profound respect which she appeared to have for religion, and her deep solemnity whenever I spoke to her on the subject. I had hoped that by conversation with her I might get a glimpse of her heart, that the peculiarity of her state of mind would casually become manifest, and thus I should learn what it would be best for me to say to her. But she was too reserved for this. After several trials I was still in the dark. I did not know what she thought or felt—what it was that kept her from attending to her salvation.

I called upon her one day and frankly told her my embarrassment about her. I mentioned her uniform taciturnity, my motive in aiming to overcome it, my supposition that some error kept her from religion, and my inability even to conjecture what it was. I said to her that I had not a doubt there was something locked up in her own mind which she never whispered to me. She seemed very much surprised at this declaration, and I instantly asked her if it was not so. With some reluctance she confessed it was. And then, after no little urgency, she said she would tell me the whole, not on her own account, but that *her* case might not discourage me from aiming to lead others to Christ.

She then said that her day of grace was past—that she had had every possible opportunity for salvation — that every possible motive had a thousand times been presented to her—that she had been the subject of deep convictions and anxiety often—that she had lived through three remarkable revivals of religion, in which many of her companions had been led to Christ—that she had again and again attempted to work out her salvation ; but all in vain. "I know my day is gone by," said she. "I am given over. The Holy Spirit has left me."

She spake this in a decided manner, solemnly and coldly, unmoved as a rock! It surprised me. And, as I was silently thinking for a moment how I could best remove her error, she went on to say that she had never before now mentioned this for a number of years—that she fully believed in the reality of experimental religion—that she believed all that she had ever heard me preach, except when, once or twice, I had spoken of religious despair—that, as her day of grace was past, she did not wish to have her mind troubled on the subject of religion at all,—and asked me to say nothing more to her about it.

I inquired how long she had been in this state of mind. She

told me she had known for eighteen years that there was no salvation for her. I inquired if she ever prayed. She said she had not prayed in eighteen years. I inquired if she did not feel unhappy to be in such a state. She said she seldom thought of it; it would do no good, and she never intended to think of it again. I asked,—

"Do you believe the heart is deceitful?"

"Yes, I *know* it."

"It may be, then, that your wicked heart has deceived *you* in respect to your day of grace."

This idea appeared to stagger her for a moment; but she replied,—

"No; I am not deceived."

"Yes, you are."

"No, I am not. Nothing can save me now, and I do not wish to have my mind disturbed by any more thought about it."

"Why do you attend church?"

"Only to set a good example. I believe in religion as firmly as you do, and wish my children to be Christians."

"Do you pray for *them?*"

"No; prayer from me would not be heard."

"Madam," said I, emphatically, "you are in an error. I know you are. And I can convince you of it. If you will hear me, lend me your mind and speak frankly to me, and tell me the grounds on which your despair rests, I will convince you that you are entirely deceived. I cannot do it now. It would take too long. You have so long been in this state, and have fortified your error by so many other deceptions, that it will take some days to demolish the defences you have heaved up around you. But I can do it. If your mind will adhere to a thing once proved to you—if, when a thing is *fixed*, your mind will let it *stay* fixed, and not just have the same doubt *after* the demonstration that it had before it, I am perfectly certain you may be led to see your error. May I come to see you again about it?"

"I had rather not see you. It will do no good. It will only make me miserable. I did not intend to tell you how I felt; but when you found out that something was concealed, I would not deceive you. But I wish to hear no more about it. *My* day of grace is past for ever."

"No, it is *not*," said I, most emphatically. "Your deceitful heart has only seized on that idea, *as an excuse for not coming to repentance.* Allow me, at least, to come and see you."

"I had rather not, sir."

"Madam, you must! I *cannot* leave you so! I will not! I love you too well to do it. I ask it as a personal favour to myself; and I shall not think you have treated me politely, if you refuse it. May I see you a little while to-morrow!"

"I will *see* you,—if you so much desire it."

"I thank you, my dear lady. You have greatly gratified me. You will yet believe what I have said to you. I *know* you can be *saved.* And you know *me* well enough to know that I am not the man to make such strong declarations rashly. All I ask is the opportunity to convince you. I will see you to-morrow."

In all this conversation she seemed as unmoved as a stone. She did not shed a tear, or heave a sigh. She could talk about the certainty of her eternal misery as if her heart were ice!

The next day when I called, I asked to know the reasons or evidences on which her dreadful opinion rested. She told me one after another, referring to many texts of Scripture; and did it with a coldness which made me shudder. Of the certainty of her eternal enmity to God, and her eternal misery, she reasoned so coolly, that I almost felt I was listening to words from the lips of a corpse!

Perceiving that she would probably decline seeing me again, and wanting time to study her case more carefully, I suddenly took leave of her. I had expected the old affair of the "unpardonable sin," or "sin against the Holy Ghost;" but I found a far more difficult matter.

I called again. Evidently she was sorry to see me. But I gave her no time to make any objections. I desired her to listen to me, and not yield her assent to what I was going to say, if she could reasonably avoid it. I then took up her evidences of being for ever given over of God, beginning with the weakest of them; and in about an hour had disposed of several in such a way that she acknowledged her deception "in respect *to them.*" "But," says she, "there are stronger ones left."

"We will attend to them hereafter," said I. "But remember, you have found your mistake in respect to *some;* therefore, it is possible you may be mistaken in respect to *others.*" This remark was the first thing that appeared to stagger her old opinion. She *said* nothing; but evidently her confidence was shaken.

I saw her time after time, about once a-week, for five or six weeks; examined all her reasons for thinking her day of grace gone by, except one, and convinced her they were false. Evidently she had become *intellectually* interested. There was but one point left. She had never in all this time expressed a wish to see me, or asked me to call again. I now called her attention summarily to the ground we had gone over, and how she had found all her refuges of lies swept away, save one, as she had herself acknowledged; and if that were gone she would think her salvation possible—and then asked her if she *wished* to see me again.

She replied that her *opinion* was unchanged; but that she *should* like to hear what I had to say abont this remaining point, which, as she truly said, I had avoided so often.

I called the next day. I took up the one point left—this last item which doomed her to despair; and as I examined it, reasoning with her, and asking if she thought me right, from step to step as I went on, the intensity of her thought became painful to me. She gazed upon me with unutterable astonishment. Her former cold and stone-like appearance was gone; her bosom heaved with emotion, and her whole frame seemed agitated with a new kind of life. To see the dreadful fixedness of despair melting away from her countenance, and the dawnings of inceptive hope taking its place, was a new and strange thing to me. It looked like putting life into a corpse. As my explanation and argument drew towards the close, she turned pale as death. She almost ceased to breathe. And when I had finished, and in answer to my question, she confessed that she had no reason to believe her day of grace was past,—instantly she looked as if she had waked up in a new world. The tears gushed from her eyes in a torrent—she clasped her hands—sprung from her seat, and walked back and forth across the room, exclaiming, "I can be saved! I can be saved! I can be saved!" She was so entirely overcome, that I thought she would faint, or her reason give way. I dared not leave her. I said nothing, but remained till she became more composed, and took my leave with a silent bow.

The next Sunday evening she was at the inquiry meeting. She appeared like other awakened sinners, nothing remarkable about her, except her very manifest determination to seek the Lord with all her heart.

In about three weeks she became one of the happiest creatures in hope that I ever saw. She afterwards united with the Church, and yet lives a happy and decided believer.

The gospel is addressed to hope. Despair must always be deaf to it. Entire despair is incompatible with seeking God. Despair cannot pray. The last effort of the devil seems to be, to drive sinners to despair. "We are saved by hope," says the apostle.

Few errors are harmless. None are safe. Truth is never injurious. And I can have no sympathy with those ministers who think an error may do an impenitent sinner good. Tricks are not truth.

XV.

Total Depravity.

ABOUT to call upon a young woman, to whom I had sometimes spoken on the subject of religion, but who uniformly appeared very indifferent, I began to consider what I should say to her. I recollected that, although she had always been polite to me, yet she evidently did not like me; and therefore I deemed it my duty, if possible, not to allow her dislike to *me* to influence her mind against religion. I recollected, also, that I had heard of her inclination towards another denomination, whose religious sentiments were very different from my own; and I thought, therefore, that I must take care not to awaken *prejudices*, but aim to reach her conscience and her heart. The most of her relatives and friends were members of my church. She had been religiously educated, and was a very regular attendant upon divine worship; I knew, therefore, that she must have considerable intellectual knowledge on the subject of religion. But she was a gay young woman, loved amusements and thoughtless society; and I supposed she would be very reluctant to yield any personal attention to her salvation, lest it should interfere with her pleasures. And beyond all this, I had heard that she possessed a great share of independence, and the more her friends had urged her to attend to her salvation, the more she seemed resolved to neglect it.

I rang the bell, inquired for her, and she soon met me in the parlour. I immediately told her for what purpose I had called, and asked whether she was willing to talk with me on the subject of her religion. She replied,—

"I am willing to talk with you, but I don't think as you do about religion."

"I do not ask you to think as I do. I may be wrong; but the word of God is right. I have not come here to intrude *my* opinions upon you, but to induce you to act agreeably to your own."

"Yes," she replied, with a very significant toss of the head, "you all *say* so; but if anybody ventures to differ from you, then they are '*heretics*,' and '*reprobates*.'"

"I beg pardon, Miss S——, I really do not think you can say that of *me*."

"Well—I mean—mother, and the rest of them; and, I suppose, you are just like them. If I *do* differ from you, I think I might be let alone, and left to my own way."

"Most certainly," said I, "if your own way is right."

"Well," says she, "I am a Unitarian."

"I am very glad to hear it; I did not know you were anything."

"I mean," said she, "that I think more like the Unitarians than like you."

"I doubt it," said I; "but no matter. Never mind what *I* think. *I* am no rule for *you*. I do not ask you to think as *I* do. Let all that go. You may call me fool, or bigot, or—"

"You are no *fool;* but I think you are a *bigot*," said she.

"Very well," said I; "I am happy to find you so frank. And you—"

"Oh!" said she, blushing, "I did not mean to say that; indeed I did not. That is too impudent."

"Not a bit," said I. "It is just right."

"Well," said she, "it is true that I *think* so; but it was not polite to *say* it."

"I thank you for saying it. But no matter what *I* am. I wish to ask you about yourself first, and then you may say anything to me that you please to say. Do you believe the Bible?"

"Yes; to be sure I do!" said she, tartly.

"Are you aiming to live according to it? For example, are you daily praying to God to pardon and save you?"

"No!" said she, with an impudent accent.

"Does not the Bible command you to pray? 'To seek the Lord while he may be found, and call upon him while he is near?'"

"Yes, I know that; but I don't believe in total depravity."

"No matter. I do not ask you to believe in it. But I suppose you believe you are a *sinner?*"

"Why, *yes*," she said impatiently.

"And need God's forgiveness?"

"Yes."

"Are you seeking for it?"

"No."

"Ought you not to be seeking for it?"

"Yes; I suppose so."

"Well, then, will you begin, without any more delay, and act as you know you ought, in order to be saved?"

"You and I don't agree," said she.

"No matter for that. But we agree in one thing; I think exactly as you do, that you ought to seek the Lord. But you don't agree with *yourself*. Your course disagrees with your conscience. You are not against *me*, but against your own reason and good sense,—against your known duty, while you lead a prayerless life. I am surprised that a girl of your good mind will do so. You are just yielding to the desires of a wicked and deceitful heart. I do not ask you to think as I think, or feel as I feel; I only ask you to *act* according to the Bible and your own good sense. Is there anything unreasonable, or unkind, any bigotry in asking this?"

"Oh no, sir. But I am sorry I called you a bigot."

"I am glad of it. I respect you for it. You spoke as you felt. But let that pass. I just want you to attend to religion in your own way, and according to God's word. I did not come here to abuse you, or domineer over you, but to reason with you. And now, suffer me to ask you if you think it right and safe to neglect salvation as you are doing? I know you will answer me frankly."

"No; I do not think it is."

"Have you long thought so?"

"Yes; to tell you the truth, I *have*, a good while."

"Indeed! and how came you still to neglect?"

"I *don't know!* But they keep talking to me,—a kind of *scolding* I call it; and they talk in such a way, that I am provoked, and my mind turns against religion. If they would talk to me as you do, and reason with me, and not be *dinging* at me, and treating me as if I were *a fool*, I should not feel so."

Said I, "They may be unwise perhaps, but they mean well; and you ought to remember that religion is not to be blamed for *their* folly. And now, my dear girl, let me ask you seriously, —will you attend to this matter of your salvation as well as you can, according to the word of God and with prayer, and endeavour to be saved? Will you do it without any further delay? If you are not disposed to do so; if you think it best, and right, and reasonable to neglect it; if you do not wish me to say anything more to you about it;—then say so, and I will urge you no more. I shall be sorry, but I will be still. I am not going to annoy you or treat you unpolitely. What do you say? shall I leave you and say no more?"

"I don't wish you to leave me."

"Well, do *you* wish to seek the Lord?"

"I wish to be *saved*," said she. "But I never can believe in total depravity. The doctrine disgusts me. It sounds so much like *cant*. I *never will* believe it. I abhor it. And I *won't* believe it."

"Perhaps not," said I. "I do not ask you to believe it. But I ask you to repent of sin *now*—to improve your day of grace, and get ready for death and heaven. I ask you to love the world supremely no longer—to deny yourself and follow Christ, as you know you ought to do. When you sincerely try to do these things, you will begin to find out something about your heart that you do not know now."

"But I don't like *doctrines!* I want a practical religion!"

"That practical religion is the very thing I am urging upon you: the practice of prayer—the practice of repentance—the practice of self-denial—the practice of loving and serving God in faith. I care no more about doctrines than you do, for their own sake. I only want *truth*, which shall guide you rightly and safely, and want you to follow it."

"Well," said she, "if I attempt to be religious, I shall be a Unitarian."

"*Be* a Unitarian, then, if the Bible and the Holy Spirit will make you one. Do not be afraid to be a Unitarian. But get at the truth, and follow it, according to your own sober judgment. Study your Bible for your own heart. Get right. Pray God to direct you. And never rest till you feel that God is your friend and you are his. I beseech you to this, because I love you and wish you to be right and happy. And now, my dear girl, tell me, will you try to do it?"

"Yes, sir, *I will*."

"I thank you for that promise. And I do trust God will bless you."

In a few days she sent for me. I found her very sad. She told me she was in trouble. She had not found it so easy a thing to be a Christian as she expected. Her heart rebelled and recoiled; and she did not know what was the matter. Her mind would wander. The world would intrude. Instead of "getting nearer to religion, she was getting further off every day." She wanted to know if other people felt so when they tried to be Christians.

I said but little to her, except to direct her to God's promises to those that seek him with all their heart. She desired me to pray with her, which I did. As I rose to depart, she affectionately entreated me not to neglect her.

About ten days after this she sent for me again. I obeyed her summons. She told me, with tears in her eyes, that she never dreamed she was so wicked. She said the more she tried to love God and give up sin, the more her own heart opposed her. Her sins not only appeared greater, but it seemed to her that sinning was as natural to her as breathing. "*What shall I do?*" said she; "I have no peace, day or night! My resolutions are weak as water."

I repeated texts of Scripture to her. "In me is thy help"—"Let the wicked forsake his way, and the unrighteous man his thoughts," his thoughts are wrong, "and let him return unto the Lord, and he will have mercy upon him, and to our God, for he will abundantly pardon"—"Strive to enter in at the strait gate."

I saw her several times. She said her troubles increased upon her, temptations came up every day, and it seemed to her "there *never was so wicked a heart* as she had to contend with." Among other things, she said, some Christian people would keep talking to her, and she did not wish to hear them. I advised her to avoid them as much as possible; and without letting her know it, I privately requested her officious exhorters to say nothing to her. But I found it hard work to keep them still. And when she complained to me again of their officious inquiries about her feelings, I requested her to leave the room whenever any one of them should venture on such an inquiry again.

She continued her prayerful attempts after the knowledge of salvation, and in a few weeks she found peace and joy in believing in Christ. She told me she *knew* her entire depravity; "but," said she, "I never should have believed it, if I had not found it out by my own experience. It was just as you told me. When I really tried to be a Christian, such as is described in the Bible, I found my heart was all sin and enmity to God. And I am sure I never should have turned to Christ, if God had not shown me mercy. It was all grace.

"Now I believe in total depravity. But I learned it alone. *You* did not convince me of it."

"I never tried," said I.

"I know you didn't; and it was well for me that you let it alone. If you had tried to prove it, or gone into a dispute about Unitarianism, I believe I should not have been led to my Saviour."

She afterwards made a public profession of religion, which she still lives to honour.

XVI.

Ignorance of Self.

IN the time of a revival of religion, a clergyman, not much known to me, called upon me, and by invitation preached for me at my regular weekly lecture in the evening. I had mentioned to him the existing seriousness among the people. His sermon did not suit me. He made careless statements; seemed to me to rely on impressions more than on truth; seemed to value his own powers, and to desire other people to rely on theirs. I perceived that he highly esteemed himself, as "a revival preacher;" and I thought he preached "revival," and prayed "revival," rather than religion.

After we had got home, and my clerical friend had retired for the night, one of my most intimate and confidential friends came in to see me, and inquired how I liked the sermon. I criticised it with some freedom. My friend then told me, that as she left the church she fell in company with one of our young ladies, who had been serious for some weeks, and who said to her, "Oh, that sermon will do me good. It was just what I wanted. I wish our minister would preach so."

I felt humbled and sad. And as my clerical friend was much older than myself, I thought it became me to consider more carefully what he had preached, and what I had been saying.

But I noticed that, from that time, the serious impressions of this young lady, who thought "the sermon would do her good," began evidently to diminish. I saw her often, and aimed to bring back the depth and solemnity of her former seriousness. It was all in vain. She grew more and more indifferent, till finally she went back to the world entirely. There she remains. Years have rolled on; but she remains a stranger to Christ.

Convicted sinners are very poor judges of what "will do them good." The very things which they think they need, are often the very things which are snares to their souls. How is it possible for "the natural man, who discerneth not the things of the Spirit of God," to tell what will do him good? He has no sincere liking for God, or the truth of God. And if likings are to be consulted, the truth must often be sacrificed. It is better to trouble his conscience, than to please his heart. A convicted sinner is the last person in the world to judge justly, in regard to the kind of instruction he needs. He will seize error more readily than truth; and if his tastes are consulted, his soul will be endangered. In consulting such tastes lies the cunning art of deceivers, who lead crowds to admire *them*, and run after *them*, and talk of *them*, while they care not for the truth: "deceiving and being deceived."

XVII.

Superficial Conviction.

THERE was much opposition to religion, at one time, among a few young men in the place where I was settled. It was in a season of revival. Probably the gospel was then preached with more than ordinary plainness. The complaint was made that there was too much said about the justice of God, the terrors of the law, and the wickedness of the human heart. They said that I "exaggerated," in respect to the danger of sinners, and made God appear as a terrible and odious Being; which was "no way to lead men to religion."

Just at this time I was informed that some young men were determined to attend the meeting in the evening, with stones in their pockets, to stone me on the spot if I ventured to preach about "depravity," and "sinners' going to hell." This was an indication, I thought, that the doctrines of divine justice and human wickedness had alarmed them, and that these arrows ought to be "made sharp in the heart of the King's enemies." Therefore I preached that evening on these two points, the wickedness of men, and the anger of God against the wicked. There was no disturbance. Nobody stoned me. The opposers were present, and were seated near together. In the first part of the sermon there was an occasional whisper among them, but they soon became attentive, and our meeting was one of stillness and deep solemnity.

Immediately after the service, I attended an inquiry meeting, to which I had publicly invited all unconverted sinners, who were disposed prayerfully to study divine truth. Some of the young men met me at this meeting. Within a few months some of them united with the Church. Among them there was one who told me, at the time of his examination for Church membership, that what had been reported of him was not true,—that he "had *not* carried stones in his pockets prepared to stone me." Said he, "I know my heart was wicked enough to do almost anything, but it never was bad enough to do that."

I noticed this expression. It was an unusual thing to hear such a remark. Directly the opposite was common. I therefore examined this young man the more carefully. But he appeared so sensible of his natural depravity, so humble, so docile, and so determined to live a life of holiness, that he gained my confidence, and he was received into the Church. I thought that he might be a true believer, and still his views of divine doctrine be erroneous; and I knew very well that many people regarded me as too strict on points of doctrine. And though I believed, and had always acted on the principle, that true experimental religion will always lead its subjects to a knowledge of the great essential doctrines of the Christian system,—indeed, that to experience religion is just to experience these doctrines,—I came to the conclusion that this principle would not adjudge him to be unfit to become a communicant.

As long as he remained in the place, about two years, he lived apparently a Christian life; but after he removed to a neighbouring city, away from his religious associates, and under a new kind of influences, he soon began to neglect public worship, violate the Sabbath, and finally became a profane and intemperate man. I called to see him, and conversed with him. He was entirely friendly to myself, but he appeared blinded and hardened. He said he did not think himself to be very wicked. "Indeed," says he, "I never *did* think my heart was so bad as some people tell of. I never did much hurt; and as to being so bad that I can't reform, I know that I can turn from sin when I please."

Probably my exertions for him did no good. The last that I

heard of him was, that he grew worse and worse, and would probably die a miserable and drunken man.

I have often thought that a truly regenerate man cannot have any doubt of the entire depravity of the heart. If he does not see *that,* it is probable that he does not see his heart. And hence his repentance, his faith in Christ, and his reliance upon the Holy Spirit, will probably, all of them, be only deceptions. My observation continues to confirm me more and more in the opinion that *to experience religion is to experience the truth of the great doctrines of divine grace.*

XVIII.

Excitement.

WHILE God was pouring out his Spirit upon the congregation to which I ministered, and upon many other places around us, two individuals belonging to my parish went to a neighbouring town to attend a "camp meeting." One of them was a young man of about twenty years of age, whose mother and sisters were members of the Church. The other was a man of about twenty-six years, whose wife and wife's sister were also communicants with us. Both of these men returned from that meeting professed converts to Christ. They had gone to it, as they told me, without any serious impressions, impelled by mere curiosity. While there, they became very much affected; so much so, that one or both of them fell to the ground, and remained prostrate for an hour, unable to stand. They earnestly besought the people to pray for them, and prayed for themselves. Their feelings became entirely changed. Instead of grief and fear, they were filled with joy and delight. And in this joyful frame of mind they returned home, having been absent only two or three days.

I soon visited them both, and conversed with them freely. At my first interview I had great confidence in their conversion. They seemed to me to be renewed men, so far as I could judge from their exercises of mind. They appeared humble, solemn, grateful, and happy. In future conversations with them, my mind was led to some distrust of the reality of their conversion. They did not seem to me to have an *experimental knowledge of the truth*, to such an extent as I believed a regenerated sinner would have. I could get no satisfactory answers when I asked,

"What made you fall? How did you feel? What were you thinking of? What made you afterwards so happy? What makes you so happy now? What makes you think God has given you a new heart? What makes you think you will not return to the world and love it as well as ever?" They had ready answers to all such questions, but they did not seem to me to be *right* answers. They appeared to have no clear and full ideas of the exceeding sinfulness of the heart, of remaining sin, or the danger of self-delusion. And yet these men were prayerful, thoughtful, serious, and happy. They studied their Bibles, forsook their old companions, and appeared to value and relish all the appointed means of grace. In this way of life they continued for months. I took pains to see and converse with them often; and though they did not appear to me to blend very happily in feeling with other young Christians, or to enjoy our religious services as if they were quite satisfied, yet my mind apologized for them, on the ground of the peculiar way in which their religion commenced. And with the exception of their imperfect views and feelings about the great doctrines of religion, I saw nothing in either of them to make me think them unfit for connection with the Church.

Some months after their professed conversion, I mentioned to them, separately, the subject of making a public profession of their faith. Each appeared to think this his duty, but each of them was rather reserved. I could not very definitely ascertain their feelings, though I aimed carefully and kindly, and repeatedly to do so. One season of communion after another passed by, and neither of them united with the Church. Their particular friends, who had made such frequent mention of their conversion, as if it were more worthy of mention than the conversion of scores of sinners around them, and who had so much rejoiced in their conversion, and had been so confident of its reality, began to be very silent about them. I found that their confidence in them was shaken.

Within a year from the time when they professed to have turned to Christ, the younger man had become entirely careless of religion; and, so far as I know, continues so to this day. The other was a little more steadfast. But within three years he had become an intemperate man, and a shame and a torment to his family; and the last I heard of him, he was a drunkard! He had ceased to attend divine worship on the Sabbath; family prayer was abandoned; his children were neglected; and his broken-hearted wife, with prayer for him still on her lips, but almost without hope that God would hear, was fast bending downward towards the grave, the only remaining spot of an earthly rest!

Mere excitements of mind on the subject of religion, however powerful, unless they arise from the known truth of God, are never safe. Excitement, however sudden or great, is not to be feared or deprecated, if it is originated simply by the truth, and will be guided by the truth. All other excitements are pernicious. It is easy to produce them, but their consequences are sad. A true history of spurious revivals would be one of the most melancholy books ever written.

The great leading doctrines of Christianity are the truths which the Holy Spirit employs when he regenerates souls. If young converts are really ignorant on such points, not having experimentally learnt them, they are only converts to error and deception. It is not to be expected, perhaps not to be desired, that young Christians should understand doctrines scholastically, or theologically, or metaphysically; but if they are Christians indeed, it is probable that their mind will be *substantially* right on such doctrines as human sinfulness, divine sovereignty, atonement, justification by faith in Jesus Christ, regeneration by the special power of the Holy Spirit, and the constant need of divine aid. God's children all have the same image, and same superscription—the family mark. Heaven has but one mould. "Beholding as in a glass the glory of the Lord, we are changed into the same image."

XIX.

Ashamed of Christ.

IN the course of my annual pastoral visitation to the families of my congregation, I called upon a married woman, not a professor of religion, whom I had seen before, and whom I had aimed to persuade to prepare for the future life. I recollected her former reserve and apparent indifference to religion, and determined, before I entered the house, to exert all my powers to lead her to an immediate attention to her future welfare. As I expected, I found her alone, her husband being engaged in his daily employ as a mechanic. I stated to her in few words the particular reason why I had called on her,—that I wished to persuade her to attend to her salvation.

"I have little time for that," said she.

"Little time!" said I. "What do you mean?"

"I mean," said she, with a very determined air, "that my time is all occupied. I have hardly a moment to spare. I have much to do for my family. I have my husband and three children to care for. We are not rich; and if we are to live comfortably and appear respectably, I must be industrious—at work almost every moment of my time. My husband works hard, and I mean to do *my* part towards getting a living."

"I am glad to hear you say that," said I. "It gives me a higher opinion of you. It convinces me that you know *one* part of your duty, and intend to do it. I am sorry that you are overburdened with work, if you are so; I am sorry that you have any hardships. But I am *not* sorry that you are not rich as you say. If you were rich I should have less hope of you; you would have more temptations and *no more* time. The gospel is for the poor; for their comfort here, and their salvation hereafter. Jesus Christ was poor. He preached to the poor. He associated with the poor. He sympathized with the poor. He loved the poor. If you had less to do I am not certain that you would be any more inclined to give attention to religion than—"

"Yes, I should," said she.

"I have no doubt you think so, but perhaps you are mistaken. How is it with other people—with those who *have* less to do? Do you see the rich and people of leisure, any more of *them* Christians, in proportion to the number, than of the poor?"

"No, sir; not so many."

"Well, are you an exception—are you not like other people? And if, on the whole, more people are hindered from religion than helped towards it by wealth and time *enough* to attend to it, is it not probable, that if you were in the very condition you wish to be in, with more wealth and less to occupy you,—is it not probable that you would be less likely than you are now to attend to religion? Think a moment. Many of your friends and neighbours, who have much time, are not pious. Many of them who have little time to spare from labour are. Somehow or other they have found time to pray, to seek the Lord, to repent. And now, my dear woman, tell me honestly, have you not as much time as they?"

"I suppose I have," said she.

"Then, can you not seek the Lord as well as they?"

After a considerable pause she answered with apparent hesitation:—

"I could, if I knew how."

"*Will* you, if I will tell you how?"

"Yes, as well as I can, in the little time I have to spare."

"Time! woman! time to spare! What is time given to you *for*, but to lay up treasures in heaven? You must find time to be sick, and time to die, whether you are prepared or not. And you ought not to treat religion as if it were a mere secondary matter, to be attended to or not, just according to your convenience."

"Oh no, sir; I do not mean *that.* I have always designed to be a Christian."

"And you have put it off from time to time, waiting for a more fit opportunity?"

"Yes, I have."

"Then, let me tell you, a more fit opportunity will never come till the day you die! No, it never will! Your idea about want of time is all a deception. You have had time, and you have lost it! You have it to-day, and you are losing it now. You have done your duty to your family *well*, and I respect you for it. I honour your feelings of anxiety and affection for your husband and children. I would not that you should do less for them. But I would that you should do *more* for your own soul, and for your God and Saviour. I tell you solemnly you *have* time to seek God. It is a deceitful and wicked heart, and not want of time, that keeps you in your irreligion. God knows your situation and all your cares. He has himself placed you as you are situated. He will accommodate the aids of his grace to all the difficulties of your situation. 'He knoweth our frame, and remembereth we are but dust.' He does not require of you *anything* which, by his grace, you cannot do. And you have a wrong idea of the merciful God, when you think he has placed you in such a situation that you have not time to attain salvation."

"I do not mean to say *that*," said she.

"Then you *have* time, and have no occasion to talk about the little time you have?"

"Yes, I have time, if I knew how."

"God has told you how. You may find his directions in his word. For example, in the fifty-fifth chapter of Isaiah, 'Seek ye the Lord while he may be found; call ye upon him while he is near.' That is one way of seeking him. You must pray. Do you ever pray?"

"Not often!"

"Ought you not to pray, as he bids you?"

"I *ought* to."

"Then *will* you? will you begin to-day? will you carefully read that chapter, and pray over it, and beseech God to lead you to salvation?"

"Yes, *I will*," said she solemnly.

"Then, good-bye. If you seek the Lord, as that chapter directs, you will not seek in vain."

A few days after this I called upon her, and found her in a very anxious state of mind. She had no more to say about want of time. She seemed deeply impressed with a sense of sin and utter unworthiness, and expressed her gratitude to God that her mind had been turned to this subject, before her life had come to a close. I conversed with her as well as I could, and aimed to lead her to Christ. She appeared to me to know her condition as a sinner so well, and to be so deeply impressed with a sense of her need of Christ, and in all respects so solemn and determined, that I hoped she would soon be brought into the peace and security of faith.

I soon called again, and found her in the same state of mind. This surprised me. I had not expected it. I laboured to find what could be her hindrance; but I questioned, and reasoned, and talked in vain.

Again and again I repeated my visits to her. She remained the same. It distressed me. I could not understand it. For months she had appeared to me to understand all the great truths of the gospel, and to feel them deeply. I could detect no error in her views. I could not find wherein she was unprepared to deny herself. I could discover no reliance upon her own righteousness, and no lack of prayer or love of the world, which might tend to hinder her from coming to Christ. She omitted no outward duty. Daily she studied and prayed in secret. Still she had no hope and no peace. And yet, as months rolled on, her seriousness and solemnity did not appear to diminish, as I expected they would. The Holy Spirit had not forsaken her.

Her case seemed to me a dark mystery. I could not understand it. I had never been acquainted with any such instance before. Ordinarily I had found those of such deep seriousness coming to repentance, or else losing their anxiety much sooner than this. She appeared to have all confidence in me, and to conceal none of her feelings from me. I knew she was a woman of good mind, and strong and deep feelings. And on that ground, after exhausting all my powers to discover her hindrance or difficulty, I said to her one day, at a kind of venture, "Mrs. K——, I have been very anxious about you for a long time. I love and respect you. I have tried with all my might to do you good. But I have failed! Something, I know not what, keeps you back from repentance and coming to Christ. Now, what is it?"

"Why," said she, with great effort, speaking as if compelling herself to speak, "I have never been baptized."

The expression startled me. I could not conceive what she meant. I knew she was a woman of good mind, and well instructed; and how the lack of baptism should keep her from turning to Christ, it was impossible for me to conjecture. Her case was a perfect riddle to me, darker than before. I answered,—

"You have never been baptized? Well, what of that—how does that hinder you from fleeing to Christ?"

"Oh," said she, "if I were really a Christian, it would be my duty to join the Church; and I never could come out, at my age, before my husband and my three children, and be baptized."

I was perfectly amazed at her.

"Why," said I, "do you mean that you should be ashamed to own Christ, and be baptized, in the presence of your husband and children?"

"Yes, I mean just that."

"And has that idea hindered you from coming to Christ?"

"Yes, I believe it has. I never could do that; and every time I think of following Christ, that turns me back. I could not endure it. If it were not for that, I believe I should be willing to follow Christ. There is no other thing that *I* know of which I should not be willing to do."

Still more amazed, I answered,—

"You utterly astonish me! I am amazed beyond measure! Is it possible, that a woman of your sense, of your character and decision is hindered by such an idea? Are you not ashamed of it?"

"I know it seems foolish," said she; "and that is the reason why I did not tell you before. I thought you would despise me; but such are my feelings. I never *could* be baptized!" She wept bitterly.

"Well, I thank you, my dear friend, for telling me now; I thank you much for it, and respect you for it. You shall never regret it. I have no disposition to despise you, or in any way hurt your feelings. But is it not strange that—"

"Yes; it is strange and foolish," said she, interrupting me; "but I cannot help it. I do feel so. Oh, how I wish I had been baptized in my infancy! But my parents were not communicants in the Church."

She still sat weeping immoderately.

"My dear friend," said I, "you are yielding to a temptation of the devil. Remember, Christ has said, 'He that is ashamed of me, of him will I be ashamed.'"

"I know it, I know it all; I have thought of it a thousand times. I wish I did not feel so; but I cannot help it." As she said this, she lifted her streaming eyes upon me, and hastily brushed away her tears, as if determined to dismiss the subject of religion from her thoughts.

"Hear me," said I. "You *must* not yield to this. Your being baptized cannot certainly be a matter of great self-denial to you; and if you were a believer indeed, you would not feel it to be so. Give yourself to Christ to be saved; and you will not hesitate then, with your heart full of love to him, to be baptized before your husband and children, and all the world if need be." She shook her head at this in a very determined manner, as if she disbelieved it, or was resolved to dismiss religion from her thoughts. Said I,—

"Well, then, since you feel so, I will remove all that difficulty, —*you need not be baptized at all*, if you do not wish to be. You need not think of it again. Repentance and fleeing to Christ in faith are your duties now; and the great adversary is keeping you from Christ, by leading you to think of what may be your duty hereafter. Dismiss all that from your thoughts entirely. You need *not* be baptized. You need not join the Church. I never will say a word to you about it, unless you do to me. Only repent. Give God your heart *now*, before he leaves you to your own way. The Holy Spirit will not always strive with you."

"Do you mean," said she, "that I need *never* be baptized?"

"Yes, I mean exactly that. You need not be baptized unless you choose to be after you have come to repentance and faith in the Redeemer. I never will mention the subject to you. And now, will you seek the Lord with all your heart, and let baptism alone?" Said she,—

"I hope I shall be enabled to do so, if I can be a Christian without being baptized."

I prayed with her, and left her. Within a very few days from that time she found peace with God. She had very comfortable evidences of her acceptance. She appeared to be a peculiarly determined and happy believer. She avowed her hope of eternal life through the atonement made for sinners by Jesus Christ—expressed her astonishment that she had lived so long in impiety—thanked me very emphatically for "delivering her out of her snare," as she called it—and blessed God that her "poor heart could now rest."

After this I saw her often. For months she continued much the same in hope, peace, and gratitude towards God.

I kept my promise to her. I never uttered a word to her about connection with the Church. One day she said to me that she should like to become a member of the Church, if I thought she "had any fitness for the Lord's table."

"But, Mrs. K——," said I, "you have never been baptized."

"Oh," says she, "don't say anything about that. I have got over all that difficulty now. I am willing to be baptized; and *I want* my husband and my children to *know* that I love Christ, and am willing to own his name."

A few days afterwards she was received as a member of the Church, and I baptized her in the presence of all the congregation.

After she had been at the Lord's table, and the congregation was dismissed, she waited for me at the door of the Church, to tell me that she "wanted to have her children baptized in the afternoon." She apologized for asking me to do it on a day in which I had so many duties; but she said she could not wait; she did not wish to have her children tormented as she had been, and she might not live till another Sabbath. She presented them for baptism in the afternoon. The next day she told me that she considered the covenant of God a very precious privilege, she could now pray for her children, as embraced in the covenant promises; and it relieved her heart to think that they would not be hindered from religion by such an "obstacle as had troubled her so foolishly."

Many convicted sinners are kept from salvation by some mere trifle. It is important to remove the obstacle. They will not be likely to seek God in earnest till that is done. The stony ground and the thorny ground need preparing before the seed is sown. The young man in the gospel valued his riches too much to follow Christ. All kinds of rubbish will gather around a wicked heart, and a sinner will yield to an obstacle which he is ashamed to mention. We have gained something when we have discovered what it is. We can then take aim, and the arrow is more apt to hit.

XX.

The Last Step.

FOR the purpose of learning as much as possible about the workings of the human heart, I have been accustomed, in conversing with those who have been led to indulge a hope in Christ, to ask them questions whose answers might be beneficial to me in my intercourse with others. "As in water face answereth to face, so the heart of man to man." It is not probable that the consciousness of such persons will always be very extensive. Some are not likely to recollect the processes of their own mind. But it is probable that such consciousness will have much truth in it, and that thereby we may sometimes get a clear understanding of the operations of the Holy Spirit, and of the difficulties or errors which keep sinners from repentance. On this matter the conceptions of an uneducated or an ignorant man are not worthy of so much regard probably as those of a well-trained and discriminating mind. Fanaticism will soon expose itself when its own consciousness is appealed to, and is compared with the truth of God.

To those who have recently indulged a religious hope, I have many times put such a question as this: What kept you so long from Christ?—or, What was your hindrance?—or, What were you trying to do in all that time while you were so anxious about religion, and had not attained the hope you have now? I have never received but two answers to that question. The answers, indeed, in the form or words of them have been various, but they might all be reduced to two in substance, if not to one.

A highly educated man, a fine scholar, and a very careful

thinker, gave me one of them,—a man, at that time an officer in one of our colleges, and who afterwards filled an important station in a public institution as a man of science. He had been for some weeks very anxious and prayerful. He had often sought conversation with me, and I had told him all the truth of God and his own duty as well as I could. Very manifestly he had disliked, if he had not disbelieved, what I said to him in respect to prayer and a sinner's dependence upon the Holy Spirit. On one occasion, after I had been urging upon his heart and conscience some of the fundamental and plain truths of the gospel, he said to me, "This is too doctrinal." I therefore concluded that just such doctrinal instruction and urgency were the very things his case required, and continued ever afterwards to employ them when I conversed with him. At another time he stated to me the speculative preferences and habits of his own mind; and expressed his opinion that such a mind needed "views of truth adapted to its calibre," as he expressed it. I therefore took pains ever afterwards to simplify everything as much as possible, and talk to him as I would talk to any unlettered man or to a child. When I referred to the Scriptures and quoted their language in its connection, and showed how one passage was explained by another, and how the truths I urged upon him were perfectly consistent with all the other Scriptures, and how these truths of God must not be set aside in our experience, but that our religious experience must mainly consist in experiencing just these doctrines or truths of God, he became silent, but I did not think he was satisfied. He appeared convinced, but not in the least relieved.

After he had reached a different state of mind he came to me again, and stated to me his views and feelings with a clearness that I have seldom known equalled. His mind seemed as light as day. "Faith is the great thing," said he. "Simplicity is better than speculation." After conversing with him for a time, I thought I should like to know how such a clear and strong mind would judge in respect to the hindrances which keep convicted sinners from salvation. I therefore said to him,—

"You have been a long time attentive to religion, what hindered you that you did not come to repentance before?"

"Allow me," he said, "to tell you about myself. I have studied religion for years. It is no new subject to me. Three or four times before now I have had my attention arrested and have been over all this process of conviction, and prayer, and anxiety, everything, but the last step."

"What was *that step?*" said I.

"Giving up all to God!" was his emphatic reply. He then went on to say, "I was like a man trying to climb over a rail fence. I went up one rail, and then another, and another, till I got to the top; and then got down again and went on, the same side as before. That has always been the way with me before now. But now I hope I have got over. I have been brought to give up all to God."

"What do you mean by giving up all to God?"

"I mean," said he, "consenting to let him rule,—to let him do with me as he pleases, and trust him to do everything for me through Jesus Christ."

"How came you to get over the fence at last?"

"Because *I* gave up all, and *God* took me over."

This was his consciousness. So far as he could himself understand the process of conversion, the turning-point lay just here—"I gave up all to God."

All true converts may not be conscious of any special act of the Holy Spirit in their regeneration. Minds are not all equally discriminating. Some are confused in respect to what passes within them. But with discriminating minds there will ordinarily be the clear impression that something has been done for the soul beyond its own power. This impression, indeed, is no unfit test in every case of religious hope. If it is entirely wanting, we may well doubt the reality of the believed conversion, no matter how it is expressed. The words are nothing, but the thing is essential. The Holy Spirit is the author of regeneration, and why should not the subject of his operations be expected to have a consciousness that a power beyond his own has acted for him, and has done for him what was never done before? That "effectual calling is the work of God's Spirit" has ordinarily constituted one of the things which true converts have learned by their own experience. In some way or another, this idea will come out as they are giving a reason for the hope that is in them. "He sent from above; he took me; he drew me out of the deep waters, and established my goings upon the rock." Moral suasion experience is a very suspicious sort of experience. There is a better kind: "*I* gave up all to God, and *he* took me over."

And more. Impenitent sinners need to be convinced of their dependence on a power beyond their own. They need this especially. It is an essential point. Such a conviction will tend to drive them off from their miserable self-reliances. It will never put them at rest, but lead them to work, to prayer. Aside from such a conviction, they will be ignorant of the extent of their depravity, their seriousness will lack depth, and their seeking lack earnestness. The just sense of the amount of their criminality for continuing in their impenitence cannot be brought home to their hearts unless the doctrine of their dependence helps to bring it there.

The Holy Spirit is their offered aid; and surely that aid is enough. They should know and feel it to their heart's core, that they are now, on the spot, to-day, under the most solemn obligations to repent, not only because sin is wrong, but because God offers them the aids of the Holy Spirit: "In me is thy help." Their impenitence not only tramples under foot the blood of the covenant, but also does despite to the Spirit of grace.

XXI.

The Persecuted Wife.

JUST before one of our seasons of communion, I called upon a woman whom I had often seen, and who for some months had entertained a hope in Christ, to have some conversation with her in reference to her uniting with the Church. She thought such a step to be her duty, for she believed the Holy Spirit had renewed her heart, and Christ had accepted her. She delighted in faith to repose upon him, and she said it would rejoice her heart to come to his table, and try to honour a Saviour whom she had neglected for so many years.

But she feared her husband would oppose it. He was somewhat intemperate, and, when intoxicated, tyrannical. She wished to unite with the Church, but she did not wish him to know it. He seldom attended public worship, and cared and said so little about religion, that she deemed it quite probable he would never know anything about it if she should make a public profession of her faith. She proposed, therefore, to unite with the Church, but to keep it a secret from him.

To this proposal I could not consent. I explained to her why I could not. There were several reasons. He was her husband, whom she was bound to honour; and though there might be much in him which she could not respect,—his irregular life and his opposition to religion,—still she was bound to treat him kindly. If she should unite with the Church without his knowledge, he would be more likely, as soon as he knew it, to be offended and treat her unkindly, and to have his opposition to religion increased. She must not be ashamed of Christ, or fear to do her duty in the face of all opposition. And if she had so little faith that she could not confess Christ for fear of any wicked man's displeasure—if her faith in God was so small that she could not do her duty, and trust him to take care of her—I could not have confidence enough in her piety to consent to her reception into the Church.

She appeared greatly cast down. She wept bitterly. "Then," said she, "I can never come to the Saviour's table!"

I replied, "I think you can, madam. In my opinion, your husband will not be so much opposed to you as you think. If he should be, you can pray for him, and He who hears prayer can remove his opposition."

She was much agitated. "What shall I do?" said she. "I do think it my *duty* to come out from the world and own Christ as my Saviour and Lord, and I long to do so; but I am afraid of my husband. I know he would never consent to it, and would abuse me if I should name such a thing in his hearing.

"You have not tried it, madam. You have nothing to fear. God loves his children, and for their sakes often restrains wicked men. Besides, your husband is not so bad a man as you think, probably."

"O sir, you don't know him! He sometimes talks to me in a dreadful manner if he finds me reading the Bible or crying."

"Well," said I, "it is nothing *but* talk. He has just manliness and courage enough to bluster and abuse a poor woman like you with his tongue, but he will go no further. If you do your duty he will not dare to injure you, and quite likely, when he sees you are firm, your example will be the means of leading him to repentance."

"What *shall* I do? I wish you would tell me."

"I will tell you, madam. When your husband comes home, take some favourable opportunity, when you are alone with him, and when he appears calm, sober, and good-natured, and just tell him seriously and kindly how you feel, what you think of your past life, what you believe God has done for you, and that you have come to the conclusion it is your duty to unite with the Church. If he is angry, or speaks unkindly to you, have no disputes, not a word of argument; hear all he has to say in silence. You may tell him, if you think best, that you have done all your duty to him as well as you could while you had no religion, and now you mean to do it better; but you think you owe duties to your God also, which ought not to be neglected. But do not say one word unless your feelings are kind, and mild, and calm. You must feel rightly, or you will not speak rightly. You can at least tell him this, and hear what he will say."

"Well, I will do it," said she, "if you think it best."

I left her. Three days afterwards I called upon her, and found her in deep depression. She had followed my advice, employing my own words as nearly as possible in speaking to her husband. At first he was silent, and she thought he was going to make no opposition. But after saying a few words, he seemed to be worked up into a dreadful passion. He swore he would never live with her another day if she joined the Church. He would turn her out of doors. He declared "the Church folks were all hypocrites;" and as for her minister, he was a *villain*, and if he ever came to his house again, to destroy the peace of his family, he would "put him out of the house quick."

"What time will he be home?" said I.

"In about an hour."

"Very well," said I, rising to go; "I will be here in an hour."

"Oh no, sir, no!" said she, "I hope not. He will abuse you. I don't know what he would not do."

"Never fear," said I. "He will not trouble me. You need not tell him I have been here this morning. And if I meet him here at noon, do not leave me alone with him; stay and hear what he will say to me."

She begged me not to return, but in an hour afterwards I returned, and found him at home with his wife. I spoke to him, gave him my hand, and conversed with him for some minutes. He was rather taciturn, appeared a little sullen, but he did not treat me with any special rudeness. I mentioned to him the altered feelings of his wife, and expressed my hope that he would himself give immediate and prayerful attention to his salvation. I solemnly assured him that, without being born again, he could not see the kingdom of God; and that though he had neglected it so long, salvation was still within his reach; but that he would soon be on the down-hill of life, even if God should spare him, of which he had not an item of security. To die as he was would be dreadful. And if he would seek God, like his wife, they would live together more happily for themselves, and would set an example for their numerous children, which certainly would be beneficial to them, and be fondly remembered by them when he and his wife were gone to the grave.

He heard all this in silence, but did not seem to be much affected by it, beyond an occasional sigh, while I was speaking. When I arose to depart he coldly took leave of me.

Before the next season of communion arrived, I called upon his wife, expecting to find her prepared to confess Christ before men. She had seen that her husband did not treat *me* as he had sworn to do, and I thought she would be convinced by that that there was nothing to be feared if she should unite with the Church, as she steadily maintained it was her duty to do. But I was disappointed. She seemed more determined than ever to yield to her husband's wishes. "He has dreadfully threatened me," said she.

"And will you obey his threats, and disobey what you yourself say is the command of Christ?"

"I do know it is my duty. I feel it. The Testament makes it plain in Jesus Christ's own words. But we are poor people. I am a poor woman without friends, dependent upon the daily labour of my husband for myself and my children. He says he will not live with me a single day after I join the Church, and I don't know what will become of me and the children. The most of them are very young. I have eight of them, and the oldest is not sixteen. And what would become of this baby if I had no house or home?"

As she said this, she was holding the little thing in her arms, and the tears gushed from her eyes, and fell in quick drops upon its little cheek. The scene was too much for me. I turned away and wept.

But repressing my emotions, I said to her: "My dear friend, I am sorry for you; but I do not fear for you. Do whatever you seriously deem your duty, and God will take care of you. Your husband will do no such thing as he threatens. He will *not* leave you. He will *not* turn you out of the house. He will *not* drive you and the children into the street. If he should, remember 'Blessed are ye when men shall revile you, and persecute you, and shall say all manner of evil against you falsely, for my sake. Rejoice and be exceeding glad, for great is your reward in heaven'—'Ye cannot serve two masters'—'Whosoever will save his life shall lose it; and whosoever will lose his life for my sake shall find it'—'Whosoever shall be ashamed of me and my words, of him shall the Son of man be ashamed, when he shall come in his own glory and in his Father's, and of the holy angels'—'If any man come to me and hate not his father and mother, and wife and children, and brethren, and sisters, yea, and his own life also, he cannot be my disciple'—'Every man that hath forsaken houses, or brethren, or sisters, or father, or mother, or wife, or children, or lands, for my name's sake, shall receive an hundred fold, and shall inherit everlasting life.' Such are some of the solemn words of Christ. I cannot alter them. It is your solemn duty to weigh them well. They appear to have been uttered for just such cases as yours. In the first ages of Christianity they were obeyed. Men and women became even martyrs for Christ. I do not know what God may call *you* to endure—not martyrdom, I believe; but if he should, it were better for you to die a thousand deaths, than to dishonour and disobey your Lord. My heart bleeds for you, but I cannot help you. Go to your God. Cast your burden upon him. Pour out your heart to him. I have told you before that I do not believe your husband will execute one of his threats. But if you cannot have faith in God, and obey his commands, come what may, do not think yourself a Christian. 'My sheep hear my voice. They follow me.' If you do not believe it to be your *duty* to come to the Lord's table—"

"Oh," said she, interrupting me, and sobbing as if her heart would break, "I *know* it is a duty. It is *my* duty. Christ has commanded me."

"Well, will you obey him?"

She did not answer. She could not. She seemed crushed beneath a burden she was unable to bear, and continued to weep bitterly.

"I will leave you," said I. "I will not even pray with you now. You are the one to pray. You can pray better than I can, on this occasion; and God will hear you."

I left her. That communion season passed by, and another, and still another. She was still undecided. I mentioned the subject to her more than once; and on one occasion she told me she did not any longer fear *anything* on her own account, for she could herself bear death even, but it was her fear about her children that kept her from her duty.

" God can take better care of them than you can," said I.

It appeared to me to be no part of my duty to urge her to unite with the Church. I never had done so. I believed God would teach her her duty, as she prayed for the Holy Spirit. But I often exhorted her to learn her duty from her Bible, and by prayer; and when she had learnt it, to do it in good faith, and fear nothing. And she always affirmed, she knew her "duty to be to confess Christ before the world."

Nearly a year after the time I had contrived to meet her husband at his house, when he had threatened to put me out if I came there, she sent for me. I went. Immediately after I entered her house she said to me,—

"I have made up my mind to join the Church, if you are willing to receive me. I know I ought to have done it before, but my faith was weak. I could not endure the thought of what is to come upon me and my children. After I got over all fear on my own account, I still feared for them. And even now I am afraid my faith will fail me, when the communion day comes. But if you are willing to receive me, and God will give me strength, I will go forward where my Saviour commands."

I said to her, "Fear not, for I have redeemed thee; I have called thee by thy name; thou art mine. When thou passest through the waters I will be with thee; and through the rivers, they shall not overflow thee; when thou passest through the fire, thou shalt not be burnt, neither shall the flame kindle upon thee. For I am the Lord thy God, the Holy One of Israel, thy Saviour."

"Precious promise!" said she; "blessed promise! God has said it, and I can trust him."

She appeared very solemn indeed, but not unhappy. She said she expected all that her husband had threatened; but she had for months been thinking of the words of Christ, which I had quoted to her; and she could not hesitate any longer. "He gave his life for me," said she; "and shall I not give my worthless life for him, if he asks it?"

I told her I had no more to say to her than I had said so often before. But she must tell her husband that I had been there, and that she was going to obey the dying command of Christ. "You may tell him, that you have done your duty to him and to the children, as well as you could, and intend to continue to do it as a good wife and mother ought." But she need not reason with him at all if he made any opposition. She must not dispute or argue. And I would call to see her the Saturday before the communion Sabbath.

I did so. She informed me that she had done as I advised her. She told her husband what she meant to do; and he replied very sullenly, "Well, you know what I told you. Not a day shall you stay in this house after you join that Church! I *will not* live with you—not a day!"

I told her to repeat the same thing to him again that night

I afterwards learnt that she did; and he merely replied, "You know what I told you—and I'll *do it!*"

Their house was situated too far from the church for her to walk, and some one must take care of the children while she was absent at church. It was now Saturday. I engaged a conveyance for her to church, and procured a woman to take care of her children on the Sabbath.

She retired to bed on Saturday night with a heavy heart. The thought would come over her mind, time after time, that she had spent her last day of peace—that before another night should come, her family would be broken up, and she and her children separated, perhaps for ever, without a home, and without a friend to lean upon. She could do nothing but weep and pray; and she wept and prayed till she fell asleep.

When she awoke in the morning her husband was gone. This alarmed her. She knew not what to expect. He had not commonly risen on Sabbath morning till a late hour; and she supposed his doing so now foreboded no good. She hastily rose, dressed herself, and looked for him. He was nowhere to be found. The children also looked for him; but all in vain. With a sad heart she busied herself in preparing breakfast, and in about an hour he came in. "Wife," says he, with a sort of careless accent, "I suppose you want to go to church to-day, and it is too far for you to go afoot. You know I am too poor to keep any horse, and I have been down to Mr. B——'s to get a ride for you in his waggon. He says you can ride with him, as well as not, if you want to go; and I will stay at home and take care of the children!"

She was so astonished that she could scarcely believe her ears. She hesitated for a moment; but as the truth burst upon her, she threw her arms around his neck and wept like a child. He wept too. But he aimed to conceal it; and making some expression about breakfast, as if to divert his own thoughts, he said he "would go back and tell Mr. B—— that she would ride with him."

She did ride with him. Her husband stayed at home and took care of the children. When she returned in the afternoon, he met her pleasantly; and when in the evening she told him, as I had directed her to do, that she had been at the Lord's table, he merely replied in an affectedly careless manner, "Well, what of that?"

Ever after that time he made no opposition to her religion, but would take pains to accommodate her to the utmost of his power. He would procure some means for her to attend church, would offer to stay with the children while she was gone, and in every possible way aimed to gratify her desires about her religious duties. He came with her to the church when she presented her children for baptism. For a time he was more temperate, and we had no small hopes that he would himself turn to the Lord. Indeed, I had confidently expected it all along. But I never knew of any decided change in his habits. Whenever I spoke to him about his wife, he seemed to be glad on her account. He said he believed "*she* was a true Christian, and no pretender; and wished all the members of the Church were as good as she." But I could not induce him to seek the Lord.

What it was that produced the sudden change in his feelings on that Saturday night I never could ascertain. But it requires no great amount of faith to believe that God interposed in behalf of that praying and weeping wife, and by the power of his own Spirit put a stop to the opposition and rage of that rebellious man. "He maketh the wrath of man to praise him, and the remainder of that wrath he will restrain."

XXII.

The Arrow Driven Deeper.

FINDING it impossible, on account of the number, to have much conversation with each individual at the inquiry meeting, I at one time abandoned the practice of conversation for a few weeks, and addressed them all together. I found this was unacceptable, and concluded, therefore, to return to the former custom. It was on one of those evenings, when about seventy persons were present, and I was passing rapidly from one to another, that I came to an individual who had never been there before.

Said I: "What is the state of *your* feelings on the subject of your salvation?"

"I feel," said he, "that I have a very wicked heart."

"It is a great deal more wicked than you think it," said I; and immediately left him, and addressed myself to the next person.

I thought no more of it till a few days afterwards, when he came to me with a new song in his mouth. He had found peace with God, as he thought, through faith in Jesus Christ. Said he: "I want to tell you how much good you did me. When I told you that I had a very wicked heart, and you answered that it was a great deal *more* wicked than I thought, and then said nothing more to me, I thought it a most cruel thing. I expected something different. I thought you would say more, and my soul was wonderfully cast down. I did not believe you. I was angry at your treatment. I thought you did not care whether I was ever saved or not; and I did not believe you knew anything about my feelings. But the words rung in my ears, 'A great deal more wicked than you think.' I could not get rid of them. They were in my mind the last thing when I went to sleep, and the first when I woke. And then I would be vexed at you for not saying something else. But that was the thing which drove me to Christ. I now know it was just what I needed. I thought, when I went to that meeting, my convictions were very deep. But I have found out they were very slight. You hit my case exactly. If you had talked to me, my burden would have been diminished. But you fastened one idea on my mind. You drove the arrow deeper, when I expected you to do just the contrary; and I could find no relief till I gave up all into the hands of Christ. I know you read my heart exactly."

After some few minutes' conversation with him, he said to me, "I want to ask you a question. I have been thinking of it a great deal, and I cannot conceive how you know what to say to each one, where there are so many. We have been talking about it some of us, and we cannot understand how it is that you can know our thoughts and feelings, when nobody has told you. How *can* you know what to say to one after another, when there are so many, and some of them you have never seen before, and they say so little to you?"

"I have only one rule on that subject," said I. "I aim to conspire with the Holy Spirit. If I perceive any one truth has impressed the mind, I aim to make its impression deeper; because the Holy Spirit has already made that impression, and I would not diminish it by leading the mind off to something else. If I perceive any error in the individual's mind, I aim to remove it; for I know that the error is of sin, and not of the Holy Spirit."

"But," said he, "our impressions are so different."

"No matter. They are of the Holy Spirit if *truth* has made them; and he can choose the kind of truth which is appropriate to any sinner, better than I can. I just aim to conspire with the Holy Spirit."

Said he, "I am confident if you had said much to me, or anything, to turn my mind away from that one thing, it would have done me hurt. You have no idea how much you increased my trouble that night. I somehow wanted you to lighten my burden, —you made it heavier. Then I was soon led to see that none but God could help me. I had partly begun to think my heart was improving. I found out the contrary, and turned to God in despair. He gave me peace, through Jesus Christ."

XXIII.

Divided Mind.

IN a season when the Holy Spirit was poured out, and there was an increasing interest in religion, and an increasing number of sinners awakened to a sense of their lost condition, two young persons, who had become serious and prayerful, were induced to forsake, in part, the services of our congregation, in order to attend those of another Church, where there was also an uncommon degree of seriousness, but too much noise and talk on the subject,—too much said about "*revival*," "*revival*." I feared the result. A divided mind has poor prospects before it. I aimed as prudently as I could to put a stop to the course of these young persons; but in vain. They were under the influence of a very zealous member of the Church, who, perhaps, had more zeal than knowledge.

The result was what I feared it would be. They were both left without grace. They attained salvation nowhere. Almost the entire number of their associates among us, with whom they had been connected in the commencement of their seriousness, became hopefully the children of God, and united with the Church; but these two remained the same as before. It appeared manifest to me, all along, that their seriousness really diminished very much as their attention was divided. And this is what I have often noticed. If our Church-members were wise, they would never lend themselves to do this kind of mischief. They would not be beguiled into it through the desire to be esteemed liberal, and above bigoted notions, or through the pride of being more engaged in religion than their brethren, and wanting to go

" where there is some life,"—" some real religion,"—" where the Holy Spirit is present."

In my opinion, these young persons were led away from their *duty*, and thus grieved the Spirit of God. Many years have passed away since that time, and neither of them has become a follower of Christ.

XXIV.

Human Resolves.

TWO young girls of my congregation, about seventeen years of age, went to a neighbouring town, where there was a religious excitement; and after remaining there about two days, returned home very happy. They thought they had attained salvation by faith in Christ.

On talking with them, I was surprised to find them so little sensible of the extent of human depravity, of the helplessness of human nature, and the necessity of regeneration by the Holy Spirit. They told me that they had been rendered sensible of their sin and danger, and had resolved to go to Christ; and the minister told them that was enough—if they really *resolved* to give up the world and to serve God, that was enough; and they *had* resolved to do so. This appeared to me to be all the reason for the hope which made them so happy.

But their religion did not last them six months. At least, they gave no evidence of it, but much to the contrary. They ceased to hope and ceased to pray.

Moral suasion is one thing, and the Holy Spirit is another. It is an easy thing for a minister to *fix a hope* in the heart of an alarmed sinner, but it is not safe. The Bible does not tell us that a sinner's *resolves* are enough. It does not tell us the resolves are regeneration.

XXV.

I Can't Repent.

ONE of the most solemn assemblies that I have ever seen was convened on the evening of the Sabbath, in a private house. It was an inquiry meeting, at which more than a hundred persons were present, the most of them young or in middle life. The structure of the house was rather peculiar. There was a spacious hall, about ten feet wide and about forty feet long, extending from the front door along the side of three parlours, which opened into it as well as into each other; and at the rear part of this hall was a staircase extending to the second storey of the house. Movable benches were introduced into this hall, and placed along each side of it, to afford seats for those who attended this meeting, and who could not all be accommodated in the parlours. After the meetings had been continued in this place for a few weeks, it became manifest that the hall was the preferred place. As the different persons came in and took their seats where they pleased, the seats in the hall would be filled, and then the stairs would be used as seats entirely to the top, and then the upper hall would be occupied, and finally the parlours. I was accustomed to stand, while addressing the assembly, in one of the doors opening from the hall, where my eye had a full view of all those in the hall, on the stairs, and in one of the parlours. Besides a general exhortation, it was my ordinary custom to speak to each individual, passing from one to another. And all those in the hall and on the stairs could hear every word which I uttered in this conversation and the most of what any one said to me. And for these reasons, as I supposed, the persons who resorted there would choose the hall or the stairs. This listening of others, to what passed in conversation betwixt any one individual and myself, was never very pleasant to me. I should greatly have preferred to converse with each one alone; as there would have been less restraint on their part, and on my own, more certainty that what I was saying would be truly applicable, and would not be applied by any one for whom it was not intended. And besides this, individuals would sometimes make expressions to me so erroneous, that I was unwilling others should hear them, lest they might be injured by it. To avoid this, I used to speak in a low tone of voice; and if the expressions of any individual were becoming such as I feared might be injurious, I usually broke off the conversation suddenly, by saying, "I will call and see you to-morrow."

On the evening to which I now allude, all the seats were filled, and three persons were seated on each step entirely to the top, and many had found their place in the hall above. It was a calm and mild summer evening, and perfect stillness reigned over the crowd assembled there, unbroken except by the long breathing or the deep sigh of some pensive soul. I thought I had never seen so still, so solemn, and thoughtful an assembly. I closed the front door, after all had entered, and took my stand in my accustomed place. I hesitated to speak. I was afraid to utter a word. It seemed to me that anything I could say would be less solemn, impressive, instructive, than that tomb-like silence in an assembly of so many immortal souls, each visited by the Holy Spirit. I stood for a time in perfect silence. The power of that silence was painful. The people sat before me like statues of marble—not a movement—not a sound. It appeared as if they had all ceased to breathe. I broke the silence by saying slowly, and in a low voice, "Each one of you is thinking of his own immortal soul and of his God." Again I paused for the space of an entire minute, for I was overawed, and knew not what to say. Then falling on my knees I commenced prayer. They all spontaneously knelt. After a short prayer, I proposed to speak a few words to each one of them, as far as it was possible, and requested all of them, except the individual with whom I should be conversing, to be engaged in reflection or in silent prayer to God. Passing rapidly from one to another, I had spoken to all those in the parlours and in the hall, till I had reached about the middle of it, where every word spoken could be heard by the whole assembly. Coming to a man, about thirty years of age, whom I had seen there three times before, I said to him,—

"I did not expect to see *you* here to-night. I thought you would have come to repentance before this time, and would have no occasion any longer to ask, 'What shall I do to be saved?'"

"I *can't repent!*" said he, with a sort of determined and despairing accent, and so loudly as to startle us all. Instantly I felt sorry for this expression. But I thought it would not do to avoid noticing it, and leave it sounding in the ears of so many impenitent sinners. I immediately answered, as I stood before him, as gently and yet solemnly as I could,—

"What an awfully *wicked heart* you must have! You can't repent! You love sin so well, that you cannot be sorry for it—you cannot forsake it—you cannot hate it! You must be in an awful condition indeed! You are so much the enemy of God, that you cannot be sorry for having offended him—you cannot cease to contend against him; and even now, while you are sensible of the impropriety and unhappiness of it, you cannot cease to resist the Holy Spirit, who strives with you to bring you to repentance! You must have an awfully depraved heart!"

"I *can't repent!*" said he again, with an accent of grief and intolerable vexation,—"I can't repent with such a heart!"

"That means," said I, "that you have become too wicked to desire to become any better; for nothing but wickedness makes repentance difficult. And then you just plead one sin as an excuse for another—the sin of your heart as an excuse for the *continued* sin of your heart!"

Still he insisted: "I *can't repent!* I should if I could!" and the tears rolled down his cheeks, of which he seemed to be utterly unconscious, as well as unconscious of the presence of any one but myself.

"You would if you could," said I, "is only a self-righteous and self-justifying excuse. Your deceitful heart means by it that you are not so wicked as to continue in your impenitence *willingly.* It means that you are *willing* to repent, but you cannot. You are deceived. You are *not* willing. You think you are, but you are in an error. You never *will* be willing, unless God shall verify in you the promise, 'My people shall be willing in the day of my power.' In that power lies your only hope, as I have told you before, when I urged you to pray. If you are willing to repent, what hinders you? I am willing you should repent. All of us here are willing. Every angel in heaven is willing you should repent. Christ, who died to redeem you, is willing. God the Father is willing. The Holy Spirit is willing, who at this moment strives with you to bring you to repentance. What hinders you, then? Yourself only! And when you say you can't repent, you mean that you are not to be blamed for coming here to-night with an impenitent heart. You are wofully deceived! God blames you! The whole Bible blames you! Your own conscience, though you strive to silence it, blames you! This excuse will not stand!"

"I *can't repent!*" said he again, in a harsh, vociferating voice, as if in anger.

"Then God can't save you," said I, "for he cannot lie, and he has said the impenitent shall be destroyed. *You* say you cannot repent. *He* has not said so. He commands you to repent."

He replied, with much agitation, but in a subdued tone, "I am sure I have tried long, and my mind has been greatly tormented. All has done no good. I do not see that I *can* repent!"

"Other people have repented," said I. "There are a great many penitents in the world. I find there are some here to-night, who think they have come to repentance since they were here last Sabbath evening. One of them told me *then* very much the same thing you tell me *now*—that it did not seem to him he ever could turn from sin; but he has found out he can. As to your having tried so long, the length of time will not save you. If a man has got his face turned the wrong way, the longer he goes on the worse off he becomes. He would do well to stop and turn about. Such is the call of the Bible, 'Turn ye, turn ye, for why will ye die?'—'Repent, and turn yourselves from all your transgressions, so iniquity shall not be your ruin.'—'Let the wicked forsake his way, and the unrighteous man his thoughts, and let him return unto the Lord.' Other people have turned to God, and you ought to. But your mind has seized on the idea of your trying and your trouble, and you make an excuse and a self-righteousness of them."

"Do you think I am self-righteous?" said he.

"I *know* you are; that is your grand difficulty. You have been trying to save yourself; you are trying now. When you tried to repent, your heart aimed after repentance as something to recommend you to God, and constitute a reason why he should forgive and save you. It was just an operation of a self-righteous spirit. It was just an attempt to save yourself, to have your religion save you, instead of relying by faith upon Jesus Christ, to be saved from wrath through him. This is precisely the case with every impenitent sinner. The error is one; the forms of it may be various, but in all cases it is substantially the same thing. St. Paul has given a perfect description of it: 'Going about,' from one thing to another, from one device or attempt to another,—'going about to establish a righteousness of their own, they have not submitted themselves to the righteousness of God; for Christ is the end of the law for righteousness to every one that believeth.' One man tries to establish a righteousness of his own out of his reformations; another, out of his duties; another, out of his painful attempts or painful convictions,—as you just now mentioned your own torments of mind. It is evident that you are trying to be righteous before God, through your pain and your attempted penitence. And if you should find any peace of mind in that way, it would only be a deception, not an item of religion in it. You ought to betake yourself to the Lord Jesus Christ, a poor, guilty, undone sinner, to be saved by him alone—saved by grace. You ought to go to him, just as you are, to be washed in his blood, to be clothed in his righteousness, to be sheltered from the thunders of God's eternal law in the security of his all-sufficient atonement. You ought to flee to Christ, like the man-slayer to the city of refuge, before he is cut down by the sword of the avenger of blood. You ought to go instantly, like the prodigal to his father, in all his poverty, starvation, and rags, as well as guilt. You ought to cry, like Peter sinking in the waves, 'Lord, save me!' But instead of this, you are just looking to yourself, striving to find something, or make something in your own heart, which shall recommend you to God. And in this miserable way you are making salvation a far more difficult matter than God has made it. You have forgotten the free grace of the gospel, the full atonement of Jesus Christ, by the sacrifice of himself."

"But," said he, "I can't repent and come to Christ *of myself*."

"*I* certainly never said you could, and never wished you to think you could. In my opinion God does not wish you to think so. And if you have found out that you cannot repent of yourself, aside from divine aid, I am glad of it—you have found out an important truth. Most certainly God does not tell you to repent *of yourself*. He tells you that 'Christ is exalted to give repentance.' He says to every sinner, 'Thou hast destroyed thyself; in me is thy help'—'Let him take hold on my strength, that he may make peace with me, and he shall make peace with me.' On the ground that they need it, he has promised 'the Holy Spirit to them that ask him.' God never expects you to repent without divine aid, but with it. He knows you are too wicked to do it,—that you are without strength, helpless, undone, a *lost* sinner! And here lies the very heart of your error. You have been trying to repent in a way that God never told you, just by your own powers, instead of trying to get God to have mercy upon you, and save you by his help. You have been looking to the powers within you instead of looking to the aid above you. You have trusted to yourself, instead of trusting yourself to the grace of Christ. And that is the very reason why you have failed, and now you complain that you cannot repent, while in reality you have exactly the same sufficiency as the penitent all around you. What has been their help may be your help; and the sooner you are driven off from all that self-seeking and self-reliance the better it will be for you. You are in the double error of undervaluing the character of God, and overvaluing your own. God is more merciful and more gracious than you think him to be. He is more ready to save you. And when he commands you to repent, he does not wish you to forget that all your hope lies in the immediate aid of his Holy Spirit. Nor does he wish you to attempt to dispense with that proffered assistance by your not believing that you are as utterly helpless as you really are. He does not tell you to rely upon your own shattered strength, but you have done so. And when you have failed, you then turn round and complain that you 'can't repent.' You reject his offered help—the help of the omnipotent Spirit. And for this reason you will be the more criminal if you do *not* repent. That Divine Spirit is your only hope. If he leaves you to yourself, you are lost—eternally lost! Tread softly, my dear friend. The ground whereon thou standest is holy ground. Let not the Holy Spirit, who presides over the souls here this evening, bear witness against you in the day of the final judgment,—'Because I have called and ye refused!' You *can* repent, just in the way that others repent,—just because God is your help. Trust him, and rely upon yourself no longer."

As I was saying these things, he appeared to become much less affected, but much more thoughtful. His tears and his agitations ceased, and he seemed to hang upon my lips, as if he had been listening to some new wonder. When I had done, all was hushed as death; and in a deliberate, subdued, and solemn tone he broke that expressive silence, saying,—

"I hope my God will help me."

"Let us pray," said I; and a short prayer, pleading for God's help, closed the exercises of the evening.

I afterwards found numerous reasons for believing, that that was one of the most profitable religious exercises that I ever attended. Among others was the case of my friend, whose expression had drawn me somewhat out of my proposed mode of conducting the exercises of the evening. He became, as he hoped, a true believer. He stated to me the exercises of his mind, his repentance, his faith in Christ, his peace and hope, and his reliance upon the Holy Spirit. His mind appeared to seize upon the great truths of the gospel, almost without emotion. He had no ecstasy, no exultation, no joy. He had only peace and hope. He told me that his agitations had all been useless to him; that they were not faith, and did not lead to faith; and that he thought "sinners ought to attend to the calls of God in a believing and business manner." And when I asked him what had kept him from Christ so long, he replied: "I was trying to make myself better, to have a religion instead of trusting in Christ. What you said to me that night showed me my mistake; and I went home with a deeper sense of my dependence, and a clear view of the free grace of God to sinners, through the redemption of Christ."

About six months after this he united with the Church, and has continued to manifest an established and uniform faith.

To cut off the sinner from all reliance upon himself, his merits, and his powers, and throw him naked and helpless into the hands of the Holy Spirit to lead him to Christ in faith, should be the one great aim of the ministry.

Sinners certainly ought to repent, for God commands them to repent. But in my opinion, he does not design to have them understand his command as having respect only to their own ability to repent, and not having respect to the proffered aids of the Holy Spirit. Such aids constitute one grand ground on which his command is obligatory, and sweep away every possible excuse. No man ever did repent without the Holy Spirit, or ever will; and this is no small amount of proof that no man ever can. Nothing seems to be gained by making a sinner believe that he is able to repent without divine assistance. Such a belief will be very likely to mislead him to a reliance upon his own shattered strength. And as to his conviction of criminality for *not* coming to repentance, surely there is strong ground for such conviction, since God offers him all the ability he needs,—"*In me is thy help*"—"*Let him take hold on my strength that he may make peace with me.*"

XXVI.

A Strange Snare.

A YOUNG man about nineteen years of age, a member of my congregation, was a hopeful convert to Christ, at the time of a general revival of religion. I felt a more than common interest in him, on account of my intimacy with his family, his own intelligence and education, and my hope that he would become a minister of the gospel. I had not so much personal acquaintance with him as with most of those who had been led to seek the Lord. He was very retiring, and it was not easy to know so much of him as I desired. But I had often conversed with him about his hope in Christ, and knew him well enough to know that there was something a little peculiar about his turn of mind, or way of thinking. But I saw nothing in him that led me to doubt his piety. He was very attentive to his religious duties, and to me he appeared humble and devoted. I had often conversed with him about the evidences of his faith; and just before our season of communion, he came to converse with me alone, in respect to his uniting with the Church. He deemed that to be his duty.

After considerable conversation on the evidences of his piety, and the nature and design of divine ordinances, he said to me rather suddenly, and as if he had just thought of it,—

"My opinion is, that immersion is the right way of baptism."

"Indeed," said I. "What makes you think so?"

"Christ was immersed," said he.

"I do not believe he was," said I. "There is not an item of proof that he was. There are strong reasons for believing the contrary. But suppose he was immersed. So he was *crucified.* But *why* was he baptized?"

"I don't know," said he; "for an example to us, I suppose."

"What makes you suppose so?"

"Why—why—I thought so," said he, hesitatingly.

"And did you think he was *crucified* for an example to us?"

"Oh no!"

"Why not? If his *baptism* was an example for us to follow, why not his *crucifixion* also?"

"I don't know. I never thought of that."

"Does the Bible teach you that Christ's baptism was an example for us to follow, any more than his crucifixion, or his fasting forty days?"

"I never thought of that," said he.

"Was Christ baptized for the same reason that his followers are to be baptized? or was he baptized as an official induction into the priestly office, as Aaron and his sons, and the Levites, were ordered to be sprinkled with water?"

"I don't know," said he.

"What does our baptism mean?" said I.

"It is a sign of the washing away of sin," said he.

"Was Christ a sinner?"

"Oh no!"

"Why, then, was such a sign applied to him?"

"Indeed I cannot tell. I never thought of it."

"Was Christ's baptism Christian baptism? was the Christian dispensation established at that time?"

"I cannot answer."

"Had the Jewish dispensation come to an end?"

"I cannot answer that."

"Was Christ baptized in the name of the Father, the Son, and the Holy Ghost?"

"I never thought of that."

I then said to him, that I had no objections to make against immersion, no fault to find with those who practised it, and no objections to his uniting with that excellent Christian denomination. But it was manifest that he had not studied the subject very much, and it would be best for him to take time and examine it well, before he united with any Church. He would then be better satisfied with himself than if he acted hastily.

He cordially assented to this, and afterwards came to me repeatedly, naming some passages of the Bible which he thought favoured immersion; and as often as he came I gave him my views upon them, which he confessed appeared to him just and fair. He could find no fault with them. In this way we examined all the passages of the Scriptures which he thought related to the subject. He said he could find no more; and could not disprove or dispute the explanations I had given.

I then presented the passages and the arguments on the other side of the question, telling him to detect any error into which I might fall, and that I was willing to be a Baptist myself, if the Bible would make me so. But he did not pretend that anything I said was inconclusive.

Some months had passed since he began to study the subject and come to me with his texts on baptism, when he said to me one day—

"What objections have you to immersion?"

"None at all," said I. "In my opinion immersion is a baptism acceptable to God, if those who practise it are conscientious; but I do not believe it is the *only* acceptable baptism."

Said he, "Would *you* be willing to baptize any one by immersion?"

"Yes; three things being out of the way, I should. *First*, if there were no Baptist Church in the place that the individual could attend. *Second*, if he had *not* been baptized in infancy. *Third*, if I thought he were truly conscientious in the matter, and were not making too much of that ordinance, that is, placing an undue reliance upon it."

"Would you be willing to immerse *me?*"

"Yes, on these conditions."

"Well," says he, "I have never been baptized, and there is

no Baptist Church here for me to attend. These are two of the conditions."

"But," said I, "do you think immersion needful, when you cannot, as you confess, bring a single passage of the Bible to prove it, and cannot answer one of my arguments and proofs to the contrary? You will have hard work to convince me of your conscientiousness and sincerity, if you are not going to be governed by a fair interpretation of the Scriptures. A believer must have a Bible conscience. And if any one talks to me about conscience in any religious matter, and leaves his Bible behind him, I shall be very apt to think his conscience needs a baptizing with the Holy Spirit before I will baptize him."

"I do *mean* to be conscientious," says he.

"According to the Bible?"

"Certainly," said he; "that is the only rule."

"Very well, go to work. You have to convince me of your piety and of your conscientious belief in immersion, as being taught in the Bible; and when you have done so, I will immerse you, if you desire it. But if you become a Baptist, I advise you to join the Baptist Church, not ours."

"I could not do that," said he. "They reject infant baptism, and hold to close communion, and I do not agree with them."

After this he often called upon me, and finally he did convince me that he was sincere and conscientious about immersion. He confessed he could not show that immersion was the Bible mode of baptism, and could not pretend that I had misinterpreted a single text in defending my practice. But after all, he said it did appear to him that immersion was right; he should be better satisfied that he had done his duty if he were immersed, and begged me to immerse him.

"Not yet," said I. "A few questions first. What does baptism mean?"

He replied, "Just what you have often explained it—a sign and seal of the covenant of Christ, a representation of cleansing from the pollutions of sin by the Holy Spirit."

"Well, in your opinion, is it essential on what day of the month or of the week it is done?"

"No. The New Testament does not limit us to any particular day."

"In your opinion, is it any matter what o'clock it is when one is baptized?"

"Why, no!"

"In your opinion is it any matter how many *ministers* are present, when baptism is administered?"

"Why, no!"

"Well, then, in your opinion is it any matter how many *other people* are present? If a minister and the person to be baptized are alone, like Philip and the eunuch, would that be good baptism?"

"Certainly, I think so."

"Very well. Put on your hat. Let us go down to the river, and I will baptize you now." He hesitated. "Come, it is a fine, warm day—nobody will see us—I never will tell of it—it shall remain a perfect secret—come, let us go." I had risen, put on my hat, and opened the door. "What do you hesitate for? Come on."

"What! *now?*" said he, sitting still.

"Yes; *now*. I want your conscience to be satisfied; and we have spent months enough studying this matter. Come on. Let us go to the river."

"What! all alone?"

"Yes; like Philip and the eunuch. You said it was no matter whether anybody was present or not."

He seemed confounded. But he would not go. I urged him. I appealed to his conscience, which demanded immersion. I exhorted him not to violate his conscience by neglecting his duty—not to destroy his peace of mind. But I could not start him. There he stood, mute, confused, and ashamed. I urged him to tell why he would not go; but he gave no answer. The more I insisted, the more he seemed resolved not to be baptized.

After spending half an hour in this way, I said to him, "You have lost my confidence entirely! A little while ago I believed you sincere; but I do not believe it now. If you were sincere, actuated by conscience, by a sense of duty, as you pretend, you would not hesitate to go with me and be baptized. But I cannot baptize you now by immersion, or in any other mode. I have lost my confidence in you. Have patience a moment, and I will lift the veil that hides your heart, and give you a little glimpse of what lies within. You thought it would be a fine thing to be immersed, to have the credit of an independent mind; or perhaps you were tickled with the idea, that I and all the people should parade away down to the water on Sunday, yourself the hero of the scene, to be talked about among us. Such a baptism would make a good deal of noise here, and you liked it in your vanity. That is your heart. You may study it at your leisure. But never talk to me about conscience again while under the influence of such a heart. You may go. I have no more to say to you."

He left me, seeming to feel that he had escaped out of the paw of the lion.

It was not three months after this before I heard of his extravagant levity, and his sneers at religion. He became apparently very hardened; and in this course of life he continued for months.

But God did not leave him at peace in his sin. He was arrested in his career, and finally became hopefully a convert to Christ. He came to me to tell me his altered feelings. And finally, when he was examined for admission into the Church, he told me he was fully convinced of the truth of what I had said to him about his heart, at the time when he wanted to be immersed. He said he felt ashamed to own it, but it was true, that his desire for immersion arose very much from pride and vanity, and a desire to be popular. If he should be immersed, he would be unlike others; and he was then pleased with the idea that people would talk about him with wonder, and think him something uncommon in penetration and independence. But he hoped he had repented deeply and sincerely of all this; and now he did not wish to be immersed.

He united with the Church. I baptized him, but not by immersion. He still lives a reputable Christian, after twenty years of trial.

The snares of the devil are very numerous. Perhaps none of them are more common or more dangerous than those which are addressed to pride and vanity. Young persons especially are exposed to these. When they begin to be attentive to religion or entertain hope in Christ, if their pride becomes connected with religion or religious things, they are greatly exposed to take the gratification of their pride for the comforts of piety. A passion for popularity the desire to be noticed, and known, and talked about, has led many a sinner into strange delusion. Spiritual pride is the worst of all pride, if it is not the worst snare of the devil. The heart is peculiarly deceitful just on this thing, pride.

XXVII.

Fanaticism.

A YOUNG woman, who was a member of my Church, came to me with the urgent request that I would visit her sister, who was in a very anxious state of mind, and would be glad to see me. Learning that her sister had been a communicant in another denomination, and very seldom attended our Church, I declined going, as I was unwilling even to *appear* of a proselyting spirit. But she was so urgent, that I finally consented.

She lived in a neighbourhood some miles distant, where most of the people belonged to another denomination. I immediately rode to her house. She entered the room where I was, and her sister, after introducing her to me, left us alone, that she might speak freely to me. I perceived she was very much agitated, trembling and sighing. I said to her, "You seem to be very much troubled. What is it that distresses you?"

Said she, "I have been converted three times, and I feel as if I needed it again!"

"Take care," said I, "that you do not get converted again *in the same way*. All that has done you no good. Has it?"

"No," said she; "not at all!"

"Then, do not get converted *so* again. You want a religion that shall last,—a religion to die with; and I advise you to get an entirely new kind."

I conversed with her for some time, aiming to teach her the nature of religion, and to quell the excitement of her mind, which appeared to me to arise more from an agitation of her sensibilities than from real conviction of sin. Her affections, more than her understanding and conscience, were excited. I visited her afterwards; and for some time her impressions appeared to me to become more scriptural and deep, and to promise a good result. But she was drawn away again among her old associates, at an exciting assemblage in the evening, where she professed to have become converted again. She was as joyful and happy as she had been before, and her religion lasted this time about six months.

The heart that has once been drunk with fanaticism, is ever afterwards exposed to the same evil. It will mistake excitement —any fancy, for true religion. Fanaticism is not faith.

When the affections, or mere sensibilities of the heart are excited, and the understanding and conscience are but little employed, there is a sad preparation for false hope—for some wild delusion or fanatical faith. The judgment and conscience should take the lead of the affections; but when the affections take the lead, they will be very apt to monopolize the whole soul,—judgment and conscience will be overpowered, or flung into the background; and then, the deluded mortal will have a religion of *mere impressions*—more feeling than truth—more sensitiveness than faith—more fancy and fanaticism than holiness. Emotions, agitations, or sensibilities of any sort, which do not arise from clear and conscientious perception of truth, will be likely to be pernicious. The most clear perception of truth, the deepest conviction, is seldom accompanied by any great excitement of the sensibilities. Under such conviction, feeling may be deep and strong, but will not be fitful, capricious, and blind. To a religion of *mere impressions* one may be "converted three times," or three times three; to a religion of truth, one conversion will suffice. In my opinion, my young friend was all along misled by the idea that religion consisted very much in a wave of feeling Her instructors ought to have taught her better.

XXVIII.

A Mother's Prayer.

AS I was very much engaged, at one time, in calling from house to house among the people of my charge, I called upon a young woman to endeavour to direct her attention to the subject of her salvation. I attempted to draw her into conversation upon religion, but did not succeed. She would converse freely about anything else; but on this subject she was very mute, only deigning a brief answer to my questions, and sometimes not even that. I knew that she was very partial to me,—a very warm personal friend,—and I wondered at her obstinate silence. On visiting her again, a day or two afterwards, I found her in the same state. About religion she was wholly reserved. As days passed on I made many attempts to persuade her to deny herself and follow Christ; but my attempts were all in vain. Almost the whole of her youthful associates had become Christians, as they hoped, or were prayerfully seeking the Lord. She remained almost alone, and I became very solicitous about her. I tried with all my power to affect her mind. I explained the character of God, the law, sin, the work of Christ, the prospects of sinners. I showed the vanity of the world. I employed the promises, and aimed to melt her heart. Time after time, with the Bible in my hand, I directed her own eyes to the passages, and got her to read them to me. I marked passages, and desired her to read them alone, carefully, and with prayer. Polite, amiable, and kind as she was, she appeared entirely unmoved by all that I could say to her. I understood, also, if anything was said about religion in the family, she would retire to her room. She would leave the table as soon as she could without manifest rudeness if the subject of religion became a topic of conversation. Her mother told me she would not hear a word from her on that subject when they were alone, but would leave the room if she spoke of it at all. She had also abandoned all religious meetings except on the Sabbath, and sometimes she was absent then.

Finally, one day, I called and said to her, "I have called to see you once more, in order to speak to you again about your salvation."

"I am always happy to see you," said she.

"And are you willing to talk with me on the subject of your own religious duty?"

"You can talk to *me* if you please."

"That is not enough. I *have* talked to you many times, and you are silent. You force me to talk in the dark, because I cannot find out what you think or feel. You will not even answer the questions I put to you. And it seems to me that you must deem me intrusive, impolite, and unkind, to be so often speaking to you on a subject which appears unwelcome to you."

"Oh no," said she, "not at all."

"Then are you willing to talk freely with me, as you do on all other subjects?"

She gave me no answer. I told her that at present I had no time for any other than religious conversation; that when I had I should be happy to see her, but that now there were many persons wishing to see me, and willing to converse with me freely about the way of salvation; and if she did not wish to see me on that subject I would excuse myself from calling on her again. She made no reply, and I began to fear she was going to cast me off entirely. I asked her,—

"Do you wish me to come to see you again?"

She appeared to be affected, but gave me no answer.

"I hope you will allow me to call on you again."

She made no reply. Said I,—

"My dear girl, I have tried to do you good; I wish still to try

I have loved you and respected you; I hope you will not cast me off in this way. I ask it as a favour that you will allow me to call on you again, and aim to persuade you to attend to your salvation.

She manifested much emotion, but remained silent. Said I,—

"It is for you to say whether I shall call on you again or not. I will not force myself upon you."

I rose to depart, and, offering her my hand as she accompanied me to the door, I said to her,—

"May I come to see you once more? I do no not like to be cast off so by one that I love so much. What do you say—may I come? I ask it as a favour."

She wept, but she did not answer. I paused and repeated the question, "May I come?" but she made me no reply, and I bade her good-bye.

The next day, as I passed the house, her mother saw me, and came after me in the street, through the deep snow, and begged me to call and see her daughter. She was greatly distressed about her. She feared nothing would induce her to seek God. I told her how she had refused to give me permission to come to see her again, even when I had begged it as affectionately as I could, and therefore I could do no more. I could not intrude myself upon her. It would do no good. And unless her daughter expressed a willingness, at least, to see me, I never should trouble her any more. The mother wept like a child.

"Oh!" said she, "what will become of her? She refused to hear *me* say anything long ago, and now *you* are going to give her up! What shall I do?"

"You can pray for her," said I. "God can reach her heart."

She begged me not to forget her poor child, and turned back towards her home, with tears streaming from her eyes,—one of the most heart-broken mothers I have ever seen."

The next Sabbath evening that girl was at the inquiry meeting. She was entirely overcome by her emotions. She bewailed herself as an undone sinner. She said she had resisted God—she had broken her mother's heart—she had destroyed herself, and feared there was no mercy for her.

After some weeks she entertained a hope in Christ; but her mind soon became darkened and bewildered with doubts and fears, and for some years she never made a public profession of religion. More than ten years after she came to that inquiry meeting I took some pains to visit her. She still entertained her hope, and still lived a life of prayer.

The cause of her yielding, when she first came to the inquiry meeting, seems to have been that *she was let alone.* Her mother had ceased to say anything to her about her salvation; her minister was cast off; her companions had ceased to solicit her attention to her religious duties. She was left to herself. Nothing opposed her. And she found she was opposing God.

The Holy Spirit leads to self-inspection. Such inspection is just the operation of a convicted sinner's mind. Sometimes, if he is just left to take his own course, nobody to oppose him, his own conscience will be the more apt to do that office. Aside from a deep sense of accountability, there will be little or no conviction. But it was prayer, a mother's prayer, that availed for her. That mother said to me, "I went to my room after you told me you could do no more, and that we could only pray; and I prayed as I *never* prayed before. I felt that God only could help me; and if he did *not* answer me, I could not think myself a Christian any longer."

XXIX.

Easy to be a Christian.

IN conversation with a young woman who was awakened to a sense of her sin and danger, I was much surprised at the perfect clearness of her perceptions. She appeared to perceive her guilt as a sinner, her depravity and alienation from God, her opposition of heart to his law, her need of the blood of atonement and of the help of the Holy Spirit. I could make none of these truths more plain to her, or more forcible. In telling me how she felt she preached more powerfully to herself than I could preach to her. I was afraid to say much to her, lest my words should diminish her impressions, instead of giving them more depth. But I insisted upon it that God was willing to save her; that her bondage in sin was her own fault, not his; that she was unwilling to come to Christ, or renounce the world, or give up sin, or be indebted to Christ for pardon, or set her whole heart to seek God, or trust her heart to the power of the divine Spirit; that there was some such hindrance of her own—that God did not hinder her. Still she did not think so. She said she had such an awful fear of God's wrath, and such a desire to be a Christian; that she could *think of* nothing which she would not do in order to be saved." "Yes," said I, "you would do everything but one,—that is, consent to *do nothing*, and let Christ save you. You are just 'going about to establish a righteousness of your own,' and that is the great reason why you have not 'submitted yourself to the righteousness of God; for Christ is the end of the law for righteousness to every one that believeth.'"

I left her abruptly, not giving her time for any reply.

I called upon her the next day. The first words she uttered when she saw me were, "Oh, how easy it is to be a Christian! You have only to be willing, and it is all done. How easy! how easy it is!"

"Yes," said I, "'My people shall be willing in the day of my power.'"

"Is that in the Bible?" said she.

"Yes; in the 110th Psalm."

"I wish I had known it before," said she; "then I should have known where to go. But no matter; I know it now. I found that when I was really willing it was all done. And when I prayed God made me willing. It *was* he. It was all of God. I did nothing, I *know* I did nothing but come to him humbly. He gives me peace, as I trust in Jesus alone. It is easy to be a Christian when you are willing."

Self-denial is indispensable to religion. "If any man will be my disciple, let him deny himself." And whatever difficulties there may be, and there are certainly many, in turning to God, it would be no easy thing to show that not one of them lies very much in the will. A perverse will is the sin and hindrance of unconverted sinners. They are not willing to be converted sinners. They ought to know it.

XXX.

Proselyting.

DURING the progress of a revival of religion, I remarked the absence of the young people of one family from our meetings, which they had been accustomed to attend, and in which their attention had been turned towards religion. They had become serious inquirers about the way of salvation. I had conversed with them. Their solemnity appeared to be deepening, and I was surprised at their absence. I soon found they had been very urgently requested to attend similar religious meetings of another Church, and had yielded to the solicitation. They preferred to attend there. The young minister of that Church was particularly attentive to them, visiting them almost daily, and sometimes oftener, and taking special pains to induce them to attend all his religious exercises. He would invite them, and urge them, and sometimes send for them. One of their parents told me, "how very much interested" they were in Mr. B——, and expressed the opinion, they "ought to go to the church where they feel most interest. And then, Mr. B—— is *so* attentive. They love him dearly. The girls think there never *was* such a minister. They can talk about nothing else but Mr. B——."

I replied, that I should rather hear they were "interested" about Christ than about him; and inquired how they appeared to be affected on the subject of salvation.

The reply was, "Mr. B—— thinks they are getting along very well; and they seem so happy when they come from his meetings."

I asked whether they believed that God had given them a new

heart, and was answered, "No, not yet; but they seem very much engaged."

It was manifest, as I thought, that their favourite, Mr. B——, was tickling their vanity and pride by his visits and other attentions, which were encouraged by parental influence. Through the medium of a trust-worthy friend of the family I aimed to have some influence upon them; but it was all in vain. These three young persons were sometimes in our religious meetings, but it was manifest that they were dissatisfied there; and we thought their influence upon our other young people tended more to levity than solemnity, to fanaticism than to faith. But they did not annoy us long. They continued their preference for Mr. B——; they became his "converts;" and within a year from that time, they had thrown off all the restraints of religion, and one of them all restraints of parental authority.

An interest *about* religion may be very different from an interest *in* it. Men talk of being "interested," and "interesting meetings." This is all suspicious. It is commonly a mark of either fanaticism or pride, or of both. True religion is solemn and humble. And if it is happy, it is happy in truth, in God, in duty. To mislead souls is no trifle. The kisses of an enemy are deceitful.

XXXI.

The Obstinate Girl.

THERE are periods when the minds of unbelievers are more than ordinarily ready to attend to the concerns of eternal life. It is an important duty to improve such seasons. Having called one morning upon several young people, and found their feelings tender on the subject of religion, I determined to keep on in this service. I therefore called upon a young woman who attended my Church; and introducing, as gently as I could, the reason which brought me there, I found that her mind was fully set against any personal attention to her salvation. I reasoned with her, as well as I could, explained to her some texts of Scripture, and affectionately besought her to give immediate attention to the great concerns of a future life.

She replied to it all in a very opposing and insolent manner, which I did not resent in the least. The more impudent *she* became, the more polite and gentle *I* became,—thinking in this way to win her, or at least, that she would become ashamed of her want of politeness. But it turned out very differently. My gentleness seemed to provoke her to increased insolence. She found fault with Christians,—called them hypocrites; spoke of ministers as bigoted, and domineering, and proud; and "wondered why people could not mind their own business." She became personally abusive to myself; and in her abuse I believe she made some capital hits, as she drew my character. I bore it all with perfect gentleness and good nature; but tried politely and gently to persuade her to try to be saved herself, let what would become of the rest of us. Whenever I got an opportunity, for she was very talkative, I answered her objections and cavillings as briefly as possible, determined to enlist her own reason against her disposition, if I could. For example, she said to me with a bitter sneer:—

"What examples your Church members set!"

I answered, "I want you to be a Christian, and set us a good example. You are under as much obligation to set *me* a good example as I am to set *you* one."

"I have a right to my own way," said she.

"Then," said I, "other people must have a right to theirs. But surely you do not mean to say you have a *right* to be *wrong*. A wrong right is a queer thing."

"Well, I am *sincere*, at any rate."

"So was Paul when he persecuted the Church. He was very sincerely wrong, and afterwards was very sorry for it."

"I am accustomed to mind my own business."

"I thought just now you were minding *mine*, when you talked so freely about me," said I; "and as to minding your own, let me tell you, your *first* business is to seek the kingdom of God."

"I *abhor cant!*"

"Those were the words of Christ that I uttered. I should be sorry to have you call them cant."

"Oh, you are mighty cool!"

"Yes; I should be very sorry to be angry with you, or injure you, or treat you impolitely. I have no feelings toward you but those of kindness and good-will."

"You have got all the young people running after you in this excitement, which you call a revival of religion. In my opinion there is not much religion about it! But I'll tell some of them better. I'll let them know what you are!"

"You may know me better yourself, perhaps, before you have done with me. And as to the young people, I am happy to know that many of them are trying to flee from the wrath to come; and if we are mistaken about the matter of religion in this revival, I hope you will become *truly* religious yourself, and thus give us an example and be prepared to tell us our error."

In this mode I aimed to soften her asperities. But, for the most part, she took the lead in the conversation, and kept on with a more abusive talk than I ever received before.

I took my leave of her, saying I would do myself the pleasure of calling again soon. She replied, with a triumphant air, and with an accent of bitter irony, "I should be *very* happy to see you, very *indeed!*"

After I left her I thought over the interview, and studied her character with all the carefulness and penetration I could muster. I knew that sometimes convicted sinners would become opposers, just because they *were* convicted,—being led to vent upon other people the dissatisfaction they feel with themselves. And in such cases I have always thought it best to treat them with kindness, and aim to overcome their opposition by good-will, and by letting them find nothing to oppose. But I did not think this was *her* case. She had manifested no dissatisfaction with herself; and though she was "exceeding fierce," I did not believe she resembled those whom the devils tore, before they came out of them.

This young woman was very rich, having a large property of her own, which she used as she pleased. She lived in the midst of elegance; and several of the expressions which she used while talking to me appeared to me to indicate that she was proud of her affluence, presumed upon it to give her respectability, and was fully resolved to enjoy the pleasures of the world. The costliness and elegance of her dress rather sustained this idea; which was still further impressed upon my mind by my knowledge of the kind of accomplishments she had aimed at, while pursuing her education.

On the whole, I came to a fixed conclusion as to the manner in which I should treat her, if she ever ventured to talk to me in the same manner again. Evidently she felt that she had triumphed over me, and was proud of her triumph. Little as such a triumph might be, I was afraid the pride of it would still further harden her, and thus I should have done her an injury. Her mother was a member of my Church. I had always treated her and her daughter politely; and I knew, or thought I knew, that the young lady supposed herself able to overawe me. And if I should allow her to go on in this way, and to feel that she triumphed, she would probably become the more haughty, and hardened, and worldly. However, I rather supposed that on reflection she would be sorry for what she had said, and be careful not to repeat it again. I very much hoped that she would. But if she should commence such a course again, my duty was plain, and I resolved to aim to discharge it.

Accordingly I called upon her the very next day, and stated to her my desire to have some conversation with her, if agreeable to her, very frankly and kindly, on the subject of her duty to God, and to her own soul. I found her in much the same mood as before. She soon commenced her abusive style of remark about professors of religion, and ministers, and revivals. I allowed her to go on in her own way, without saying much myself, for about half an hour. I only aimed to pacify her opposition by mildness, and lead her to speak more reasonably and feel more justly. She seemed to take courage from my forbearance, to be the more bitter and abusive. When I thought the fit time had come, I requested her to pause a little, and just hear what I had to say to her.

I then talked to her as severely as I was able. I told her there was not much truth, and not an item of sincerity, in all she had been saying,—that I knew it, and she knew it herself;—that she knew she had been saying things which were not true, and affirming opinions which she did not entertain;—that she was just wickedly acting out the deep-seated and indulged wickedness of her heart against God,—a wickedness which, I was surprised to find, had led a lady of her sense and accomplishments to forget the dignity of her sex, and descend to mean and low abuse, of which she ought to be ashamed, and would be ashamed, if she had any delicacy left;—that I had entered her house in a gentlemanly manner, with respectful and kind feelings towards her, and had treated her politely and kindly in every word and action, both yesterday and to-day; while she had disgraced herself and her family by her abuse and coarseness, which were unworthy of any one who pretended to the least respectability;—that, on my own account, I did not care one atom what she thought of me, or said to me, for she was entirely incapable of hurting my feelings; but that I felt exceedingly sorry for *her*, to find her acting like a poor, wicked fool, "foaming out her own shame," and boasting of her sincerity, when there was not an item of sincerity about her;—that, as for her influencing other young people against me, and turning their hearts away from religion, as she had yesterday threatened to do, I would take care to see to that; she might do her worst, I would caution them against her; and any slanders she might utter against me would only exalt me in the opinion of any one, whose opinion I cared anything about;—that she might indulge her wickedness, and rail against Christians and Christian ministers as long as she pleased;—I never would attempt to stop her again, for if this was to be her course, I was now in her house for the last time;—that I was sorry to speak thus to her,—I had never done it before to any person in my life, and never expected to have occasion to do it again; but I felt it to be my duty now,—a duty which I owed to her own soul, for I had never, in all my experience, witnessed such hardened and silly wickedness as I had seen in her, for which she would soon have to give an account unto God;—that if she had known no better, I could have had some respect for; but she did know better, she spake what she knew was not true, just indulging the enmity of her heart against God;—that her pride would soon be brought low, and if she did not repent and flee to Christ, the time was not far distant when God would leave her to her own way, and at last she would have her just portion "in shame and everlasting contempt?"

As I went on to speak in this strain, she at first appeared to be taken by surprise, to be utterly confounded, as if she could not believe her own ears. But in a little time her eyes were cast down to the floor; she buried her face in her handkerchief, and wept and sobbed as a child.

I did not heed this at all. I continued to speak in the same manner till I had finished all I had to say. I then told her that I had done all my duty to her, and was now going to leave her for ever. I had only to say, that so far as I was myself concerned in her vituperation, I freely forgave it all, and hoped God would forgive it; but that I very well knew it all proceeded from her enmity against God, which he only could forgive; and I besought her to seek his forgiveness, before it was too late.

While uttering this severe rebuke, I had stood with my hat in my hand, ready to depart; and when I had finished, I bade her good morning, and turned towards the door. She sprang from her seat, and reaching out both her hands to me, she begged me, with tears coursing down her cheeks, not to leave her so. She began to entreat my forgiveness. I stopped her instantly.

"I will not allow you to beg my pardon," said I. "You have not offended me at all. If I have said anything wrong, I will beg *your* pardon."

"No, no!" said she, while she clung to my hands in great agitation, sobbing aloud.

Said I, "I must go, if you have nothing to say to me."

Said she, "I hope you will consent to stay a little longer. Don't leave me, don't leave me. I beg of you to stay."

I did not intend to stay; but she appeared so overwhelmed, and I had really talked to her so severely, that I began to relent. I could not bear to add another burden to her heart.

We sat down, and she immediately thanked me for my plainness with her, and confessed she deserved it all. She continued to weep most piteously, and with an imploring look she asked me, "What shall such a poor, wicked creature do?"

I was entirely overcome. I wept with her. I could not avoid it. But I could not now converse with her. After several attempts I said to her,—

"I *cannot* talk with you now. If you wish it, I will come to see you when I am less agitated."

"Will you come this afternoon?" said she.

"Yes, I will, if you desire it."

"I *do* desire it. Now be sure to come. Don't forget me. Come immediately after dinner, or as soon as you can. I have much to say to you."

I left her. When I returned in the afternoon, she met me at the door, bathed in tears. She gave me her hand affectionately, but in silence. She could not speak. Her proud spirit seemed crushed. She was all gentleness. As soon as she could subdue her agitation, she expressed her joy at seeing me. She had been watching for me, and should have gone after me in a few moments if I had not come. She thanked me again and again for what I had said to her. She told me that when I began to talk to her so plainly in the morning, she was surprised, she did not expect such an address. "But as you went on," said she, "I was confounded. I knew what you said was true, but I was amazed that you should know my heart so well. I thought you knew it better than I did; and before you had done, if you had told me *anything* about myself, I should have believed it all. It seemed to me that you just lifted the covering from my heart. I felt myself in a new world. And it does now seem to me that I am the most wicked sinner that ever was. Will God have mercy upon me? What shall I do? What can I do?"

I saw her many times after this, and all our intercourse was most kind and pleasant. She sought the Lord and found him. In a few months she united with the Church. I knew her for years afterwards, a lovely and consistent Christian, and one of my own most precious friends.

This is the only instance, save one, in which I have ever ventured upon such a course of severity. I do not know that I should do it again. I thought it wise at the time, and the result pleased me exceedingly. After she became a member of the

Church, and an intimate friend, I conversed with her on the subject of my treatment of her at the time when she said I "uncovered her heart;" and she expressed her opinion that nothing but such treatment could have arrested her in her career. She said, that while I was talking to her, at first she perfectly hated me; but before I closed, she perfectly despised herself, and feared that God would have no mercy upon her.

There can be no question that the power of the gospel lies in its kindness and love, and that through such affections, rather than the opposite ones, souls are to be wooed and won to Christ. But kindness and love can censure as well as smile. There are circumstances in which censure is demanded, and duty cannot be discharged without it. And yet, to censure and reprove are things so uncongenial to the love-spirit of the gospel, and are apt to be so congenial to some of the worst feelings of human nature, that few duties are so difficult. None but a truly affectionate believer can wisely trust himself to utter words of severity to those who oppose religion. St. Paul had tears, but no taunts, for the enemies of Christ.

XXXII.

Conviction Resisted.

AT the request of a neighbouring minister, I went to preach for him a day or two in a time of revival among his people. Some of those who were concerned about their salvation came to me for the purpose of personal conversation, after the close of the first meeting I attended. The number of these continued to increase. But my ministerial friend seemed very sad. He would put all the services upon me; I could scarcely induce him even to offer a prayer, in public or in the family. On the second day that I was there, he came into the room I occupied, locked the door, and with much agitation told me the cause of his distress. He said he was afflicted beyond measure, his soul was cast down to the ground. He had a daughter about eighteen years of age, whose mind had been serious for months, and whose determination to gain an interest in the great salvation appeared to become more and more fixed, till about two weeks before, when her seriousness appeared to diminish; and now she seemed resolved to resist all divine truth and divine influences. She would not converse with him any longer; and if any one said anything to her about her attending any religious service, she would contrive to stay away. He had come to the conclusion to say no more to her, and he desired me not to mention the subject of religion to her personally, lest her heart should be set against it still more.

I carefully inquired what had taken place to change the current of her feelings so much, but he could give me no information, or even conjecture. He had tried in vain to ascertain. I told him I thought he might safely leave it to me, whether I should speak to her or not. I felt inclined to do so. He objected to it, but finally left it to me; "for," says he, "she will give you no answer, if you try to talk with her."

I met her once or twice, for a moment, in the course of the forenoon, as we casually came together in the hall or parlour She did not go to church. After dinner I seized an opportunity in the parlour to talk with her; but I said nothing about religion. Afterwards I saw her in the garden, and joined her in a walk there. But while I aimed to become acquainted with her, and aimed to please her, I said nothing about religion. She stayed away from religious worship in the afternoon. She did not appear to avoid me any longer. After tea she came into the parlour, where I was sitting alone, and we had a very pleasant interview for half an hour. Not a word was said on the subject of religion; only she told me she believed she "would go to church in the evening."

"Well now," said I, "you can do me a favour. It is difficult for me to know what sermons to preach, away from home. I will bring down my bundle, and get you to look at the texts and the titles, and tell me which one to preach."

Without waiting for an answer, I went for them. When I returned, I put them into her hands familiarly, and asked her to choose. She looked a little confused; but I went on talking familiarly about the sermons, and finally asked which she would have. After some little urgency necessary to my purpose, because she modestly declined making any selection, she handed me one, saying, "I should like to hear *that one.*"

"Oh!" said I, "I beg your pardon for giving you *that.* I preached that this afternoon. However, it is all the better; for if you wish to hear it, perhaps you will allow me the pleasure of reading it to you at home."

"I should be glad to hear it," said she, with a smile, "but I cannot trouble you to do that for me."

"Ah," said I, "that is your polite way of getting rid of listening to a dull composition. But you are right; I will not bore you with it."

"Indeed I should not consider it a *bore.*"

"You are a very rash girl to say that before you have tried it; 'Let not him that putteth on the harness boast himself, as he that putteth it off.' But see here,—you and I must be a good deal *alike.* The very sermon *I* chose for the afternoon, *you* chose for the evening. You are only half a day behind me. You must try to catch up. I know we can walk together, and not quarrel, —we think so much alike. But choose me another—any one you select I will preach."

Said she, "I am afraid it will be a foolish selection."

"Well, now! that is a pretty compliment to my sermons!—'a *foolish* selection!'"

She laughed at this, but answered,—

"I did not mean the *sermon* would be foolish."

"Well, foolish or not, I must preach some one of them; so, please to tell me which."

She chose one. And I apologized for being so impolite as to leave her alone, by telling her that I must read it over before going to the pulpit.

By this time we had become quite familiar. Her reserve had worn off, and she appeared to feel at ease in my presence. It seemed to me that it was about time to name the subject of religion to her; but on the whole I concluded to wait another day, and see if she would not *herself* commence conversation on that subject, which I should much prefer.

She attended church in the evening, appeared just as usual, and the next day, morning and afternoon, she attended and heard my sermons. I kept up my acquaintance with her at home, got her to select sermons for me, and tell why she selected the particular ones she chose, and debated the matter with her, whether she had hit on the right ones for the object she had in view. This was the mode by which I first got a glimpse of the state of her mind. I became much interested in her. Her quickness of mind, her taste and refinement, her fine education, and her amiability, together with an air of pensiveness, which hung around her, and seemed to creep over her unbidden, made me feel attached to her as a friend, and ready to sympathize in all she felt.

As she started to go to church in the evening, I motioned her father out of the way, and gave her my arm. She seemed surprised, for she had evidently intended to avoid me. We had about half a mile to walk; and as she had started before the fit time, there was full liberty for us to walk very leisurely.

I immediately commenced speaking to her on the things of the gospel, in the most delicate and affectionate manner that I could. At first she was mute, but in a few minutes she told me frankly all about her feelings. She said that she had been very much interested about her salvation, but her interest was all gone. She had ceased to pray. She had become disgusted; and she supposed the Holy Spirit had left her. At any rate, she felt no concern now, as she had done for many weeks, when she was sensible of her sin; and for some days she had not allowed any one to speak to her on the subject.

"Perhaps," said I, "you did not wish *me* to mention it. If you are *unwilling* to hear me, just say so, and I will be still. But I have become attached to you, as a friend; you have interested me very much; and if the thing *is* allowable, I should like to ask what disgusted you with religion."

"I would rather not tell."

"I wish you *would* tell me. I give you my promise that all you say to me shall be sacredly confidential; and I assure you I will treat you kindly, and you may speak to me *anything* you think or feel."

"I *was* very anxious for a while, but I am not now; and you would think me foolish if I should tell you what disgusted me."

"Not at all," said I. "I shall think you dislike and distrust *me*, if you *don't* tell."

"Well," said she, "it was what a young man said to me. He attends college. He was here a few days, attended prayer meetings, and sometimes made addresses, as he is going to be a minister; and one day, when he asked me about my feelings and I told him, he talked to me very harshly, because I had not come to repentance, and said that his prayers for me would sink me deeper in hell."

"And what did you say to that?"

"I told him, I hoped then he would not pray for me."

"That was right," said I,—"that was right. I thank you for saying it. You taught him a good lesson. He had no business to be talking to you in that manner. If you took that for an example of religion, it is no wonder that you were disgusted. I am sure it sounds disgusting to *me*."

"And then," said she, "after I told him *that*, he became still worse in his language. He told me I was the vilest creature on earth—he wondered I was not in hell—and I should be there soon. I was disgusted and angry, when he said a great many such things to me. I would not attend the prayer meeting afterwards where he was. I thought if that was the way and feeling of religion, I would have nothing to do with it; and since that I have thought but little about it."

"When he told you that you would soon be in hell, what did you say to him?"

"I said it was well for me that *he* could not send me there."

"Very well. I am glad you said it. It will do him good, if he has sense enough to profit by it. You have done rightly. *He* was in fault, not *you*. He is probably a proud, silly, impudent young man."

"*I* think so," said she. "And I was amazed to hear my father speak so very highly of him, and commend his faults, as I thought them."

I then reasoned with her on the impropriety of her being influenced at all by *anything* that such a heartless young man could say; and the impropriety of judging of *religion* by such a specimen of *irreligion*,—for surely his *talk* was anything but religion, be his heart what it might. I besought her to take her own way, the way of her own conscience and good sense, uninfluenced by any man or minister on earth. I told her to think of it, how she was manifestly wrong in being influenced as she had been. She said she knew it was wrong. I then besought her to seek the Lord now, as she very well knew she ought to do; and not regard what *I* said, or anybody else said, but follow her own reason, and look to God, and he would bless her. She said she would candidly think of it.

By this time we had reached the door of the church. I preached the sermon she had selected. Before pronouncing the blessing, I came down from the pulpit to the desk below, and invited all those who had no hope in Christ, and were willing to begin now to seek God prayerfully, to remain in their seats after the blessing was pronounced, for I had something more to say to them. I made an address to all unconverted persons, on the duty of seeking God now; and besought every one of them not to be influenced by anything but a sense of their duty to Christ and their own souls. And to furnish them a little time more for making up their mind, deliberately, whether they would seek the Lord or not, I proposed to sing a hymn which I would read, and make some few remarks as I read it. I then read the hymn:—

> "'Come, humble sinner, in whose breast
> A thousand thoughts revolve;
> Come, with your guilt and fear oppressed,
> And make this last resolve;
>
> I'll go to Jesus, though my sin
> Has like a mountain rose;
> I know his courts, I'll enter in,
> Whatever may oppose.'

"'Choose ye this day whom ye will serve; if the Lord be God, follow him; if Baal, then follow him.' Go the one way or the other. 'Now is the accepted time; now is the day of salvation.'

"'Prostrate I'll lie before his throne,
And there my guilt confess;
I'll tell him I'm a wretch, undone
Without his pardoning grace!'

"'The Son of man is come to seek and to save that which was lost,'—lost sinners! lost! lost to holiness! lost to God! lost to happiness! lost to heaven!—lost!—lost!—lost!

"'Perhaps he will admit my plea,
Perhaps will hear my prayer—'

"'Perhaps?'—there is *no* '*perhaps*' about it. God says there is none! 'Hear, and your soul shall live. I will make an *everlasting* covenant with you, even the sure mercies of David.' There is no 'perhaps' in the matter. Eternal life is *certain* to the sinner who will seek God with all his heart. The *hymn* is right. It represents what a sinner feels when he is just resolving to go to Christ. But let him fling his '*perhaps*' to the winds! and let him *know* that Christ will accept him, if he comes. 'Come ye to the waters'—'If any man will, let him take of the water of life freely.' Still *he* does not feel so. Hear him:—

"'Perhaps he will admit my plea,
Perhaps will hear my prayer;
But if I perish, I will pray,
And perish only there.'

"And if you perish *there* you will perish where a sinner *never did* yet! You will be the *first* that ever went down to hell from the foot of the cross!

"'I can but perish if I go,—'

"'*Perish?*'—sooner shall heaven and earth pass away! '*Perish?*'—the sceptre of Immanuel shall be shivered into pieces —the throne of the Redeemer Jehovah shall sink, if you perish there!

"'I can but perish if I go,
I am resolved to try;
For if I stay away, I know
I must for ever die!'

"'Stay *away?*'—forbid it, O God of mercy! Draw every one of us by thy love. May not *a soul* stay away to-night:—

> "'For if I stay away, I know
> I must for ever die!'"

As I read this hymn and made these remarks, an awful solemnity seemed to rest upon the congregation. All was still as the house of death. There was not a sigh or a tear!

The hymn was sung, and then I requested all the members of the Church to retire, and all others, except those unconverted sinners who were resolved to begin *now*, if they had not already begun, to seek the Lord earnestly and prayerfully. Those who would thus seek God, I requested to remain in their seats. I pronounced the benediction.

My young friend, who was in the pew just before me, remained standing still for a moment—then made towards the door—then paused, and sat down—then immediately rose again, as if to mingle with those who were leaving the church—opened the door of the pew—then paused—then stepped out into the aisle—and finally turned back into the pew and sat down, bowing her head upon the pew before her, evidently in deep emotion. As her father, who stood by my side, noticed this action of his daughter, he burst into tears, sunk down into his seat, and covered his face with his hands.

About forty persons had remained, almost the whole of whom became members of the Church before the close of the summer. I made a short address to them, offered a short prayer, and dismissed them.

As they were leaving the church, I perceived that my ministerial brother was making his way towards his daughter, as if to speak with her, his eyes streaming with tears. I took him by the arm and held him gently back, till I could get before him. I met her myself at the door of the church, offered her my arm, and we walked home in silence.

I conversed with her a few moments the next morning before leaving the place, and never saw her afterwards.

Some months after this, her father told me that a week after I left there she entertained a hope in Christ, had since united with the Church, and "is now," said he, "the happiest mortal in the world."

It is important to be wise in aiming to win sinners to Christ. The Bible is the only safe guide. Its spirit is love. It utters no denunciations against any who are disposed to treat the gospel offer seriously. To lead sinners to condemn *themselves* is one thing, for us to condemn them is quite another. If their reason and conscience do not very much second what we say to them, our words do not hit their case.

The snares of the devil are very deceitfully contrived. This young woman was right to dislike some of the things said to her, but she fell into a subtle snare when she allowed them to turn her mind from truth, duty, and God. How strange that she should suffer herself to be influenced so much by the very man whom she disapproved and despised. Such is human nature.

I have every reason to believe that this young girl was of a most affectionate and amiable disposition, and therefore the coarse and heartless language of that young man was the more revolting to her. If what he said was appropriate to her conscience, it was not appropriate to her heart; and if the matter of it resembled the truth of the gospel, the spirit and manner of it certainly had no resemblance to Christianity. Religion needs no such advocates.

This young man was a revivalist. He was fond of talking and praying about "revivals," and "revival spirit," and "revival measures." We have had so much of this in some parts of the country, that many Christians have been led into serious errors; and while, like this young man, they have adopted strange modes of expression and action, they have thought, and felt, and even prayed just as if sinners could not be converted except in revivals, and thus the irreligious have been led to think it vain to seek God at any other time. An office-bearer of my Church once told me that he himself had "*waited for a revival ten years,*" because he "had been led, by the way in which Christians talked, to suppose there was little reason to hope for a blessing at any other time." By such notions about revivals repentance is delayed, prayer discouraged, the Spirit grieved, souls ruined, and revivals corrupted! The Church and the world ought to know that sinners may seek God and find him at any time, as easily as in revivals.

XXXIII.

Determination.

AT the close of a religious service held in the evening in a large public room, I requested all those who were not members of the Church, but were disposed to attend to the matter of their salvation, to remain in the place after the benediction was pronounced, and give me an opportunity to converse with them. I did this for the sake of convenience, as there were so many at that time, it was not easy for me to call upon all of them at their homes so often as they might perhaps desire to speak with me. And besides, it was quite likely that some just then, while the truth preached was upon their minds, and its impression had not worn off by their mingling with the world, might be induced to begin to seek God by a request to take their stand at once. This, their instant duty, was urged upon them affectionately and earnestly. About sixty remained. Though it was impossible to have much conversation with so many, yet as there were some whom I did not know, and whose residences I wished to learn for the purpose of visiting them, I passed from one to another, speaking to them such things as I found to be called for by their state of mind.

While I was thus employed, and the assembly was peculiarly still and solemn, we were startled by the heavy and rapid tread of a person upon the steps leading up to the front door of the room. The rude footsteps ascended the stairs,—sounded along the wooden platform,—the door burst open as if by violence,—a young man rushed in with an excited, wild look, stamped up the aisle hastily, and flung himself into a vacant seat. He breathed heavily; and with his head erect he stared wildly around, with such a look of iron determination as I never saw. Till that moment I had supposed that he was some evil-minded person, who had come in to disturb us. The heavy tread upon the stairs, and stamp along the floor, so rude and hasty, contrasted strangely with the quiet and solemnity of the place and the occasion. But as the young man sat still, and only looked wildly and breathed strongly, those who had been startled at his entrance became composed; and I began to think that he might have come there with no wicked or unfriendly intention. I kept my eye on him as he sat with his head erect, but said nothing to him till I had finished what I had to say to all the rest. Still doubtful of his intentions, I went to him, offered him my hand, which he seized with the grasp of a madman, and seating myself by his side, inquired whether he wished to see me.

Said he, "I have had a dreadful struggle. I have known this *month* that I ought to attend to my salvation. I went home from this place to-night, and when I got there I could not go in. I turned about and came back here; and when I got to the door, I could not enter. I turned about to go home; but it was hard work. I got over the bridge; but when I was going up the hill to the gate, my knees failed me, my heart gave way,—I felt as if I had been fighting with God! I turned about and came back here to the door; but I could not get in, to save my life; I was ashamed to be seen here. I thought everybody would laugh at me, if it should be known; and I could not bear that; and I was afraid I should not hold out if I began; and then I should be ashamed of myself to go back to the world. So I gave it up, and went off *determined* to think no more about it. But I could not help thinking. I stopped on the bridge, and stood there a long time, looking first one way and then the other, and I could not stir a step either way. A man came along and passed me as I stood there in the dark, and I went on after him up the hill, till I got my hand upon the gate. But I could not open it; I thought I was opening the door of hell to go in! I determined I *would* come back, or *die* in the attempt. But I was afraid to trust my resolution, so I ran with all my might, and stopped for nothing till I got my seat here. I am a dreadful sinner! I have opposed God. If I do not gain salvation now, it will be too late for me! I have struggled against the Holy Spirit for a month! My heart has been too stout for me; but I have made out to get here."

I conversed with him for a few moments, and dismissing the assembly, accompanied him to his own door, and bade him good night. In my conversation with him, I aimed to convince him of the mercy of God to sinners through Jesus Christ,—of the necessity of faith in Christ, and repentance for sin,—of the free offer of salvation to be accepted at once,—of the hardness, wickedness, and obstinacy of his heart, which was every instant resisting truth and the Holy Spirit.

The next morning early my door-bell rang violently. I opened the door, and there he stood, pale and trembling. "I can't live so," said he, with a look of agony; "what *shall* I do?"

"Mr. R——," said I, "you are very much afraid of going to hell, but—"

"Hell?" said he,—"I never *thought* of it! It is this *heart*," said he, smiting upon his breast,—"my dreadful heart! It fights against God! That is what puts me in this awful agony!"

Said I, "Your only hope must be in the power of the Divine Spirit to subdue your rebellion."

"I find it so, sir. I have tried all night, and I am as much at war with God as ever! If he does not save me, I am gone. Pray for me."

This young man became at peace very soon. Two days afterwards I found him calm. He afterwards became a member of the Church; and for the ten years that I knew him he was one of the most devoted and consistent Christians I have ever known. Remembering the struggle of that night, when he ran to our meeting, lest his heart should get the victory over him, he was accustomed to insist upon "decision, decision, decision," to every anxious sinner whom he addressed. Said he, "If you expect God to help you, you must be perfectly *decided*."

Decision is a vastly important matter with a convicted sinner. The Bible treats it as such: "Choose ye this day whom ye will serve." A sinner must choose, or he must be lost. Nobody else can choose for him. Nothing can excuse him from doing this duty at once. If he will not do it, he may expect the Divine Spirit to depart from him, and leave him to his own way.

XXXIV.

The Miserable Heart;

OR, DELUSION AND INFIDELITY.

MY duty required of me, as I thought, to preach, on one occasion, upon the subject of Church discipline. Late in the evening of the day on which the sermon was preached, my door-bell rang; and as my family had all retired, I went to the door, supposing some sick person had probably sent for me. As I opened the door I was surprised to behold a young lady, a member of my Church. I instantly thought some one of the family must have become suddenly ill, or some calamity must have occurred, to bring her to my house at such a late hour. I instantly inquired what was the matter; and I felt the more anxious because I noticed that she was very much agitated. She did not answer very readily. She said the family were well, and nothing sad had happened. I could not conjecture what had brought her there. She refused to come in. As she stood trembling in the hall I told her she *must* tell me what was the matter, offered her any service I could render, and tenderly endeavoured to soothe her agitation. Finally she tremblingly and hesitatingly said—

"I have come to ask if you are going to discipline me."

"Discipline *you!* my dear girl; what do you mean? No. Why should *you* be disciplined?"

"Why," says she, "you have been preaching to-day about Church discipline, and I thought you were going to discipline me."

"No, no! Why discipline you? What have you done to deserve it?"

She gave me no answer, but trembled so greatly that I thought she would fall upon the floor. I was astonished. She belonged to one of the most respectable families of the place, was a very modest and amiable girl, not twenty years old, and I had never heard a syllable against her. I could not induce her to take a seat in the parlour, nor could I persuade her to tell me why she had thought that she was to be disciplined. I assured her that I had never thought of such a thing—had never heard a lisp against her, and kindly entreated her to tell me all her thoughts, promising her the most inviolable secrecy. But she would not tell me. I soothed her agitation all in my power. I accompanied her home to her own door, and begged permission to call and see her the next day.

I went. But still she refused to tell me what led her to suppose that she was to be made the subject of discipline. And I did not succeed in getting the explantion till I had conversed with her in private more than once, had gained her entire confidence, and had promised her, that, be her case what it might, I never would make use of anything she should say to me, in any manner whatever, without her permission. She appeared so unhappy every time I saw her, so agitated and gloomy, that I pitied her very much. I thought she needed some friend to lean upon; and offering her all I could do, I had no hesitation in promising to keep her dreadful secret. She told me it *was* a secret. She had never told her mother or any one else; it was known only to herself.

She then told me that she had no religion, no hope! She knew that she ought not to be a communicant while in her unbelief; and she thought that I had had penetration enough to discover her state of mind, in some way that she knew not of, and was determined to have her cast out of the Church. She wondered at my supposed discovery, for she had never till that moment, as she said, "uttered a word about her feelings to any person on earth."

This disclosure surprised me. but it greatly relieved me. I

thanked her for it, and assured her of my fidelity to her, and the affectionate interest I felt in her.

But as I began to exhort her to seek God and explain religion to her according to the Scriptures, I soon discovered, as I thought, that I had not yet reached the bottom of the matter. Something seemed to be locked up in her own mind. I told her so. I begged her to tell me if it was *not* so. After much hesitation on her part and urgency on mine, she confessed it was so. Most affectionately I entreated her to tell me all, so that I might be able to comfort her unhappiness if possible, and might counsel her in a manner appropriate to her case.

I treated her so affectionately and tenderly, that she became evidently much attached to me; and little by little she opened her mind to me very reluctantly, because, as she said, she knew it would give me pain; and I had "been so kind to her, that she felt very unwilling to give me any unhappiness on a matter wherein I could do her no good."

I found that she was entirely an infidel. She did not believe in the Bible—she did not believe in any religion—she did not believe in the immortality of the soul, or in the existence of a God. She thought that man died and went to nothing, just as a tree dies—its trunk and its leaves and its living principle perishing together. And the failure of mind in old age she deemed a strong indication of its falling into non-existence at death.

She had become a member of the Church when she was very young, attending school,—a girl about fifteen or sixteen years old. She said she was excited, in a time of revival, as others were; wept as they wept; attended the religious meetings appointed by the minister for those of her age, ordinarily in the school; listened to his exhortations; was affected by what he said; had fears of punishment, and then hopes of heaven; and when a time was appointed for the examination of those who desired to join the Church, she went with the rest of the girls. She thought then that she was doing rightly, and never dreamed of any error or deception; but she thought now that all those feelings were the mere effect of sympathy, fear, and imagination. The examination for her reception into the Church was very little except an exhortation. Only one question was put to her, "How long have you had a hope?" to which she replied, "About four weeks." This, she said, was the only question that any person ever asked her at all about her religious feelings; till years afterwards, when I first saw her, and finding she was a member of the Church, asked her if she thought she was growing in grace. She joined the Church, and had gone regularly to the communion ever since,—a period of about five years. She had not stayed away, because of the great repugnance she felt to being made the subject of remark; and for the same reason she had not mentioned the state of her mind to any person whatever. She had been exceedingly miserable all the time; had felt the need of some one to talk with; and now, for the two or three weeks since she first began to open her mind to me, sad and gloomy as she still was, she was happy beyond anything she ever expected to be. She had long felt conscious that she was unfit to be a communicant,—that there was a wrong and a meanness in professing what she did not believe; and she despised herself for it. But she supposed, if she should reveal her feelings and opinions, they would make her a subject of discipline, or, at least, everybody would be talking about her, or pointing at her as an apostate; which disgraceful notoriety and scorn she felt that she could not bear—her whole nature shrunk from it. And this was the afflictive idea which had compelled her to go to my house at that late hour of the evening, when she thought no one would know it, and when she came to me with such a burden on her heart. "Oh!" said she, "if I could have borne it, I never should have gone there. It was a hard trial!"

By this time I had become well acquainted with her, and could judge of the power and character of her mind, and the natural turn of her disposition. She was no ordinary girl. She had an uncommon degree of intellectual power, and especially of keen discrimination. She was a severe reasoner. She grasped the points of an argument with the hand of a giant, after she had discerned them with the eye of an eagle. Often afterwards I had occasion to be humbled before the penetration and strength of her uncommon mind. She was modest and timid to a fault. Mind —reason, was her forte. She had not much poetry about her. Her taste, however, was correct; not only, as might be expected, from the severe correctness of her intellect, but it was gentle and refined also, as might be expected from the amiableness of her affectionate disposition. A truer heart never beat or bled. She was all woman, all affection. A stranger might not think so, because she was timid and reserved in her manners, which cast over her an aspect of coldness. She had a fine education, moved in polite society, and was universally esteemed. The more I knew of her mind and heart, the more I esteemed and loved her.

She was now perfectly miserable. She was ashamed of being in the Church, and would be ashamed to leave it. What to do she did not know, and saying, with a flood of tears, "Now, my dear pastor, I have told you all,—what I supposed I never should tell anybody, but carry it with me, a dreadful secret, to my grave;" she cast herself upon my kindness and sense of duty, to treat her as I pleased. "Disgrace me if you will. I know you will do right!"

Being resolved to spare no pains to do her good, if God would deign to bless my poor attempts, and fearing that her sensitive mind would be too much diverted from the one thing needful if she should have her feelings excited by the idea that people were talking of her, I enjoined upon her to say nothing to any one about her religious feelings,—to keep on just as she had been doing,—to attend church,—to go to the communion,—and not be troubled about anything but her own private religion. I had some doubts about giving her this advice to attend the communion. But she was a member of the Church,—her covenant called her there,—now, she was going there only for a season, unless her mind became different,—and if she did *not* go, I was fully convinced that she would become too much agitated and diverted in mind for a just consideration of the matters which I was going to urge upon her attention. She was peculiarly sensitive. Her feelings were very delicate. She had been tormented for years with the idea of her condition. She had despised herself for going to the Lord's supper, and thus deceiving people by professing to be a Christian, while she did not believe in any religion ; and yet she could not endure the idea of being exposed and made the subject of remark. Moreover, she felt that it was not *her* fault that she was a member of the Church. She had only done what her minister, and others older than herself, had urged her to do; and if anybody was to be blamed for her being in the Church, the blame was not hers, but theirs. I thought so too, and frankly told her so.

In order to be as well prepared as possible to lead her mind out of its dark and miserable error, into the light and cheerfulness of truth, I wished her to tell me how her mind had been led into this infidelity,—an infidelity which really was just atheism ; for she did not believe in the existence of God. Her account was as follows:—

A few months after she became a member of the Church, her excitement having worn off, she found herself just the same that she always had been. Her mind was the same; her taste, her heart, her delights and desires were the same. Instead of finding in religion the peace of mind, the delight in God, and the love of prayer, which she had been taught to expect, "if she would go forward and do her duty," as it was called, she found nothing at all. With *her*, at least, religion was all a delusion.

Her next step was to examine into the case of her associates, those of her own age, who had joined the Church when she did. She said nothing to any one of them, but she watched them. What they did, what they said, where they went, how they felt, where they sought their pleasures and placed their affections, were all matters of her continued and close observation and study. She saw that they were under some restraint, indeed ; but so was she, and she thought it was the same with them as she knew it was with herself,—consistency with her profession restrained her. So far as she could judge, they were just like herself. If she had no religion, there was no evidence that they had any.

"Why," said she, "do you believe that Miss Susan M—— is what you call a Christian?"

"No," said I; "not at all."

"Or Miss Sally E——?" said she.

"No," said I; "not at all."

"Or Elizabeth C——?"

"No," said I.

"Or Miss D——? or Martha F——? or Miss B——?"

"No, not one of them."

"Oh!" said she suddenly, "what have I said! I beg your pardon. I did not mean to mention any one's name. I forgot myself. I am very sorry. Since I have become so well acquainted with you, and told you all my heart, I feel, when I am talking with you, just as if I were thinking alone."

"I should be sorry and half offended if you did *not* feel so. You did right to mention their names; and you perceive I answered promptly. To *you* I can say anything. I can trust you. And I want you to trust *me*."

These persons whom she named were all members of the Church, were her friends and associates, had become Church members about the time she became such, and I am sure she would not, on any account, have done them any injustice or injury. In my opinion, she judged rightly of them. I did not wish her to judge of religion by their exemplification of it, and therefore answered her frankly, because I could trust her, and because I knew, if I did not give her my confidence, I could not secure hers.

Her next step had been to look a little further. She thought of all the members of the Church whom she knew, to see if it was not with them just as she knew it was with herself, and had inferred it was with her young companions. On this point she found great difficulty. She studied it for weeks. *Some* of these people really seemed to be different from those called unbelievers. They seemed to be above the world, to have joy in religion, to be conscientious, to love prayer and other religious duties, and evidently they were sincere. It *did* appear that there might be some propriety in saying that such persons had a new heart. She could not account for these things on the supposition that religion was to them what it was to her. But she remembered that most of them were old people, who had not any longer a taste for the pleasures of life, and on this ground she could account for their sobriety and much else in them which distinguished them from other people. They expected to die soon, and it was natural that they should not greatly set their affections upon the world. "You might *expect* that my mother, at her age, would not feel about the world as I do." But then there was a difficulty; she could not believe them *insincere*—hypocrites, like herself. They evidently *believed* in religion, and evidently had some felicity in its exercises and hopes. But she recollected that it had been so with herself once; that *she* used to love prayer, as she thought, and enjoy the Sabbaths and the sermons. She had now found out that this was all a delusion with *her*, and therefore came to the conclusion that it was all a delusion with them. "The difference," said she, "betwixt myself and them seems to me to be this,—they have been so fortunate as not to find out that religion is all a deception, and I have been so *un*fortunate as to find it out fully." On the whole, she came to the conclusion that other members of the Church had really no new heart any more than she had—that they were just like herself; only they were in a happy delusion which, unhappily for her, she had found out to be a delusion. All other Churches and Christians she disposed of in the same way—"happy dreamers," was her description of them.

The next step was to examine where this delusion, called religion, came from. It manifestly came from the Bible. She then examined the Bible very carefully for weeks, and she found it so. Ministers preached the Bible. Christians talked about repentance, faith, prayer, regeneration, peace, and all religion, just as the Bible talked. But she had now discovered that all this personal, experimental *religion* was a falsehood, and therefore concluded that the Bible it came from must be a falsehood also. The *religion*—her own and that of other people—was only a delusion; and as it originated in the Bible, and was what the Bible asked for, the Bible itself must be a delusion. She therefore discarded it at a single dash.

She then found herself entirely afloat on an ocean of midnight. She had no guide and no certainty. All she could do was to reason,—and reason very much in the dark. And as she went on from one thing to another, she saw no satisfactory proofs of the future existence of the soul, and expected soon to die and cease to exist, just like a beast or a tree. She thought it more reasonable to believe that the world was eternal, than that it had been created; and that it would always go on as it does now, than that it would ever come to an end. She saw no proofs of the existence of God, and could give no account of the existence of anything else,—only that *it happened to be so.*

When urged to tell how it came about that all these chance operations were such *regular* operations, and so strongly indicative of intellect and design; to tell how conscience, for example, comes to be such a liar about a *future* and fearful accountability, since it is so truthful about things here; to tell how it came about that the very *ideas* about God and immortality ever got abroad among men, if they are only fictions and dreams; to account for the existence of the Bible, which told her with unerring accuracy the very inside of her heart, as no human being could tell;—she could only reply, that she had "no answer to give; it seemed to her that she knew nothing. All was in the dark."

I then besought her to take up this subject, and reason upon *one thing at a time* most carefully—not to be afraid to reason upon anything—not to let anything go till she was satisfied about it—and not to dismiss the matter till she had an established faith, and a hope fit to die with. I proposed to reason with her, and said I would not blame her, but commend her, for overthrowing every argument if she could. I offered to be an infidel and an atheist with her, if reason and truth would make me so; and I *promised* to lead her mind out of this darkness, if she would only attend to me. I did not care what she denied or where she began. She might deny her own existence if she pleased, and I would beat her, till she believed in it by the evidence of her own senses. But I wanted her to get some one thing settled first as a foundation on which to build another thing, or a way by which to reach another. I wished her to have a log to stand upon, in order to jump to another, and thence to another, till she got out of this dreary morass, with her feet upon solid ground. And I assured her that my *only* doubt about her perfect and happy success rested on the fear that her mind would *not stick to a conclusion* or a truth when once demonstrated to her. If it would, I knew she would arrive, perhaps not soon, at an intellectual certainty upon religion, as clear, strong, and full, as she had, or could have, upon any other subject. And I entreated her instantly to commence a careful examination.

She was very reluctant to do so. She said it would only make her unhappy, and she did not wish to think of the matter. It would do no good. She besought me to let her alone, not to care for her, but leave her to her own way; and I have always supposed that she was finally led to the examination and study I urged upon her more for my sake than her own. She had become greatly attached to me. I had treated her kindly, had sympathised with her, and she had found it, as she declared, "a precious relief, if not a delight, to have one human being to whom she could open her heart." She finally consented to examine the matter of religion again.

I at first attempted to convince her of the truth of the Bible, as the shortest way of settling the whole matter; but I soon found that some other things must for her be settled first.

By a course of reasoning I succeeded in convincing her of the existence of God. This took some time. She was a whole week over the subject. As I could not spend so much time with her in conversation as I thought she needed, and as I found that she would sometimes waver afterwards about a conclusion which she had once reached, I wrote down for her the condensed arguments, that she might examine them at her leisure, and refute them if she could, or tell me if they were not fully satisfactory. I had no need to expand them. She had fully mind enough to do all that for herself, and to understand all that they contained. I continued to do this for weeks, going over one subject after another; and she continued to examine and scrutinize with an intellectual acumen which astonished me. She fought every inch of ground, and never retreated a single step till she was fairly compelled to it, and never suffered a weak or unsatisfactory argument to escape her detection. In this mode,—*she* first suggesting her doubts or difficulties, *I* writing for her the arguments and proofs on the point; *she* reading them, and then in conversation stating her conclusions or her doubts to me, and *I* responding,—we went over a wide field. I demonstrated to her satisfaction such things as the existence of God, his infinity, eternity, immutability, omniscience, omnipotence, wisdom, justice, truth, and goodness, his creation of all things, and his providence over all things. To copy here what I wrote for her would make this sketch too long. As soon as she became fully convinced of God's existence and dominion, I insisted upon it that she should pray to him, and convinced her reason that this was her duty, and one which she ought to love. In this mode, all along, I aimed to bring in religious *practice*, as soon as I had established a doctrine or truth to found it upon. And when she made objections to prayer, which she had never attempted for years, it gave me an opportunity to show by argument addressed to reason, that her heart, instead of being as it ought to be, filial towards God, was just what the Bible says it is, enmity against him. "And here is one proof that the Bible is true." And thus I prepared the way for preaching the gospel to her by-and-by, when she should have become fully convinced that it came from God.

By arguments addressed to her reason, I convinced her of the accountability of man, of a future life and future judgment. There were some points on which I tried in vain to satisfy her fully, aside from the sacred Scriptures; such as the goodness of God, and the certainty of eternal existence. But she had now gone far enough to examine whether the Bible is God's word. Of this she became convinced in a few weeks, mainly by the evidence which it carries along with it. I preferred the internal to the external evidences, as lying nearer the heart of religion, and as constituting, after all, the real ground on which the great majority of mankind must ever receive the Bible as from God. And when she had come to receive the Bible as God's word, all the rest was easy, so far as the reality and nature of religion were concerned. Thus, after months of examination and study, she became fully settled in the belief that the Christian religion is true.

This belief did not seem to comfort her at all. She had no hope in Christ, and was as far off from peace as ever. But her mind now rested upon an undoubted certainty; and this of itself was an ineffable relief, though containing no comforts of hope.

She now began to seek the Lord with great steadiness of mind. It was no easy thing for her. She had been deceived once, and remembered the bitterness it cost her. She was for many tedious months an anxious inquirer, but she did not desist. She attained to a comfortable hope in Christ; and she yet lives, one of the most enlightened and established believers, one of my own most precious friends.

If these pages should ever fall into her hands, I am fully aware that her delicate and sensitive bosom may be agitated by them; but I know that her affectionate heart will forgive me for the publication. Only she and myself can know the original of this sketch.

She has told me,—I have it, indeed, in her own letters written to me long afterwards,—that if I had not addressed her judgment as I did, if I had addressed her fears or her hopes, or exhorted her only, she did not believe that her "mind would ever have been led into the truth." "Through my judgment," says she, "you forced a way into my heart; you made my own understanding and conscience preach to me. I wish ministers in their sermons would employ this way of *reasoning* more than they do."

As nearly as I could ascertain, in my judgment, her opinion of the course pursued with her in that revival of religion when she united with the Church, was a just opinion. She and her young associates in that school were very much separated from older persons, when their attention was particularly expected to be fixed upon religion. Little was said to them in the way of instruction, but much for the purpose of impression. The great doctrines, the fundamental truths of religion, on which all safety rests, were very little explained to them. "It seems to me now," says she, "that all they wanted was to make us weep." They were not told what repentance is, what faith is, what regeneration is,—the very things which children, especially, need to have taught to them. They were merely led on, by excited and impulsive feelings, rendered the more dangerous by the quick sympathies of early life. Against such proceedings her whole mind was now fixed. And in conversation with her, the idea was often suggested to my mind—how frequently ministers address children upon the subject of religion as they ought to address those of mature age, and address those of mature age as they ought to address children. It is children who need instruction. It is the older who need impression. Children are sufficiently ready *to feel*. The danger is, that their sensibilities will outrun their knowledge and judgment. Older persons are slow to feel. *Their* danger is, that they will not have feeling enough to impel them to obey their judgment.

Admission to the sealing ordinances of the Church, especially in times of revival, is a point of no little danger. Our ministers and Churches have too often erred on this point. It seems to be very often forgotten that then the popular feeling tends into the Church; fashion is that way and sympathy that way; and all the common influences which the young are particularly likely to feel, tend to urge them forward in the same direction. Far better would it be for the purity of the Church, and for the comfort and salvation of individuals, if some few months were allowed to pass before the hopefully converted are received into the communion, especially in times of revival. I have no reason to think that my young friend, of whom I have here spoken, judged wrongfully about the piety of her associates, whom she named to me; but I have much reason to know that her judgment was just. I afterwards sought out every one of them, and alone they opened their hearts to me.

It is a very difficult and laborious thing for a minister to deal with such cases as I have here mentioned. It will be hard for him to find time. But he ought to find it. He will seldom labour in vain; and while engaged in this field of duty, he is engaged in the best field of study. His work then lies nearest the heart; and he cannot fail to know the human heart more accurately, and learn how to apply the powers of his mind and the truth of God to souls ready to perish.

It is of vast importance to gain the confidence and affection of those whom he would lead to truth and salvation. As I suppose, this young friend never would have opened her heart to me, had I not knocked at its door with the hand of the most earnest and gentle kindness. I certainly loved her; and she certainly knew it. She yielded to love what she would not have yielded to mere reason, or a sense of duty; and that which began in kindness and tenderness of affection, ended in that peace of God which passeth understanding.

It is very unhappy for us, that we have such a reluctance to disclose our religious feelings. The disclosure would often put us upon the track of a divine benefit. Convictions are often stifled by not being confessed. Anxious sinners would always do well to be more free to tell their troubles to some Christian minister or friend. There is ordinarily either some great error or some dangerous sin lingering around the mind that sensitively seeks concealment. The communion of saints is a privilege. It is one way to attain communion with God.

XXXV.

Unconditional Submission.

ONE of the most distressing instances of anxiety about salvation that I have ever known, was that of a married woman about thirty years of age, and of excellent character, as a wife, and mother, and neighbour. Her energy of character was her most remarkable trait. Her decision, penetration, and quickness were uncommon. She had had a religious education, and was now surrounded with religious influences. Most of her relatives and acquaintances were communicants in the Church. Her husband had lately become a pious man.

She became concerned for her salvation, and seemed to me to have a peculiarly deep sense of her sins. She often expressed to me her wonder and astonishment that God had not cut her down in her carelessness. She thought that her heart was more obstinate than the heart of any other sinner could be. She was fully sensible of its enmity against God; and appeared to be fully determined to seek the Lord with all her heart. I thought, from this and from her ordinary decision of character, that she would soon find peace with God.

But month after month she lingered. At times her distress of mind was inconceivably great. Many times I conversed with her, and in every possible way aimed to teach her the way of life. With all the ingenuity I could muster, I aimed to find out what was her hindrance; but I tried in vain. In her Bible I marked those passages which I hoped would benefit her. She studied them intensely. She prayed daily and with agony. But yet she attained no hope in Christ, no peace with God or with herself.

I expected that the hopeful conversion of her husband, whose exercises of mind had very much resembled her own, would have a beneficial influence upon her mind. But when he told her of his hope and peace, and exhorted her to flee to Christ, she expressed her gladness that he had become a Christian, but her own mind did not appear to be in the least altered.

She conversed with me apparently with entire freedom, told me all her heart, and begged to be told what she should do. All I could say to her appeared to be of no avail. Her mind continued as dark and distressed as ever. And this appeared the more strange to me, because, within a quarter of a mile of her house, there had been at least twenty hopeful conversions to Christ, after she began to strive for salvation; and she enjoyed precisely the same means and opportunities as they.

As week passed after week in this manner, I expected her anxieties would diminish, and the Holy Spirit would depart from her. But her seriousness continued, and her determination to persevere in her attempt. After I had exhausted all my skill to do her good, fearing that I might have done her injury, I left her entirely alone for some weeks, not calling on her as I had been accustomed to do, not saying to her a single word about her religious condition. Still she continued in the same way. At one time I requested some other persons to converse with her; which they did, but apparently in vain.

At length she became almost frantic with anxiety. Her distress seemed intolerable; and I seriously feared that her reason would give way, and leave her to a maniac's gloom. She now began to despond. Salvation appeared an unattainable good to her; and the strange expressions of her despair, a despair which I could no longer alleviate with the promises and invitations of Christ, were enough to make any heart bleed. I knew her endure the most horrid temptations, time after time—temptations which I may not describe. . . . . .

I was now in the habit of calling upon her almost every day as she desired. I parted with her one day in the afternoon, leaving her in much the same gloom and despair as she had endured for some weeks. On entering her house the next morning, I was struck with her altered appearance; and the first thought I had was, that her reason had fled. She appeared quite as solemn as ever; but there was a composure about her look—a sort of fixedness and quietness of firm determination which I had never seen before. As I spoke to her, she answered me in few words, but quite rationally and calmly. There was no insanity there. I drew her into some conversation. She was rather more reserved than common, I thought; but evidently her distress of mind was diminished. She had no hope in Christ, she said, and never expected to have any. "Peace with God," says she, "I know nothing about; but I have done quarrelling with him." This expression led me to suppose that she had come to the determination to dismiss religion from her thoughts. But in a moment afterwards, replying to an expression I had made, she said, "I mean to do all my duty." I could not understand her; and after some half hour's conversation, still as much in the dark as ever, I said to her:—

"You seem to me, Mrs. S——, to be, after all, in a very different state of mind from what you were yesterday. How is it? what has brought you to this?"

"I will tell you, sir," said she, with a deep solemnity, and a kind of awfulness in look and manner, which I have never seen equalled. "After you left me yesterday, and I had been praying to God, and thinking for how long a time the Holy Spirit had been striving with me, I came to the conclusion that I could do nothing, and that there is no salvation for me! But I knew I was justly condemned. And I resolved to serve God as long as I live; to pray to him to help me do it; and resolved to live the rest of my life for the glory of Christ, and commend him to others. I determined to do all my religious duties as well as I can to the end of my life; and go to hell at last, as I deserve!"

"You will find it hard work," said I, "to get to hell in that way;" and immediately left her.

She now had no hope. I did not deem it my duty to give her

any hope. And it was more than a week after this before it ever entered into her thoughts that she was reconciled to God. All this time she was calm, solemn, prayerful, contented. She had made up her mind that she must be lost. She knew it would be just,—that God would do rightly,—and she was willing that he should reign. She determined to serve him till death,—to do all the good she could to others; and "go to hell at last."

But in a few days it struck her mind that she was satisfied with God; that she no longer felt any enmity against him or his law; that, in fact, she loved him, his law, and his Christ. She then began to question whether this was not religion after all; and gradually her mind was led to hope. She afterwards made a public profession of religion, and lived as one of the most determined Christians in the world.

In those gloomy months before she found rest, she was manifestly aiming, with a firmness and decision perfectly agreeing with her character, just to *save herself*, that is, to become a Christian by the power of her own will. And when she found it impossible, she as decidedly despaired. And then as decidedly gave up all to God; "I found I could do nothing more." God saved her, just when she ceased relying upon herself. True converts are born, "not of blood, nor of the will of the flesh, nor of the will of man, but of God."

There may be more truth in the idea which some of the old Hopkinsians intended to express by "unconditional submission," than many of their modern revilers suppose. It certainly is not needful that when a sinner flings down the weapons of his rebellion and becomes reconciled to God he should be without hope; for as soon as he does this, he has a promise of God to rest upon. But it certainly appears to be true that at that time he is not, in every case, really *relying* upon it at all. He is exercising submission—not faith. Or, if he is exercising faith at all, he may not be conscious of it, and, therefore, may have only half the comforts of it. And it is quite conceivable that one may have such a sense of sin and unworthiness as to exclude all expectation of eternal life, while, at the same time, he is really "reconciled to God." He has, in such a case, exercised submission, a gracious submission to God; and therefore his agitations and torments of mind have ceased: but his faith has not yet been brought into lively and conscious exercise; and therefore he has no hope. This would seem to be "unconditional submission," a "giving up of all to God." In this state of mind he certainly cannot be said to "be willing to be damned;" but it can be said of him that he does not expect to be saved.

It may not be possible for human science and skill to analyse conversion to Christ. The gospel has probably made the matter more plain than anything else will ever make it. And there are not a few things in the gospel which appear to place a *surrendry* before faith—yielding before trusting.

A poor Indian, of whom I once had some knowledge, who had been a very wicked man, but who became hopefully pious, was desired to give some account of his conversion—to tell how it was that he had been led to his hope in Christ. He described it in this way, taking his figures from his way of life, as he had been accustomed to chase the deer and the bear over mountains and through morasses:—Said he, "I was in the mud. I tried to get out; and I could not. I tried the harder; and the harder I tried, the deeper I sunk. I found I must put forth all my strength; but I went down deeper, and deeper, and deeper. I found I was going *all over* in the mire; I gave the *death-yell*, and found myself in the arms of Jesus Christ." When he abandoned all attempt to save himself, Jesus Christ saved him. This was all he knew about it. And more, this was all there *was* about it. "Let me fall into the hands of the Lord, for his mercies are great." This verily seems like "unconditional submission." But there is too much metaphysics in that phrase, for the work of hearts. Affection, like faith, is seldom metaphysical. Its depth lies in its simplicity. All speculation, which does not bring round the matter just to that spot, is useless for all *heart* purposes, —therefore for all *faith* purposes.

XXXVI.

The Unpardonable Sin.

DURING the whole of one summer, a young woman of respectable family and of religious education was accustomed to send for me, from time to time, for religious conversation. She had no hope, and her mind was uniformly gloomy. She appeared peculiarly desponding. Time after time, as I visited her, I endeavoured, as plainly as possible, to unfold the divine promises, and the fulness of Christ to meet all the possible wants of sinners who will believe in him. Still she remained as sad and downcast as ever. Her most common topic was the magnitude of her sins; she was such a sinner that there was no mercy for her. Repeatedly I showed the error of this notion, by the clear declarations of the Bible, and by the nature of salvation procured by the great Saviour; and most urgently I pressed upon her the instant duty of hearing the gospel call to repent and trust in Jesus Christ, while the Holy Spirit was striving with her. I assured her that no sinner need be lost because his sins are great, since "the blood of Jesus Christ cleanseth from *all* sin;" and if a sinner perishes, he must perish because he does not repent and believe, not because the merit of Christ is insufficient to reach the extent of his guilt, and not because Christ is not freely offered to him, in the full sincerity and full friendliness of God.

One day, as I was urging this point and entreating her to be reconciled to God by yielding her heart to the persuasions of the Holy Spirit, she said to me:—

"I believe I have committed the unpardonable sin!"

"What makes you think so?" said I.

"Why—I feel so," said she, hesitatingly.

"What makes you feel so?"

"The Lord would have forgiven me before this time, if there was any forgiveness for me."

"He will forgive you *now*, if you will repent of sin and trust in the redemption of Christ."

"No!" said she, "I have committed the unpardonable sin! There is no forgiveness for me!" She wept and sobbed aloud.

Said I, "How long have you been thinking that you have committed the unpardonable sin?"

"I have known it a long time."

"What is the unpardonable sin?"

"The sin against the Holy Ghost, which hath never forgiveness, neither in this world, nor in the world to come."

"What is the sin against the Holy Ghost?"

After much hesitation, she replied, "It is the sin that Jesus Christ mentioned—speaking against the Holy Ghost."

"Have you been speaking against the Holy Ghost?"

"Oh no! I have not done that," said she.

"What then do you mean? What is your unpardonable sin?"

She gave no answer, and I continued to ask, "When did you commit this unpardonable sin?" She said nothing. "Tell me what it is." She said nothing. "How came you to commit it?" She said nothing. "What makes you think you have committed it?"

"God would have forgiven me before this time, if I had not committed it."

"Before *this time?* What do you mean?"

"Why, I have been a great while seeking religion."

"And because you have been so long seeking it, you think it is no present fault of yours that you have not found it; but that God will not forgive you, because, months ago, you committed the unpardonable sin—is that what you mean?

"Yes. sir."

"Very well," said I, "I suppose you want nothing more of me, if you are unpardonable. I can do nothing for you if that is the case. I may as well leave you. You may go to your closet, and tell God, as you kneel before him, that you are willing to repent; that you are willing to trust in Christ, and willing to obey God in all things; and that it is no fault of yours that you are not a Christian. Tell him that the only thing now in the way of your salvation is that *old unpardonable sin*, which he will not forgive. Good-bye."

I left her at once. The next day she sent for me again. I found her, as I did not expect, in the same state of mind, brooding sadly over the unpardonable sin. After much conversation and aiming to remove the difficulty, and assuring her of her error, she still insisted, "I have committed the unpardonable sin,—I know I have,—I know I have,—I know I have."

I desired her, after a few moments, to quit her agitation, and fix her thoughts on the things which I was going to say to her. Said I, "I shall speak very plainly. You will understand every word of it. Some of the things which I shall say may surprise you, but I want you to remember them. All along through the summer I have treated you with the utmost kindness and indulgence. I have always come to you when you have sent for me, and many times when you have not. And it is because I feel kindly towards you still, and wish to do you good, that I shall now say some very plain things which you may not like, but they are true:—

"*First*, You say you have committed the unpardonable sin; but you do not *believe* what you say. You believe no such thing. You know, indeed, that you are a sinner; but you do *not* believe that you have committed the unpardonable sin. You are not honest, not sincere, when you say so. You do not believe it.

"*Second*, It is pride, a foolish pride of a wicked heart, which makes you say that you have committed the unpardonable sin

Influenced by pride you half strive (only *half* after all) to *believe* you have done it. You wish to exalt yourself. You pretend that it is some great and uncommon thing which keeps you from being a Christian. It is the unpardonable sin. Pride lies at the bottom of all this.

"*Third*, You have no occasion for this pride. There is nothing very uncommon about you. You are very much like other sinners. It is not likely that you *could* commit the unpardonable sin, if you should try. I do not think you *know* enough to do it."

"Why," said she, "is there not such a sin?"

"Yes;—but you don't know what it is; and you don't know enough to commit it.

"*Fourth*, You are one of the most self-righteous creatures I ever saw. You try to think that you are not so much to blame for your irreligion—that you are willing to be a Christian, and would be one, if it were not for that unpardonable sin, which you try in your pride to believe you have committed. You pretend that it is not your present and cherished sin which keeps you in your impenitence. Oh, you are good enough, surely, to repent; you would repent, indeed you would, if it were not for that unpardonable sin. *That* is your heart; self-righteousness and pride.

"*Fifth*, Your wicked heart clings to this idea of the unpardonable sin, as *an excuse* for your continued impenitence, for your living in the indulgence of sin, unbelief, and disobedience to God, every day. Your excuse will not stand. You make it insincerely. It is not the unpardonable sin which hinders your being a Christian; but your wickedness of heart, your pride, vanity, and insincerity. I shall never again have anything to say to you about the unpardonable sin. If you had any real and just *conviction* of sin, you would never name the unpardonable sin."

Some months after this she called upon me in deep trouble. But now her complaint was that she had a wicked, deceitful, and hard heart, opposed to the law of God. She became, finally, as she believed, a true penitent, and professed her religion publicly

But in all her religious exercises there appeared nothing very peculiar, and she never named to me the unpardonable sin.

True light in the conscience is one thing, and a deceitful gloom in the proud heart is quite another. When a sinner has any just sense of his condition, as alienated from a holy God, he will not be apt to think of the unpardonable sin. Spurious conviction is common but useless.

XXXVII.

Election.

AT the close of the service on the Sabbath, I gave an invitation, as I had frequently done, to any persons not members of the Church, who were seriously disposed to attend to religion, to call and see me at my own house at an appointed hour. In giving the notice, I explained briefly the reasons for the invitation, and besought those who were yet without hope to give their instant and earnest attention to this momentous subject. Among other things I stated, as one of the reasons for this invitation, that difficulties which occur to some minds on the subjects embraced in religion, could often be more happily removed in conversation than in any other way. At the time appointed, and on the evening to which I now allude, a young man about twenty-three years of age called upon me. Adverting to my invitation, he directly told me his design in coming. He said that his mind had been occupied with the subject of religion for several months; that he had felt much dissatisfied with himself,—with his own course of worldliness; that he was fully convinced of the necessity of religion; that he had come to a determination to put off the duty no longer. But he had met with difficulties which he "could not get over." The more he had tried, the more his thoughts had become perplexed; and though he had made up his mind on some points, yet on some others he was troubled and dissatisfied. "I thought," said he, "I would accept the invitation you gave us to-day, though I have not much expectation of being satisfied about many things which come up."

He seemed disposed to talk, and I did not think best to interrupt him. He went on to say that some doctrines troubled him, and he could never agree with me in respect to them. He must have his own way of thinking, and had a right to it. "Yes," said I, "if you think *right;* but you have no business to think *wrong*. If a man thinks wrong he *is* wrong; and no man can have a right to be wrong if it *is* his own way. God calls on the unrighteous to forsake their thoughts. Their thoughts are wrong, and he tells them they are not like his."

"I know that," said he, "but I mean my way of thinking about predestination, and all those doctrines that are so hard to swallow, and that make a man unable to do anything, nothing but a mere machine. I do not believe in election and foreordination, as it is called. Such things have done *me* no good, and, in my opinion, never will do me any. They only confuse me for nothing, and for my part I do not believe them. I wish ministers never would preach them. I cannot see how anybody can attempt to do anything to try to be a Christian, if he believes in such things as election. Such a doctrine takes away a man's power, and then condemns him for not using it."

In this manner he continued to talk for some minutes, till he appeared to have no more to say. There was no appearance of any deep seriousness about him. He did not seem to me to have any very special concern about his condition, as a sinner needing forgiveness of God. Evidently he was annoyed and perplexed, but he had not said a word about his being a sinner against God, or in danger of his wrath, or unfit to meet him in judgment, or his need of any reconciliation to him. Some of his expressions reminded me of an anonymous letter which I had received a few weeks before, complaining of my having preached several times within a few months on the doctrine of election, and containing some other erroneous statements. But I did not tell him so. I made no mention of the letter. But recollecting its contents, I felt more sure that I understood his state of mind by reason of that epistle, and felt that I had an advantage of him of which he was not conscious. After he had said all that he seemed disposed to say, I inquired of him,—

"How long a time is it since you began to be attentive and prayerful on the subject of religion?"

"I have been thinking about it for four or five months."

"What was it that first turned your attention to this subject?"

"It was a sermon which you preached on predestination."

"Then there may be some use in such preaching after all, if it leads people to attend to their salvation."

He appeared much confused at this answer, and remained silent for a moment, as if he knew not what to say. But seeming to recollect himself, he replied, "Did I say there was no use in preaching about predestination?"

"No, I believe you did not exactly say that, something near it, however. But people often have said it and *written* it, and *you* just said you did not agree with me in some doctrines, and 'did not believe in the hard doctrines which make a man unable to do anything—nothing but a mere machine.' And I wished to know what it was that first turned your own attention to religion. I am glad to find that the doctrine of predestination has aroused you, after all other kinds of preaching had been for so many years in vain. I shall be encouraged by this example to preach on the subject again."

"But I don't believe in it," said he, with much emphasis.

"Then certainly it need not *trouble* you, if you do not believe in it, and we will drop the subject. Have you been *praying* to God to forgive you? do you pray daily?"

"I can't say that I have *prayed* much. But I have read the Bible, and thought and studied about religion a great deal."

"Have you prayed to-day?"

"No, not to-day."

"Do you expect to be saved without prayer?"

"No. But I have no heart to pray."

"Indeed! then your heart needs your attention, quite as much as the doctrine of election. The Bible makes prayer a duty, and we ought to esteem it as a great privilege. As sinners, we do infinitely need God's blessing; and without it, all our attempts in religion will be ineffectual. It is no matter of wonder that you are not reconciled to God, if you have not even prayed for his grace to guide you. If sinners would be right, and would be saved, they must obey God. And his requirement is plain, 'Seek ye the Lord, while he may be found; call ye upon him, while he is near.' You must call upon him, you must pray, if you would have any ground at all for expecting his favour."

"But the prayers of the wicked are an abomination to the Lord," said he.

"That," said I, "is your own declaration. God has not said so. Such a declaration is not to be found in the Bible, though people often suppose it is, and though there may be some expressions which appear to resemble it. The *ordinary* complaint of the Bible against sinners is, not that they pray with bad hearts, but that they do no pray at all, or seldom. They are said to 'cast off fear and restrain prayer.' It may be a sin in you to pray, with such a heart as you have; but it is a worse sin if you neglect prayer. The Bible commands you to pray; and if you try to obey it, manifestly you are not quite so wicked as if you do not try at all. The command stands in the Bible, and will stand there. Your want of a good heart does not repeal it, nor does it excuse your disobedience. Moreover, you need God's aid for attaining a better heart; and certainly you have more reason to expect that aid if you ask for it than if you do not ask at all. 'Ask, and ye shall receive; seek, and ye shall find; knock, and it shall be opened unto you.' If sinners would be saved, they must consent to follow God's directions. You put your wisdom in the place of God's wisdom. His wisdom directs you to pray; your wickedness refuses to pray; and then your deceitful heart weaves an excuse for neglecting prayer, out of the badness of your heart—out of the very thing which constitutes the strongest of all possible reasons why you *should* pray. Your having a wicked heart, instead of being a reason for *not* praying, is the very reason why you should pray the more earnestly. Besides, your excuse is itself the offspring of self-righteousness and pride. You wish to be heard, because of your praying so well—with such a good heart. You are too proud and self-righteous to think of being heard when there is nothing in you to deserve a hearing. You want to make a merit of your prayers. A sinner must be more obedient and humble than this. At least, you must *try* to obey God, as you are not trying now. I do not say that you ought to pray with an impenitent heart; but I say, if you have an impenitent heart, you ought to pray, and the rather on that account. One sin must not be offered to excuse another. And I say further, that you have no prospect at all of having a better heart, if you will *not* pray. Besides, you are inverting the order of the Bible and of common sense. You wish to *receive* the gift of a good heart *first*, and then you will consent to ask for it. The Bible expects you to *ask* first. You wait to have a good heart first, and then you intend to pray for a good heart! Strange inconsistency of a sinner's mind! A little more simplicity of obedience, and a little less of such proud and self-righteous and foolish speculation, would be far better.

"With respect to my preaching and my doctrines, no matter for your disagreeing with *me*, I am not your standard, and certainly you are not mine. I ask nobody to think as I do. I only ask everybody to agree with the Bible. If I do not preach the gospel, I am wrong; and you ought to reject all that I say which disagrees with the word of God. No matter what *I* think. Let all that go,—stick to the Bible. It seems very strange that a man in your state of mind should mention your disagreement with me, while at the same moment your own practice so much disagrees with the word of God that you do not even pray."

He appeared scarcely to know what to say; but rallying a little, he replied with some composure, "I believe I ought to pray; but I want to know the truth about religion, before I begin in it."

"You *do* know the truth about it, my dear sir; enough to know that God commands you to pray, and to use all the appointed means of salvation. And you can have no excuse of ignorance on that matter. Moreover, you take the wrong way to learn what you do *not* know. The Bible way is, 'If ye will do the works, ye shall know of the doctrine whether it be of God.' As fast and as far as one knows the truth, he ought to obey it. That is the way to learn other truths. And that is just the way in which every sinner on earth *must* practise, if he would ever gain anything in religion. What good would it do any one to learn more truth, if he will not act upon the truth which he knows already? Such acting is necessary, indispensable, in religion. Truth is to be learnt by it, which can be learnt in no other way. The lessons of experience are the best lessons; and many times, what is to be learnt in that way only, is a necessary pre-requisite for learning even intellectually the things which lie beyond. You wish to 'know all the truth about religion before you begin in it.' You wish for an impossibility. Religion concerns not your mind only, but your conscience, your heart, your habits, your worldliness, and pride, and vanity, and above all, your self-righteousness. If you will not aim to lend your conscience to it obediently, and your heart, and your habits, you might as well think to understand all about music without your ears, or all about beauty without your eyes, or all about sensibility without your heart. You never will understand the full significance of the divine precepts, till you aim to obey them; nor the full meaning of the divine promises, till you take them for your own. 'Taste,' and then you will 'see that the Lord is gracious.' The practice will give you light, and such light as you cannot spare, when you are aiming to understand other lessons beyond. And because you have not been trying to practise the truths which you *do* understand, it is no wonder that your mind has become the more perplexed, as you said a little while ago. You perceive how it is. You have been disobedient, you have not renounced the world; you have not given your heart to God; you have not come to repentance; you have not fled to

Christ, to save you from the condemnation of God's law;—and therefore, God has not led you out of perplexity and given you peace. You have studied religion, but you have stuck to sin. You know you are a sinner, and know you ought to repent and flee to an offered Christ."

"But," said he, "if I am not predestinated to salvation, all my trying would do me no good."

"Indeed! that is a strange thing for *you* to say! You have just told me that you did not believe in predestination; and I have been trying to persuade you to let alone. You said you must have your own way of thinking; and you did not believe in the 'hard doctrines, which make a man unable to do anything—nothing but a machine.' And now, when I am trying to persuade you to do something (just what God bids you, and what your own way of thinking bids), you very strangely bring up the doctrine of predestination as an excuse for your disobedience! You say if you are not predestinated your trying will do you no good!"

He appeared very much confused and ashamed. He remained entirely silent; and I left him to his silence as long as I could with politeness. I then said to him very gently and kindly, "It is manifest, my dear friend, that you have fixed on no system of belief or practice. You do not know whether you believe in predestination or not. Your thoughts are perplexed and contradictory; and I am very glad you have come here to-night. I am sorry for your perplexity; but you will come out of it. I advise you to let the doctrine of predestination alone for the present, if you can. You have more important duties than studying it now. If your mind will be satisfied to leave it entirely for the present, and seek peace with God, you will be far more wise. I hope you will dismiss it from your thoughts, and seek God with all your heart. It is one of the deep mysteries of God; and you will not be likely to find your ideas clear upon the subject, till you become a sincere penitent for sin.

"The Bible presents this doctrine of predestination, as I think, only for three purposes. *First,* to teach men the character of God,—his grandeur, wisdom, and incomprehensibility; and thus lead them to render to him the homage which belongs to him. If the doctrine is deep and mysterious, so is God. Whoever believes in the existence of God at all, believes in an infinite mystery. And since he is himself such a mystery, we ought to *expect* mystery in his plans and providence, and not quarrel where we ought to worship and bow down before him, filled with awe at his amazing grandeur.

"The *second* purpose is, to repress the audacity of the wicked. God would have the wicked know that they cannot outreach him, —that with all their malignity, they cannot even sin but he will foil them. 'He maketh the wrath of man to praise him, and the remainder of that wrath he will restrain.' He lets them know that his eternal counsels are deeper than their malignity. If they will sin, he leads their mind back behind the curtain which veils his eternal majesty, and lets them know that his eternal plans are not to be thwarted by the wickedness of man or malice of devils. He shows them that his plans encompass them as with a net; that he has his hook in their nose, and his bridle in their mouth; and that if they will sin, their malice will be foiled,—they shall not sin an item but God will overrule it all for his glory, and all their disobedience and hardihood shall only defeat their own purposes, and bring just judgment on the heads of the willing perpetrators. You have an instance of this solemn and instructive use of the doctrine, when an apostle addresses the crucifiers of Christ: 'Him being delivered by the determinate counsel and foreknowledge of God, ye have taken, and by wicked hands have crucified and slain.' Their '*wicked* hands' could only carry out his determinate coun sel.' The counsel was his,—the wickedness was theirs. This doctrine shows the wicked that there is a plan which lies back of their wickedness,—that they cannot overreach God, that they are hemmed in on every side by the plan and the predestination of the Eternal One.

"The *third*, and main purpose of this doctrine is, as I suppose, to comfort God's people. The grand trial of a life of religion is a trial of the heart. We have sins, we have weaknesses and temptations, which tend to a dreadful discouragement. Sin easily besets us. We easily wander from God. Holiness is an up-hill work. Our feet often stagger in the path of our pilgrimage, and tears of bitterness gush from our eyes, lest such weak, and tempted, and erring creatures should never reach heaven. Devils tempt us. The world presents its deceitful allurements, and more deceitful and dangerous claims. What shall cheer us when our heart sinks within us? Whither shall we fly for comfort, when our hearts are bleeding, when our sins are so many, when our gain in holiness is so little, when our light goes out, and the gloom of an impenetrable midnight settles down upon our poor and helpless soul? We cannot, indeed, mount up to the inner sanctuary of God, open the seven-sealed book, and read our names recorded in it by the pen of the Eternal. But we can know that such a book is there; and that the pen of our Father has filled it with his eternal decrees, not one of which shall fail of accomplishment, as surely as his own throne shall stand. And when we find in ourselves, amid our tearful struggles, even the feeble beginnings of holiness, we know that God has commenced his work for us,—a work which he planned before the world was; and that he who has 'begun a good work in us, will perform it until the day of Jesus Christ,' carrying into effect his eternal plan. Just as well as we know our likeness to God, we know our election of God. We know that our holiness is *his* work, a work which he purposed from the beginning. If he had purposed it but just when he began it,—if it were a work undertaken from some recent impulse, then we should have good reason to fear that some other impulse would drive him to abandon it. But when we know it forms a part of his eternal counsels, and is no *sidework*, no episode, no interlude, or sudden interposition not before provided for—then we are assured that God is not going to forsake us; and deep as is our home-bred depravity, and many and malignant as are our foes, we are cheered with the assurance, that God will bring us off victorious, and 'the purpose according to election shall stand.' We love to see our salvation embraced in the eternal plan of God; and we know it is embraced there, if we are his children by faith in Christ Jesus. We cannot read his secret counsels; but we can read his spiritual workings within us. We know the counsels by the evidence of the workings; and then we are cheered and encouraged amid our trials, by the idea that God will no more abandon us than he will abandon the eternal plan which his wisdom formed before the foundation of the world. 'Who shall lay anything to the charge of God's elect?' He had their names in his book before they had shed a tear, before a devil existed to tempt them.

"If you examine *the order* of the Scriptures, you will find that they never break ground with predestination. Predestination comes in afterwards. They do not present it to the mind of a sinner at the outset. Indeed, they seem to avoid it. And in my opinion, a sinner should avoid it also, because he should follow the manner of the Bible; and because predestination contains nothing in itself which can interfere with the plain and practical duties of Christianity; and because, if he will go out of the way of his duty, to meddle with what God intends about his destiny, he will be very apt to stumble in his first starting, and never take one safe or satisfying step in the pathway of a true discipleship. See how the order of truth stands in the Epistle to the Romans, the most orderly, methodical, and demonstrative of all the sacred writings. Paul goes over the matters of sin, the fall, the law, the covenant, Christ, repentance, justification by faith, atonement, holiness, hope, the Holy Spirit, depravity, the resurrection; and *after* all these, and not till he gets into the eighth chapter, does he preach the doctrine of predestination. He then presents it to comfort and encourage believers, not to direct unbelievers. The comfort is simply this: if they have an item of holiness, they may know that their names are in God's eternal book; that he has begun to do for them what he purposed to do from all eternity; and that they are just as safe as he is unchangeable. 'For whom he did foreknow, he also did predestinate to be conformed to the image of his Son. Whom he did predestinate, them he also called; and whom he called, them he also justified; and whom he justified, them he also glorified.' Not a link is left out. The whole chain is finished, and lifts to glory. 'If God be for us, who can be against us?' Thus the apostle comforts believers by leading them to know that the whole matter of their salvation was a matter of plan, and purpose, and provision, before they were born; that it is not an affair which comes in amid any uncertainties and fluctuations of time, but stands above time, as it stood before time was, in God's book; and all the agitations of worlds and all the sweep of centuries cannot touch it. You may find the same thing in the other epistles. I beg you to notice how uniformly the doctrine of predestination is recorded just for the comfort and confirming of Christians—for the gladsome cheering of way-worn and struggling believers, trying to get the mastery over sin. It is *not* preached for the direction of impenitent sinners. I beg of you, therefore, not to meddle with God's eternal decrees."

My young friend listened to all this most attentively. He occasionally asked some question, not necessary to be recorded here; and I thought he appeared inclined to follow my advice. When I had finished all that I wished to say, he replied in a pensive and half musing manner: "Really I have got a strange heart! I do not know what to think. What *shall* I do, if I am to dismiss God's foreordination?"

Said I, "I have already told you. You ought to obey the gospel, deny yourself, take up your cross and follow Christ, seek God, and serve him with all your heart. It is the call of the gospel which is addressed to impenitent sinners. God sends to them a message of peace and pardon from heaven—an offer of eternal life, and lays it down, sealed with his own signet, at the door of their hearts. The message assures them of the good-will of God, of a propitiation for sinners full in itself and freely offered; and bids them welcome to all they can want. You have only to take the message, and you will secure the favour—only to agree with God, on the Christ-conditions which he proposes, and he will agree with you.

He *calls* you to this faith in the blood of atonement; and if you will but believe him, and venture your soul where he has embarked his love and ventured his honour, you have the pledge of all the truthfulness there is in God that you shall be helped on to heaven. The Holy Spirit will aid you. Divine wrath will never reach you. A child of God, adopted, loved, cherished, you shall have all the securities which the power of God can furnish, and enjoy the smiles which he bends upon his children. *To this call* of the gospel you ought to attend. This is your duty. You may mistake the decrees, but you cannot mistake the duty. If the counsel of God is dark, the call of God is clear. And I hope, therefore, you will attend to the call, and not meddle with the counsel, till you reach the fit time for considering. If you *can* do so, you will be much happier. If you cannot, if your foolish mind, through temptation, will keep running off into predestination, then, go into the subject to your sickening over it, and till you have found by experience that you have mistaken your beginning-spot. And remember, after all your attempts you will have to come round to this at last. As long as you neglect the gospel call, and attempt to grapple with the gospel counsels, you will only plunge deeper and deeper into intricacies you cannot unravel. Let God wield his own thunder. You have only to hear it, and tremble. You cannot employ it. It was not made for an arm like yours. Lay aside your captiousness, and employ your conscience. Leave the decrees, and take to the duties. The decrees are God's rules for his own action, not for yours. Let me hope, when I shall see you again, to find your heart fixed to do as God bids you, and to let Him do the work which he has decreed for himself. Just be wise enough to mind your own business, and let God mind his."

He left me. I felt confident that he would follow my advice. The next Sabbath evening he called on me again. There were about ten other persons present. I conversed with each one for a few minutes, commencing with the one most distant from him, in order that he might be influenced by their thoughts, and the truths of God which I should utter for their direction. I thought nothing could have been more happily adapted to do him good than what was said by some of these persons. One of them spoke of the wonderful goodness of God towards him during all his life, and mourned that he had himself done nothing but abuse it, ungratefully forgetting God. He wondered that God had spared him, such an unworthy sinner. Another said that her heart would not *feel.* She could not make it feel. She had tried, but though she knew she was a sinner, justly condemned by the law and graciously invited to Christ, still her base heart would neither break by God's awful terrors nor melt under his amazing love. Another said that all his attempts in religion had been in vain—that his prayers and resolutions had all failed him—that the opposition of his heart to God had seemed to increase, until he had been led to see there was only one hope for him,—*God had promised to save guilty sinners, who would trust to Christ.* Now, he just rested on that promise, and was troubled and tormented no more. His heart was at peace. He looked to Jesus Christ to save him, and blessed God that the Holy Spirit had led him to this rest. He would not go back to the world for all it could offer. Another said that he feared the anger of God. He knew he deserved it. He feared there was no mercy for him. He would give all the world, if it were his, to be the meanest and most miserable Christian there is in it.

As the young man listened to these expressions, and the replies which were made to them, he became very uneasy. He changed his position often. A cast of impatience spread over his countenance. His eye was restless. A cloud hung upon his brow. Before I spoke to him I determined not to allow him to utter any cavils about election in the ears of those who were present. As I asked him whether he had accepted the proposals which God makes to sinners, to save them by grace through Jesus Christ, he answered with an abruptness and in a tone which surprised us all, "If God foreordains everything, I can't see why we are to be condemned for sin."

"St. Paul," said I, in a slow and solemn manner, "has given

an answer to that, and I have no other to give. When one said to him, 'Why doth God yet find fault? who hath resisted his will?' Paul answered, 'Nay but, O man, who art thou that repliest against God?'" And without giving him time for another word, I addressed myself to the next individual. I said no more to him. And after prayer I bade him good night at the door; taking care that he should leave the house when the others left it, having no further opportunity to speak to me.

The next evening save one, he came to see me again. He apologized for calling so soon, saying he could not wait till Sunday, and he wished to see me alone. He immediately began to speak of election. He said he had tried, but he could not expel the idea from his mind. It would come up. He believed the devil put it into his mind, for it would occur to him in prayer, in reading, in all that he attempted to do or think of. He said he could not make up his mind about it; but he wanted to tell me what would occur to his thoughts, and see if I could assist him. He then went on to say that he believed in God's foreknowledge, but *decrees* troubled him—he could not reconcile predestination and free-will. Another time he would think, if he was to be saved he would be; if not, he could not help himself. Sometimes he thought the doctrine discouraging, and felt opposed to God, as if he were a hard master. At other times he felt vexed with himself. So he was tossed about without peace, and often tormented with the fear that he should never have any religion. And he wanted me to tell him what was the matter, and what he had to do, and what he should think about this doctrine of election. After he had said all that he wished, I replied to him—

"I am glad to see you. I thank you for coming to me. I am sorry you find yourself in so much unnecessary trouble; and I am perfectly willing to tell you all I know about the doctrine which troubles you. But before I enter upon the subject, I wish to tell you again that probably I cannot satisfy your mind at all. I can drive you from some of your errors, but I cannot satisfy you."

"Why not?" said he anxiously.

"Simply because *you are not satisfied with God.* You are opposed to him. There lies your whole difficulty. The idea of his eternal sovereignty brings him clearly to your mind; and you dislike the doctrine just because your heart dislikes God. Your head may be wrong in many things, but your heart is wrong in everything. You need a new heart. If you were truly reconciled to God you would be reconciled to predestination,—not as you have mis-stated it, but as it is in truth. And I wish you to remember this; and remember what I told you before, that after all your studying, and questioning, and battling about the *divine decrees,* you will be obliged, at last, to come round to the *divine call* to begin with,—a call which bids you repent, and bids you welcome to all that full and free salvation which God has provided for you. Let me tell you a fact. Not long since a clergyman of your acquaintance came down from the pulpit in the city of New York, after he had been preaching on the sovereignty of God, when a woman of excellent mind and education came up to him at the foot of the pulpit stairs, and thanked him very warmly for that sermon. 'O sir,' said she, 'it has done me good. All my life I have been troubled with the doctrine of election. I have studied it for more than twenty years in vain. But now I know what has been the matter,—*I have never been entirely willing that God should be God.*' And when you are entirely willing that 'God should be God,' election will trouble you no longer.

"I desire you to remember, also, that I do not preach predestination to you to-night (as I am about to do) by any choice of my own, but because you will have it so,—because you cannot be persuaded, by all I have said to you, not to meddle with dark and inscrutable counsels, but attend to God's plain and practical call. I can correct some of your errors, but I cannot make a carnal mind, which is enmity against God, satisfied with God's eternal foreordination, and with God himself."

"I assure you," said he, "I tried to dismiss the subject, but I could not. And I am very anxious to have you settle my difficulties, if you can. At least tell me what you think about such things as I mentioned when I came in."

"Then hear me," said I, "and I will be as brief as I can.

"First, let me say, the doctrine of predestination is not mine. It is God's. He has put it in his sacred book, and neither you nor I can put it out. He put it there because he wanted it there; and whatever men may think of its uselessness, God does not need their instructions. He will not receive their criticisms. He will frown upon their contentions. Such words as 'election, purpose, predestination,' are in the Bible. They mean something. We are bound to know what they mean, and to love the meaning. The doctrine is in the Bible. Predestination and the word of God will stand or fall together.

"Predestination is God's eternal purpose to rule his universe *just as* he does rule it. If any man is satisfied with God's *ruling* as he does, I cannot understand why he should have any *dissatisfaction* with his *pre-determination* to rule just so. His pre-determination is only the eternal plan of his government,—only his eternal decree.

"The decrees of God are rules for his own action,—not for ours. They are nothing more than his own wise plans, eternal and unchangeable, according to which he chooses to act. If he had no such plans he could not be wise; he would be acting at mere hap-hazard, not knowing why he made the world, or what was going to be the result! If he has formed his plans or changed them *since* time began, then he is a changeable Being, his dignity is sunk, and all security to the universe is sunk with it. For he may change again; and what will come yet, or what *he* will become, no mind can conjecture! So far as government is concerned, it is nothing to you whether he forms the plan for his day's work every morning or formed it from eternity. Plan he must have before he acts, or else he is the least wise of all intelligent beings in the universe! Until he acts you know nothing of his plans, his predestination; and therefore, so far as plan or execution of it is concerned, it matters not to you whether he is now foreordaining moment by moment, or from all eternity foreordained whatsoever comes to pass. His decrees are not laws for his creatures, but rules for *himself.* They are not statutes addressed to *will*, and demanding obedience or compelling it. They are only his wise, holy, and eternal purposes, wherein he has determined beforehand what he will do, and how he will do it. You may not like the method by which he makes the sun shine, the ocean heave, or the lost Pleiad go out,—by which he directs the earthquake, the storm, the death-wing of the pestilence, or manages his angels, men, and devils. But he has a way of his own, he has considered it well, he has not asked your advice, and you will do well to pause a little before you venture any more criticisms upon 'that high and lofty One who inhabiteth eternity!' Just consent to *let God be God.*"

"Do you say," said he, "that the decrees of God affect only his acts? do they not affect ours also?"

"I say that they are *rules* for only his own acts, and do not affect ours *directly*. How *can* they affect ours? They are ever unknown to us. They are his secret purposes, locked up in his own mind, and never known to an angel in heaven till he chooses to make them known. A secret purpose in my mind cannot affect you. You do not see it, feel it, hear it, or know anything about it. It cannot affect you. You may think I *have* it, and the thought of it may affect you; and that is all. Just so it is with God's foreordination. It touches nobody. No one feels it. It does not hit a man's head, or feet, or fingers, or heart—it absolutely affects *nothing at all*, until God pleases to proceed to *act* upon it, and carry it into execution. It is this execution *only* which affects anything. It is God's *government*, and nothing *but* his government which is felt, or which influences anybody. If, therefore, you must complain, shift your ground of complaining. Complain of God's government, of his providence, and not of those secret decrees which you know nothing about, and which never touch you."

"Well," said he, "this is new to me. I never thought of it

before. But, if I understand you, we have nothing to do with the decrees of God."

"Nobody ever told you we had anything to do with them,—except to consent that God should *have* them, and execute them. I am sure I tried, with all my might, to persuade you not to meddle with them, but to obey the gospel call, and let God take care of his decrees."

"But how," said he, "do you reconcile foreordination and free agency?"

"I never try, for the best of all reasons,—they *need* no reconciling. They are not at war with each other. If you will get them quarrelling, I will soon put them at peace. Things need reconciling only when they conflict. Here are but two propositions. *First*, God foreordains whatsoever comes to pass. *Second*, Man is a free agent. One of these propositions does not contradict the other. If it did, one or both would be false, and we would abandon the falsehood. But there is no conflict or inconsistency between them. I defy you to show any. I know, indeed, men have often said it, and sung it,—

'God can't decree
And man be free;'—

but they have never *proved* it, and never will. They have never shown any inconsistency between election and free-will. In our Church standards, which explain how we understand the Bible, we have one chapter 'on God's eternal decree;' another 'on free-will.' One affirms, "God, from all eternity, did unchangeably ordain whatsoever comes to pass.' The other affirms, 'God hath endued the will of man with that natural liberty, that it is neither forced, nor, by any absolute necessity of nature, determined to good or evil.' God foreordained that man should be a free agent,—and he is one. The eternal decree has secured his free agency. God predestinated the freedom of the human will. Hence, man is free when he sins, and free when he repents of sin; he is free when he hates God, and free when he loves him; he is free when he neglects the great salvation, and free when he loves God with all his heart. His bondage in sin is a willing bondage. And yet it is true that he cannot save himself, but infinitely needs the direct power of the Holy Spirit, to renew his obstinate will, and 'persuade and enable him to embrace Jesus Christ' for salvation. Aside from this Holy Spirit there is not an item of hope for him, as there is not an item of ability in him. 'He hath wholly lost all ability of will to any spiritual good accompanying salvation.' But, he is free. If he sins, he sins freely—he chooses to sin.

"But take another view of this matter. Truths are always consistent, and must be so. Here is one truth: God predestinates. The Bible says so; and aside from the Bible, I know it by my own reason, just as well as I know that God is wise enough to have some plan for his actions. That, then, is a truth; God predestinates.

"Here is another truth: Man is free. He knows this by his own consciousness. He knows that he acts of his own free choice, just as well as he knows his own existence. He feels accountable for his actions. The laws of both God and man hold him accountable. All his neighbours deal with him as a free and accountable being. He has not himself a doubt on the subject. If he believes he is not free, he is not an ordinary man—he is either a fool or a madman, and I would as soon reason with a rock. If a man tells you he is not free, that he does not act of his own free-will, give him a blistering cap and a strait-jacket, and send him to the mad-house. The man is a maniac. He is unfit to be at large.

"Here, then, are two truths:—God decrees; Man is a free agent. Each of them is fully proved. Each of them is just as certain to every sane and intelligent man as any truth in the universe. Therefore, they must be consistent. They need no reconciling."

"I know I am *free*," said he.

"And you know God foreordains?" said I.

"Yes," said he; "it must be so. The Bible says so; and he could not be a wise God if he didn't."

"That, then, is enough," said I. "What more do you want?"

He sat a long time in silence, manifestly in deep thought. At length he asked very modestly, "But if God foreordains to eternal life, why have men got anything to do in order to be saved?"

"Just because God foreordained they *shall* have something to do in order to be saved. God has not more certainly foreordained the end than he has foreordained the means. He decrees no end without decreeing the means to reach it. Though St. Paul, as instructed by God, had promised those in the ship, that no man's life should be lost, yet he afterwards said, when the sailors were about to flee out of the ship, 'Except these abide in the ship, ye cannot be saved.' The promise and the predestination could not save them, if the predestinated means failed. And you will notice how the Bible, whenever it enters into any explanation of this matter, never leaves out the *means:* 'God hath chosen us in Christ, before the foundation of the world, *that we should be holy, and without blame before him in love,* having predestinated us *unto the adoption of children by Jesus Christ to himself,* according to the good pleasure of his will.' He hath not merely chosen us to heaven, but, 'that we should *be holy, without blame, in love.*' The means for heaven, and qualifications for heaven, are as much decreed as the heaven itself. Just so it stands in that passage in Romans which I named to you once before: 'For whom he did foreknow, he also did predestinate,' not merely to heaven, but '*to be conformed to the image of his Son.* And more,—'whom he did predestinate, them he also called; and whom he called, them he also justified; and whom he justified, them he also glorified.' Not a link is left out. The whole chain is perfect. Predestination reaches both means and ends together; —*never* the one, without the other. If your salvation is foreordained, your repentance, your faith, and holiness, and willing obedience to God are foreordained also. And so is your *willing* and prayerful use of all the means of eternal life. And this brings to mind one of your expressions, 'If I am to be saved I shall be saved, do what I will; according to this doctrine.' That is utterly false. This doctrine says no such thing. It says directly the contrary. It unites means and ends,—repentance, faith, prayer, humility, love, goodness, holiness, as means; and heaven, as the end. 'If I am to be saved I shall be, do what I may!' that is not our doctrine. You never heard it preached so. No man ever preached it so. No man ever believed that. Election does not dispense with the means of salvation, and *you* cannot dispense with them. You will repent willingly, 'in the day of God's power;' you will pray, you will flee to Christ, you will 'strive to enter in at the strait gate,' if you are going to be saved. I cannot see for you the end; I cannot lift the curtain that hides eternity, and show you your place in the world of spirits; but I *can* see your duty here, the means of salvation, which ought to engage all your efforts. And, by the promise of the God of truth, I can know that if you employ the means, as he bids you, you cannot fail of the end,—eternal life. 'He that soweth to the Spirit, shall of the Spirit reap life everlasting,' because God hath *foreordained* it shall be so.

"This predestinating of God is the most comfortable truth in the Bible. Strange that men should quarrel with it. There is no other truth which carries with it a single gleam of comfort to shine on the wide world of futurity, and make man die in peace. *Everybody wants God to predestinate;* for everybody wants him to *promise.* Every promise of his *is* a predestination of his—it is only a determination and a commitment of himself to carry it out. God cannot promise without predestinating; and it is predestination, therefore, which alone lights up a single gleam of gladness beyond the shores of Time, to shine on that ocean, Eternity, where the immortal spirit shall soon be launched. In utter darkness must it launch there, if God does not predestinate. All the promises are blanks, if predestination is gone!

"You spoke to me once, about being troubled that this doctrine makes man 'a mere machine.' What a superficial, what a silly idea! If you are not a crazy man, you know you are free. You came here to-night freely. You will depart freely. You never acted, and cannot act, but by the choice of your own mind. God decreed from all eternity that you should be a free, moral agent; and you always have been so, in all your sin. God has appointed the means of salvation, and solemnly, sincerely, and affectionately calls on you to employ them voluntarily; while, as you are doing so, his predestinating promise throws the cheering of its light over all the eternity before you. The doctrine of the divine decrees does not represent man as a mere machine. It is predestination which secures him his freedom of will, and secures to him, by *predestinating promise*, the eternal rewards of evangelical obedience—'sow to the Spirit—reap life everlasting.'"

After some few minutes of thoughtful silence again, he said to me, more in the accent of serious inquiry than of captiousness, "What is the use of praying?"

Said I, "What is the use of breathing? Breathing is the means to an end. Praying is the means to an end. Predestination does not secure life without breath, and does not secure eternal life without prayer."

After another pause, he replied, "If sin is foreordained, how can men be blamed for sinning?"

"Because they *choose* to sin," said I. "They sin willingly. They know it. And they *know* they are blameable, as well as they know anything. God foreordained they should be blameable if they sinned."

Another pause ensued. Finally, he said to me: "*I cannot understand this thing! Is* it not more correct to say that God foreknows everything, than to say he foreordains everything?"

"No, not so much so; if you intend by this, to make foreknowledge mean anything *less* than foreordination. What is knowledge? It is the ascertainment or recognition of some certainty, some reality. All knowledge is founded on certainty. It cannot be *foreknown* that anything shall take place, unless it is *certain* that the thing shall take place. What has *made* that certainty? If it is *God* who has made it, then he is a foreordaining God. If it is *not* God who has made it, then there is something above him, *fate*, or something else, and he is God and Governor no longer. Then he has no right to *promise*—he can, at most, only *predict*. And then we have nothing to thank him for, in time or eternity; and all gratitude, love, and prayer, become supreme foolishness! How can you utter a syllable of prayer, if God does *not* govern, if he does not control all the certainties which *can* be foreknown? But he does control. His decree has *made* the certainties, which his foreknowledge recognises. It could *not* recognise, could not foreknow, if God had not foreordained."

After a few moments, he rose from his seat with the declaration, "I have no more to say. I am glad I came here. I understand some things now, which I never did before. But this is still a dark subject. I know I am a sinner, and yet I cannot see how I am to be blamed, if God foreordained it. You say he foreordained my free agency and accountability, and that I have sinned of my own choice. I suppose it is so. I know I act freely, for I feel it. But I am perplexed, and know not what to do."

"Do what God bids you," said I. "Obey the invitations of his grace. Flee to Christ and be saved."

He left me. I did not see him again till about a month afterwards, when he called on me and told me he hoped that he had been led to choose Christ as the portion of his soul. He did not mention the subject of election at all, till I asked him how he had extricated himself from his troubles of mind in respect to it. His answer was memorable. Said he, "I dismissed it from my mind entirely. I found that my wicked, worldly heart was resorting to the doctrine of election as *an excuse* for my not turning to God. It was nothing but an excuse to me for my prayerlessness, my love of the world and of sin. But since I have had a hope in the mercy of God, I am glad that God reigns as he pleases. Election troubles *me* no more. In my opinion, if a *man is reconciled to God, he will be satisfied with predestination.*"

He afterwards made a public profession of his religion. He still lives a communicant in the Church. More than once he has said to me, "Your explanation settles everything, 'predestination is God's eternal purpose to rule his universe just as he does rule it.'"

There is a mode of contending for the great doctrines of truth, which may almost be said to substantiate them and neutralize them at the same time. Such doctrines are susceptible of demonstration; and for one purpose the demonstration is often indispensable. And yet this purpose is only semi-religious. It may be necessary to make full intellectual demonstration of doctrines, for the purpose of silencing cavils and scepticism, by showing that Christianity can withstand all the assaults of argument and all the onsets of reasoning, which can possibly be brought to bear against her. There may be some benefit in this. But it is only the benefit of *defence*, or, at most, only *clearing the way*, in order to get at the position and real work of religion. That work lies far more in vanquishing depravity than in enlightening the intellect. By the stern and severe logic of reasoning, by carrying on a vigorous warfare of mere argumentation, it is quite a possible thing to silence every cavilling of captiousness, and compel the understanding of an unconverted man to acquiesce in the doctrinal truths of Christianity. And this is not to be undervalued. If we have silenced the battery of an opponent, we have taken one step towards getting him to cease from an open and avowed hostility. But this is a very different thing from taking a single step towards such a victory as we wish to gain over him. We do not wish merely to silence and stop an enemy; we wish to convert him into a friend. We would have him *love* the truth, and not simply make to it a cold and constrained obeisance. He may, indeed, deem such an obeisance an honour to Christianity; but, in reality, it is only a dishonour and disgrace. Christianity deserves something more. It is quite a possible thing, and quite a common one, too, that the truths of God should be acquiesced in, while, at the very same moment, they are not realised. The acquiescence is little to the purpose, if that is all. It is not a living faith. And the most that can be said of it is, that it is a dead orthodoxy. Our main business with any doctrine of religion is, not to prove it, but to proceed upon it—not to understand it, but to apply and employ it. No doctrine is ever revealed to us in the Bible for its own sake merely, or for our understanding of it merely. The great object lies beyond. Something should be *effected* by it. And if we regard the doctrine itself as the end, our contest in its behalf will be carried on with a very different spirit, and managed in a very different manner from what would prevail if our mind were fixed on the momentous and eternal design for which the doctrine has been revealed to us. If we can induce any man to study for the sake of practice, the end he has then in view will help him over many a difficulty. To have his end practical, is the very way to get right in the principle. And when we wage our warfare with him, as if the principle were the main thing, we shall be apt to induce him to stop far short of his just landing-place. It would be far better to set him out in an honest, and earnest, and instant inquiry, about the way of his own salvation. That motive standing first, and being seconded by all the deep urgencies that fitly bear upon it, there will be little danger of his failing to get right in his principles, if he prayerfully keeps the Bible before him. If he will attend to the duty, he will soon get right in the doctrine. But if he will only attend to the doctrine, he will be very apt to miss it, or misunderstand it. Engaged in an honest and earnest attempt after salvation, he will rise above all mere scholarship, as he aims to find out where the truth lies. He will discover often what the truth *must* be, in order to meet the necessities of his own nature. He will ask God to teach him, and God will honour the asking. And thus, not studying the truth in captiousness, but in candour—not in curiosity, but in carefulness—not in pride and prejudice, but for practice, and for a permanency as durable as immortal life—he will both avoid the fogs which would obscure one half of it, and the counteraction which would neutralize the other half; for there will always be fog over every item of God's truth when it is *not* studied for the heart; and there will be counteraction from the heart itself to make void even all its enlightening virtue. And besides all this, there are things not a few, among the doctrines of God, to which we shall labour in vain to make a sinner reconciled, until he is reconciled to God himself. If he is led truly to realize the necessities of his own nature, he will lose half his objections and sink half his difficulties. If he becomes reconciled to God in Jesus Christ, the other half will not trouble him much longer.

XXXVIII.

The Brown Jug.

IN the course of my pastoral visits, I called upon a man who was a member of my congregation, a farmer, between fifty and sixty years of age, a plain man, accustomed to daily labour. He was not a communicant, and I had no reason to think him to be a pious man. He was a regular attendant upon the religious services of the Sabbath; but I had never seen him in any religious assembly at any other time. He was regarded as a respectable man, I believe, in all respects. His wife was a pious woman, whom I had sometimes conversed with, and who had expressed to me her anxiety in regard to the religious state of her husband. He had been for so many years living under the means of grace, without being led to repentance and faith in Christ, that she was afraid his mind had settled down upon some ruinous error, or into a strange stupidity, so that he never would become a Christian. She said she had often talked to him on the subject of his religious duty; but he seldom entered into any free conversation upon it,—indeed, "he would say almost nothing at all about himself." He would *hear* what she had to say without any opposition, and with apparent willingness; but he seldom made any reply, except to make some general acknowledgment of the importance of the subject. He had a family of children, the most of whom had already arrived at the years of manhood, and none of them manifested any disposition to obey the gospel in spirit and in truth. They were a moral and industrious family. The sons were much like their father, with the exception that they less frequently were seen at church. The family resided some distance from my residence, and I had not known them very intimately, except the mother, as the rest of the family were usually absent in the field when I called at their house.

Before the time to which I refer, I had never found this man at home; nor had I been able to converse with him at all in reference to his religious duty. Soon after I entered the house, his wife retired from the room, and left me alone with him. I immediately addressed him on the subject of religion. He appeared candid and solemn. I found that he had no hope in Christ. He said that religion had, for many years, appeared to him as a solemn and important duty. He wished he were a Christian. He said he was fully sensible that he was a sinner in God's sight, and was exposed to his righteous justice. He referred to the sermons which he heard from Sabbath to Sabbath, and said it was a wonder to him that they did not influence him more. But he supposed that he had "little true conviction of sin," and little sense of his real condition, or he should be a different man. In this manner he spake of himself very freely for a long time.

He appeared to me to be a man of respectable mind, rather slow in thought and in his sensibilities, but of sound judgment, and of some discrimination.

I urged him to give his instant and prayerful attention to his salvation; but he did not seem inclined to yield to my solicitation. I pressed it upon him strongly. I recited to him the promises of God made to them that seek him; and the threatenings of God against the neglecters of salvation. Still he appeared unmoved. I then concluded to put together, in a manner adapted to his cast of mind, some of the most urgent appeals that I could think of. I commenced. Said I,—

"You are already somewhat advanced in life. Your remaining years will be few. You have no time to lose. You have lost enough already. If you do not become a follower of Christ soon, you never will. You have a family of children. You have never set them an example of piety. You have never prayed with them as you ought to have done. Your neglect goes far to destroy all the influence which their mother might have over them. They copy your example. God will hold you accountable for a father's influence. You may be the cause of their ruin, because—"

"That often troubles me," said he, interrupting me in the middle of what I designed to say.

"It *ought* to trouble you. It is a serious matter for a father to live before his sons without acknowledging God, without prayer, without hope,—just as if he and they had no more interest in the matter of religion than the beast, whose 'spirit goeth downward to the earth.'"

"Yes, indeed it is," said he. "And I am now getting to be an old man. I wish I could get religion."

"You *can*. The whole way is clear. God's word has made it so."

"I *will* begin," said he, emphatically. "But I wish you would make a prayer with us. I will call in Mrs E—— and the boys."

He immediately called them.

After my saying a few words to each of them, and briefly addressing them all, we knelt together in prayer. As we rose from our knees, he said to his children, very solemnly: "Boys, I hope this visit of our minister will do us all good. It is time for us to think of our souls." I left them.

The next Sabbath they were all in church. At the close of the morning service I had some conversation again with the father. He appeared to be honestly and fully determined to "deny himself, take up his cross, and follow Jesus Christ."

He continued very much in this state of mind for some months, sensible of his need of Christ to save him, and prayerful for divine mercy. I saw him and conversed with him many times. He did not appear to make any progress either in knowledge or sensibility. He did not go back; but he was stationary. He prayed in secret. He prayed in his family. He studied his Bible. He conversed with me freely. He sought opportunity for conversation. Uniformly he appeared solemn and in earnest. But he found no peace with God, no hope in Christ. Evidently he was in deep trouble of mind.

As he was not a man of much cultivation of mind, I aimed to teach him the truth in the most plain and simple manner. I proved everything, and explained everything. It was all in vain. Months rolled on. He continued in the same state. It was impossible to discover or conjecture what kept him from Christ. His condition filled me with solicitude; but I studied it in vain.

I made inquiries about him among his friends and neighbours, to learn, if possible, his whole disposition and his character of mind. But I soon discovered, as I thought, that I knew him better than anybody else.

More than six months after he began to give his prayerful attention to his salvation, as I was riding towards his house, just at a turn in the road, where it wound round a hill, which hindered our seeing each other till we were close together, I suddenly met him. He was riding in his one-horse waggon towards the village. I stopped my horse to speak to him, and I thought he appeared disposed to pass on. But as the road was narrow, and I had stopped my carriage, the wheels of our vehicles almost touched each other, and he could not well get by. We had a long conversation, as we sat in our carriages, in that retired and romantic spot. But I discerned no change in his religious feelings. He was as determined, but as hopeless as ever.

At length my eyes happened to rest on a brown jug, which might contain about two gallons, and which was lying on its side under the seat of his waggon. The thought came into my mind that he might be accustomed to the use of stimulating drinks, and that that might be an injury and a hindrance to him in his religious endeavours. I had never heard or suspected that he was an intemperate man. Probably the idea never would have occurred to me that strong drink might be his hindrance, had I not been utterly unable to account for his stationary condition in respect to religion. I instantly resolved to speak to him on that subject. But it was an awkward business. I did not know how to begin.

I would not insult him, and I did not wish to injure his feelings. He was an old man, near sixty—old enough to be my father; and to suggest the idea that he might be guilty of any excess would seem to be cruel and uncalled for. But I thought it my duty to make some inquiry. So I began:—

"Mr. E——, where are you going this morning?"

"I am going to the village—to the store."

"I see you have got a jug there, under your seat; what are you going to do with that?"

He cast his eye down upon it, a little confused, for an instant, as I thought; but he immediately replied:—

"I am going to get some rum in it."

"Are you accustomed to drink rum?"

"I never drink any to hurt me."

"You never drink any to do you any good."

"I have thought it *did*, sometimes. I do not drink much."

"Do you drink it every day?

"No, not every day, commonly. We had none to use in the field this year, in all our haying, till we came to the wet meadow, when the boys said we should get the fever if we worked with our feet wet and had nothing to drink."

"So you have used it since that time. You carry it into the field, I suppose?"

"Yes, we commonly do, in haying and harvest."

"Well, at other times of the year do you keep it on hand in your house?'

"Yes; I always *keep* it. But it is only a little that I drink; sometimes a glass of bitters in the morning,—or when I am not well, and feel that I need something."

"Mr. E——, when you are perplexed, annoyed, or in some trouble, do you never take a drink on that account?"

"I am very apt to. It seems to keep me up."

"Well, now, just tell me; for a good many months back, since you have been troubled on the subject of religion, have you been accustomed to resort to it, 'to keep you up?'"

"Yes; at times. I feel the need of it."

"In my opinion that is the *worst* thing, my dear friend, that you *could do!*"

"Why, I only drink a *little* at *home*. I have not carried it into the field, except in haying time."

"So I understand. But one question more: Have you not often at home, when you have felt downcast in mind on account of sin, taken a drink *because* you felt thus troubled?"

"I believe I have done it sometimes. I cannot tell how often. I never thought much about it."

I had become convinced by this time that he was at least in danger, and that it was not at all an improbable thing that his drinking just kept him from repentance. I told him so; and then began, with all my sagacity and power of persuasion, to induce him to quit all intoxicating drinks *for ever*. At first he appeared not to believe me at all. He heard me just as if he had made up his mind, and did not care what I said. His eyes wandered carelessly around, over the fields and trees, and then turned upon his old horse, as if he had been impatient to start on, and get out of the way of a lecture which he disbelieved. After a time, however, and while I was stating to him some facts within my own knowledge, to show the uselessness of strong drink, he became apparently interested in what I was saying. He listened, and I went on with my plea. As I explained the effect of intoxicating drink upon the mind, and upon the feelings and the conscience of men, he hung down his head, and appeared to be lost in thought. After a while, as I kept talking, he cast a glance at his jug; then looked up, and then his eyes fell back upon his jug again. I kept reasoning with him; but he did not look at me any longer,—he did not appear to be thinking of what I was saying. He appeared rather to be engaged in deep thought, and his eye often turned upon his jug. By-and-by he slowly reached down his hand, and took hold of it. With a very solemn countenance, and without saying a word,—he had not spoken for half an hour,—he placed the brown jug upon his knee. I talked on, watching his silent motions. He turned his head very deliberately around, one way and the other, as if he were looking for something; his eyes glancing here and there, as if he did not see what he desired. I kept on talking to him.

Just at the spot where we were, the road swept politely round a huge stone, or side of a rock, which rose about ten feet above the path; and as those who formed the road could not get it out of the way, the path made rather a short turn round it. This rock was within three feet of his waggon. His eye fixed upon it, and then glanced back to the jug upon his knee. Then he looked at the rock, and then at his jug again, and then at me. And thus his eye continued to wander from one to another of these three objects, as if it could not get beyond them. At first I was in some doubt which of the three was the most attractive to his eye,—the rock, the brown jug, or myself; but in a little time I noticed that his eye rested on the brown jug *longer* than on me; at length *I* was lost sight of altogether, though I continued talking to him, and his eye glanced backward and forward, from the brown jug to the rock, and from the rock to the brown jug. All this time he maintained an unbroken silence, and I kept on with my lecture.

Finally he seized the poor jug by its side, wrapping the long fingers of his right hand half round it, and slowly rising from his seat, he stretched up his tall frame to its full length, and lifting the brown jug aloft, as high as his long arm could reach, he hurled it, with all his might, against the rock, dashing it into a thousand pieces! "*Whoa! whoa! whoa!*" said he to the old horse. "Hold on here. Whoa! whoa! Turn about here. Whoa! We will go home now." The horse had suddenly started forward, frightened at the clatter of the brown jug, and the pieces which bounded back against his legs and side. The start was very sudden; and as my long friend was standing up, it came near to pitch his tall figure out of the waggon backwards. However, he did not fall. As he cried "Whoa! whoa!" he put back his long arm upon the side of the waggon, and saved himself. He soon stopped his old horse; and deliberately turning him round in the road, till he got him headed towards home, he put on the whip, and without saying a word to me, or even casting a parting look, he drove off like Jehu! I drove on after him as fast as I could; but I could not catch him. He flew over the road. And when I passed his house, about a mile from the jug-rock, he was stripping off the harness in a great hurry. We exchanged a parting bow as I drove by, and I never spake to him about rum afterwards.

Within a single month from this time that man became, as he believed, a child of God. His gloom and fears were gone, and he had peace, by faith in Jesus Christ.

About a month afterwards, as I passed the spot where such a catastrophe came upon the jug, and where my long friend came so near to be toppled out of his waggon, I noticed that some one had gathered up some pieces of the unfortunate brown jug, and placed them high up on a shoulder of the rock. I saw them lying there many times afterwards, and thought that my friend had probably placed them there as an affecting memorial,—he might have done a worse thing.

XXXIX.

The Harvest Past;

OR, THE DYING UNIVERSALIST.

MORE than sixteen years have now passed away since the occurrence of which I am now to write made its first impression upon me; but I am still unable to recall the scene to my mind without the most painful emotions. There was something in that whole scene too horrible for description. And I would much rather, were I to consult my own feelings, pass it over in silence, and let a veil be drawn over it for ever, than have the recollection revived by copying the notes made respecting it. But several of my friends have urged the publication; and I yield to their judgment.

I was hastily summoned to the bedside of a sick man, by the urgent request of his mother. He was yet a young man, I suppose about twenty-six years of age, was married, and the father of one little child. I had never spoken to him. I knew there was such a man, but I did not know him personally. His mother, who was a communicant in the Church, had often mentioned him to me; and his wife, who was a woman of very serious turn of mind, though very modest and reserved, had sometimes mentioned to me her husband, in a manner that showed me that his treatment of the subject of religion was a matter of sorrow to her. But I had no personal acquaintance with him. Whenever I had visited the family, he had either been absent from home, or intentionally kept himself out of my sight,—which, as I suppose, he had often done. Sometimes, but very rarely, I had seen him at church, not knowing, at the time, who he was. And I did not suppose he had ever been in church for years; till, when I saw him on his sick-bed, I recognised him as one whom I had seen in church, and had taken for a stranger. He was an industrious man, prosperous in his business, and as a man of the world, bore a good character.

His father was a Universalist, and the son had imbibed his principles. I had known this before. His mother had mentioned it to me, with much sorrow. She had also requested me to converse with the old man, her husband, and I had more than once attempted to do so; but he very soon excused himself, by pretending that his business was urgent, and he could not spend the time. I had also known him to leave the house and go off into the field, when he knew that I had called to see his family, and when he had good reason to suppose that I would request to see him. I have no doubt that he did this on purpose to avoid me. His son, who was now sick, had also, as I suppose, avoided me in the same manner. He still resided in the house with his parents, who had also another son, a lad about twelve years of age. These persons, with an infant child of the sick man, made up the whole household.

As I approached the house, I was startled at the groans of the sick man. I could hear them distinctly in the street. As I entered the door, his mother met me, calm in her deportment, but evidently in the most heart-rending distress. She looked the very image of woe. She briefly told me how her son was; and it was very easy to perceive that she expected he would die. She did not wish him to know that I had come at her request. She had not told him that I was coming. But she desired me to go in immediately, and converse with him and pray with him.

As I entered the sick man's room, and as she called my name and told him that I had come to see him, he cast a sudden look at me, appeared startled, and turned away his face towards the wall, without uttering a word—as if he regarded me with horror. I approached him familiarly and kindly, offered him my hand, which he seemed reluctant to take, and feeling his feverish pulse, aimed to soothe him as much as I could.

He had been taken suddenly ill with a fever, accompanied with violent pain in the chest, back, and head. He was in the most excruciating agony, tossing from side to side, and his groans and shrieks would have pierced any heart. He was a large, robust man, and his whole appearance indicated a vigour of constitution seldom equalled. His gigantic frame was yet in its full strength, and as he writhed in his spasms of pain, I thought I had never seen such an instance of the power of disease. This man of might was shaken and tossed like a helpless leaf.

When he became a little more quiet I inquired about his sufferings, and aimed to soothe and encourage him, expressing the hope that he might soon be relieved In an accent of intolerable agony he exclaimed, "*Oh! I shall die! I shall die!*"

"I hope not," said I, "by this sickness. I see no reason why you should not get well. And I think the doctor will be able to relieve you in a few hours."

"The doctor has done what he could," said he. "My time has come! I cannot live! Oh! I shall die!" And raising himself up suddenly, leaning for a moment upon his elbow, he threw himself back upon the bed and drew the covering over his face, holding it there with both his hands.

I again attempted to soothe his agitation, gently requesting him to be as quiet as possible, and assuring him I did not think that the doctor regarded his case as hopeless. Whether he gave any attention to my words I could not tell; for he kept his head buried in the bed-clothes, and firmly resisted the gentle attempts of his wife and his mother to remove them. In this manner he lay for several minutes, still groaning in agony. I asked him several questions, but he made me no answer.

Thinking that he might perhaps feel embarrassed at my presence, after speaking to him for a few moments, I took my seat in another part of the room, and conversed familiarly with his wife and his mother, aiming to remove his embarrassment, if he had any, by proposing something for his relief, and by such an ease and familiarity as should lead him to regard me as a friend. This had the desired effect. He gradually removed the bed-clothes from his burning face, and attentively listened to our conversation. With an imploring and despairing look, he stared at his wife and then at his mother. Time after time his fixed gaze was turned from the one to the other; but I noticed his eyes never rested on me. He seemed to avoid looking at me. If his mother or his wife spoke, his eyes would turn upon them at the sound of the voice; but if he heard a word from me, he did not notice me at all.

I had retired from his bed-side and taken my seat by the window, as I thought that would be a more delicate mode, than to stand by him, at least for a few minutes. He became more composed, and entirely still. After he had uncovered his face and listened for a few minutes, I rose to approach him. His mother, anticipating my design, and as I thought sensible of his reluctance to speak to me, rose and approached him before me. Calling him gently by name, she told him that I had come to see him, and inquired if he "would not like to have me pray with him." Instantly stretching both his hands towards the heavens, he raised himself on his bed, and holding his hands still aloft, as far as he could reach, he uttered the single syllable, "*Oh!*" with a dreadfulness of accent and a prolongation of the sound which made my blood curdle in my veins. His wife and mother turned pale—the former sinking into a chair from which she had just risen. This sudden and singular action of the sick man led me to believe he was in an agony of mind. It did not seem like the action of bodily distress. It was altogether different. Thinking it the best way to induce him to express his feelings to me, I inquired:—

"Has your pain returned?"

Still holding his hands aloft, and without looking at me, he exclaimed in a tone of horror, "Oh! oh! oh!"

"Are you in great pain?" I asked.

Another groan was his only answer.

"I am sorry to find you so ill," said I.

He uttered another groan—a dreadful shriek.

His wife, sobbing aloud, left the room.

I then said to him, "God is merciful. He is the hearer of prayer; and if you are—"

"*Oh!*" was the dreadful sound from his quivering lips which interrupted me; it was a shriek, which rang through the house; and every one of the family hurried into the room where he was. Among others was his little brother, who was the only person he seemed to notice. He glanced once or twice at him; and thinking he was about to speak to him, I remained silent. As he sat thus erect in his bed, with his hands stretched aloft to the utmost of his power, his eyes fixed on vacancy before him, and his lips uttering only his dreadful monosyllable, as a scream apparently of horror, he was the most pitiful object my eyes ever beheld.

"Shall I pray with you?" said I.

He flung himself back violently upon his bed, turned his face away from me towards the wall, and again drew the clothes over his head. We knelt by his bed-side, and continued some time in prayer. He had not spoken to me at all. But it appeared to me that his agony was quite as much mental as bodily; and I aimed to pray in such a manner, that he might be soothed and encouraged by the idea of the mercy of God towards sinners through our Lord Jesus Christ. During prayer he remained entirely still; but I could distinctly hear his deep breathing, and feel the bed shake, as a long breath rushed from his lungs. I continued in prayer for some six or eight minutes, I suppose; longer than I should have done, had not this exercise appeared to quiet him, and had it not been the only mode by which I appeared to be able to make any religious idea find access to his mind.

When we rose from our knees his face was uncovered; and turning his eyes upon me, then upon his mother, then back upon me again, he seemed to be on the point of speaking to me. and I stood by him in silence. With a look and tone of decision, he exclaimed, as he fixed his eyes firmly upon me :—

"It will do no good to pray *for me*, sir."

I waited for him to say more, but as he did not appear to be inclined to do so, I replied :—

"God is the hearer of prayer : he has encouraged us to pray to him : *he* has not said that it will do no good to pray."

"*My* day has gone by !" said he. "It is too late for me !—it is too late !"

"No, sir, it is *not* too late. If you want God's mercy, you may have it. God himself says so : 'Whosoever *will*, let him take the water of life freely.' You ought to think of the death of Christ for sinners,—of the mercy of God."

"*Mercy ! mercy !*" he vociferated, "that is what makes my situation so dreadful ! I have despised mercy ! I have scoffed at God ! I have refused Christ ! If God were only *just*, I could bear it. But now the thought of his abused mercy is worst of all ! There is *no mercy* for me any longer ! For years I have refused Christ ! My day has gone by ! I am lost ! I am lost !"

"You think wrong," said I ; "God has not limited his invitations. Christ says, 'Come unto me, *all* ye that labour and are heavy laden.'"

"My day has gone by !" said he.

"No, it has *not*," I replied, in a voice as firm as his own ; "behold *now* is the accepted time—*now* is the day of salvation."

"That is not for *me !*" said he. "I have had my time, and lost it ! I have spent all my life for nothing ! I have been a fool all my days, and now I am dying ! I have sought for nothing but this world ! I have refused to attend to God, and now he has taken hold of me, and I cannot escape !" The family, much affected, retired from the room.

"You have time still to seek him—to repent and flee to Christ. You have time *now—to-day*. 'The blood of Jesus Christ cleanseth from all sin.' Pray to God. You may be saved."

"You think so," said he, "but I know *better*—I *know* better! It is too late! I am dying, sir!"

"Christ accepted the dying thief," said I. "God is so rich in mercy that he pardons sinners at the eleventh hour."

"The eleventh hour is past!" said he. "This is the *twelfth* hour! God's time of vengeance has come! I have had my time, and lost it! It is all gone! I have loved the world only, and now I must leave it! O fool! fool! What is the world to me? Oh, how could I live so? I have been a fool all my days!"

He uttered these desponding expressions in the most firm and decisive tone. And as I was aiming to convince him of the mercy of God, and referring to the Scriptures, all I could say did not seem to weigh a feather with him.

His wife and his mother, hearing our conversation, had returned to the room, and seated themselves in silence at a distance from his bed. And just as he was uttering some exclamations about his love of the world and his folly, his father entered the room, and hearing his expressions for a little while, he approached the bed, saying to him,—

"Why, you need not feel so bad; you have never done any hurt to anybody."

"*Don't talk to me*, father!" said he in a tone of authority, or rather of hatred and anger. "You have been my worst enemy! You have ruined me! You led me to disobey God, and neglect the Bible! You led me into sin when I was only a little boy! You took me off to fish, and hunt, and stroll around the fields on Sundays, when mother wanted me to go to church. You told me there was no hell,—that all men would be saved. And *don't come here now to try to deceive me any longer! You have done your work! You have been my ruin!* Oh, if I had minded mother, and not *you*, I should not have come to such an end! Don't cry, mother, don't cry so"—he heard her sobbing. "You are a good woman; you have nothing to be afraid of. God will take care of you. Don't cry so. Oh, I would give a *thousand worlds*, if I owned them, to have your religion—or any part of it—or anything like it! But I am lost! I am lost! You told me, father, there was no hell; and I tried to believe it. I joined you in wickedness when I knew better. I have laughed at hell, and now hell laughs at me! God will punish sinners! He has taken hold of me, and I cannot get out of his hands!"

His father attempted to say something to him, but the son would not allow him to finish a single sentence. The moment he began to speak, the son exclaimed,—

"*Quit, father! Don't talk to me!* Your lies cannot deceive me any longer! You have ruined my soul! Where is my brother?"

As he made this inquiry, his wife rose, and coming near to the bed-side, replied,—

"He is out in the garden, I believe. What do you want of him? shall I call him?"

"Yes; call him. He is young. I want to tell him not to believe what father says to him—not to be influenced by him. He will lead him to hell. Now, when he is young, I want him to know that what Universalists say is false. I don't want *him* to be led into sin, as father led me. I want him to believe what mother says to him, and read the Bible, and pray before praying is too late, and not break the Sabbath day, and attend church, so that he may not die as I am dying."

His father, looking at me, remarked,—

"He has had so much fever and pain that his mind is not regular."

"Father, I *am no more crazy than you are!* You need not deceive yourself with that notion! But you are *not* deceived. You know better! You *try* to deceive yourself, just as you try to believe there is no hell. You pretend that all men will be saved, but you don't believe it. You led me to talk in the same way, and laugh at the warnings in the Bible against sinners. When I was a little boy you began to lead me into sin! Don't come here to torment me with your falsehoods now, when I am dying!"

At this moment his little brother, about twelve years of age, whom he had asked for, entered the room. Calling him by name, and looking tenderly upon him, vastly different from the look he had just bent upon his father, he said,—

"Come here, my brother. I am going to die very soon, and I want to tell you something. I wish you to remember it after I am dead. You are young now, and I want you to begin to live in the right way. I have been a very wicked man. Don't do as I have done. Read the Bible. Never swear, or take God's name in vain. Always go to church on Sundays. Always mind what mother says to you. Father will lead you into a very bad way, if you are not very careful. He led me into sin when I was a little boy like you. He has led me to ruin, because I was fool enough to yield to him. If I had done as mother wanted me to do, I might have died in peace. She is a good woman. Don't cry, mother; do not cry so." Sobbing aloud she left the room. "If father ever says there is no hell for the wicked, don't believe him. There is an awful hell! Remember that I told you so when I was dying! If father ever says that all men will be saved, never believe a word of it. The wicked will be turned into hell! Dear boy! It is a pity that he should be led to ruin. Never believe what the Universalists say. Believe your mother, and don't let father lead you into sin. Be a good boy. If I could live I would tell you more another time. But I must die!"

The young brother had stood by him weeping, manifestly struggling hard to control his emotions, till, entirely overcome, he cried aloud in a burst of grief, and rushed out of the room.

While he was talking to his little brother, the father listened for a time apparently unmoved, and then with a sort of stealthy tread went out.

It was one of the most affecting scenes. His mother, who had returned again to the room, his wife, and myself, subdued to tears, sat for some time in silence. It was enough to melt a heart of rock. But the sick man never shed a tear. I had hoped, when he spake so tenderly to his mother, and when he began to talk so affectingly to his little brother, that his own sensibilities would have been excited in a tender manner, and be a means of overcoming the stern and dreadful stubbornness of his resolute despair. But there was none of this. His voice never faltered. His eye never moistened. His burning brow never quivered.

I again attempted to converse with him, but he manifested no disposition to hear me. He did not even reply to any question. Recollecting how he had appeared a little while before, when I prayed by his side, I proposed to him that I would make a short prayer with him before I left him.

"Not here!" said he firmly. "Pray in the other room if you wish to pray. Do not pray here. I cannot pray. And I will not pretend to do so. I am beyond praying! My day is gone by! The harvest is past! Mother, I wish you would go into the other room if you want to pray."

We retired to another room, where we found his father, who had probably heard all that he had said. The old man appeared to be unaffected. And when I spake to him about the necessity of preparation for death, he seemed as indifferent as a stone. As the rest of us kneeled in prayer, he sat looking out of the window.

Before I left the house I returned again to the room of the sick man. He appeared very uneasy and restless, but I did not think his pain was bodily. The doctor came in, felt his pulse, asked some questions, prescribed for him, and saying he thought he would "be better to-morrow," left him.

"I shall be *dead* to-morrow!" said he firmly, without changing his position, or appearing to regard the presence of any one.

Briefly assuring him again of the mercy of God, the readiness of Christ to save him, and exhorting him to prayer, I bade him good-bye, to which he made no answer, and left him.

After I had retired, as I afterwards learnt, he remained very much silent, seldom even replying to any question, but from time to time tossing from side to side, and groaning aloud. His father brought him a paper, as I was told, which he wished him to sign as his will. He refused to sign it. Again the father brought it. It was read to him. Witnesses were called. He refused to sign it. "Father," said he fiercely, "you have led me into sin, into the snares of the devil; you have ruined me for ever! And now you want me to sign that paper, to take away from my wife and child all their support! *You know* it would not be right for me to sign it. Take it away!"

Repeatedly during the night his father urged him to sign that will. He steadily refused to do so, and sometimes stated the reasons for his refusal. But at last he signed it, wearied out with the ceaseless importunity, or, what is more probable, in a moment of insanity, unconscious of what he was doing. Be this as it may, the will was set aside afterwards by the court.

Early the next morning I returned to see him. The doctor had just left him, still giving his friends encouragement that he would recover, though he said he had "not expected to find him so bad as he was, but his symptoms were not unfavourable." I suppose he formed his opinion without regard to the state of the sick man's mind; and on this ground I have not a doubt his opinion was right.

As I entered the room I was struck with his altered appearance. He looked ten years older than when I left him the previous afternoon. He was evidently fast approaching his end. His voice was sunken and husky—his breathing short and laboured—his strength diminished—his look wild and delirious. He talked incoherently, his words running upon all strange matters by turns, as I understood had been the case with him, at times, through the whole night.

He had manifestly some lucid intervals. In one of them I attempted to converse with him, but he did not appear to regard me at all. I offered to pray with him, and he answered:—

"Prayer comes too late now—the harvest is past!" He immediately turned himself on the bed with a distressing shriek, and lay with his face towards the wall; and a moment afterwards he gave utterance only to delirious ravings! I may not here record what he said in his delirium; but it may be remarked, that his thoughts seemed to run much upon his father in an unhappy manner.

I stayed in his room for a long time. When he seemed to have a lucid interval, I conversed with his mother and wife, hoping that he might attend to what was said, as he had apparently done the day before; but he did not seem to notice it.

I particularly noticed his manner towards those who were around him, as I had done the day before. When his mind was not wandering, he appeared the same as on the previous day. He would not speak to his father, but with great reluctance, and as if he detested him. He appeared unwilling to have him in his presence. He would follow him with his eye, as he came into the room or retired from it, with a look of hatred. Towards his mother his manner was entirely different. He spake to her affectionately. He would gaze upon her for minutes together with a look of tenderness and intense interest. If he saw her in tears, he would sometimes strive to comfort her. He was manifestly affectionate towards his wife and his little brother. His eyes would rest upon *them* with a look of fondness, but fix upon his *father* with the look of a fiend.

After I had retired from his room for a few minutes, we returned again; and I found him sinking so fast, that I thought it my duty to tell his mother and his wife that I did not believe he would live out the day. They seemed surprised, and immediately sent for the doctor. When he came he found him dead! He had survived about three hours after I left him, growing weaker and weaker till he breathed his last, with the words of delirium upon his lips.

"When the harvest is past, and the summer is gone,
And sermons and prayers shall be o'er;
When the beams cease to break of the sweet Sabbath morn,
And Jesus invites thee no more;

When the rich gales of mercy no longer shall blow,
The gospel no message declare;—
Sinner, how canst thou bear the deep wailings of woe!
How suffer the night of despair?

When the holy have gone to the regions of peace,
To dwell in the mansions above;
When their harmony wakes, in the fulness of bliss,
Their song to the Saviour they love;—
Say, O sinner, that livest at rest and secure,
Who fearest no trouble to come,
Can thy spirit the swellings of sorrow endure,
Or bear the impenitent's doom!
Or bear the impenitent's doom!"

It does not belong to us to decide upon the condition of this departed man; but who would wish to die like him? "Let me die the death of the righteous; let my last end be like his."

I have no reason to suppose that the religious character of that father was ever essentially altered. At the funeral of his son he appeared very much affected, and I hoped that his affliction and the serious exercises of that solemn and tender occasion would have an abiding and salutary impression upon his mind. But when I visited him the next day, I found him occupied with the papers of his son, and the will which he had induced him to sign on the night before his death; and though his wife expostulated with him against such an employment at such a time, he still kept on. And afterwards till the day of his death, I never found any reason to believe that he ever became a different man.

But it was not so with that little brother, to whom the dying man gave such a solemn and affecting caution. The boy seemed to have treasured every word of it in *his heart*. He was very respectful and obedient to his father, in all things but one. In all that pertained to religion he was as fixed as a rock against his father's influence. He would instantly leave him if his father uttered a word on that subject. He could not be induced to neglect church or violate the Sabbath, by any influence or authority of his father. Without explanation or words of any sort, he would quietly disobey him, when he thought his requirements were contrary to the law of God; while in all other things he was most respectful and obedient towards him. I knew him well for years. His Bible and his mother were his counsellors; the Sabbath was his delight. He sought the Lord, and found him. And when giving me an account of the manner in which his mind had been influenced in respect to his salvation, he referred to what his dying brother had said to him. But he made this reference with evident reluctance and pain, weeping in bitterness of spirit. I have every reason to believe that both he and the widow of his departed brother are the children of God, through faith in our Lord Jesus Christ.

XL.

Doctrines and Death.

A FEW years after I was settled in my congregation, a family moved into the place from another part of the country, and took a seat in our church. The husband and wife both brought letters of introduction from the Church where they had lived, and became members of our Church. I soon became acquainted with them, and much interested about them. They were little more than thirty years of age, active, wealthy, and of good education, had seen much of the world, and were energetic in all that they undertook; and I thought them capable of doing much good. I therefore took the more pains to know them well. They entered very readily into our plans and ways, and their aid was beneficial to us.

But it soon became manifest to me that the wife was not well satisfied. She did not much complain, or find fault, so far as I know; but many of her expressions, uttered in conversation with myself and others, indicated a dissatisfied mind. Whether this dissatisfaction was personal towards myself, or had reference to the congregation, I could not at first even conjecture. In her youth she had been educated in another denomination, whose forms of worship differed from our own in some degree; and I deemed it probable that she did not feel quite at home among us. I respected her the more on this account. I did not think it would be wise to let her know that I perceived her dissatisfaction; but I determined rather to be faithful and friendly to her, and let her dissatisfaction wear off, as I trusted it would. She had never mentioned it to me, and if I should mention it to her, I thought it quite likely that she would throw off all restraint, and be confirmed in her unhappy dislike. I therefore always treated her just as if she were satisfied with me, and with her fellowship in the church.

As time passed on, I became more and more convinced that her dislike had respect to myself. I aimed to conjecture what it was in me that did not suit her; but I could form no opinion. She might dislike me as a man, or she might dislike me as a minister—I could not tell which; or her dislike on either one point might lead to dislike on the other. But as she never disclosed her feelings to me, I never disclosed my knowledge of them to her.

But after she had remained with us about three years, I supposed that I had discovered clearly the grounds of her dissatisfaction. She did not like some of my preaching; indeed, very little of it suited her. I could at times perceive this when she was listening to my sermons. And in conversation with her, when she adverted very modestly to my preaching, and expressed her opinion that some particular sermons were likely to do good, and that she did not believe some others were so appropriate, I perceived that she disapproved of the greater part of my sermons. She disliked those which she called "doctrinal." Such themes as human sinfulness; divine sovereignty; justification by faith in Christ simply; regeneration, not by baptism, but by the Holy Spirit aside from baptism; the unbending nature of the law of God; the justice of God in the condemnation of sinners, and the obligation resting upon sinners to repent, especially because God proffers to them the aids of the Holy Spirit—these doctrines did not appear to be acceptable to her. My mind apologized for her dislike, by the fact that she had been educated in another denomination, and by the recollection of the strength of our early preferences. However, as she had not *complained* of my preaching, but had only spoken in the way of inquiry and suggestion, all I could do was, first to refer to the Bible, and show that in my preaching I had not given to such subjects a greater proportionate regard than the divine writers had; and then to explain to her how such subjects were the most important and practical of all possible things, because they were the *facts in the case*, because they *addressed men's hearts*, and laid the foundation of religion *there*, in the heart's experience of God's truth, by the power of the Holy Spirit. This explanation appeared to cut her to the heart; but she did not complain.

By many things in her appearance and conversation, I was convinced, after a time, that some change was taking place in her religious views and feelings. The nature of the questions she sometimes put to me, about experimental religion especially, convinced me of this. She had never told me so, however, in any very plain manner; and I did not deem it best to make any inquiries about it. But she became a personal friend to me very evidently, not only as a man, but especially as her minister. And she used to urge upon the attention of her friends, as I learned, the truths which I preached; and used to urge them to "attend the church, and listen to every word so as to understand." In this friendship and confidence, her dissatisfaction all gone, she continued to live in the Church, manifestly a growing and happy believer, till the day of her death. The very doctrines which she had disliked became the delight of her soul; and she often requested me to go to some other places which she named, and preach there the sermons which she had listened to at home; "for," said she, "the people there do not hear these truths, and do not know how precious they are. I did not use to hear them when I was there."

At one time a friend of hers, a young person, had united with the denomination to which she formerly belonged. But though this young person stood in such relation to her, that it would naturally have been expected that such a profession of religion would have been made known to her at the time, yet it was kept a secret from her—she knew nothing of it till some little time after her young friend had been to the communion. She then ascertained that her own mother had advised the young person to this step. It grieved her much. She could not think it was right. She thought that some stronger evidence of fitness than her young friend possessed was requisite for Church membership.

In the pain of her heart, she spoke to the old lady about it: "Why, mother," said she, "how *could* you advise it? I think it is just the way to deceive souls! You seem to suppose that baptism and the Church ordinances are everything. I thought you had learnt better. That is just the way you brought *me* up; and if I had not learnt better, I should have been ruined for ever. And now, you have just led this young creature astray; and I am afraid she will never find it out, till it is too late!" This she told me herself with deep affliction and tears, and asked me if she had said anything disrespectful, or what was wrong in such a case. She said she wished to "honour her mother, but she could not avoid speaking, when she was so much afraid this poor young creature would be led to ruin."

When she came to her last illness I saw her often. Her sufferings were very great continually. Her patience never forsook her for a moment. She never uttered a single syllable of complaining —not a murmur escaped her, though her exceeding pain sometimes compelled her to shriek. As I visited her from time to time, for conversation and prayer, she was accustomed to speak freely to me; and after I had left her, I used to write down some of her expressions, part of which I here transcribe.

About ten days before her death I found her in the most excruciating agony. She said to me, "I am in great pain. I never knew what pain was before. But my God sends it; and I know it is good for me, or he would not bring it upon me so dreadfully. I do not complain. I sometimes scream, because I cannot help it. But do not think me impatient because I scream. If I could avoid it I am sure I would. I am afraid my friends will think me impatient, and think religion is not such a support as I tell them; but it is only my poor *body* that troubles me. My mind is at peace. Christ sustains me, or I could never endure this. And, as you have often told us in your sermons, that afflictions are benefits to God's children, I find it so now. Indeed, I can see now, as I look back, that in all my life God has given me my richest mercies in the shape of crosses. Very often I did not know it at the time; but I know it now. I praise him for it all. He sustains me. I have dreadful pain; but I have precious peace. My Saviour makes good to me his promises, as you have so often assured us he would. I find now that it is true. I believe it now in a way that I never believed it before."

A day or two afterwards she said, "I am glad you have come. I want you to pray with me, and thank the Lord for his goodness. I am in no less pain; but I am supported wonderfully. I find that I know a great many things about religion now, which I never understood before. You have taught us a great deal about the promises, and living by faith; and now I know what it means. Faith is everything. It gives me patience, it gives me love, and leads my heart to rest. You have not taught us too much about it, nor said too much about Christ. He is all in all to me.

"When I have a little more strength, as I hope I shall have before I die, I want to say something to you about yourself. I can't say much now. If you will come in another time when you can, I will say more. I want to tell you something about your preaching. It was a long time before I could be reconciled to your way. I did not like it. I was blind, and did not understand why you should preach so much about Christ, and the atonement, and our evil hearts of unbelief, and the Holy Spirit, and sovereign grace to justify us, and prayer. But I understand it all now; and I find it all true, as I hope to be able to tell you more particularly at another time."

The next day when I went in, she seemed, after a little while, to muster her remaining strength, and gather up her thoughts for what she called "something particular." She said to me, speaking with great effort, and slowly and solemnly, "I wish to thank you for instructing me as you have done out of the Scriptures. I hope you will continue to press upon your people, as you are accustomed to do, the Bible itself. The forms of religion are nothing. Since I have been sick, it has been a great comfort to me to go to the Bible. I can remember the chapters I have heard you read in the church, and the texts, and the doctrines I have heard you preach; and now they comfort me. Many a time when I have gone to church, I should have been pleased, I suppose, to hear you preach some fanciful sermon, as some ministers I know do; but you would come out with some Scripture doctrine, and urge us to examine the Bible, and see if these things were not so; and it has done me a great deal of good. I think it has been the means—one great means, of fixing my faith just on the Scriptures; so that now I am comforted by them. If you had not done so, I never should have had this strong faith in my God. I might have got it, perhaps, in some other way, if you had not preached so, and insisted upon the Scriptures so much; but it seems to me that I never should. And I want you to keep on so, and God will bless you in it. I want you to continue to urge upon the people, as you used to do, the Bible truths and doctrines. They will not all like it any better than I did at first; but I hope the Lord will instruct them to hear his great truths. They have done me good,—great good. They comfort me now. Some ministers talk about other things, such as the lives of men; but that does not do me any good,—except the lives of those mentioned in the Bible. Your preaching led me to examine God's word, to see if the things you preached were so there; and I found them so. I thank you for it all. I hope you will urge it still upon the people to turn to the Bible, and find the truths you preach there. The Bible is enough. It is precious to me. It contains all I want. I hope you will not be discouraged, if the people do dislike some of them, your humbling, solemn way. Keep on. They may learn better as I did. And then they will have precious promises, and precious doctrines to lead them, and not care about forms and ceremonies, or speculations and fancies."

On another occasion, when I saw her, she spoke of herself: "I am to die very soon; and I am ready to die. I did not think, last night, that I should be here to-day. I slept a little. This dreadful pain had exhausted me; and when I waked up, I was sorry to find myself here. I hoped I should have been with Christ. I would not be impatient; but I hope God will take me away soon. I do not fear death. Some people speak of it as a dark valley; and so I suppose it is of itself. I believe the Scriptures call it so. But it is no dark valley to *me*. It is all light. The promises shine on it. They shine beyond it. Christ is with me, and I trust *him*."

The day but one before she died, she said to me: "I took the Bible to read this morning, and I came upon the place where Paul speaks of being 'clothed upon with our house which is from heaven.' It led me to think of what I am just coming to. I hope I have got almost home; and I trust I shall not be disappointed. I am now ready to go. God has been very merciful to me, keeping my mind in this perfect faith and peace. When I was first taken sick, I had been in a cold, backsliden state; and I murmured for some time. But I am fully satisfied now. My trials have been good for me,—all good. God does all for me that I want, through my Lord Jesus Christ. *He* has brought me to these sufferings, and I thank him,—I thank him for it all. He has been with me, and kept me full of peace and joy. I have settled all my worldly affairs; and I have nothing now to do, but to think of God and heaven. I have given up all.

"I have been surrounded with kind friends,—nothing but kindness all the time; and their kindness overcomes me, and brings these tears. I have found it difficult to be reconciled to part with them, and give them all up; but I have been able to do it satisfactorily. Some of them I hope to meet in heaven. She mentioned their names. They are professors of religion, and I hope true Christians. But what grieves me most of all is, that I must leave some of them, not knowing that we shall ever meet again! She mentioned their names. They are not professors, and I suppose are not Christians. I do not know that I shall ever see them again! This grief overwhelms me. I don't know what will become of them. But grace is all-sufficient,—I leave them with God.

"I have always felt that a Christian ought to die rejoicing. In dying, we are going home to our Saviour. Christ is with me all the time, and gives me peace,—sweet peace to my soul; and I hope he will not leave me in the last hour. I trust he will not. I have been afraid my faith would fail then, when I come to the waves of Jordan; but I trust *him*, and I am happy to think I have got so near home."

Such were some of her death-bed expressions. Her joy increased as she neared her end, till it became the most triumphant and rapturous exultation; and she died with the words of joy and ecstasy literally upon her lips,—an *unfinished word* of praise and exultation being the last word she attempted to utter. It was commenced on earth, and finished in heaven!

A PASTOR'S
Sketches 2

A PASTOR'S
Sketches 2

Conversations with Anxious Souls
Concerning the Way of Salvation

Ichabod Spencer

Solid Ground Christian Books
PO Box 660132 ~ Vestavia Hills, AL 35266

Author's Original Preface

The following Sketches have no necessary connection with those formerly published, and contained in another volume. Each volume is complete by itself, though, it is believed, the two are fit companions for each other.

The favorable reception which the former volume met with from the public; the numerous testimonials of its usefulness to private individuals, which have been received from many different parts of the country; and more especially the similar testimonials received from many of his ministerial brethren, have induced the author to believe it to be his *duty*, to issue this additional volume. The former one has a thousand-fold more than realized every expectation that was ever entertained by the author respecting it; and although this volume may be less interesting in tender and affecting incidents, it is believed there are some reasons to hope, it will not prove less useful.

The author has aimed to present here such sketches as are *unlike* those of the former publication; so as to avoid, as much as possible, the needless repetition of the same ideas and arguments, and to make the volume a fit companion for the one which preceded it.

In these volumes, the author is not to be understood as professing to exhibit all the phases of Christian experience. To the varieties of such experience there is no assignable or *conceivable* end. Experiences are varied and modified by a thousand circumstances, which no pen can describe; by age, by condition, by illness, by peculiarities of mind and disposition, by the kind of preaching which has been heard, by associations, by habits of life, and perhaps, by the sovereign and infinite wisdom of the Divine Spirit, in His enlightening and saving influences. Sometimes one doctrine, or class of truths, and sometimes another, will take the lead in the reflections of an anxious mind, and so varied will these reflections become, that (it is believed), no wise man will ever attempt to describe religious experiences, which shall embrace all possible varieties. The circle of religious experience is immense, if not infinite. But this fact need discourage no inquirer, need embarrass no minister of the Gospel. The truth of God, after all, is simple: there never *was* a soul to which it is not applicable, and it is the sole instrument of the Spirit in the sanctification of the soul; and therefore there will be *points* of very distinct resemblance in all the *saving* experiences of men. And if what the author has written upon this subject tends to show, that the same truths are applicable to all souls; his work may not be valueless in illustrating the simplicity of the Christian religion, in conducting bewildered minds to the path of truth and salvation, and in showing, that the power and excellence of the Gospel lie in the great doctrines of grace, doctrines applicable to all souls who would find the way to Christ and eternal life.

The purpose of this book is not sectarian. It is confidently believed, that nothing here written can give any just offence to evangelical Christians of any denomination. Not willingly would the author wound the feelings of any human being; and he has aimed here, to deal only with the religion of the heart, and the truths which promote it.

It is not probable, that all readers of this book will entirely approve the *mode* of the author's conversations with the inquiring. He has only to say, that his reliance has been placed upon the *truth alone*, as the instrument of the Holy Spirit in leading sinners to heaven; and consequently his aim, in these conversations, was simply to cause the truth to be understood, felt, and received, as the sole and sure guide. The *matter* of his teaching can be better judged of, by this book, than the *manner* of his teaching. The propriety of manner has respect to the person, his age, state of mind, and other things; and to give such a minute description of all these personalities as to justify the manner in which he spoke, the author knew full well would make the book too large, and diminish the power of its truth. But he has always been unwilling to utter a single sentence, which could wound the feelings of an anxious inquirer after truth, aiming to find his way up to the Cross, and perplexed and harassed with the doubts, and difficulties, and darknesses of his own troubled mind. And he may be permitted to say, that some of the expressions contained in this book, (and the former one also), which, to a mere reader, will probably sound abrupt, and perhaps *severe*, are expressions which assumed their peculiar style, from the supposed propriety of it in the case. It was felt to be an important thing to *condense* the truth, to make it plain, and pointed, and incapable of being misunderstood; but he hopes and trusts there are no expressions here which will be found offensive to refined taste. Christianity, certainly, is kindness, and good manners, and good taste; and the author is confident, that he never uttered an unkind expression upon the ear of any inquirer, and never unnecessarily wounded the feelings of any one, who ever did him the favor to come to him. About the *mode* of conversation, men will entertain opinions somewhat unlike: the author can only say, he aimed to impress the truth upon the mind in the most effectual manner; and he feels fully satisfied with the kind regards towards himself which are entertained by those who have been led to Christ under his ministrations. They both prize and love him far more than he deserves.

Some of the conversations recorded here, (as well as those contained in the former volume), have a character which they could not have possessed, had it not been for an advantage, which the author always strove to improve. Whenever it was practicable, he studied the subjects beforehand. Having met an individual once, and expecting to meet him again, he carefully considered his case, aimed to anticipate his difficulties, studied the whole subject intensely, and, in many cases, wrote sermons upon it, the substance of which afterwards came out, to a greater or less extent, in the conversation. Thus, the conversations aided the sermons, and the sermons aided the conversations. If he might be permitted to do so, the author would commend this mode of ministerial action to younger ministers of the Gospel.

What is here presented to the public, has been submitted to the inspection of some of the author's ministerial brethren, in whose judgment and taste he has great confidence; and, without their approval, these pages would never have been printed.

If this humble volume, by the blessing of God, shall be the means of aiding sinners in the way of salvation, and of any little assistance to the younger ministers of the Gospel, in directing the anxious, and guiding the perplexed, and comforting the broken in heart, the author's hopes will be realized.

Dr. Ichabod S. Spencer
Brooklyn, NY,
March, 1853

A PASTOR'S SKETCHES.

Second Series

Contents

I. The Universalist's Daughter 11
II. The Lost Child; or, Affliction Sanctified 20
III. The Stormy Night; or, Perseverance 44
IV. The Choice: Hold On or Let Go 49
V. *The Neglected Bible 52
VI. No Escape 66
VII. The Date of Conversion 71
VIII. My Old Mother; or, Conscience in Trade 87
IX. One Word to a Sinner 96
X. "Nobody Said Anything to Me" 98
XI. Family Prayer 100
XII. Doctrines Reconciled; or Freedom and Sovereignty 102
XIII. "I Can't Pray" or, The Two Sisters 108
XIV. "I Can't Feel" 126
XV. Willing to be Lost 130
XVI. The Bird of Paradise 141
XVII. Superstition 152
XVIII. The Whistling Thinker 154
XIX. Unconscious Conversion 167
XX. Ceasing to Pray 181
XXI. Continuing to Pray 185
XXII. Human Ability 188
XXIII. The Faults of Christians 204
XXIV. Trying to Find God in the Wrong 213
XXV. Delay; or, The Accepted Time 222
XXVI. Physical Influence 226
XXVII. Treatment of the Desponding 229
XXVIII. Unknown Presence of the Spirit 236
XXIX. A Revival is Coming 240
XXX. The Broken Resolution 242
XXXI. What Can I Do? 250
XXXII. Religion and Rum 253
XXXIII. The Word of a Companion 255
XXXIV. God Reigns; or, Despair 257
XXXV. The Last Hour 262
XXXVI. The Dawn of Heaven 270

Appendix 1 - Fasting and Prayer (an additional chapter)
Appendix 2 - * Sixteen Short Sermons (from The Neglected Bible)

A PASTOR'S SKETCHES.

I.

The Universalist's Daughter.

THERE was something, as I thought, not a little peculiar in the religious aspect of a young married woman in my congregation, whom I sometimes visited, and strove to influence on the subject of religion. She was not a pious woman, but greatly respected religion, and was a constant attendant at church. It was her seriousness which first made me particularly acquainted with her; though before that time, I had sometimes urged her to attend to the concerns of a future life. At her solicitation, as I understood, her husband, with herself, had left my congregation about six months before, and they had attended another church, until they were induced to come back to our church one evening, by the expectation of hearing a clergyman from a distance. As she found I was to preach, for the stranger clergyman was not there, she whispered to her husband, proposing to leave the place and go home; but he refused to go, for he said it did "not look well." They constantly attended our church after that evening; and when they became seriously disposed to seek the Lord, I became more intimately acquainted with them. She had become deeply serious, but appeared strange to me. I could not discover precisely what it was that was peculiar about her, but there was *something*. She was uniformly solemn, appeared to me to be frank and candid, was an intelligent woman, had become prayerful, and was at times deeply anxious about her future welfare; and yet, as weeks passed on, she appeared to make no progress, but remained in much the same state of mind,—unsettled and without peace.

She had no resting-spot. Whenever her thoughts were directed to the subject of religion, a pensiveness would spread over her soul, like the shadow of a cloud over the summer landscape. I pitied her. She was an interesting woman. Her naturally fine mind had not been neglected. She had received the accomplishments of a careful education. She was young, she was beautiful, she was tasteful; and the ease of her manners threw an additional gracefulness over her tall and graceful person. But a cloud was on her brow. It was out of its place—it had no right there. Such a brow ought to be bathed in the sun-light. A heart like hers ought not to be the victim of some secret and mysterious sorrow, and such a soul as hers ought to find in the kindness of Christ the balm for its sorrows.

She had been married about a year, and her husband, like herself, had become interested in the subject of religion. But they were very unlike in their religious successes. He seemed to get onward; she remained stationary and sad. They were about the same age (twenty-seven, perhaps), and in other respects much resembled each other; but they were unlike in religion.

She had been born and educated in a distant part of the country, and among people of somewhat different manners; and I thought that she might perhaps have some feelings of melancholy and loneliness, as she had come to reside among strangers. But I found she had no such feelings. On the contrary, she was delighted with her new home; was easy, and familiar, and friendly in her social intercourse with her new acquaintances. Several times I called upon her, and aimed to discover what made her so downcast in mind, and especially what hindered her from attaining peace with God through faith in our Lord Jesus Christ. But I could gain no light on the subject. After all my conversation with her, the peculiarity which hung around her was as mysterious to me as ever.

At one time I suspected that her seriousness might arise more from mere fear than from any just sense of her sin; and therefore I aimed, by explanation of the law of God, and by application of it to her own heart, to render her conviction more deep and clear But, to my surprise, I found that her sense of sin and unworthiness, and of the wickedness of her heart, appeared to be more than usually deep and solemn.

At another time I feared that she might have a very imperfect idea of the freeness of divine grace, and therefore I aimed to show her how "the *kindness and love of God our Saviour*" offers to every sinner pardon and eternal life as a free gift, by us unmerited and unbought. And again, to my surprise, I found that her ideas on this point also appeared as clear and as strong as any that I could express.

So it was with her, as it seemed to me, on every part of evangelical truth. I could discover in her mind no error or deficiency, and could not even conjecture what kept her from flying to Christ in faith. Evidently the Holy Spirit was with her, but she yet lingered; and her state appeared to me the more wonderful, because her husband had become, as we believed, a follower of Christ, and was cheerful and happy in hope.

As I was conversing with her one day about her state of mind, she somewhat surprised me by suddenly asking,—

"Will you lend me the Presbyterian Confession of Faith?"

"Certainly, madam," said I, "if you want it; but I advise you to let it alone."

"I want to know," said she, "what the Presbyterians believe."

"They believe just what you do, I suppose," said I; "they believe the Bible,—they believe just what you hear me preach every Sabbath."

"Other denominations," said she, "who disagree with you, profess to believe the Bible too."

"Yes, that is all true; but I do not wish you to agree with either, but to agree with the Bible. I have no desire to make a Presbyterian of you. I only wish you to be a Christian, and I am fully content to have you judge for yourself what the gospel teaches, without being influenced by the Presbyterian Confession of Faith or any other human composition. The Bible is the rule. If we agree with it, we are right; if not, we are wrong. You will understand it well enough to be saved, if you will study it prayerfully, and exercise your own good sense. You have to give an *account of yourself unto God*, and it matters little to you what other people believe."

"Why are you unwilling," said she, "that I should read your Confession of Faith?"

"I am *not* unwilling, madam,—not at all, if you wish to read it, I will bring it to you with pleasure at any time you desire it. But I am only expressing my opinion, that it will do you no good at present. I think the Bible is far better for you to read just now. At another time the Confession of Faith may be of service to you, but not now."

"I was not brought up in the Presbyterian Church, sir. My father is a Universalist, and my mind is not settled about the doctrines of religion."

"Are you a Universalist too?"

"No, sir, I don't think I am; but I don't know *what* to believe," said she, most mournfully.

"Do you believe the Bible is God's word?"

"Oh yes, I believe that."

"Well, the Confession of Faith is *not* God's word, though, in my opinion, it substantially agrees with it; and I advise you to take the Bible and lay its truth upon your own heart, with all candour and with sincere prayer. If you get into the Confession of Faith, I am afraid you will not understand it so well as you can understand the Bible; and I am afraid your understanding alone will be employed, and not your heart; or, at least, that you will have more of the spirit of speculation than of heart religion, and will leave your sins, your Saviour, and salvation too much out of sight.

"O sir, I don't mean to do that."

"I think, madam, that you know perfectly well that the Bible demands of you a repentance, and a faith. and a love of God which you do not exercise, and your first business should be, not to examine the Confession of Faith about a great many other doctrines, but to get your *heart* right,—and what that means the Bible teaches you, and you painfully feel its truth."

"But, sir, I ought to know what a Church believes before I unite with it."

"Most certainly you ought. But you are not prepared at present to unite with any Church. You do not think yourself to be a true Christian at heart—a true penitent—a true believer—a sinner born again, and at peace with God through Jesus Christ. Come to these things *first*. Get a *heart* religion, and after that you will be better prepared to examine the Confession of Faith. But don't allow your mind to be led away into a wilderness of doctrines, to the neglect of your present, plain duty. You are an unhappy woman,—a sinner without pardon. You have no peace of mind. And first of all,—yes, *now* on the spot, you ought to give up your heart to Christ, penitent for sin and trusting to the divine mercy. Here lies your present duty. Don't you think so yourself?"

"Yes, sir, indeed I do," said she, sadly; "*I wish I were a Christian.*"

"I will send you the Confession of Faith, if you desire it, but in my—"

"No, don't send it," said she, interrupting me; "I will not read it yet."

"You said your father was a Universalist, but you did not think you yourself were one? I have no desire to say anything to you about that doctrine. It is unnecessary. If you will read the Bible with candour and common sense, and with humble prayer for the direction of your heavenly Father, you certainly *can know* as well as any one what the Bible teaches about that. I leave that to your own judgment. If you find any difficulty on that, or on any other subject, I shall be happy to tell you hereafter just what I think. But I am sure you cannot mistake the meaning of God's word about the everlasting punishment of sinners."

"Do come to see me again," said she, with a sad earnestness, "I am not satisfied to rest where I am. I will try to follow your advice."

After a short prayer I left her. In subsequent conversation with her, I discovered nothing to make her peculiarity or hindrance to repentance any more intelligible. I did not suppose that the religious opinions of her father were exerting any influence upon her mind; for it seemed to me, and to herself too, that she had entirely abandoned them.

Just at this time her father paid her a visit, and remained with her for more than a week. He probably noticed that she was unhappy, and probably knew the cause; but he said nothing to her on the subject of religion. He was one of the prominent men and liberal supporters of a Universalist Church in the place of his residence; and, as she afterwards told me, she longed day after day, while he remained with her, to talk with him about religion, and about her own feelings; but he seemed to avoid all conversation which would lead to the subject, and she "could not muster courage enough," as she expressed it, "to speak to him and tell him how she felt." Every day she thought she certainly *would* do it, but every day she neglected it, and every night she wept bitterly over her neglect. Said she to me, "He is a very affectionate father; he has always treated me most kindly; but I could not tell him how I felt—my heart failed me when I tried."

The morning at last came when he was to leave her. He prepared for his departure, and she had not yet told him of the burden that lay on her heart. He bade her good-bye very affectionately, gave her the parting kiss, passed out at the door, and closed it after him. Suddenly her whole soul was aroused within her. She "could not let him depart so." She hastily opened the door and ran after him through the little yard before the house, to the front gate. She flung her arms around him, "Father, O my father!" said she, the tears streaming from her eyes, "I want to ask you one question; I can't *let* you go till you tell me. I have wanted to ask you ever since you came here, but I couldn't. I am very unhappy. I have been thinking a great deal about religion lately, and I want to ask you one thing. Tell me, father, what you truly think—you *must* tell me—do you really believe that all people will be saved hereafter, and be happy in another world? *Don't deceive me,* father; tell me what you really believe."

"Elizabeth," said he, with evident emotion, which he struggled to conceal, "I think it is very likely that some will be *lost for ever!*" and lifting his hand to his brow, he instantly turned away and left her. He could not tell his daughter, as she hung upon him in such distress, that dangerous falsehood which he professed to believe.

His tearful daughter returned into her house, the last prop knocked away, the last refuge gone! "Now," as she said to me afterwards, "she could look to nothing but Christ, and have hope only in sovereign mercy. My last deception was gone." And it was not long before she became as happy in hope as she had been sad in her perplexities and fears. She was a firm and joyful Christian.

She united with the Church, and for more than twenty years has lived as a happy believer. Her children have grown up around her; and some of them, the delight of her heart, are the followers of their mother's Saviour and their own.

But her father returned to his home and his former place of worship, professing still before the world to believe in universal salvation,—a falsehood which he could not tell his daughter when she wept upon his bosom.

After her hopeful conversion she wrote to her father, giving him a simple and affectionate account of her religious experience, thanking him for his kindness in telling her his real opinion, and entreating him to forsake a congregation where he himself knew he did not hear the truth—beseeching him to turn to Christ, that he might be saved from everlasting punishment. His reply to her letter was kind, but evasive. He made no response at all to the real burden of her letter. She then wrote to him again. In the most kind and touching manner she recapitulated her experience, told him of her sweet peace of mind, her joy and hope, and asked him whether he was willing that she should unite with the Presbyterian Church, as she proposed to do, or would rather that she should be a Universalist. In his reply, he adverted to what he had said to her on the morning when he parted with her, and very plainly assured her that he would rather have her join the Presbyterian Church than his own. But still he avoided saying anything about *himself*. Again she wrote to him, and appealing to the declaration of that morning, and to his letter, she affectionately entreated him to obey the truth as it is in Christ Jesus, and not go down to death with a lie in his right hand—a thing the more dreadful because he *knew* it was a lie!

But all this did no good. He remained in the Universalist Church. Though for a time he appeared to waver, and occasionally for some weeks together would attend the Sabbath ministrations of another congregation, and sometimes wrote to his daughter in a manner which encouraged her to hope he would become a Christian; yet all this passed away, and the last time she mentioned her father to me, she told me with bitter tears, "He has gone back to the Universalists, and I am afraid he will be lost for ever!" "Oh!" said she, "he *knows* better—they all know better—they *try* to believe their doctrine, but they don't believe it." I shrewdly suspect there is no little truth in her declaration.

The course of this man at first appeared to me very astonishing. I marvelled at it beyond measure. I could not doubt that he told his daughter the truth, when he said he "thought it very likely that some would be lost for ever." But while entertaining such an opinion, and while unwilling that the daughter whom he fondly loved should be a Universalist, that he should himself still continue to be a supporter of that system of falsehood appeared to me most surprising. But I have ceased to wonder at it. He only followed the inclination, as I suppose, of his wicked heart. He did not obey his conscience. He only strove to pacify it with a delightful deception. He did not love the truth. And with some dark and indefinite notion about the salvation of all, he strove to hide himself from the power of the truth, which he both feared and hated—hated, *because* he feared. Any man who will be wicked and hardened enough thus to trifle with truth, and thus to run counter to conscience, and thus aim to "believe a lie," may be left to do the same thing. Human depravity, fostered and indulged, has immense power, and will lead in strange ways to the eternal ruin of the soul.

Sinners are sometimes kept from repentance by a hindrance which they do not suspect. This woman was. She afterwards recollected that the idea had sometimes come floating over her mind, and had lingered around it, "Perhaps all will be saved." And this it was that half stilled her fears, and half pacified her conscience, and threw a sort of dimness and doubt over the whole field of religion. On this account she lingered in her sins and away from her Saviour. She knew not her own heart till it sunk within her as her delusion fled. But she soon came to Christ after her delusion was dissipated by the words wrung from the conscience of her father on that memorable morning,—"Elizabeth, I think it is very likely that some will be *lost for ever!*"

II.

The Lost Child;

OR, AFFLICTION SANCTIFIED.

I RECEIVED a very polite and fraternal note from a neighbouring clergyman, whose kindness and confidence I had experienced many times before, desiring me to attend the funeral of the only child of a gentleman and lady, who had formerly been attendants on his ministry, though at that time they had come to reside nearer to myself. Another duty called him to a distant part of the state, and he commended these afflicted parents to me. I had never seen them, and I believe they had never seen me; but the brief note which commended them to me, prepared me to have a high respect for them, and to sympathize in their sadness, as they were now bereft of the only child they ever had.

The person who brought me the note and engaged my services for the funeral could tell me but little about them. They were not communicants of any church, though my clerical friend in his note gave me to understand that they were persons of a serious turn of mind, and at times felt some personal anxiety, one or both of them, on the subject of religion.

I felt no hesitation about my duty. Indeed I could not mistake it, and had no desire to avoid it. But I was burdened with the impression that it was a difficult duty for me to discharge with acceptance and propriety. It is a delicate thing to go to strangers in the day of their deep sadness. A friend may carry the balm of consolation to hearts that have often opened to him, but how can a stranger dare to meddle with the tenderness of grief? I feared that their hearts would be shut up against me—*must* be, from the very nature of the case; or would recoil from me as an intruder, if I should attempt at all, stranger as I was, to meddle with the sacredness of their sorrow, or should even try to lay the consolation of the Lord's mercy upon the grief-spot of their smitten bosoms. And I was the more embarrassed on account of what their messenger had told me respecting the child they had lost. She was a little gem of earth,—a most beautiful, intelligent, and amiable little girl about four years old, with a maturity of mind far beyond her years; and her parents were peculiarly cast down now when death had snatched her away. I knew that I could sympathize with them; but I did *not* know that they could receive my sympathy. Affliction seldom resorts to a stranger. It seeks solace in solitude, or the sympathy of some long-tried friend; and I was not a little afraid that their tender and hallowed sadness would shrink from me if I should attempt even to comfort them. They had no faith, as I supposed; and I knew that nothing but the truths of Christianity could afford them anything better than a fictitious and deceptive comfort, worse than none. I knew that mere reason would be dumb over a corpse,—that no philosophy could grapple with grief and the grave.

At the hour appointed I went to their house. It was filled with people. I spoke with the parents for a few moments, and before the funeral services commenced there was put into my hands the following letter:—

"DR. SPENCER,

"Rev. Sir,—We thought we should like to give you a few particulars in regard to our only child. She was of uncommon promise, and, for her age, possessed a mind much matured. During her illness of two weeks she was a great sufferer, without murmur or complaint. Her mind continued perfect until the last, and she would often say, 'Mamma, comfort your little daughter.'

"Previous to her last sickness she had enjoyed unusual health, with a heart full of mirth, tenderness, and sympathy. She was a favourite, and beloved by all. We have never known her to speak an untruth. She loved to do right, and was very conscientious in regard to her conduct on the Sabbath. She loved to talk of God and heaven; and a few weeks since, while an uncle was very ill, she said, 'Mamma, when we die, if God would only take us in his arms and carry us right up into heaven, so we should not have to be put into the dark coffin, how happy it would be!' We trust she is now there."

———.

I read this affecting note, signed by both the parents, and the funeral services were conducted in the usual manner. Before prayer, I aimed to say such things as I thought might be profitable to the assembled multitude, and such especially as I had some hope would bring at least a gleam of comfort to the crushed and bleeding hearts of these parents, now stripped of their precious treasure. It was a most solemn and tender occasion. The little coffin was placed near the folding doors, which opened between the parlours. I had looked into it just as I entered the room. Its slumbering tenant was lovely even in death. She looked as if she were asleep, and appeared more pure and beautiful than the flowers which were placed beside her and on the coffin lid. But that marble brow was cold; and those lily lips, which seemed as if ready to utter some syllable of love, would never speak again. I could not look upon it. I turned away and wept.

After the religious exercises were closed, I sat where I could see the countenances of the multitude, who came one after another and looked into the little coffin. I did not see one who turned away without eyes suffused with tears. Every one was affected. Old men, with stern and severe faces, wept over it. And when the parents came to take their last look, and the mother bent down over the coffin to give her last kiss to such a child, I felt that her heart must break. Tears streamed from her eyes; her whole frame shook like an aspen leaf with the dreadful violence of her agitation. There were no noisy outbursts of grief, but such a deep and dreadful sorrow as seemed too much for nature to endure. She retired from the coffin supported by her husband; and tear-dimmed eyes followed her as she went up to her chamber—a childless mother!

Promising to call on them the next day, I left the melancholy scene; and this sweet child was conveyed to the tomb.

The next day I called at the house. Business had compelled the father to leave home, but the mother met me with a heavy heart. She could scarcely utter a syllable for some moments. She gave me her hand with a look of despair that horrified me.

"I have called to see you, madam," said I; "for I sympathize with you in your heavy trial, and if I could, I would say something to comfort you."

Evidently struggling to conceal her emotions, she answered,—

"I am glad to see you, sir. I feel very wretched. I never expected such a trial as this. My child was everything to me. Our hearts were wrapped up in her, and now she is gone! I do not know how to endure this. I cannot endure it—I feel that I *cannot!*" and she wept bitterly.

"It is *God*, madam, who hath taken away your child. I am sorry for you—my heart bleeds for you. I do not blame you for mourning, and God will not blame you for it. You cannot avoid it, if you would; and you would not, if you could."

"Oh no, sir," said she, weeping; "she was such a lovely child—so affectionate and intelligent, and—my *all!* She had a maturity of mind far beyond her years. I wanted you to know something about her before the funeral, and because we wished you to know something of her, we wrote you that little note."

"That letter," said I, "affected me very much. I shall answer it as soon as I have time. It was put into my hands just after I came in here yesterday, and as I glanced over it and found her expression about being taken right up into heaven without being buried, I could not repress my emotion. I could scarcely command composure enough to conduct the funeral exercises with propriety. I am sorry for you,—I can weep with you; but God alone can do you any good. Do you think you are submissive to his will?"

"I am afraid not, sir. I know his will is right; but I cannot feel reconciled to it as I ought. It is such a stroke to me; I know not how to bear it. I never knew what affliction was before. We were very happy. I am afraid we loved our child too much. I often thought how much I had to enjoy in my husband and my child; but now God has taken her away, and I am perfectly wretched." She sobbed aloud.

"My heart bleeds for you, my dear friend; but I want you to remember that God only can comfort you, or make your affliction beneficial. You must not murmur. You must not rebel or repine. You are not forbidden to mourn. I do not blame your grief, and do not wish you to blame yourself for it; but I want you to be satisfied with God, and especially I want you to be profited by your dreadful trial. God *means* something by sending it; and I want you to ask him *what* he means, and be led by this sad providence nearer to himself, in faith that rests on Christ and will fit you for another world. Do you think you have *any* faith?"

"Oh no, sir. My mind is *all* dark. I have no comfort, no peace. It seems as if I could think of nothing but my child."

"I do not blame you for thinking of her. You cannot help thinking; but you ought to be led by this affliction to seek the Lord. Have you been praying to him?"

"I have tried to pray, sir, but my prayers seem almost like mockery. My thoughts wander, and God seems to be *very far off*. I am entirely cast down. My heart seems broken, and I think there is no comfort for me in this world, now my child is gone."

"I assure you, my dear friend," said I, "I feel your affliction deeply and tenderly, and that makes me the more anxious for you, to have you fly in faith to that Saviour, to that God and Father, who I know has comfort for you, and will lay the balm of a precious solace upon that deep sorrow of heart, which no other friend can reach. Fly to him as a child to a father. He will not cast you off. He will love and comfort you—I know he will."

"I am very miserable," said she. "It seems to me that my trial is more than I can endure."

"God will enable you to endure it, and to profit by it, if you give up sin and the world, and betake yourself to him in faith. He invites you to his arms; he wants you to lean upon him confidingly and affectionately, as a child. He asks you to 'cast all your care upon him,' drawn by the power of that blessed argument, 'for *he careth for you.*'"

"I do feel as if I needed comfort," said she.

"God only can comfort you," I replied.

"My child was my treasure," said she.

"Prepare to follow her to another world, madam."

"I wish I could. When you were speaking yesterday at the funeral, your words went to my heart. It was so sweet to think she is happy now, and may be hovering near us to do us good. I could have heard you speaking as you did of my angel child all night—any length of time. It gave me the only comfort I have, to think she is for ever happy with God."

"Waiting there," said I, "to welcome *you* into heaven, and rush into your arms in a little while, if you will only give up the world, and, as a sinner to be saved, flee now to the Saviour who calls you. Do you mean to do so?" Mournfully she replied,—

"I hope I shall try. The world all seems different to me now. I was happy; but now all is dark to me, for this world and the other! I cannot think of anything but my lost child."

"*Not lost*, madam; not *lost*, but gone before. Do not think of her as lost to you, but think of your *duty* to prepare to follow her."

"I feel entirely discouraged. If I try to seek God, it is in vain. My prayers are not answered. Everything is dark. I can think of only one thing."

"My dear friend," said I, "you *must* not let this affliction be lost upon you. Turn *now* to God with all your heart. He will pity you. He will hear your prayers and comfort your heart, if you will come to him in faith. Do you intend to do so?"

"My thoughts have been directed to the subject of religion,

but I do not seem to have any faith. All is dark to me; and now, my loss is more than I know how to bear."

"You cannot bear it rightly but by the help of God. 'In me is thy help,' says he; and you will find help there, if you will only seek him with all your heart. He has directed your attention to the subject of your salvation before, and now he has given you such an affecting call, that surely you ought to heed it. I hope you will. Go to him—tell him all your wants and sorrows. He is of infinite love and kindness, and you have no need to be discouraged. He will not let you sink."

Very much in this manner our conversation continued for some time. I strove to comfort her, for I felt that she had a very sore trial, in which I could not but sympathize with her grief. She was a perfect picture of woe, if not of entire despair. Her intelligence, too, and her frankness and simplicity, had deeply interested me; and I especially strove to persuade her to make a just use of her bitter affliction. But it was very noticeable how her mind rested upon but one thing. Whatever I said, she would come round to that. Her lost child absorbed all her thoughts, all her heart. If I spake of God, her mind would turn upon her child. If I spake of submission, it took only a moment for her to get her thoughts turned back to her child. If I spake of her duty to improve her affliction, or of the kindness of God; or spake of Christ, or comfort, or prayer, or the Holy Spirit, or sin, or faith, or heaven, a single expression would bring round her thoughts to the same melancholy theme—her lost child.

I felt it to be no easy thing to deal with such a heart rightly. To soothe and comfort her crushed spirit, and at the same time to lead her to make a just use of her affliction, appeared almost impossible. If I should attempt to lead her mind off from her lost child, all a mother's heart would be against me. If I should attempt nothing more than to condole with her, she might indeed be soothed a little by the sympathy, but that soothing would not lead her to salvation. I strove, therefore, to find some-hold upon her sensibilities, some link which should unite her sorrow and her Saviour—which should neither do violence to a mother's bleeding heart nor peril her everlasting interests. And before I left her, one of her own expressions had, as I thought, furnished me what I desired. I resolved to employ the idea afterwards—it was the idea of her own child now in heaven.

Before I left her I prayed with her, as she requested me to do, that their affliction might be sanctified to her and her husband.

As soon as I was able, I sent an answer to the letter which was given to me at the funeral, and in the answer I aimed to comfort and counsel my sad friends as well as I could.

Pressing engagements hindered my seeing her again, except once for a few moments, till nearly a fortnight after the funeral. It was a Saturday when I called upon her again; and I found her, if possible, more miserable than before. In answer to my inquiry, she replied,—

"I feel perfectly miserable, and there is nothing that can comfort me. I feel my loss more and more every day."

"I am sorry for you, my dear child. Your loss is indeed great, and I do not wonder at your feeling it. I do not blame your sorrow. I should blame you if you had none. God would have you mourn. Jesus wept at the grave of Lazarus, whom he loved. But God can comfort you, and I hope he will. The Holy Ghost is the holy Comforter. Have you been praying to him?"

"Yes, I have tried; but my thoughts are wandering. It seems to me that God will not hear such prayers as mine. My mind is all dark. I have tried to pray, but it does me no good."

"What have you been praying *for?*"

"I have prayed that our affliction may be sanctified to us."

"Do you think it will be?"

"I am afraid not. God does not answer me, and my heart appears to me to be very hard."

"Have you any comfort in praying?"

"No, none at all; and I am discouraged in *trying* to seek God."

"You need not be discouraged. If you seek him with your

whole heart, he will be found of you. He has promised that, and he will be true to his word."

"But my heart is so senseless. I try to believe, but it seems as if I had no faith. I read the Bible, but it is dark to me. I try to pray, but my heart is not in my prayers; and I am afraid God will never hear me."

"Do you think you have been led to know and feel that you have a *wicked* heart, and need God's help to make it different?"

"I *know* it, but it seems to me that I do not *feel* it at all; and I wonder at myself."

"Do you wish to feel it?"

"Yes, I do. I have prayed to be enabled to do so. I know I am a sinner, and I wonder I do not realize it more. I think I never have had conviction enough."

"How much conviction does a sinner need, in order to be prepared to come to Christ? He needs just to know and feel that he cannot save himself. If he knows he is a lost sinner, he knows all the truth about himself that he needs to know; and he ought instantly to accept the offer of God, trusting Christ to save him. Do you think you feel your need of the atonement that Christ has made for sinners, in order that you may be forgiven and saved?"

"Yes, I do. I can do nothing for myself."

"Well, then, let Christ do everything for you. *Trust* him to do everything for you. He *offers* to do everything for you. Come to him *just as you are,* with all your sin—with all your darkness—with all your unworthiness—with your cold and unbelieving heart—and let him give you another heart. He waits to receive you, and your delaying is unnecessary. Your waiting to gain more distressful feelings about yourself will not make you any better prepared to give up the world and trust in him. Come to him now—not to be lost, but to be loved—not to be cast out, but to be comforted *and saved.* Come now, while the Holy Spirit strives with you."

"I *need* his blessing," said she. "I feel very miserable. God has taken away the only child I ever had; and I believe he has done it to show me my sins; but I am afraid it will be in vain to me. I cannot feel *anything*. My heart seems hardened."

"But, my dear friend, your child is better off than you; and your duty now is to prepare to meet her in heaven. God has spread a cloud of gloom over this world, to turn your heart to a better one. But you do not give God your heart; you are still hesitating, fearful, and unbelieving. If you remain thus, all your affliction will only be lost upon you. I am not a little afraid it will. Do you not know that the instances of conversion to Christ are far less than the number of mourners?—that very few persons are ever led to religion by such afflictions! Affliction goes everywhere—death goes everywhere. You see it all around you. 'Who has not lost a friend?' Parents die, and children die; and yet how seldom do bereavements profit the living. Such trials do *Christians* good; but they seldom bring unbelievers to true religion. You *know* this is true; you see it to be so all around. And even now, when the only comfort you have is to think of the little gem you have lost,—now a gem in heaven,—I am afraid your affliction will not lead you to Christ."

"My heart," said she, "is very hard. I am miserable; but it seems to me I cannot feel my sins. I have tried to seek God, but something keeps me from thinking of anything but one."

"Give God your heart just as it is,—remember, *just as it is*,—and let him make it feel. 'Turn unto the Lord, and he will have mercy upon you; and to our God, for he will abundantly pardon.' You must have faith. You must *believe* what he says to you. You must trust his promises, and fall into his arms. Salvation is all of grace. Do not wait for feeling. Have the faith first, and let the feeling come afterwards. Receive Christ as your own, affectionately, and as a child; and then you may expect your hard heart will melt. The Holy Spirit strives to bring you to this. 'Now is the accepted time.' Flee to Christ to day, and be prepared to follow your child to glory."

As her thoughts hung constantly around her child, I aimed, with all my might, so to connect the idea of her loss with the idea of her personal obligation to religion, that she should not be able to think of her child without thinking of her own salvation. I may not here record all my exhortations to her—it would tire the reader. But I strove to make every recollection say to her, " Prepare to meet your child in heaven." I hunted her soul with that thought, and linked the thought with every recollection. I made it come up with every sigh, and burn in every tear. I associated it with the last look she took of her child, and with that coffin-kiss which I thought would break her heart. I wrote it upon the little grave, and made the green grass that grows over it say to her, " Prepare to meet your child in heaven." The past uttered it to her, the future uttered it. Love, hope, disappointment, grief, every little memorial, was made say to her, " Prepare to meet your child in heaven." I aimed to people the whole universe for her with that one thought, " Prepare to meet your child in heaven." I linked this thought with the morning, the evening, the bed-room, the books,—with all this wilderness world. I painted to her her lost one now bending over the battlements of heaven, and looking down upon her, and saying, " Mother, prepare to meet your child in heaven." I represented to her that lost child now, perhaps, hovering around her as a " ministering spirit" sent forth from heaven, in some mysteriou manner to minister for her as an " heir of salvation," and waiting to carry the tidings of her repentance on high, that there might be a new " joy in the presence of the angels of God."

After beseeching her in this manner to fly to Christ, and praying for her, I took my leave, saying to her with solemn tenderness, " Prepare to meet your child in heaven."

The next morning I perceived that she and her husband were in church, and appeared very attentive to the sermon.

It was not possible for me to call upon her on Monday or Tuesday, as I had intended. Late in the evening of Tuesday, a messenger brought me the following letter :—

"Dr. Spencer.

"Rev. Sir,—I have taken the liberty of addressing a few lines to you. Allow me, in the first place, to *thank* you for your kindness and sympathy towards us, strangers as we were to you. I shall never forget your consoling words; they fell like balm upon a bruised and broken heart. The light and the joy of our home was taken; but the fond hope which your words inspired, that our dear child 'might be hovering over us, missioned from heaven in some mysterious manner to minister to our spirits,' seemed to animate and encourage me not to be weary in well-doing. When I saw you on Saturday, I felt that I was still far from God. I had no heart to read the Bible, no heart to pray. I was overwhelmed with grief; my child was gone, and what had I to live for? It seemed that one thought had taken the place of every other; but I still continued to pray, although my lips uttered words which I thought my heart did not feel. On Sabbath morning, before entering the church, I prayed that God would bless to me the words that I might hear spoken. 'Faith and grace' [alluding to the sermon], they were just what I most needed; but the door of my heart was closed, and they could not enter in. After dinner, I took up a book, and one piece that I read, 'Waiting for conviction,' made me feel that I was standing in just that position. I had been relying upon my own self-righteousness,—waiting for something, I knew not what. I felt as if you were talking to me; every word came home to my heart. I went to my room and prayed, as I had never prayed before, 'God be merciful to me, a sinner.' I was a good deal cast down, and it seemed to me as if I must not retire to rest that night until I had made my peace with God. I passed a restless, weary night; the words kept sounding in my ears, 'Prepare to meet your child in heaven.' I could but cry, Lord have mercy! When I awoke near morning, after a short and restless sleep, I felt as if the work must be accomplished before another day passed over. During the day I felt better, had some comfort in reading the Bible, felt that God had answered my prayers, unworthy as they were. He had convicted me of my sin, and I seemed to have more faith; but still unbelief held its sway. I prayed earnestly for more faith and grace; and as I sat alone in my room in the twilight hour, I thought over all my past life. I had done nothing for God, and he had done everything for me. He had given me a most precious gift, and I had never once thanked the Giver, but went on, in my own pride and self-love, building fond hope and joy for the far-off future; and in a little time she was stricken from my sight. It appeared to me that God had taken that means to bring the parents to repentance; and I felt that it was but right and just. While I thus sat holding communion with my own thoughts, recalling the blessed promises of the Bible, all at once such light, and love, and hope, shone into my heart, it seemed as if I must clap my hands and sing aloud a new song:—

'His loving-kindness—oh, how great!'

"I could kiss the hand that had smitten. The heavy load of sin is gone. Will you, dear sir, be kind enough to call and see me to-morrow? I have no words to thank you for your kindness. I am as a little child just entering upon a new world, and I am afraid my feelings will not last."

———.

In accordance with the request contained in this letter, I called upon her the next morning. She met me with a smile of gladness. Her downcast look was gone—not a trace left of that deep and settled melancholy, which had formerly rested upon her countenance and made her such an image of woe. Her joy and peace seemed to have transformed her into another being. She was perfectly happy. Peace filled her heart, and her countenance was lighted up with the beams of an ecstasy which she could neither repress nor conceal. She was solemn, but "her joy was full." Smiles of peace unbidden would spread like a beam of light over her features; her step, her mien,—the whole woman was changed.

"I wanted to see you," said she—with a look and in an accent of rapture—"I want to tell you how happy I am. I can bless God now. He has been very gracious to me, and I can praise him for all he has done. I can see his goodness in all my affliction. I thought, yesterday, I must go and see you, and have you rejoice with me."

"What makes you so happy?" said I.

"Because God has heard my prayers, and removed my dreadful burden of sin, and given me peace with himself. I know it is not anything that *I* have done—it is the mercy and grace of God. He has heard me, and given me faith and love. I cannot be grateful enough."

"Do you think you have faith now?

"Oh yes, I have faith. I believe and trust Him; for he

has shown me the way, and brought me to this delightful peace. I was very wretched, and could not feel reconciled; but now I see the hand of his kindness in it all. I see the leading of his providence all along, in sending us here and directing us to you. I cannot be thankful enough. I feel very grateful to you for your kindness to us in our affliction. I was afraid to have you come when my child died. You were a stranger to us, and I did not know that you could enter into our feelings; but when I heard you speak at the funeral, my fears vanished; and when you came afterwards and talked to me, I thought God had sent us here, and taken away our child, on purpose to have us led to repentance. I thank you for all you have done."

"Do you *love* God now?"

"Oh yes, I do. I cannot thank him enough. I can submit to his will now, though my loss is so great. I see he meant it for my good."

"Does your heart rest on Christ alone to save you?"

"Yes, I trust him entirely. I have nothing else to trust in. I know I am a great sinner; but he has heard me, and answered me. He has set my heart at rest."

"Have you this peace of mind and joy in God all day long?"

"Sometimes I am afraid I am deceived for a little while; but generally I am very happy. At first I felt as if I could not restrain my feelings. I did not want to come down to tea: I was afraid they would think me crazy, for I knew I could not conceal my joy, my looks would betray me; and I was afraid I should lose my happy feelings.

"I want you to see my young friend. I want you to tell her that she has only to come to Christ,—that she 'need not wait to get ready,' as you told *me* on Saturday. It all seems to me *so easy* now —only to come to God in faith—not wait to get ready. I wonder people do not see it. I wonder that I did not see it before. But I had not faith. Now I can see the way all clear; and this light and peace with God make me very happy. I feel my loss, and cannot but weep; but I know God has done it for my good, and

I am resigned and happy. I thank and praise him for his kindness."

"Have you any doubts or fears to trouble you?"

"Yes, I have at times, for a little while; but when I go to God in prayer, my joy returns. Sometimes I am afraid my feelings are not the right ones, and that I am deceived. I know my heart is deceitful; but I trust in God, and then I am happy. I feel as if I were a little child, and want to be led. I have only just begun to learn. I know but very little, and I am afraid these joyful feelings will not last. God has afflicted me; but now he comforts me."

"You recollect I told you on Saturday that *such* afflictions were very seldom of any benefit to unbelievers."

"I know you did; and it made me feel very sad."

"But you know it is true," said I.

"Oh yes, I know it is true. A great many have lost children, and never come to repentance; and that made me feel the more anxious to improve the time."

Again and again, when I saw her, she conversed in the same happy strain,—affectionate, grateful, and simple-hearted as a child. She was peculiarly desirous that other members of her family should have the same faith and peace of mind which made her so happy. She told them how she felt, with an earnestness, affection, and simplicity which could not be surpassed, and with the manifest impression fixed upon her mind that salvation was freely offered to them, and they had nothing to do but to believe it and accept the offer.

As I was talking with her at one time, in the presence of a young woman in whom she felt a deep interest, and to whom she had done me the favour to introduce me, I thought many of her expressions must reach the young woman's heart. I asked her,—

"Do you still feel the same happiness that you have had?"

"Oh yes, most of the time. Sometimes I have a little darkness, but it soon passes away, and my happy feelings return. God answers my prayers. I go to him for everything. I have just begun. I am a little child, and want to be led all the time. I want some one to teach me whether my feelings are right. But I feel very happy."

Said I, "I wish to ask you one question. You have given some attention to the subject of religion before this time; it has often been on your mind, and you have tried to seek the Lord; and after your child died, you were for some time in great distress and darkness. Now I wish to ask you this question: What kept you so long in darkness—what hindered you, that you did not come to Christ sooner?"

"Oh," said she, "I was *self-righteous:* I had not *faith:* I was trying to do something for myself,—*to get ready* to trust in God."

The eyes of the young woman filled with tears, her breast heaved with emotion, and I could not but hope that the truth, which I had elicited from the lips of her happy friend, would lead *her* to a happiness as precious. At least, she was taught that she *need not* "*wait to get ready*."

Notwithstanding the severity of her affliction, this bereaved mother was uniformly happy. She seemed to live on high. In prayerful communion with God, and in contemplation of heaven, she spent her days in peace. She could not forget her child, and she could not cease to mourn; but her grief for her loss was mingled with joy in God, and many times have I seen tears and smiles blended together on her expressive countenance. She was a most affectionate mother. She loved deeply and tenderly. Her peace of mind, her submission and joy, were not in the least the results of a stupid or a stoical heart; but they were the gift of God, and in the exercise of them she was no less tender and affectionate as a Christian than she was as a mourning mother.

Her deep and tender solicitude for her irreligious friends was a most interesting feature in her character. From the commencement of her seriousness, I had aimed to awaken in her heart an interest in the salvation of others. Several of her "nearest and dearest friends" were, as she said, still in unbelief. From the first she manifested much interest in their eternal welfare; but before the time when she came to her own sweet hope in Christ, her thoughts seemed to be called back from them to herself, and she found an almost insuperable obstacle in her way, whenever she attempted anything for them, even in prayer. Her thoughts were drawn back, and her feelings were borne down by the sadness and gloom of her own mind. But after she came out of that gloom, her heart turned to the subject of *their* salvation with much tenderness and strength of affection. She was not only willing, but prompt and joyful to second any of my attempts to bring them to Christ.

A few weeks after she began to find Christ her refuge, she expressed some of her reflections in the following letter:—

"Dr. Spencer.

"Rev. Sir,—I will intrude upon your time but for a few moments. We have been looking for a visit from you for some days. It has been so pleasant to have you come in and see us, that it really seems as if you had almost forgotten us. I shall ever hold in grateful remembrance your kindness to me; and those consoling words, which fell like balm upon my bruised and sorrowful heart, will never be forgotten. They were the first words that made me feel deeply; and through God I feel that you have been the instrument of opening my eyes—'Whereas I was blind, now I see.' Oh, how beautiful is the plan of salvation! —to be redeemed, to be bought with the price of a Saviour's blood!—to be justified, adopted, and sanctified!—to call God our Father! and when our hearts go forth to him in prayer, to feel that he is so near to us! Oh, that I may be wholly his! My earnest desire is to be a whole-souled Christian, not a half, undecided one. When I look at my poor sinful heart, so prone to wander, so vile, and so full of sin, I almost despair, sometimes, of ever attaining the only worthy end for which to live; but with God all things are possible, and I can but pray to be purified,—'Wash me, and I shall be whiter than snow.' I have spent many calm and peaceful hours in my retirement, communing with my own thoughts and with God, thinking of my angel child as she walks the golden streets of the New Jerusalem. Hers was a bright and joyous spirit on earth, and how much more bright and beautiful there! Heaven does not seem so far off as it once did.

"I often ask myself, when the time comes for me to mingle again with the world, if my heart will be as near to God as it is now. I hope that he will ever guide me. I must watch and pray. Prayer and the precious Bible must be my refuge. How beautifully the hymn,—

'Jesus, lover of my soul,'

warms the heart, and makes it feel indeed that—

'Thou, O Christ, art all I want,—
All in all in thee I find.'

"God has supported and directed me. He seems to know just what I most need. . . . .

"But it seems to me that I know too little of divine truth. I want to be fed with the bread of life, to drink deeper from the fountain of living waters. My health has been such that I have not been able to attend divine service, and I thirst for more knowledge of the Bible. . . . .

"'How beautiful are the feet of him that bringeth good tidings; that publisheth salvation!' I know, my dear sir, that you have often been made very happy, and have felt doubly paid for all the toil and trouble, when sinners have come to you with faith and joy beaming in their countenance, and told you that they had found their God. My request, therefore, will not afflict you, though it should add to your labours. . . . .

"I know your time is much occupied, and you will please pardon my intrusion upon you."

———.

I visited her often. It was delightful to witness her joy. She seemed to live in the sunshine of peace. Seldom were her skies overcast; and when a cloud did darken her heavens, it was only for a moment, and only served to make the returning light more sweet.

"I have sometimes a little darkness," said she.

"And what do you do then?"

"Oh, I pray to God, and the light returns."

"Do you *love* to pray?"

"O yes, I always love to pray. It seems to me such a precious privilege. Whenever I am sad, thinking of my child, or my mind is downcast, I find that when I pray, God answers me and I am comforted. I just go to him with my trouble. It is a precious privilege."

"Have you ever any doubt whether God has given you a new heart?"

"At times I have, for a little while. But the most of the time I cannot doubt; I have such sweet peace in thinking of God, Christ is so precious to me, and all my feelings are so different from what they used to be. I know I am still a sinner. I sin every hour; and I know my heart is deceitful; but I trust in Christ, and God comforts me with hope."

Such were her feelings week after week. Her joy was full. Her faith appeared to grow stronger; and while her humility became more deep, the tenderness of her love and her *confiding* became more and more peaceful.

When our communion season came, she did not unite with the church. She thought it best to defer the public profession of her faith for a time. But she was present at the administration of the ordinance of the Lord's supper. A day or two afterwards I called upon her, and she adverted to it with a very manifest delight.

Said she, "I had a happy day last Sunday. When I saw those young persons come forward to unite with the Church, I longed to be with them. I thought it would be such a privilege, to confess my faith in the Lord Jesus Christ, and aim to honour him before so many people. And when the members of the Church were partaking of the bread and wine, they all appeared so solemn and happy,—I wondered that anybody *could stay away*. It was the happiest day I ever saw. I thought the Lord was there to comfort his people. It seemed to me that they had the peace of heaven; and I hoped the time would come when I should myself be with that great company and partake of their joy."

"Such occasions," said I, "have been profitable seasons to us."

"Oh, I think they must be," said she. "Though I was only a spectator, I felt it was good for me to be there; and I did not wonder when you said that you scarcely recollected a communion season when there was not at least some one sinner awakened to seek the Lord. It seems to me that nobody could have witnessed the exercises of last Sunday unmoved. I should think that every spectator would be convinced of the presence of Christ, and the happiness of communion with him. I look forward with delight to the time when I shall come myself to that solemn spot, and give away myself to our Lord Jesus Christ."

In due time she *did* come. Years have since rolled away, and she still lives a happy believer—one of the *few* whom bereavement has called out of the world's allurements, and aided towards Christ and heaven.

If this publication should ever meet her eye, I am aware it may open afresh the fountains of her grief,—and that is the only idea which makes me hesitate about giving this narrative to the world. But I am sure she will *know* that it is not in my heart to afflict her, by exposing to the world the sacredness of her sorrow, or by recalling to her mind a scene which grief burnt upon her memory; and I am sure she will pardon me the liberty I have taken, when she shares with me the hope, that some *mourning mother* will be led to Christ by this narrative of THE LOST CHILD—not lost, but gone before.

'Twas a gem fit for love,—'twas the gift of her God,
But no thanks did the gift e'er excite;
Death snatched it away—she sunk under the rod!
All her world was a chaos of night!

Then there whispered a voice from the land of the blest,
Oh, my mother, my mother! on high
I wait to receive thee to this land of sweet rest
Oh, my mother, prepare thee to die.

I'm not in the dark coffin,—Christ spread his arms round me,
I awoke 'mid this light and this love,
Where the bright beams of heaven spread their glory around me;
For *I* died to allure *thee* above.

She heard it; she felt that attraction of heaven,—
It was peace: she can now kiss the rod;
She flew to her Christ—she's a sinner forgiven,—
They shall meet in the bosom of God.

This is one of the few instances that have come within my own knowledge, wherein the sorrows of mourning have been of any lasting spiritual benefit to an unbeliever. To God's people bereavements and sorrows are sanctified. This is general, if not universal. Our observation can behold it, and we often hear the testimony from their own lips. But to the "children of this world," their days of mourning are very much in vain. They can bury their friends, and with a depth and tenderness and bitterness of mourning weep over their loss; but in a few brief days their hearts turn back again upon the world, and they go on as carelessly and gaily as before. The place of the funeral is a very hopeless place for preaching the gospel to unbelievers. I recollect but two instances before this, in a ministry of more than twenty years, in which anything that I ever said at a funeral has been the means of arousing and leading to Christ a single impenitent sinner. The hope which irreligious persons so frequently indulge, that some future affliction, when it shall come, the loss of some loved and valued friend, will lead them to religion, is almost universally a hope of entire vanity and deception. They do not know their own hearts. Both observation and experience prove such a hope to be delusive. Bleeding hearts are not necessarily penitent ones. Among hundreds whom I have heard, at the time of their reception into the Church, giving an account of the manner in which they had been led to religion, I recollect *only two* who mentioned the death of a friend as the means of leading them to seek God. The member of a family dies, but the survivors do not become pious. Indeed, so common is this—such an ordinary historical fact, that scarcely a man among us can point to a single instance where the doings of death, and the effectual workings of the Holy Spirit to convert to Christ, have gone side by side. Indeed, unbelieving hearts, crushed with a burden of sorrow in the dark and dreadful days of mourning, are more apt to be injured than benefited by the bitterness of their sad experience. I knew of a woman, many years since, whose attention had been earnestly directed to the subject of religion, and who, for some weeks, had been prayerfully attempting to seek the Lord, when she was suddenly summoned to the death-bed of one of her children in a neighbouring state. She came home from the funeral of that child; and immediately after her return, several other relatives of her own family were brought to her house, disfigured corpses, having been killed by a steamboat explosion. No one could have been more shocked, or more deeply plunged into anguish than was she. "Now," said she, referring to her loss a day or two afterwards, "I give up the world; it is nothing to me any longer." But when, by the lapse of time, her grief had somewhat lost its poignancy, her seriousness was all gone. Her grief had dissipated her religious anxiety: she had forgotten the subject of her salvation; and relapsing into her former indifference, she went on for months and months in her irreligion and prayerlessness, as unconcerned as ever.

Such things appear strange and wonderful to many people. At the first thought, probably, such a thing appears wonderful to everybody. But I think it is a thing susceptible of a very intelligible explanation. Sorrow leads the mind one way, and seriousness about salvation leads it quite another. Grief for a lost friend is one thing, and grief on account of sin is quite another thing. When a sinner is seeking salvation, his thoughts are turned upon his sins, his soul, his eternity, his God and Saviour; but when he is overwhelmed with personal affliction and sorrow, his thoughts are turned upon his loss. Then, it is not his *sin* that troubles him; no, he is just thinking of his loved one dead, —his child, his sister, or his father taken from him, and now buried in the deep, dark grave. His mind is now called off from the state, the guilt and danger of his own immortal soul, from his need of Christ to save him, and of the Holy Spirit to "renew a right spirit within him." *Whatever* it may be that leads him to forget his sins, does him an injury. Any diversion of his thoughts to a new channel does him an injury. The channel may be *more* dark, more distressful, more dreadful to him; but his attention has become diverted to a new object, and that "one thing needful" is at present crowded away into the back-ground of his contemplations, or forgotten entirely. And hence, the deeper his sorrow, the more dangerous its influence becomes. His affliction just makes him forget his sins and his soul.

And thus it is, as I suppose, that we behold, all over the world, the mourning of unbelievers so seldom attended or followed by any religious benefits. Their thoughts are on their loss—their earthly loss. The death of their friend has spread a gloom over the world. Their house lacks an inmate,—their heart lacks a friend to lean upon along the pilgrimage of life. Another star has gone out, and left a dark spot in their heavens, which once appeared so bright and beautiful to their eye. A seat is left vacant at the fire-side,—a friend is absent from the table, a familiar voice is missed in the family circle. But all these are earthly griefs. They are not spiritual ones to an unbeliever. The mourning unbeliever *never* much prized his now lost friend, as an aid to his holiness and salvation; he prized him only for earthly reasons. He *never* loved the lost one as a companion to go hand in hand with him to Jerusalem, or along the vales of Palestine, amid the fragrance and beauty of "the rose of Sharon and the lily of the valley." He *never* loved his companionship because his lips were vocal with the melody of "another country, even an heavenly," which he hoped to reach; but simply because his companionship made earth more pleasing, not heaven nearer. And, therefore, when death has snatched away his now lost companion, only an earthly sorrow takes possession of the heart,—just that "sorrow of the world which worketh death." And when he turns away from the grave of his buried friend, or, in the dark days that follow, thinks of him so mournfully, the whole effect of his sorrow is just to make the world more dreary; not the world to come more gladsome and inviting. If he had lived with his friend *as a Christian*, it would have been very different with him now, when his friend is no more; and the death he deplores would have made his thoughts hang more fondly around the *religious* things, in which he and his friend used to aid and comfort one another. But he did not; he was an unbeliever (*himself*, whatever his lost friend may have been); and, therefore, the death which has saddened him just confines his thoughts to this dark and dreary *world*, instead of leading them towards the *world* of immortality.

God is infinitely willing to sanctify to men their sorrows, and bring the beams of gladness over the dark days of their mourning. But men misuse their times of sorrow. The sad history of thousands of hearts that have bled, demonstrates but too plainly this melancholy truth,—our piety seldom springs from the grave that our tears have watered.

III.

The Stormy Night;

OR, PERSEVERANCE.

THE most remarkable instance of protracted and determined perseverance in seeking God that has ever come within my knowledge, was that of a young married woman, whose seriousness commenced soon after I had visited her at her own house for the first time. The conversation that I then had with her, as she afterwards told me, "led her to make up her mind that she *would* seek the Lord, and would not stop till she believed her salvation was secure." The one consideration, and, so far as I could ever ascertain, the only one, which had any special influence to lead her to form this resolution and begin to act upon it, was taken from the assurance I gave her in my first conversation with her, that salvation was within her reach,—that she might be a Christian if she would,—that she would not seek the Lord in vain, if she only sought him with all her heart. "You told me, sir," said she to me, years afterwards, "I should not seek God in vain. Your words were (I remember well, and always shall), '*I know*, Mrs. E——, that you will be saved, if you seek God with all your heart.'"

She tried to do so. She came to my house, for conversation with me about her salvation, almost every Sabbath evening for nearly two years. In the depth of winter, on a cold, stormy night, the wind blowing violently, the snow drifting into the path, in some places more than two feet in depth (as I found on accompanying her home),—one of the most unpleasant and even terrific nights for a woman to be abroad,—she came nearly half a mile to my house alone. As I opened the door for her admission that stormy night, I uttered an expression of surprise,—"Why, Mrs. E——! are you here on such a night?" And I shall never forget the severe, *deserved* rebuke, which she unwittingly gave me some time afterwards, in reference to that expression. "It stumbled me," said she. "I did not know what to make of it. You had invited us there, and I thought you would be expecting me. I thought you ought not to be *surprised* to see me there, if sinners were in danger of the everlasting wrath of God and might escape it, as you had preached that day. It was a long time before I could get over that stumbling-block. I thought, if you had *believed* what you preached, and felt about it as I did, you would *expect* to see me. I know it was a stormy night, and I was afraid; but I kept thinking as I went, that the day of judgment would bring a worse storm, as you said once in your sermon—'Hail-stones and coals of fire.'" This she said to me more than a year afterwards, and after she had attained hope in the mercy of God through Christ Jesus.

At the same time she told me another thing, which added keenness to her unintentional rebuke. She said that her husband, at that time an irreligious man, was very unwilling that she should venture out on that stormy night, and strongly urged her to stay at home, when he found she proposed to go. "But," said she, "he told me afterwards that my going to your house that night was the first thing which brought him to reflection; for he thought there must be *something* about sin and religion which he did not know anything about, if I would go to your house in such a storm all alone. I did not know it at that time; but when he told me afterwards, I remembered that he looked very cross when I came home, and I thought he was angry because I went. But I was not going to mind *that*. I knew I had done rightly, and I was not going to let anything turn me aside from trying to be a Christian. And don't you remember, three Sunday nights after that, he came to your house with me?"

Month after month this woman's deep anxiety continued. I never could discover why she lingered so long in her unbelief. Again and again I aimed, with all possible carefulness, to tell her all the truths of the gospel, and to discover what error, sin, or temptation kept her from repentance and peace with God. But I never could discover her hindrance; and she never could tell me, then or afterwards, of any difficulty or temptation which had troubled her, except the expression I made to her on that stormy night. And in justice to her I ought to say, that she did not mention that as having been a hindrance, though she called it a stumbling-block; but mentioned it casually and in another connection—not to find fault with me, and not to account for her continuing so long in unbelief. Far from this. She was one of the most modest of women, and one of the most affectionate and devoted friends I ever had. Nothing, I am sure, could ever have tempted her to find fault with me, or utter a syllable with any intent to censure me or wound my feelings. *Before* that memorable night of storms, when her presence surprised me, she had been for months an anxious inquirer.

It was a most painful and perplexing thing to discharge my pastoral duty to this woman. I could not understand her state of mind. She was frank, she concealed nothing, she told me all her heart, she was desirous of being interrogated. She was, moreover, an intelligent, well-educated woman, and had been trained in early life by religious parents. But I could not even conjecture what kept her in her unbelief, since for so long a time she had known the truth, and had such powerful strivings of the Holy Spirit. And what then could I say to her? How could I hope to do her any good?

She came to me so many times, and I had so many times told her all that I knew about the way of salvation, and so many times presented to her every motive of the gospel, and invited and urged her to cast herself upon Christ, that I did not know what more to say or do; and time after time I was half sorry to see her come into my house, and then ashamed of myself because my heart had such a feeling. I knew not what to do. At one time I was on the point of telling her that I had nothing more to say to her, and she need not come to me again. But I could not do it. She was so miserable, so sincere, so determined, docile, and confiding, that it was impossible for me to cast her off. I afterwards rejoiced that I had not done it. Her husband became pious, her sister, and others of her friends, all of whom began to seek God after she did; and yet, there she stood, the same unhappy, unconverted sinner. She did not advance, and she did not go back. Time after time I assured her that her lingering was unnecessary, and would gain her nothing,—that she had but to trust herself to the arms of Christ outstretched to receive her, —that "without faith it was impossible for her to please God," or gain an item of profit to her own soul. A hundred times I cautioned her most solemnly against putting any trust in her perseverance, for that she was persevering in the wrong course while in her unbelief, and the further she went, the worse would be her condition. Time after time, the Bible in my hand, and she in tears before me, as a minister of God, and on his authority, I offered her a free salvation, and demanded her heart's faith, and instant submission to divine authority and unbounded love. Her mind, her conscience, her heart, I besieged with all the kindness of Christ. I explained to her such passages of the Scriptures as "the marriage which a certain king made for his son,"—and "the prodigal," who, in a far country, "began to be in want." All would not do.

As far as I could discover, she had for many weary months a full conviction of all the great doctrines of the Bible,—of the entire depravity of her heart, of her sin and danger under the law as a condemned sinner, of the impossibility of her salvation but by Christ, and of the full and free salvation offered to her in the love of God, on the ground of the great atonement. I have never spent half as much time with any other awakened sinner, or uttered to any other one half as many threatenings and promises of God, or kneeled with any other half as many times in prayer. But, so far as I know, she never received any benefit from it all, unless that was a benefit which she one day suggested to me long afterwards, when she said, " If *you* had been discouraged with me, *I* should have been discouraged,—and should have given up trying to be saved."

She persevered. She became a child of hope and peace. She united herself with the people of God ; and now, after more than thirteen years, she still lives in the enjoyment of Christian hope. Neither she nor I—nay, nor her husband—will ever forget that *stormy night.*

Ministers ought never to despair of the salvation of any sinner. To despair of any one, is just the way to make him despair of himself. Many have been ruined in this way, probably. We ought to *expect* sinners to repent,—and treat them accordingly. Who shall limit the Holy One of Israel? It took me long to learn the lesson, but I have learnt *never to give up a sinner.* We must urge the duty of an immediate faith and repentance, as the Bible does so continually; but we should be careful to enjoin this duty *in such a manner* that, if it is not immediately *done*, the individual shall not be led or left to cease seeking God. Many a sinner turns back, when just at the door of heaven.

IV.

The Choice:

HOLD ON, OR LET GO.

MANY months after the foregoing sketch was all written, together with the reflections I have made upon it as they are printed above, I had an opportunity for conversation with my persevering friend, and I made another attempt to learn, as I had sometimes tried to learn before, what it was that kept her in her unbelief for so long a time, in those dark days of her wearisome perseverance.

"You have asked me that," said she, "more than once before, and I never could tell you. I have often thought of it, but it always seemed mysterious to me. I believed the Spirit had led me, but I did not know how. But a while ago, in one of my backslidings, I thought I found out something about it."

"Well, how was it?"

"I was in a cold state," said she. "I had lost all the little light I ever had. I knew I had done wrong. I had too much neglected prayer, my heart had become worldly; and for a good many weeks I was in trouble and fear, for I knew I had wandered far from God. Then I thought I felt just as I used to feel before I had any hope, when I was coming to your house so often. And then I tried to recollect what I did to come to the light at that time, so as to do the same thing now. But I couldn't remember anything about it. However, while I was trying, one thing came to my mind which did me some good. You know your sermon that you preached just before I came to have any hope,—I don't remember the text,—but it was about wandering sinners lost on the mountains."

"No, indeed, madam, I have no recollection of it."

"Well, I can't tell you what it was; I can't repeat it; may be I can tell enough to make you remember. I know you represented us in that sermon as lost sinners,—lost in the woods, wandering over mountain after mountain in dark and dangerous places among the rocks and precipices, not knowing where we were going. It grew darker and darker. We were groping along, sometimes on the brink of a dreadful precipice, and didn't know it. Then some of us began to fall down the steep mountains, and thought we should be dashed to pieces. I know *I* thought so. But we caught hold of the bushes to hold ourselves up by them. Some bushes would give way, and then we would catch others, and hold on till they gave way, broke, or tore up by the roots; and then we would catch others, and others. Don't you remember it, sir?"

"Partly. But go on."

"Well, you said our friends were calling to us, as we hung by the bushes on the brink, and we called to one another, '*Hold on—hold on.*' Then you said this cry, '*Hold on—hold on*,' might be a very natural one for anybody to make, if he should see a poor creature hanging over the edge of a precipice, clinging to a little bush with all his might, if the man didn't see anything *else*. But you said there was another thing to be seen, which these '*hold on*' people didn't seem to know anything about. You said the Lord Jesus Christ was down at the bottom of the precipice, lifting up both hands to catch us, if we would consent to fall into his arms, and was crying out to us, '*Let go—let go—let go.*' Up above, all around where we were, you said they were crying out, '*Hold on—hold on.*' Down below, you said, Jesus Christ kept crying out, 'Let go—let go;' and if we only knew who he was, and would *let go* of the bushes of sin and self-righteousness, and fall into the arms of Christ, we should be saved. And you said we had better stop our noise, and *listen*. and hear *his* voice, and *take* his advice, and '*let go.*'"

"Don't you recollect that sermon, sir?"

"Yes, only you have preached it better than I did."

"Well, when I remembered that sermon last spring, in my dark, back-slidden state, I tried to obey it. I 'let go' of *everything*, and trusted myself to Christ; and in a little while my heart was comforted,—my hope came back again. And afterwards, when I was wondering at it, I thought perhaps it was just so when you preached that sermon a great while ago, when I was first led to have a hope of salvation. But I never thought of it before; I don't know how I found peace and hope the first time, if this was not the way. I suppose we have to make our choice whether to 'hold on' to something which can't save us, or 'let go,' and *fall into the hands of the Lord.*"

The efforts of a legal spirit are directly the opposite of an evangelical faith. By nature every sinner resorts to the law. It cannot save him. He must let go of that, and fall into the arms of Christ. *Faith* saves, and Jesus Christ is the sole object of faith.

V.

The Neglected Bible.

IN the month of February 18—, I called at the house of a family, which I had several times visited before. I knew them well, and my purpose was to make another attempt to do them good. They were very poor, their home was very uncomfortable, their apparel dirty and ragged; and what was most mournful of all, these evils were manifestly occasioned by intemperance. The husband and father was an intemperate man, as all his acquaintance knew, and as anybody would know by the sight of him; and the wife and mother was an intemperate woman, as I was frequently told, and as her appearance but too plainly indicated. Such they had been for more than a score of years. They had several small children, who were miserably clothed and repulsively dirty, appearing to be little cared for by either father or mother. They had one daughter, the eldest of their children, a very worthy girl, of about eighteen years, who was a seamstress, supporting herself in a very respectable manner, and moving in respectable society. But she seldom or never went home. She had left her parents, because she could not live with them any longer. She once told me that she could not endure the pain of seeing her father, and especially her mother, in such a condition as they were; and when she had sometimes gone home to see them, after she left them, they only complained of her, and reproached her for her pride, because she had dressed herself in a decent manner, and because she would not consent to board at home any longer. Her mother had once requested me to induce her to return to them; but after learning all the circumstances, and hearing the daughter's touching story from her own lips, I had no heart to do it,—I could not attempt it,—I told the poor girl that in my opinion she was right in staying away. She could do them no good. She had tried it. She was only reproached if she called upon them. The treatment she received made her the more unhappy; and she once told me, with bitter weeping, that when she went there at all, she "came away with such a feeling of shame, that it made her wretched for a month." It was a very delicate thing for me, and a very painful one, to mention the subject to her; but I trust I was enabled to do it in such a manner as to wound her feelings but little, and to gain her respect and confidence entirely. She certainly gained mine.

On the morning to which I now allude, I knocked at the door, and the old woman opened it and looked at me without uttering a word. She did not even respond to my "good morning;" and when I inquired more particularly how she was, in as kind and respectful a manner as I could, she scarcely made any reply. She did not ask me to walk in; but as the door was open, and she did not forbid me, I passed into the house. Thinking that she might perhaps be a little disconcerted by my coming at a time inconvenient for her to see me, I told her, as I went into the house, that "I would not hinder her long; I had called for only a minute, to see how she was."

"I am glad to see you," said she, with a low voice and a very sullen look. She appeared so different from what I had ever seen her before, so downcast and sad, that I thought she might be unwell, and therefore inquired particularly if she "was sick."

"I am well," was her brief and solemn reply, uttered in a low and sepulchral tone.

In order to make her feel at ease, if possible, I seated myself upon a chair. It was covered with dust; and her whole room, as I had often found it before, was so far from being decently clean, that I hesitated to sit down in it. Everything was in disorder.

The floor had not been swept, apparently, for a week,—the ashes were scattered over the hearth-stone,—the scanty furniture was most of it broken, and resembling one of the chairs, which had but three legs, and was lying on its back; the ceiling was festooned with cobwebs, that had caught the floating dust, and as they waved to and fro in the wind, they appeared like a mournful token of the wretchedness which seemed to have taken possession of her heart.

I made several attempts to lead her into some conversation, but it was all in vain—she spake only in muttered monosyllables. This surprised me. I had many times visited her before, and had supposed that my attention to her, my familiarity and kindness, had entirely won her esteem and good-will. Indeed, I had supposed myself quite a favourite with her. Though I had sometimes reproved her very plainly, I had always done it affectionately, and she had always treated me politely, and as a friend. But now all was changed. She was cold and mute. She appeared very much as if she had been angry, and moved about the room adjusting her little stock of furniture, as if too sad or too sullen to be conscious of my presence. She scarcely noticed me at all.

Most sincerely I pitied her. I saw she appeared very wretched. I thought of her poverty, of her better days, of her youth, of her children, and of her sins and her soul. She was of a respectable family, and had received a respectable education in her youth. I had often thought, in my previous conversations with her, that she possessed a superior mind. And now to behold her in this miserable condition, and no prospect before her of any relief, a disgrace to herself, to her children, wretched and heart-broken, was too touching a thing to allow of any other feelings than those of compassion and kindness. My heart bled for her. I could not have uttered a word of censure, even if my principles would have allowed it. I resolved to soothe and console her for a moment, if I could, before I left her. Said I,—

"Mrs. B——, do you remember what I was speaking to you about, when I was here the week before last?"

"*Yes*," said she, with a low and sepulchral voice.

"You know I told you that you had no reason to be discouraged."

"I know you did," said she mournfully.

"I told you that I thought you a woman of superior sense, and capable even yet of doing a great deal of good to yourself and your family."

"What can *I* do?" said she, in a tone of despair.

"My dear friend, I *told* you when you asked me the question the other day. With God's blessing, if you will seek it, you may do *anything* you wish—you may be respected and happy here, and be saved in the world to come."

I paused, but she made no reply. Said I,—

"Have you thought of what I told you *then?*"

She gave no answer. Said I,—

"Have you any disposition to try to seek God, and aim to gain everlasting life?"

Still she was silent. Rising from my seat, and stepping towards the door, I said to her,—

"I am aware that I have called on you rather early in the morning, and I will not hinder you any longer now. If you will allow me, I shall be glad to call on you at another time."

I offered her my hand to bid her good-bye; but instead of taking it, she placed her hand against the door to hinder me from opening it, saying, in a firm and solemn tone, "*Don't go.*"

"I will stay longer," said I, "if you wish me to do so. I will do anything in my power for you, Mrs. B——, most willingly; but I suppose—," lifting my hand to the latch—

"*Don't* go," said she, placing her shoulder firmly against the door, to keep it from opening.

"What can I do for you?" said I.

She did not answer.

"Is there anything you wish to say to me, Mrs. B——? I hope you will speak freely to me. I assure you I will treat you with all kindness, and I think you know me well enough to trust me."

Still she did not answer. She stood like a statue of stone, her eyes fixed on the ground, her large frame slightly bending forward, and her countenance strongly indicative of deep thought and melancholy emotions. She seemed lost in her own contemplations. I considered her for a short time in silence. She moved not—she spake not—she never raised her eyes upon me—she scarcely breathed. I knew not what to think of her. She appeared angry, and yet it was not anger. Her solemn look, fixed and indescribable, made her resemble one wrought up to an iron determination for some mighty purpose. Said I,—

"Mrs. B——, you appear to feel unhappy this morning. What has occurred to trouble you? or can I assist you in any way?"

She drew a long breath, but remained as silent as ever, lost in thought, or in some wilderness of emotions. I did not know what to make of her. Evidently she was sober. At first I had thought she was angry, but her voice gave no indication of anger in the few syllables which she had uttered. I could not leave her, for she stood motionless by the door, in such a position that I could not open it without swinging it against her, to push her out of the way. She held me her prisoner.

I knew not what to say, but concluded to make another attempt to find what was occupying her thoughts. Said I,-

"Mrs. B——, I wish you would tell me what makes you so unhappy. I should think you *would* tell me; I have always been a friend to you, and I think you have reason to confide in me."

"I know you have," said she, as unmoved and solemn as ever.

"Then tell me what is the matter,—what troubles you?"

"I am a *great sinner!*" said she, slowly and with deep solemnity.

"That is true, and a much greater sinner than you think."

"I am *such* a sinner!" said she, with a countenance as fixed and cold as marble.

"Yes, I am glad you have found it out; for now you will see the necessity of fleeing to that Saviour of whom I have spoken to you so many times, as your only ground of hope."

"I am *undone for ever!*" said she, with a look of cold, fixed despair.

"You *would* be, if there were no mercy in God, and no Christ Jesus to save. But God is able and willing to save all sinners who repent of sin and forsake it, and put all their trust in Christ."

"I have sinned a great while!"

"And God has borne with you a great while, simply because he is 'not willing' that you 'should perish, but come to repentance.' Have you been praying to God to save you?"

"Yes; I prayed a long time last night, and I have been praying this morning till you came in."

"What did you pray *for?*"

"I prayed that God would forgive me."

"And do you think he will?"

"I am afraid not! I am a very great sinner."

"Jesus Christ, madam, is a very great Saviour. He will save all that come to him in faith. The *greatness* of your sins cannot ruin you, if you will but repent of them and forsake them, trusting to the great Redeemer of sinners for pardon, through his atoning blood. 'The blood of Jesus Christ cleanseth from *all* sin.'"

"*Will* God have mercy upon me *now*, after all I have done?" said she, for the first time lifting her eyes upon me, with a beseeching look.

"Yes, he will; he *says* he will. 'Though your sins be as scarlet, they shall be as white as snow; though they be red like crimson, they shall be as wool.'"

"I have been an awful sinner! I am a poor creature, unworthy of anything but God's curse!"

"True, all true, madam; but Christ is infinitely worthy, has borne the punishment due to sinners, and is willing to save you."

"I wish I could think so," said she, with the same fixed and despairing look.

"You *may* think so; God thinks so."

"There is no mercy for me any longer!"

"So *you* think, but God thinks differently. You and he do not think alike. He thinks right, and you think wrong. You must fling away your own thoughts and act on his. And that is what he means in that expression in Isaiah, 'Let the wicked forsake his way, and the unrighteous man his *thoughts:* and let him return unto the Lord, and he *will have* mercy upon him; and to our God, for he *will* abundantly pardon. For my thoughts are not your thoughts, neither are your ways my ways, saith the Lord.' Your *thoughts,* madam, your most sincere and sober thoughts, are to be *forsaken.* Your thoughts are wrong. Fling them away, and use God's thoughts. His thoughts are right. You think differently from him, and therefore your thoughts are not to govern you. 'Let the unrighteous man forsake his thoughts.' You think wrong about God, and wrong about yourself, and wrong about sin, and wrong about forgiveness. I do not mean that you think yourself a greater sinner than you are, for you have not yet seen the half of your guilt and danger; but you think wrong about God's readiness to forgive you. Remember that he says, 'Let the unrighteous man forsake his thoughts.' And then, a little after, he says again, 'My thoughts are not your thoughts;' and goes on to say, 'for as the heavens are higher than the earth, so are my thoughts higher than your thoughts.' What does he mean by all this? He means that it does not belong to *you* to tell what God will do or will not do. If you undertake to tell, you will be sure to tell wrong, because you think wrong. You must let *him* tell what he will do. And he is telling in that very passage about the forgiveness which you say you cannot think there is for you: 'Let him return unto the Lord, and he will have mercy upon him.' But the sinner does not think so; and therefore God says it over again, as if he would beat it into the poor sinner's heart, 'Let him return unto our God, for he will *abundantly* pardon.'" She shook her head with a slow desponding motion, as I went on. "You do not think so, but God does. He *tells* you, 'My thoughts are not your thoughts, neither are your ways my ways.' Your thoughts this minute are, 'I am a great sinner;'—God's thoughts are, 'I will have mercy upon her.' Your thoughts are, 'I have sinned too long to be forgiven;'—God's thoughts are, 'I will abundantly pardon her.' I should like to show you that whole chapter. I want to read it to you. Have you got a Bible, Mrs. B——?"

Without uttering a word, she slowly moved from the door to the other side of the room, placed a chair beneath a high shelf, that was made of a single rough board, and hung up on rude wooden brackets, almost up to the ceiling of the room. She then stepped upon the chair, and reaching her hand upon the shelf, felt along till she found it, and took down her Bible. She stood upon the chair, and gazed on it as she held it in her hand, with a fixed look. Then she slowly stepped down from the chair holding her Bible in her hand, and stopped and gazed upon it, motionless, and without uttering a word. It was covered all over with dust, soot, and cobwebs, appearing as if it had not been handled for years. I thought her heart smote her, as she held it unopened and looked down upon it. I thought I could see "the iron enter into her soul." I did not disturb her. I was willing she should meditate and remember. There she stood, motionless as a stone, with her eyes fixed upon her Bible, and I did not think it was best for me to say anything to her,—the dusty, cobwebbed Bible was speaking! The tears gushed from the eyes, and fell in quick drops upon its blackened board. Slowly she lifted her tattered apron, and wiped off the tears and the dust, and deliberately turning towards me she extended to me the book—"*There* is my *Bible!*" said she, with a bitterness of accent that I shall never forget. She turned from me, with both hands lifted her dusty, ragged apron to her face, and wept aloud.

I could not but weep too. It was a scene surpassing, I am sure, the genius of any painter.

When she had become a little composed, I requested her to sit down by me, and then directing her eye to the expressions, I read and explained to her the fifty-fifth chapter of Isaiah.

I attempted some further conversation with her, but she did not seem so much inclined to talk as to listen. At her request I prayed with her; and when I was about to leave her, I inquired,—

"How long have you been in this state of mind, Mrs. B——, feeling that you are such a sinner?"

"Since last night."

"What led you to feel so last night?"

"It was a little book that I read."

"What book was it?"

"Sixteen Short Sermons."

"Whose sermons were they?"

"I don't know. I came across the book somewhere about the house. I don't know where it came from."

"I mean who *wrote* the Sermons?"

"I don't know."

"Where is the book? I should like to see it."

"It is not here. I lent it this morning to Mrs. A——" a near neighbour.

"Did Mrs. A—— ask to read it herself?"

"Yes. She was in here, and would make me tell her what was the matter with me; and after I told her, she said she wanted to read the Sermons too. So I lent it to her, a little while before you came in."

Taking leave of Mrs. B——, I went immediately to call on Mrs. A——. I found her in tears. She had become alarmed about her condition as a sinner against God. She frankly expressed to me her convictions and fears, adding with great emphasis, "What *shall* I do?" Of course I conversed with her, and explained the way of salvation. But she said nothing about the book, until, as I was about to leave her, I inquired what it was that had inclined her to attend to her salvation. "It was a little book that

Mrs. B—— lent me this morning," said she; and taking it from under her Bible that lay on the table, she put it into my hand. Then I discovered that it was a tract, bearing the title, "Sixteen Short Sermons,"—one of the publications of the American Tract Society, which I had entirely forgotten, if I had ever read it, so that I did not recognise it by the title.

After this I often visited Mrs. B——, and had many an interesting conversation with her. In one of these conversations she referred gently and humbly to her daughter, and not, as I had formerly heard her, with manifest anger and ill-will. She said, "I should like to see her,—I have not seen her for many months; but I suppose it hurts the poor child's feelings to come home and find us—as we have been. I hope we shall not always be so." I immediately went to see her daughter, and alone, and in as delicate a manner as I could, I told her of her mother's altered feelings, and suggested the propriety of her going to see her. She wept bitterly and long. It was almost impossible to comfort her at all; and before I left her, I found it was not her mortification and shame about her mother, so much as her anxiety about her own salvation, which caused her distress. She had already heard of her mother's seriousness, and that was one of the causes of her own. But she did not go to see her mother. I pointed her to Christ as well as I could, and left her.

A few days after this I called upon the daughter again. I went to tell her of her mother's happy hope in Christ, which she had just expressed to me for the first time; and to my no small joy and surprise, I found that the daughter had been led to the same sweet hope also. "*Now,*" said she, the tears of joy coursing down her youthful and beautiful cheeks, "*now*, I can go tc see *my mother*."

She did go. She opened the door, and found the old woman alone. "My *mother!*" said she,—and she could say no more. In an instant they were clasped in each other's arms, both bathed in tears of unutterable joy.

That humble dwelling soon became as neat as grace had made

its inmates happy. The daughter went home. She aided her mother in all her domestic duties with a glad and grateful heart. She made their house as attractive as it had been repulsive. She made clothes for the younger children, and having assisted her mother to dress them in a neat and respectable manner, the old woman went with them herself to the Sabbath school, and requested to have their names put on the roll; "for," said she, "they will be here every Sabbath if you will be so kind as to teach them the Bible."

That house and its inmates were very different in June from what they had been in February. Neatness and peace reigned where there had been filthiness, and clamour, and contention, through year after year of misery. The whole appearance of the woman was changed. She did not look like the same being. She became dignified, lady-like, intelligent, easy in her manners; and, though always solemn, she was uniformly contented and happy. "It seems to me," said she, "that I need but one thing more, and my cup is full; if my husband would only quit his ways, and turn to God, it seems to me we should be happy enough." But he never did. He continued his intemperance. I exerted all my skill to persuade him to forsake his ruinous course; but I met him thirteen years afterwards, staggering in the street.

Eight months after the time when I found this woman so suddenly awakened to a sense of her situation, by "a little book that she had read," I baptized both her and her daughter, and they were received into the Church together. Mrs. A——, her neighbour, who borrowed the book, was received and baptized at the same time. When the old woman presented herself in the church for the reception of baptism, her neighbours and friends, who had been acquainted with her for a score of years, did not know who she was,—her appearance was so altered; and I found it difficult the next day to make them believe that it was verily their old neighbour, whom they had pitied and despaired of so long.

There was nothing of any marked peculiarity in this woman's religious experience, unless it was her deep humility and her iron determination, manifest always from the very beginning of her conviction; and after her conversion, her unbounded gratitude to God. "Who could have thought," said she, "that God would have had mercy upon such a creature as I?"

That "little book," the "Sixteen Short Sermons," lent from house to house through the neighbourhood, did good service in that season of a revival of religion, which I have always supposed originated from its influence, more than from any other thing. However this may have been (and I believe there is a great deal of foolish error abroad among the Churches in attempting to account for revivals of religion, and trace their origin), the name of Mrs. B—— stands recorded in my private book, the very first name in the list of the hopeful converts to Christ in that revival —a list containing more than two hundred and fifty names.

As long as I continued to be her pastor, Mrs. B—— always appeared to me to be a humble and happy Christian. There was uniformly an air of deep solemnity about her, of profound humility, and a cast of mournfulness too, whenever she adverted to her past life, or the time of her hopeful conversion. The remembrance of what she was seems to have thrown a sombre shade over her character. Twenty years have passed away, and she still lives, enjoying the Christian confidence and affection of her Church.

I have sometimes called upon her, since I ceased to be her pastor and removed to another and distant place. At one time I visited her after an interval of thirteen years. I did not expect she would know me. I knocked at the door—she invited me in —and taking a seat, I asked some business-like questions about two or three of her neighbours. She responded readily to my questions, but kept her eyes fixed upon me, with a kind of curious and doubtful inquisitiveness. This questioning and answering and inspecting continued for several minutes, till I supposed that the nature of my questions had thoroughly concealed my identity. Finally, I asked her,—

"Have you got a Bible?"

Adjusting her spectacles to her eyes with both her hands, she replied,—

"Ain't *you* priest *Spencer?* Them are the same eyes that used to look right through me. How *do* you do? I am glad to see you."

"I am no *priest*," said I.

"Well, we used to *call* ministers so when I was young. It is just like you to come and see me. But I didn't expect it."

I inquired whether she still kept her "Sixteen Short Sermons."

"Oh yes," said she; "*that* is next to the Bible."

I told her that I should like to have that same book, and asked if she would be willing to give it to me. Said she,—

"I will give you anything else I've got; but I should be unwilling to give that, unless I could get another just like it. I read it over every little while."

She produced the same old tract which I had seen in her house more than seventeen years before. It bore the marks of age and of much service. It had become almost illegible by use, and time, and dust. "It has been all around the neighbourhoood," said she. "I have lent it to a great many folks; and sometimes I have had hard work to get it back again."

I gave her two new copies of the same tract, and also the whole bound volume which contains it; and after carefully examining the two, leaf by leaf, "to see if they were just like it," as she said, she finally consented to part with her old, time-worn, rusty one. "I thought," said she, "I never should part with that book,—but these new ones are better; I can read them easier, and I can lend them to more folks. Some people will read these, who would not read one so dirty and old as that."

I felt half guilty for taking her old companion, and was sorry I had ever asked for it. As I parted with her and came away, I noticed that her eyes kept fixed upon the "Sixteen Short Sermons" that I held in my hand. I hope yet to be permitted to return it to her.

There were two things in the character of this woman worthy of very special notice,—her determination and her dependence. So firmly was she fixed in her resolution to abandon the habit, which had so long been her sin, and the cause of her misery, that after her first seriousness on that memorable night, she never once tasted the cup of her shame. She would not see anybody else do it,—she would not go where it was,—she would cross the street to avoid passing the door where it was sold,—she would not even *look* at it. And so entire was her dependence on God to keep her from it, that she gave this memorable description of her course,—"*Drink anything?* no! if I ever *think* of it, I immediately go to prayer." I recommend her example to every reader of this book: "Drink anything? no! if you ever *think* of it, immediately go to prayer."

VI.

No Escape.

IN conversation with a young man, who desired to unite with the Church, he surprised me very much by a reference which he made to his former "detestation of religion," as he called it, and by mentioning the manner in which he was first led to any considerable concern in reference to his salvation. I had known him with some intimacy for several months, had frequently conversed with him as a serious inquirer, and afterwards as one who entertained a hope in Christ. But he had never before mentioned to me so definitely the means of his awakening, and his previous opposition to religion.

He belonged to a pious family; his parents and several of his brothers were members of the Church; he was a moral, staid, industrious, intelligent young man, always attending church, and was a teacher in the Sabbath school. I had not supposed that his feelings of opposition to religion had ever assumed the strong character which he described to me now; and I had never known the means of their alteration. I happened to ask him,—

"Mr. H——, what was it that first called your attention definitely to religion, when you began to make it a matter of your personal concern?"

"I found there was no escape,—I could not get away from it."

"What do you mean, when you say, 'There was no escape?'"

"Why, the subject met me everywhere. Wherever I went there was something to make me think of it."

"Yes," said I, "there are things to bring it to mind all around us and always, if we would heed them. God has filled his world with things suggestive of himself."

"O sir," said he, "I don't mean *that* at all. It is true, that *now* almost everything makes me think of God and my duty; but I mean things that were done *on purpose* to catch me. It seemed to me that I was pursued everywhere. There was no getting away. If I went to church on Sunday, you never let us off with a descriptive or literary sermon; you always had something about faith or repentance, or depravity, or the duty of sinners to fly to Christ. If I went to my shop on a week-day, thinking I should escape *there*, because I had something else to attend to, my partner would have something to say to me about religion, or something to say in my presence which I knew was meant *for me*. If I met you in the street, you were sure not to let me pass without bringing up that subject in some way or other. If I went home to dinner or tea, religion would be talked of at the table. If I was spending any part of the evening in the family after I left the shop, it was the same thing again: religion, religion would come up; every one had something to say which made me think of religion. If I went off to bed as I did many a time to get out of the hearing of it, my sister had put a tract upon my pillow. I could not bear all this. I often avoided everybody and went to my room, where I could be alone, and think of what I pleased; and *there* the first thing to meet me would be some religious book, which my mother, or one some else, had put in the place most likely to attract my attention,—and perhaps left it open at some passage marked on purpose for me. After several of my young associates had become Christians, and began to talk about religion, I avoided them and sought other company, and pretty soon *they* began to talk of religion too! I was provoked at it!"

"Did those people who endeavoured to influence you, treat you rudely or impolitely?"

"Oh no! That was the worst of it. I hoped they would. If they had been meddlesome and impudent, I should have had something to find fault with, and should have told them to mind their own business, and keep their religion to themselves. I should have said that religion makes men ungentlemanly, and unfit for society,—and so should have excused myself. But there was none of that. There was little said to me. All that was done was only calculated to make me think *for* myself, and *of* myself; and so I could not complain. But religion came up before me on all sides; whichever way I turned, morning, noon, and night, it was there. I could not escape from it."

"Had you a strong *desire* to escape from it?"

"Yes, I had. I turned every way. I avoided Christians. One Sunday I stayed away from church; but that contrivance *worked the other way*, for I could think of nothing but religion all the morning; and so in the afternoon I went to church, to see if I couldn't forget it there. When I came home I went into an unoccupied room, because they began to talk about the sermon in the parlour; and the first thing that met me was *the Bible*,—laid open at the second chapter of Proverbs, and a pencil-mark drawn round the first six verses. 'This is some of mother's work,' said I. Finally, I resolved to give up my business, and get away into some place where I should not be *tormented about religion* any longer. I began to make arrangements for selling off."

"Well, sir, what altered your mind?"

"Why, just as I was in this trouble to get away from religion, resolving not to live any longer in such a place as this, I began to think what I was after,—why I desired to get away. And then I soon found out it was because I desired to get away from the truth and away from God. That alarmed me, and shamed me. I thought, then, that if there were no escape from men here, there could be no escape from God anywhere. And though it cost my pride a hard struggle, I made up my mind that I was all wrong, and I would attend to my salvation. Then I began; but I don't think I ever should have begun, if I had not been pursued in every place where I tried to escape."

"Had you any more temptation to neglect religion after that?"

"No. I immediately took my stand. I went among the inquirers openly. Then I was disappointed to find how little I cared any longer for the world, for what people would say, and all such things, as I used to think would be great trials to me. And I believe *now*, there is very much gained by getting a sinner to *commit himself* on this matter. Then he will not wish to get off."

"What way do you think is most likely to succeed for inducing any one 'to commit himself' to attend to his religion?"

"Oh, I cannot answer *that*. Any way is good, I suppose, which will lead people to *think*. Judging from my own experience, I should suppose that no irreligious person in the world could put off religion any longer, if his way were hedged up as mine was, so that he could not avoid *thinking* of the subject."

Such was a part of my conversation with him. He united with the Church; and I have some reason to suppose, that since that time he has aimed to "lead people to think," in such a manner that there could be "no escape."

Thoughtlessness is the common origin of unconcern. We do a far better office for men when we lead *them* to think, than when we think for them. A man's own thoughts are the most powerful of all preaching. The Holy Spirit operates very much by leading men to *reflection*—to employ their own mind. I should hesitate to interrupt the religious reflections of any man in the world, by the most important thing I could say to him. If I am sure *he* will *think*, I will consent to be still. But men are prone to be thoughtless, and we must speak to them to lead them to reflection.

But the instance of this young man contains, as I think, a most important lesson. It appears to show that Christian people may easily exercise an influence upon the minds of the worldly; and I have often thought such an influence is the very thing which the Church needs, more than almost anything else. There is many a member of the Church, having faith, having benevolence, and sincerely desirous of the conversion of sinners, who never has once opened his lips to commend religion to the careless, and has never in any way attempted to lead them to serious reflection. It is not too much to say that this is *wrong*. Surely it *cannot* be right for the people of God to wrap their talent in a napkin and hide it in the earth! In *some* mode, almost every Christian in the midst of us is able to influence the thoughts of the careless every day. By conversation, by timely remarks, by books, by tracts, and by a thousand nameless methods, the people of God have opportunities to impress religious truth upon indifferent minds. There is too much neglect of this. The irreligious often notice this neglect; and whenever they notice it, they are very apt to have a diminished esteem for religious people, if not for religion itself. A minister cannot go everywhere and speak to everybody in the community, but private Christians can. Such Christians are meeting the ungodly daily, they know them, they associate with them, work with them, trade with them, and it would be easy for them to awaken many a sinner, whom a minister cannot reach. Such exertion is one *great want* of the Church. There are few irreligious persons in the midst of us who are compelled to say, "There is no escape."

VII.

The Date of Conversion.

IN a very remote and rural part of my parish, several miles from my own residence, and by the side of an unfrequented road, there lived a married woman, whose state of mind on the subject of religion interested me much, the first time I visited her. I thought I discovered in her a sort of readiness to obey the gospel, if I may use such an expression. She was about thirty years of age, full of vivacity, enthusiasm, and kindness, simple, beautiful, graceful; and when she became animated in conversation, her clear blue eye beamed with intelligence and sweetness of disposition, which flung an indescribable charm around all that she uttered. She and her husband had been religiously educated. She was a woman of refined manners; and to me she appeared the more interesting, because she evidently never supposed herself to have any refinement at all. Her politeness, which I have seldom seen equalled, was not the politeness of the schools, but of nature; not the polish of art, but the prompting of simplicity and an affectionate disposition. In all things she appeared unaffected, natural, simple. She was willing to appear just what she was, and therefore always appeared to advantage. Her manners would have graced the most refined society. She made no pretensions under the promptings of pride or vanity, uttered no apologies for her appearance, and felt no bashfulness in the presence of a stranger. Too far removed from any school to be able to send her children, she taught them herself; and her three little boys, for intelligence, kindness, and propriety of manners, might have served for models to almost any other in the parish. I found the little things a short distance from the house, plucking the wild flowers in the woods, to entwine in their mother's hair, which they claimed the privilege to adorn in that manner, and which might be seen thus adorned, according to their taste, almost any day, from the early spring time till the frost had nipped the last blossom of the year. Eight summers had not passed over the head of the eldest. They were the children of nature—simple, fearless, artless. The frank, gentle, and affectionate demeanour of these little creatures, especially towards one another, gave me, as I thought, some insight into the character of their mother. I judged of her by her little pupils, and afterwards found that I had judged justly. I took them as bright miniatures of herself. And I did not think the less of *her* when I perceived the evident pleasure and exultation, if I may not say *pride*, which she had in them.

I visited her as her minister. I was a stranger to her. She was evidently glad to see me at her house, and the more so as she had not expected it. After making some inquiries about her husband and her children, I inquired of her,—

"Are you and your husband members of the Church?"

"No, sir," said she, with a downcast look.

"Neither of you?"

"No, sir."

"And why not? Are you still living without religion?"

"I suppose we are. I have wished a great many times for *fitness* to be a communicant."

"And why are you *not* fit?"

"Because I have no saving faith. I could not go to the Lord's table without faith?"

"No, but you ought to go *with* faith. Jesus Christ is offered to you in the gospel, to be your Saviour. Your duty is to believe in him. And are you still, at your time of life, an unbeliever?"

"I suppose I am," said she, with a pensive look.

"And are you going to continue so?"

After a long pause, during which her thoughts seemed very busy, she replied, with an accent of sadness,—

"Indeed, sir, I cannot tell."

"Are you *willing* to continue so?"

"No, sir, I am not satisfied with myself. I think about religion very often, but—"

"And do you pray about it very often?"

"No, sir, not *very* often, since I was a child."

"Have you prayed to-day?"

"No, sir."

"Did you pray last Sabbath?"

"No, sir. I read my Bible. I sometimes pray, but my prayers are not answered."

"What do you pray *for?*"

"I have prayed for forgiveness and the Holy Spirit; but it was all in vain to me."

"And so you ceased to pray?"

"Yes, sir. I thought I could *do* nothing without the Holy Spirit."

"But, my dear madam, it was the Holy Spirit that led you to prayer. *God* was calling to you at those times when you were constrained to pray."

"I have never thought so, sir."

"Then he has been more kind towards you than you have thought."

"I wish I *were* a Christian."

"You may be one, if you will; but not without earnest prayer. Will you seriously attend to your salvation, beginning *now?* With the Bible to guide you, and the Holy Spirit to pray for, will you *at once* begin to seek the Lord?"

A long pause followed this question. She seemed to be lost in thought, and I did not choose to disturb her thoughts. She appeared downcast; but after a little while I thought I perceived a sort of obstinacy manifest in her countenance, and fearing that she was about to utter some objection, I suddenly rose to take my leave.

"What!" said she, "are you going?"

"I *must* go, madam."

"Shall I ever see you again?" said she, beseechingly.

"Do you *wish* to see me again?"

"Yes, sir, I *do*," said she, emphatically.

"Then I will come to see you as soon as I can. But before I come, I hope you will have made up your mind fully, and will have turned to Christ."

A month afterwards I called upon her. She appeared much as before. At times she had prayed, but not daily. I talked to her plainly and affectionately, prayed with her and left her.

I had now little hope of doing her any good. However, about three months afterwards, being in that neighbourhood, I called upon her. I could find little alteration in her feelings or habits, except that she seemed to have a more tender spirit, and was more accustomed to prayer. But nothing I could say appeared to make much impression upon her. She assented to all the truths of religion. She had known them from her childhood, when her religious parents taught her. A pensiveness and solemnity hung around her; but she had no deep anxiety. In various ways I strove to affect her; but it was all in vain, till I appealed to her conscience and sensibilities as a mother. I said to her,—

"You have three precious children intrusted to you, and your example will have great influence over them. They will be very much what *you* make them. If you are irreligious, they will be very likely to remain so too. If they see you living a life of faith and prayer, the example will not be lost upon them. You ought to be able to teach them religion. But how can you teach them what you do not know yourself? Allow me to say,—and I am glad I can say it,—I have been delighted to notice your conduct towards your children. In my opinion, *few mothers do so well.* I think you are training them wisely in all things *but one.* May I say it to you, I know of no children of their age who please me so much. In their excellence I see your own; and this compels me to respect and love you the more, and be the more anxious that you should train them for heaven. I am very sorry that you are *an irreligious mother!*"

She burst into tears, and rising suddenly from her seat, turned her face towards the window and wept convulsively. I left her without uttering a word.

It was more than six months before I could see her again. When I called upon her, after this long interval, she told me that she had tried to repent and flee to Christ, and had prayed daily, but that her heart remained the same, and she was amazed at her stupidity.

"I am insensible as *a stone*," said she. "It seems to me that I feel nothing. I wish to love God, and be a Christian; but I am fully convinced that I have no power at all over my hard heart. And yet I have some faint hope that God will have mercy on me, after all my stubbornness and stupidity, and will yet grant me the Holy Spirit. Is it wrong for me to have such a hope?"

"Not at all, my dear madam. I am glad you have that hope. Hold it fast. Only let all your hope be in God through Jesus Christ. Let nothing discourage you for an instant, while you attempt to obey the gospel. I believe God has good things in store for you. You may say, 'Will he plead against me with his great power? no, he will put strength in me.'"

"Oh, that I knew where to find him!" said she.

"He is on his throne of grace," said I. "'Then shall ye go and pray unto me, and I will hearken unto you. And ye shall seek me, and find me, when ye shall search for me with all your heart; and I will be found of you, saith the Lord.'"

"I *do* seek, sir; but why does not God give me the Holy Spirit?"

"He *does* give it, madam. He calls you. He strives with you. He shows you your sin, your stupidity, your strange heart."

"But, sir, do you think the Holy Spirit is sent to one alone, and when there is no revival?"

"Strange question for you to ask! *Yes*, my dear friend, most unquestionably. Is the offer made only to a multitude? Is it not made *to every one* that asks him?"

"I know it is. But it seems to me that it would be too much to expect God would regard me *alone*, when there are no others inclined to turn unto him."

"Then your unbelieving heart does an injustice to his kindness. He is a thousand-fold better than you think him. He 'waits to be gracious unto you.' He 'calls, and you refuse.' Because you do not know of others disposed to seek God, you have little courage to seek him, though you know that his promises are made, and invitations given to each individual sinner like yourself,—*to you*, as much as if you were the only sinner in the universe."

"But if others were attending to religion, if my husband and neighbours were, I should have more expectation of succeeding."

"Madam, I am not sure of that. I will not too much blame you for thinking so; but see here,—you do *not know* how many others feel just as you do, and wait for *you* just as you wait for *them*. You mentioned your husband. I am going to see him, and I have not an item of doubt that before I have left him he will confess to me that he is waiting for *you*."

"Why, I never thought of that," said she, with surprise.

"I suppose not. But it is time for you to think of it. You and he are waiting for one another. Which shall begin first? I would not afflict you, or say an unkind word to you,—I have not a feeling in my heart that would allow me to do it; but I tell you seriously, you are *a hindrance to your husband*. He may be a hindrance to you,—I suppose he is; but you are a hindrance to him."

"I do not *intend* to be a hindrance to him."

"But you *are*, and you will continue to be, more or less, as long as he thinks you to be an unconverted sinner, living in your indifference and stupidity."

"What shall I do?"

"I will tell you what to do. First give your own self to the

Lord. Did you ever talk with your husband on the subject of religion?"

"Oh yes, a great many times."

"Have you lately? and have you told him how you feel about your own heart, your sin, and your salvation?"

"Oh no, sir, I have not said anything to him about *that.*"

"So I supposed. And now I will tell you what to do. When he comes in, and you and he are alone together, just tell him plainly and affectionately how you feel, what you have done, and what you intend to do. Open your whole heart to him. When he hears you talking so, *he* at least will know of one sinner who intends to seek the Lord. And thus you will hinder him no longer."

This was quite an unexpected turn of thought to her. She sat in silence for a little time, as if meditating the matter, and then inquired,—

"Did you say you would see my husband *to-day?*"

"Yes; and he will tell me you are a hindrance to him, just as you say he is a hindrance to you."

"But, sir, I did *not* say exactly *that.*"

"True, madam, you did not. I have expressed the idea a little more plainly than you did, and much less politely. You said it in your kind way, and I in my coarse one. I have not essentially altered it. You *did* mention what an *encouragement* it would be to you if your husband were attending to his salvation. He feels precisely so about his wife, in my opinion. And what I want of you both is, that you should encourage and aid one another."

"I should be *very* glad if he were truly a Christian.

"He would be very glad if you were truly a Christian. But will you do what I have just told you? Will you tell him your feelings?"

After a short pause, with her eyes fixed on the ground, and a look of ineffable solemnity and tenderness, she replied emphatically,—

"*Yes*, my dear pastor, *I will.*"

"Good-bye," said I, and reaching her my hand, instantly left her.

I soon found her husband in the field, at work among his corn; and shaping the conversation according to my previous intent, it was not long before he said to me,—

"Well, if my wife thinks it is time for her to attend to religion, I shall certainly think it is time for *me*, when my poor health reminds me so often of my end."

"I have been talking with her, and I assure you that, in my opinion, she would certainly be quite ready, were it not for one thing."

"What is that?" said he, with surprise and concern.

"That one thing is yourself! It is you who are a hindrance to her. You do not follow Christ, and she has not the encouragement of your example."

"That need not stand in *her* way."

"But it does stand in her way. She follows your example. She naturally looks to you as a guide, and her affectionate disposition catches your feelings. As long as you remain an irreligious man, your influence tends to make her remain an irreligious woman. You may be assured of this. You yourself have just told me, that if she thought it was time for her to give her heart to religion, you should certainly think it was time for you; and is it not natural that she should think so too? You are the husband. She looks to you as a guide. She looks to you *more* than you look to her. She feels your influence more than you feel hers. Thus you are a hindrance to her, when you ought to be a help."

"She never said anything to me about it."

"And did you ever say anything to *her* about it?"

"No, nothing in particular. But I have been thinking about religion a good deal, as I told you when you came here in the winter; and I do not feel contented. I am not prepared to die, and the thoughts of it make my mind gloomy."

"You *may* have such thoughts as to make your mind glad.

The gospel is 'good tidings of great joy,' and 'for all people,'—*for you.* And when you go home, I want you to talk with your wife on this subject, as you know you ought to do; and tell her what you think. Will you do so?"

"I will think about it."

"But will you *do* it?"

"I can't say, I can't say."

"Well, aim to do your duty in the fear of God; aim to lead your wife and children to the kingdom of heaven." I left him.

This man was of a very sedate and cautious disposition. He was amiable, but he was firm. He was no creature of impulses. His wife had more vivacity, more sprightliness, more ardour, while she was by no means deficient in decision of character. I hoped that the vivacity of the one would stimulate the slowness of the other, and that the thinking habits of the man would steady and temper the ardour of the more impulsive woman.

Without much hope of being able to influence them at all, I called upon them again the next week—sooner, probably, than I should have done, but for a sort of curious desire to know the result of their next meeting after I left them. The wife met me at the door with evident gladness.

"I am very happy to see you," said she, "I have something to tell you. My husband is serious, and I *do hope* he will become a Christian."

"And I suppose he hopes you will become a Christian."

"I wish I *were* one, but I am as stupid as ever. My husband is much more like a Christian than I am."

"Then his seriousness has not done you the good you expected from it."

"No, and I am astonished at myself. But I must tell you. After you went away last week I did not know what to do; I felt very strange about speaking to him as I promised you I would. I did not know how to *begin.* I thought of it a long time. At last I came to the conclusion to begin as soon as he came in, and tell it all over, just as it was. So when I heard him coming through the gate, I went out and met him there under the tree. Said I, 'Mr. Spencer has been here talking with me, and I want to tell you, my dear Luther, how I feel.' He stopped and looked at me without saying a word, and I told him all about myself, since the time when I was a little child. He listened to it all, looking at me and then on the ground; and when I had got done, I asked him if he did not think we ought to live differently. I was *so delighted* when he answered right off, 'Yes, I do.' I could hardly keep from weeping for joy, it was so different from what I expected. I said, 'My dear Luther, let us not neglect salvation any longer.' Said he, 'I don't mean to do so; I am determined to do all I can to lay up treasures in heaven.' After dinner we had a long talk. Almost the whole afternoon he sat here reading the Bible, and talking with me. Sometimes he did not say a word for a long time, but would read, and then stop and think. As soon as he went out, I went alone and prayed, and then for the first time in my life I was glad to think I *might* pray. In the evening he sat here with me and the children, without saying much, only he asked me some questions about the atonement, and the Holy Spirit, and faith in Christ. And when it was time for the children to go to bed, I whispered to him, 'Shall we not have family prayer?' He got right up, without saying a word, took down the Bible, told the boys to wait a little while, and then turned to the third chapter of John, and read it aloud. Then we all kneeled down, and he made a prayer. *Such a prayer!* I could not help weeping. After we rose from our knees, and were sitting in silence a little while, our second boy went to him and put his little arms around his neck. 'Father,' said he, 'I wish you would pray so *every* night.' He looked very serious; and when the boy waited for an answer, looking right in his face, he told him, 'I am going to do it every night and every morning too.' Since that time I have been more happy than I ever was before. I know I am not a *Christian*, but I hope God will have mercy upon us, and lead us to Christ."

Such was her simple story; and she told it in a manner that would have affected any heart. Her little boys clustered around her, wept at seeing her weep, and I should have despised myself if I could have avoided weeping with them. Her husband soon came in from the field, and after some little conversation, I prayed with them, and left them.

Months passed away before I saw them again. They then appeared much alike. They had little hope, but they did not seem unhappy. They only hoped that God would yet bring them to repentance. If now they had no faith, it did not seem to me that they had any slavish fear; and I could not say a word to discourage or alarm them, for I certainly did hope for them, since God is "a *rewarder of them that diligently seek him.*" After this I left them to themselves.

Just before a communion season, which came about six months after my last interview with them, I was very agreeably surprised by an unexpected visit of this man and his wife, who called upon me at the time publicly appointed for conversation with those who desired to unite with the Church. They had come on that account. They believed that God had led them to faith in his Son, and they wished to commemorate the Saviour's death at his table. I had much conversation with them. They could not tell when their faith or hope *commenced;* and that was their greatest trouble, and the only ground of their hesitation about making a public profession of religion. They had been very much alike in their feelings. For months they had been happy, not by the belief that they were Christians, but in the exercises of the means of grace, and in the hope that God would lead them in his own way and time to religion. In this confidence they had rested, and loved to rest. The Bible, and prayer, and religious conversation were their delight. And it was not till they had passed month after month in this happy manner, that the idea occurred to either of them that they were the children of God. The wife thought of this first, and the thought made her unhappy. "I was afraid," said she, "of a false hope, and I *tried to feel* as I *used* to do, when I was afraid of being lost for ever." She mentioned her fears to her husband, and was astonished to find that he had the same fear about himself; because he, too, had almost half hoped that he was reconciled to God, but had been banishing the hope as a snare of the great adversary. Then they wanted to see me; and as I did not visit them, the wife proposed that they should come to see me that very day, for she "wanted to know whether she was a Christian or not." After much conversation, her husband told her that no man could tell her that, for God only could read the heart, and it would be better to examine themselves alone for a while. And a week or two afterwards he objected to coming to me at all on such an errand, because the Bible says, "Examine *your own selves*, whether ye be in the faith; prove *your own selves*." Said he, "Let us pray, 'Lord, search me, and know my heart, and lead me in the way everlasting.'"

Week after week their peace of mind grew more uniform and sweet. They found, as they thought, that they loved God, that they trusted in Christ for pardon, that they hated sin, and found their greatest felicity in the divine promises, and in the thoughts and duties of religion. Both alike, they were determined to serve their Lord and Master as long as they should live. And because they found, as they believed, the evidences of religion in themselves, they came to the conclusion that they were Christians.

But when they came to me, the husband said, "We have, after all, one great trouble. We are not fully sure that we have had the gift of the Holy Spirit. We have never been sensible of any *sudden change*, and we have had no strong feelings of distress on account of sin, or of great joy on account of having faith. If I have any religion, I want to know when it *began*."

"Can you tell, sir, when your corn *begins* to grow?—or when your wheat *begins* to come up? Could you tell, my dear madam, when those beautiful violets and pinks under your window *began* to come up?"

She smiled upon me, with a countenance radiant with new intelligence and joy, and burst into tears. Said her husband, after a serious, thoughtful pause, "I know my corn *has* come up, and I know my wheat *does* grow."

"Very well," said I, "I have no more to say."

The wife turned to her husband, after a few minutes, saying, "I *should* like to know *when* I began to love God; and, Luther, it seems to me that we have been Christians ever since that first night when you prayed."

They united with the Church, though uncertain of the date of their conversion. He became a very staid and thoughtful Christian. She was a Christian of light and smiles. Both were contented and happy. "I am glad we live in this retired place," said she to me a year afterwards; "we can enjoy religion here, and nobody comes to trouble us. We have some kind and pious neighbours a little way off, who are a great comfort to us; but my Bible, my boys, and my flowers are enough to make me happy. I would not give up my little home, my cottage, and my woods, for the richest palace in the world;" and tears of joy coursed down her cheeks when she said so. Adverting to her former troubles she said, "I have come to the conclusion that it is *best for me* that I have never yet been able to fix the time of my conversion; I am afraid I should trust too much to it, if I could. Now I trust to nothing but to continued faith, and to living in happy fellowship with my God, my heavenly Father. My husband is happy too, and what can I want more except the conversion of my children?" As she said this she turned away and wept.

Her husband died in peace, as I have been told; and his precious wife, now a widow, has unspeakable comfort in two pious sons,—her joy, and her earthly crown. They will soon be her eternal crown in the kingdom of heaven. I cannot doubt it.

These instances of conversion are here given as examples of an extensive class. In making my first visit to the families of my congregation, I met with a number of persons who appeared to me to have some readiness to give their attention to the gospel call. They were not anxious, not alarmed, or, in the common acceptation of the term, serious. They evidently did not consider themselves the subjects of any special divine influence, or as having any particular inclination towards religion. But they appeared to me to be candid and conscientious, and to have a kind of readiness to obey the gospel. There was an indescribable *something* about them, I know not what, which made me have more hope for them than for others.

To the names of about twenty such persons I attached a private mark in my congregational book (containing the names of all my congregation)—a mark to indicate to *me* their state of mind, and prompt me to visit them again as soon as possible; but the meaning of which no one but myself could understand. If I may say so, they seemed *ready to become Christians*,—I know not how to describe their state of mind by any more just or intelligible expression. If, in the time of a revival of religion, they had said the same things which they now said, had presented the same appearances, and manifested the same impressions, no minister or Christian, as it seemed to me, would have hesitated to ascribe their impressions to the influences of the Holy Spirit. And, therefore, why should I not *now* have that opinion respecting them? and why not *treat* them in all respects as I would have done in the time of a revival? and why not *expect* the same results?

These were serious and troublesome questions to my own mind. By conversation with older and more experienced pastors I aimed to get some instruction on this subject; but all I could learn did not satisfy me,—indeed, it did not seem to do me the least good. I found I must teach myself what nobody appeared able to teach me. And, however just or unjust may have been the conclusion to which, by continued and intense reflection, my mind was at last brought, I retain the same opinions now, after a score of years has passed away, which I formed at first. I believe those persons had their cast of mind through the influences of the Divine Spirit. Almost every one of those to whose name I attached my private mark within the space of two years became hopefully converted to Christ.

I often visited them, conversed with them, and entreated them to be reconciled to God. And the greatest obstacle, as it seemed to me, that I had to encounter, was their uniform impression that God had not given them the Holy Spirit, and that it would therefore be in vain for them to attempt to seek the Lord. It was an exceedingly difficult thing to convince any one of them that the Holy Spirit was present, and that their serious impressions, and occasional fears, and occasional prayers, were the effects of a divine influence and the very substance of a divine call. But I had myself been led to this conclusion. I thought that they themselves ought to be convinced of this, and ought not, through ignorance and error, to be left to misimprove the day of their merciful visitation, waiting for a revival of religion. In almost every instance,—indeed, I do not remember a single exception,—the commencement of an earnest and hopeful attempt to gain salvation originated in the conviction, which I strove hard to impress upon the mind, that the Holy Spirit was already striving with them as really as if there had been a revival all around.

To the name of the woman whom I have mentioned in this sketch I attached my mystic mark the first time I ever saw her; and to the name of her husband the first time I ever saw him. And on this account I was led to see them the more frequently. I am very certain that I was not at all the instrument of their *conviction*, or that of the conviction of twenty more like them, whatever assistance, in other respects, the truths which I uttered may have been to them in leading them to Christ. Probably many, very many sinners, who *never think of it*, are visited by the Holy Spirit. Probably not a month passes when there are not strivings of the Spirit with unconverted sinners in all our congregations. And if such sinners, instead of allowing every trifle of the world to dispel their serious thoughts, would only cherish them, conspiring with the Holy Spirit, there is every reason to believe that they would become the happy children of God. Oh, if they but knew how near God is unto them, and how infinitely willing he is, in his kindness and love, to lead them into the ways of salvation, they would not suffer these seasons of promise to pass by unimproved, especially the young, whose kindness of heart has not yet been all poisoned, or all blasted by the world, would not so often turn a deaf ear to the *still small voice of the Spirit.*

"Their happy song would oftener be,
Hear what the Lord has done for me."

VIII.

My Old Mother;

OR, CONSCIENCE IN TRADE.

A YOUNG man, who at that time was almost an entire stranger to me, called upon me at a late hour in the evening, and, after some general conversation, said that he wished to talk with me in reference to a matter which had troubled him for some time. He came *to me*, as he said, because a few days before he had heard a member of a neighbouring Church railing against me, and, among other things, saying that I was stern and severe enough for a slave-driver. "So," said he, "I thought you would tell me the truth right out."

He was a junior clerk in a dry goods store—a salesman. He had been in that situation for some months. He went into it a raw hand. His employer had taken some pains to instruct him in its duties, and had otherwise treated him in a very kind manner. But he was expected, and indeed required, to do some things which he "did not know to be quite right." He stated these things to me with minuteness and entire simplicity. He had been taught by his employer to do them as a part of the "necessary skill to be exercised in selling goods," without which "no man could be a good salesman, or be fit for a merchant."

For example, he must learn to judge by the appearance of any woman who entered the shop, by her dress, her manner, her look, the tone of her voice, whether she had much knowledge of the commodity she wished to purchase; and if she had not, he must put the price higher,—as high as he thought she could be induced to pay. If there was any objection to the price of an article, he must say,

"We have never sold it any cheaper;" or, "We paid that for it, madam, at wholesale;" or, "You cannot buy that quality of goods any lower in the city." With one class of customers he must *always* begin by asking a half or a third more than the regular price, because, probably, through the ignorance of the customer, he could get it; and if he could not, then he must put it at a lower price, but still above its value, at the same time saying, "That is just what we gave for it;" or, "That is the very lowest at which we can put it to you;" or, "We would not offer it to anybody else so low as that, but we wish to get your custom." In short, a very large portion of the service expected of him was just this sort, and, as I soon told him, it was just to *lie* for the purpose of cheating.

Whenever he hesitated to practise in this manner behind the counter, his employer, ordinarily present, was sure to notice it, and sure to be dissatisfied with him.

He had repeatedly mentioned to his employer his "doubts" whether "this was just right," and "got laughed at." He was told, "Everybody does it,"—"You can't be a merchant without it,"—"All is fair in trade,"—"You are too green."

"I know I am green," said the young man to me in a melancholy tone. "I was brought up in an obscure place in the country, and don't know much about the ways of the world. My mother is a poor woman, a widow, who was not able to give me much education; but I don't believe *she* would think it right for me to do such things."

"And do *you* think it right?" said I.

"No,—I don't know,—perhaps it may be. Mr. H——," his employer, "says there is no *sin* in it, and he is a member of the Church; but I believe it would make my old mother feel very bad if she knew I was doing such things every day."

"I venture to say that your mother has got not only more religion, but more common sense, than a thousand *like him*. He may be a member of the Church,—the Church always has some unworthy members in it, I suppose; but he is not a man fit to direct you. Take your mother's way, and refuse his."

"I shall lose my place," said he.

"Then lose your place; don't hesitate a moment."

"I engaged for a year, and my year is not out."

"No matter; you are ready to fulfil your engagement. But what *was* your engagement? Did you engage to deceive, to cheat, and lie?"

"Oh, not at all."

"Then certainly you need have no hesitation, through fear of forfeiting your place. If he sends you away, because you will not do such things for him, then you will know him to be a very bad man, from whom you may well be glad to be separated."

"He says he will have his business done in the manner *he* chooses.

"Very well; you have no objections to *that;* let him do his business in the way he chooses, but he has no right to make you use *your tongue* in the way he chooses; and if he complains of you because you do not choose to lie for him every hour in the day, just tell him that you have not hired out your conscience to him, and you will not be guilty of committing any crimes for him. Ask him if he expects you to *steal* for him, if he should happen to want you to do it."

"When I told him I thought such things wrong, he said, 'That is *my* look out.'"

"Tell him it is *your* look out whether you please God or offend him—whether you do right or wrong—whether you serve the God of truth or the father of lies."

"If I should say that, he would tell me to be off."

"Very well, *be* off then."

"I have no place to go to, and he knows it."

"No matter; go anywhere—do anything—dig potatoes—black boots—sweep the streets for a living, sooner than yield for one hour to such temptation."

"He says, 'Everybody does so,' and, 'No man can ever get along in the way of trade without it.'"

"About everybody doing so I know better. That is *not true.*

Some men are honest and truthful in trade. A man may be honest behind the counter as easily as in the pulpit. But if a man can't be a merchant without these things, then he can't be a merchant and get to heaven; and the sooner you quit that business the better. And in respect to his declaration, that 'no man can get along in the way of trade without such practices,' it is false—utterly false! And I wish you to take notice of men now when you are young, as extensively as you can, and see how they come out. You will not have to notice long before you will be convinced of the truth of that homely old maxim, "Honesty is the best policy." You will soon see that such men as he are the very men *not* to 'get along.' *He* will not 'get along' well a great while if he does not alter his course."

"Oh, he is a keen fellow," said the young man smiling.

"So is old Satan a keen fellow, but he is the greatest fool in the universe. His keenness has just ruined him. He is an eternal bankrupt, and can't 'take the benefit of the Act.' He is such a known liar, that nobody would believe him under oath. And your employer's keenness will turn out no better. He may, indeed, probably prosper *here*. Such men sometimes do. But the Bible has described him—'They that will be rich fall into temptation, and a snare, and into many foolish and hurtful lusts, which drown men in destruction and perdition.' He 'will be rich;' that is what he wants; his 'will' is all that way. And he has fallen into the 'temptation' to lie in order to get rich. And this is a 'snare' to him—it is a trap, and he is caught in it; and if he does not repent and get out of it, he will be 'drowned in destruction and perdition.' But I was going to speak of his worldly prosperity. I am no prophet, nor the son of a prophet. I do not believe that God will work any miracles in his case; but I *do* believe *that man will fail.* Mark him well, and remember what I say, if you live to notice him ten or twenty years hence. In my opinion you will see him a poor man, and probably a despised man."

"What makes you *think so?*" said he, with great astonishment

"Because he is not honest—does not regard the truth. His lying will soon defeat its own purposes. His customers, one after another, and especially the best of them, will find him out, and they will forsake him, because they cannot trust his word. He will lose more than he will gain by all the falsehoods he utters. I know a dozen men in this city, some of them merchants, some butchers, some grocers, some tailors, whom I always avoid, and always will. If I *know* a man has lied to me once, in the way of his business, that ends all my dealings with him; I never go near him afterwards. Such is my practice, and I tell my wife so, and my children so. And sometimes—yea, often, I tell them the *names of the men.* If any of my friends ask me about these men, I tell them the truth, and put them upon their guard. And thus their custom is diminished, because their character becomes known. This is one reason why I think Mr. H—— will not prosper. But whatever the mode may be, his reverses will come. Mark my words, they will come. God will make them come."

With great depression he replied, "I don't know what I *could do* if I should lose my place. I don't get but a little more than enough to pay my board,—my mother gives me my clothes, and if I lose my situation, I could not pay my board for a month."

"Then," said I, "if you get so little, you will not lose much by quitting. I do not pretend to know much about it, but in my opinion Mr. H—— *wrongs* you, does you a positive *injustice*, and a *cruel* one, by giving you so little. And if you quit, and cannot pay your board till you get something to do, tell *me*—I will see to that." He never had occasion to tell me.

"If I quit that place so soon," said the young man, "it will make my old mother feel very bad; she will think I am getting unsteady, or that something else is the matter with me. She will be afraid that I am going to ruin."

"*Not a bit of it,*" said I. "*Tell* her just the truth, and you will fill her old heart with *joy;* she will thank God that she has got such a son,—and she will send up to heaven another prayer for you, which I would rather have than all the gold of Ophir."

The young man's eyes filled with tears, and I let him sit in silence for some time. At length he said to me,—

"I don't think I can stay there; but I don't know what to do, or where to look."

"Look to *God* first, and *trust* him. Do you think he will let you *suffer* because, out of regard to his commandments, you have lost your place? Never! Such is not his way. Ask *him* to guide you."

"I am pretty much a stranger here," said he with a very dejected look; "I know but few people, and I don't know where I could get anything to do."

"For that very reason ask God to guide you. Are you accustomed to pray?"

"Yes, I have been at times lately. Some months ago I began to try to seek the Lord, after I heard a sermon on that subject, and ever since that time, off and on, I have been trying. But I didn't know what to do in my situation."

"Will you answer me one question, as truly and fully as you are able?"

"Yes, sir, if I think it is *right* for me to answer it."

"The question is, Has not your seriousness, and has not your trying to seek God, sometimes been diminished, *just when* you have had the most temptation in the shop, leading you to do what you thought wrong, even if you did it for another?"

He sat in silence, apparently pondering the question for a few moments, and then replied,—

"Yes, I believe it has."

"'Quench not the Spirit,' then," said I. I then entered into particular conversation with him about his religious feelings, and found that his convictions of sin and his desires for salvation had rendered him for some weeks particularly reluctant to continue in an employment where he felt obliged to practise so much deception. And I thought I could discover no little evidence, in the history he gave me of his religious impressions, that the way of his daily business had been hostile to his attempts to come to repentance. And after I had plainly pointed out to him the demands of the gospel, and explained, as well as I could, the free offers of its grace and salvation, to all which he listened with intense attention and solemnity, he asked,—

"What would you advise me to do about my *business?*"

"Just this: go back to your shop, and do all your duties most faithfully and punctually, without lying. If your employer finds fault with you, explain to him, mildly and respectfully, that you are willing to do all that is right according to the law of God, but that you cannot consent to lie for anybody. If he is not a fool, he will like you the better for it, and prize you the more; for he will at once see that he has got one clerk on whose veracity he can depend. But if the man is as silly as he is unconscientious, he will probably dismiss you before long. After that you can look about you, and see what you can do. And, rely upon it, God will open a way for you somewhere. But first, and most of all, repent and believe in Jesus Christ."

The young man left me, promising soon to see me again. He did see me. He was led to seek the Lord. He became a decided Christian. He united with the Church. But he did not remain long in his situation. His mode did not please his employer.

However, he soon found another place. He established a character for integrity and promptness, and entered afterwards into business for himself. He prospered; he prospers still. It is now thirteen years since he came to me at that late hour in the evening, and he is now a man of extensive property, of high respectability, has a family, and is contented and happy. I often hear of him as an active and useful member of a Church not far distant. I sometimes meet with him. He is still accustomed to open all his heart to me, when we are together; and it is very pleasant for me to notice his deep interest in religion, his respectability and happiness.

His employer became bankrupt about seven years after he left him, and almost as much bankrupt in character as in fortune. He still lives, I believe, but in poverty, scarcely sustaining himself by his daily toil.

I attribute this young man's integrity, conversion, and salvation to his "old mother," as he always fondly called her. But for the lessons which she instilled into his mind, and the hold which she got upon his conscience before he was fifteen, I do not believe I should ever have seen him. In my first interview with him, it was evident that the thought of his mother touched him more tenderly than anything else; and to this day I scarcely ever meet him, and speak with him of personal religion, but some mention is made of his "old mother."

The instance of this young man has led me to think much of the dangers to which persons so situated are exposed; and I think I find in his history the clue to an explanation of a melancholy fact that has often come under my notice. The fact to which I now refer is simply this, that many young men are, at times, evidently the subjects of the alarming influences of the Holy Spirit, who, nevertheless, never become true Christians. And this young man's history goes far to convince me that the Holy Spirit is quenched and led to depart from them, by some unconscientious proceedings in their business. If this young man had yielded to his employer, who can believe that he ever would have yielded to the Holy Spirit?

It was not strange that this young man should have felt a great anxiety about his earthly prospects and prosperity. He was poor. His "old mother" was poor. He had no friend to lean upon. In such a situation I could excuse his anxiety; but, in such a situation, it was most sad to have the influences which were around him every hour of the day turning his anxiety into a temptation to sin. Before I knew him, he had almost come to believe that falsehood was a necessary thing in the transaction of business. He had noticed the eagerness of his employer to be rich. He had been sneered at and ridiculed as "too green," simply because he chose to act conscientiously; and this was a trial and a temptation very dangerous for a young man to encounter. It was a difficult thing for me, with all I could say, to pluck him out of this snare of the devil. And I deem it quite probable, that large numbers of our young men are kept from seeking God, by an undue anxiety about worldly things,—an anxiety fostered and goaded on to madness by the spirit, example, and influence of their employers. By this unwise and uncalled for anxiety to be rich, the heart is harassed, the conscience is beclouded by some smooth sophistry, the Holy Spirit is resisted, and heaven forgotten; and all this at that very age when the heart ought to be happy, and when, as the character is forming, it is most important that God's word and God's Spirit should not be unheeded. By this anxiety to be rich, the bright morning of youth is overhung with dark clouds of care, and the immortal soul is bound to the world as with chains of iron! No young man should feel himself qualified or safe, in entering upon the business of the world, till his hope is fixed on Christ, and his unalterable determination is, to obey God, and gain heaven, whatever else he loses. And it would be well for every such young man, when surrounded by the influences of an eager and craving covetousness and its thousand temptations, to hold the world in check, and be led to prayer, by the remembrance of his "Old Mother."

IX.

One Word to a Sinner.

I HAVE known few seasons of greater coldness and less promise, in respect to the prosperity of religion, than was the time when a young woman called upon me, to ask what she should do to be saved. Her call somewhat surprised me. I had not expected it. I had never noticed any particular seriousness in her. But now, she was evidently very much awakened to a sense of her duty and danger, and was evidently in earnest in seeking the favour of God.

After some conversation with her, and giving her such instruction as I thought adapted to her state of mind, I asked what it was that had induced her to give her attention to the subject of religion now, any more than formerly. She replied, "It was what you said to me one evening as we were coming out of the lecture-room. As you took me by the hand, you said, '*Mary, one thing is needful.*' You said nothing else, and passed on but I could not forget it." I had forgotten it entirely, but it had fastened one thought deep in her mind.

The sermon, which I had just preached, and to which she had listened, had been of no avail to her; but she could not forget the personal address to herself,—"Mary, one thing is needful." She is now, as I trust, in possession of that "one thing."

How much more efficacious is a message than a proclamation—a personal than a public address—a letter than a newspaper! The one is to the heart, but the other scarcely appears designed for it. The one is *to us*, peculiarly, especially; the other to everybody—to us, indeed, as we form a part of the multitude, but that is very seldom what the heart wants or likes. One word to a sinner is often more effectual than a score of sermons. Indeed, the secret of convicting sinners lies just in this—leading them to a *personal* application of the truth.

Yet let us not despise sermons. They are the appointment of God, and the great means of conversion. The sermons which Mary had heard were probably the very things which *prepared* her to be awakened by a private word, and without which that word, probably, would have been in vain. Still, it is quite probable that the sermons would have been in vain without that private and personal monition,—"Mary, one thing is needful."

X.

Nobody said anything to Me.

THE title which I have given to this sketch is taken from the lips of a young man, who afterwards became a member of my Church. He had called upon me for conversation upon the subject of his religious duty; and after conversing with him, and saying such things to him as I thought appropriate to his state of mind, I asked him how it came about that he had not given his prayerful attention to the subject of religion before.

"Nobody said anything to me," said he.

"Yes," I replied, "*I* have said a great many things to you."

"I know you have, in *sermons;* but I mean nobody said anything to me in *particular*, before yesterday."

"Who said anything to you yesterday?"

"Henry Clapp," said he, naming a young man who had recently entertained a hope in God.

"What did Henry say to you?"

"As I met him in the street he stopped me, and told me he had something to say to me, and asked me if he might say it. I said, Yes, he might. And then he said, 'It is high time for you to begin to seek the Lord.'"

"And what did you answer?"

"I hardly had time to answer at all, for he passed right on. But I said to him, when he had got a few feet from me, 'So it is, Henry.' He turned back his face partly toward me, looking over his shoulder, and answered, '*Do it then*,' and went right on."

"Have you seen him since?"

"No, sir."

"You say, nobody said anything to you before. If he, or some one else, had spoken to you before, do you think you would have begun before?"

"I believe I should."

Such was the opinion of this young man. To this opinion he adhered long after. The last time I spoke to him on that subject, he said to me that he believed he "should have sought the Lord *years before*, if anybody had spoken to him about it."

Here, then, was a young man, living in the midst of a Christian community till he was more than twenty years old, a regular attendant at church, known to scores of Christian men and women; and yet, "nobody said anything to him!" The first sentence that was uttered to him was not lost upon him.

There are few points of duty more difficult for wise and engaged Christians to decide, than it is to decide what they shall say, or whether they shall say anything, to the irreligious persons whom they are accustomed to meet. Many times they are afraid to say anything to them on the subject of religion, lest they should do them an injury by awakening opposition or disgust.

No man can teach them their duty. What may be the duty of one, may not be the duty of another. The question depends upon so many things, upon character, upon intimacy, upon time, place, occasion, age, and a thousand other circumstances, that no wise man will ever attempt to lay down any general rule upon the subject. But if a Christian's heart longs for the conversion of sinners as it ought, he will not be likely to err. If he speaks to an unconverted sinner, in love, and alone, and without disputation, and in humility, and in the spirit of prayer, his words will do no harm. He may not be able to do good, but at least he can *try*. The unconverted in the midst of God's people, meeting them every day, their friends, their associates, and neighbours, certainly ought not to be able to declare, "*Nobody* said anything to me,"—"No man cared for my soul."

XI.

Family Prayer.

A MAN of my congregation, about forty years of age, after quite a protracted season of anxiety, became, as he hoped, a child of God. There was nothing in his convictions or in his hopeful conversion, so far as I could discern, of any very peculiar character, unless it was the distinctness of his religious views and feelings.

But this man did not propose to unite with the Church, as I had supposed he would deem it his duty to do. One season of communion after another passed by, and he still remained away from the table of the Lord. I was surprised at this, and the more so on account of the steady interest in religion and the fixed faith in Christ which he appeared to possess. I conversed plainly with him upon the duty of a public profession of his faith. He felt it to be his duty, but he shrunk from it. He had a clear hope, was regular in his attendance at church, was prayerful,—but he hesitated to confess Christ before men. All the ground of hesitation which I could discover, as I conversed with him, was a fear that he might dishonour religion, if he professed it, and a desire to have a more assured hope. What I said to him on these points appeared to satisfy him, and yet he stayed away from the Lord's table, though he said, "I should feel it a great privilege to be there."

In aiming to discover, if possible, why a man of such clear religious views, of such apparent faith, and so much fixed hope in religion, should hesitate on a point of duty which he himself deemed obligatory upon him, I learned to my surprise that he had never commenced the duty of family prayer. He felt an inexpressible reluctance to it—a reluctance for which he could not account. He wondered at himself, but still he felt it. He blamed himself, but still he felt it. This cleared up the mystery. I no longer wondered at all at his hesitation on the matter of an open profession of religion. I had not a doubt but his fears of dishonouring religion, and his waiting for greater assurance of hope, all arose from the neglect of family prayer. I told him so, and urged that duty upon him as one that should precede the other. His wife urged it; but yet he omitted it. Finally, I went to his house, and commenced that service with him. He continued it from that time, and from that time his difficulties all vanished. Before he united with the Church he said to me, "It was a great trial to me to commence praying with my family, but now it is my delight. I would not omit it on any account. Since I have commenced it I find it a joyful duty. It comforts and strengthens me." He had now no hesitation in coming out before the world, and openly professing his faith in Christ.

Neglect of one duty often renders us unfit for another. God "is a rewarder," and one great principle on which he dispenses his rewards is this—through our faithfulness in *one* thing he bestows grace upon us to be faithful in another. "To him that hath shall be given, and he shall have abundance."

XII.

Doctrines Reconciled;

OR, FREEDOM AND SOVEREIGNTY.

I CASUALLY met a member of my Church in the street, and the nature of some conversation which was introduced led him to ask me if I recollected the conversation I had with him at the time when he first called upon me for conversation upon the subject of religion. I had forgotten it entirely. He then referred to the period of his trouble before he entertained any hope in Christ, and mentioned the particular subject about which he came to consult me. But I had no recollection of what I had said to him. He then stated the conversation in his own way, and I afterwards solicited of him the favour to write it down for me, which he kindly did (omitting the name of the minister he mentioned), and I here transcribe it from his letter, which lies before me:—

"At a time when my thoughts were led, as I trust, by the Holy Spirit, to dwell more than had been usual with me on God and eternity in their relations to myself, and I was endeavouring to get light from a more particular examination of the doctrines of the Bible than I had ever before made, great difficulties were presented to my mind by the apparent inconsistency of one doctrine with another. I could believe them, each by itself, but could *not* believe them all together; and so great did this difficulty become, that it seemed to me like an insuperable obstacle in a narrow path, blocking up my way, and excluding all hope of progress. But I was still led to look at this obstacle with a sincere desire, I believe, for its removal.

"While in this state of mind a friend solicited me to converse with a minister of much experience and high reputation for learning. I visited him in his study, and was cordially invited to make known my feelings, with the promise of such assistance as he could render. I then asked if he could explain to me *how* God could be the ever-present and ever-active sovereign of all things, controlling and directing matter and spirit, and man be left free in his ways and choice, and responsible for all his actions. He replied that he thought he could explain and remove this difficulty, and commenced a course of argument and illustration, the peculiar mode and nature of which I have now forgotten, but in which my untrained mind soon became utterly lost and confused as in a labyrinth. And when, after his remarks had been extended many minutes, he paused, and asked if I now apprehended the matter, I felt obliged to confess to him that I did not understand anything about it. He then (without any discourtesy, however) intimated that my mind was not capable of mastering a logical deduction of that nature; and I retired somewhat mortified, and in much doubt whether the fault was in myself, the subject, or the reasoning I had heard.

"A short time after this I called upon another well-known minister, who had invited any to visit him who were desirous of conversing on religious subjects. After a little general conversation I repeated to him the same question that I had before addressed to the other minister, adding that I had been told that it could be clearly explained, and asking him if he could thus explain it to me. After a moment's pause he made this reply: '*No,*—nor any other man that ever lived. If any man says he can *explain that* he says what is not true.' This short and somewhat abrupt answer, spoken with great emphasis, produced a remarkable effect upon my mind. A sense of the incomprehensibility of God seemed to burst upon me with great power. His doctrines now appeared to me as parts of his ways, and his ways as past finding out. I felt as if I had suddenly and almost violently been placed on the other side of the obstruction, which, with others of its kind, had blocked up my path. And although they were still there, and still objects of wonder and admiration, they were *no longer in the way.*

"After a few moments my instructor added that he thought he could convince me of the *truth* of the two doctrines I had named in connection; and by a short and simple course of argument, beginning with God as the author of all things, he made more clear and distinct to my apprehension the entire sovereignty of God over all his works; and also on the other point, beginning with every man's consciousness of freedom of will, he showed me the indisputable evidence on which that truth rests. And then alluding to the axiom that all truth is consistent with itself, and separate truths with each other, he left the subject to my reflections.

"I may be permitted to add that I do not pretend to judge of the wisdom of the *modes* adopted by these two ministers, as applied to other minds than my own,—but in my own case I very well know that the most laboured reasonings and explanations could not have been half as effectual in resolving my difficulty, as that plain, direct answer before quoted.

"Although years have elapsed since these conversations occurred, the one last mentioned is still vivid in my memory, and its permanent usefulness to me is frequently realized, when vain speculations on subjects not to be understood intrude themselves upon my mind."

Things hidden belong to God: things revealed belong to us. Little is gained by attempting to invade the province of God's mysteries. Every man will *attempt* it. Such is human nature. Mind will not willingly stop at the boundaries which God has for the present prescribed for it. But in vain will it strive to overpass them. "We know in part. When that which is perfect is come, then that which is in part shall be done away."

There is one great reason *why* we cannot know everything—simply because we are not God. The only real religious utility which grows out of the attempt to understand things not revealed to us, is to be found in the fact that such an attempt may humble us: it may show us what inferior beings we are,—how ignorant, how hemmed in on every side; and thus compel us to give God his own high place, infinitely above us, and hence infinitely beyond us.

If I am not mistaken, those men, those ministers who so strenuously aim to vindicate God's ways to man, to make clear what God has not revealed, do, in fact, degrade our ideas of God more than they illuminate our understandings. They make God appear not so far off, not so much above us. If they suppose that they have shed any light upon those unrevealed things which belong to God, it is quite probable that they suppose so, very much because they have levelled down his character and ways towards the grade of their own. Thus they may lead us to pride, but not to humility; they have not brought us nearer to God, but have done something to make us feel that God is very like one of ourselves; they have not given us more knowledge, but convinced us (erroneously) that we are not quite so ignorant and limited after all. This is an unhappy result. It would be better to have the opposite one,—to make us feel that God is God, and therefore inscrutable. "He holdeth back the face of his throne, and spreadeth his cloud upon it." Better far to show a sinner "the cloud," and hold his eye upon it, and make him stand in awe, and feel his own ignorance and insignificance, than to make him think (erroneously) that there is no "cloud" there.

Somewhere the human mind *must* stop. We cannot know everything. Much is gained when we become fully convinced of this; and something more is gained when we are led to see clearly the line which divides the region of our knowledge from the region of our ignorance. That dividing line lies very much between *facts* and *modes*. The facts are on the one side of it, the modes are on the other. The facts are on *our* side, and are matters of knowledge to us, because suitably proved; the modes are on *God's* side, and are matters of ignorance to us, because not revealed. "*How*" God could be an efficient and sovereign ruler over all things, and yet man be free to will and to do, was the question which troubled this young man, when he first began to seek God. It was not a question of *fact*, but of *mode* ("how?"), and therefore not a thing of duty; and therefore a thing of difficulty to him, if he chose to meddle with it.

Now, what should I say to him? It seemed to me to be at once honest and wise to tell him *the plain truth:* "*No,*—nor any other man; no man ever did explain it, or ever will. If any man *says* he can explain it, he says what is *not true.*" That was the fit answer, because the true one. The young man in his account of that answer very politely calls it "somewhat abrupt;" but he might very justly have called it by a less gentle name—*blunt.* In my opinion that was the very excellence of it; that is the reason why the answer served its purpose. It was the truth condensed and unmistakable. At a single dash it swept away his army of difficulties. It showed him that he had been labouring at an impossibility, at a thing beyond man, a thing with which he had nothing to do, but believe it and let it alone, and let God take care of it. He says, "A sense of the incomprehensibility of God seemed to burst upon me with great power. His doctrines now appeared to me as parts of his ways, and his ways as past finding out." Again he says, "The most laboured reasonings and explanations could not have been half as effectual in resolving my difficulty as that plain, direct answer." Its excellence consisted in this—it *was* plain, just the whole blunt truth. *He* says it was "permanently useful" to keep him from "vain speculations." Its utility was just this—it led him to give God the place which belongs to him, and take his own.

His trouble undoubtedly was, that he could not see "how" the doctrines he mentioned were reconcilable. But they did not *need* any reconciling. They do not quarrel. *God is an efficient sovereign over all*—that is one of the doctrines; and it was easily demonstrated to his entire satisfaction: anybody can demonstrate it. *Man is free and accountable*—that is the other doctrine; and it was easily demonstrated: anybody can demonstrate it. Both the doctrines are *true*, therefore, and hence they need no reconciling. There is no inconsistency betwixt them. That is enough.

If any one choose to attempt to go beyond this, and, by any metaphysical explanation of God's sovereign efficiency on the one hand, and man's freedom on the other, explain "*how*" the two things *can* be true, he will "darken counsel by words without knowledge."

An unconverted sinner is not reconciled to God, and this is the very reason why he is not reconciled to the doctrines of God. In my opinion these doctrines ought *always* to be presented in such a manner as to indicate their high origin, as to show they are *like* God. *Then*, an unconverted sinner will be apt to see that he dislikes the doctrines just because he dislikes God; and thus his convictions of an evil heart will become more fixed and clear, or, at least, he will perceive that the doctrines are just such as he ought to *expect*, because they precisely accord with their infinite Author. Let him be reconciled to God, and he will find little trouble with the doctrines. But let him be reconciled to

God *as he is*, an incomprehensible sovereign, an infinite mystery to a finite mind, "the high and lofty One who inhabiteth eternity." If he is reconciled to false notions of God, all his religion will be likely to be false. A comprehensible God is no God at all, for what is comprehensible is not infinite. Let men beware of "intruding into those things which they have not seen, vainly puffed up with their fleshly mind."

XIII.

I Can't Pray;

OR, THE TWO SISTERS.

I HAPPENED to be seated in the library of a literary institution with an intimate friend, when two young ladies entered the room, whom he introduced to me as sisters, who had come from a distant state to be pupils under his care. I had never heard of them before. The elder one appeared to be about twenty years of age, and the other, perhaps two years younger. My friend was soon called out of the room for a few moments, and I was left alone with them. I thought the opportunity too good to be lost, and felt it to be my duty to speak to them on the subject of their salvation. In a brief conversation upon common topics, which I endeavoured to shape in such a manner as to prepare the way for my design, I was much pleased with them. I thought they manifested more than an ordinary share of talent, and I was particularly pleased with the frankness and simplicity of their manners, and more than all with their manifest sisterly affection.

I inquired whether they were members of any Church. They were not. "And do you think you are yet living without any religion?" said I. "We are not Christians," was the answer. Their mother was a member of the Church, and they told me that they had themselves "studied religion," as they expressed it, "a great deal," and "thought about it very often," but, they said, "we are not Christians." "And why not?" said I. The question appeared to confuse them a little, and I endeavoured to relieve their embarrassment by some general remarks, such as demanded no specific reply. I asked permission to call and see them.

A little more than a week afterwards I had an interview with them. I was still more pleased with them than I had been before. They were frank, gentle, simple-hearted, and without affectation. But in respect to their religious inclinations I found little to please me, and still less in respect to their religious opinions. Their minds appeared to be stored with a species of metaphysical ideas on the subject of religion, which I could not reconcile with the Bible or with common sense, but to which they tenaciously adhered, as being in accordance with the teachings which they had always heard from the pulpit. As I entreated them to give their attention to their salvation immediately, all I could say appeared to be warded off, or its truth rendered vain, by a single idea. That idea would constantly come out in some such question as "How *can* we seek God with such hearts?" or, "How can we do anything without the Holy Spirit?" or, "What can *we* do, if God does not give us the right motives?" This was their one difficulty. They maintained, with true metaphysical courage and acumen, that they could do nothing, and any attempt to seek the Lord must be useless, because their hearts were wrong; and they could not therefore "seek him with the right feelings," as they expressed it. No act, no attempt, no thought of theirs, "could possibly be acceptable to him," or of "any avail" for themselves. They clung to this idea constantly and tenaciously.

I supposed at first that this was only a casual thought which had occurred to them, but in a second interview, I found them just the same as in the first. The idea which hindered them from any serious attempt in religion, had become interwoven with all their religious thoughts and feelings,—had been entertained so long, and employed so often, that now it came up spontaneously, and spread itself over every thought about personal religion. They presented it so naturally, so easily, and in such varied shapes and connections, that I began to despair of having any influence over them. However, I resolved to try.

I took care to assure them of the deep interest I took in them already; which I certainly could do with entire sincerity, for they had won my esteem, and it made me sad of heart to see two such estimable girls entangled in the snares of such a deception. I aimed to win their confidence; and before I left them, having now learned their cast of mind, and their peculiar religious difficulty, I assured them most affectionately that they were mistaken in many of their notions, and that they certainly might find the favour of God, if they would seek it in the Bible way. To give some practical point and direction to their thoughts, I desired them to read carefully and with prayer the fifty-fifth chapter of Isaiah, as proof of the truth of what I told them, and especially as a specimen of the manner in which their heavenly Father calls to them and counsels them, in his infinite "kindness and love." They both promised to *read* it, but I noticed that they did *not* promise to *pray* over it, as I had requested them to do.

They were very much alike in all their ideas about religion. Their hindrance was the same. I resolved, therefore, to converse with each one separately after this, because I perceived that they mutually hindered each other; for when one of them would say, "I can't seek the Lord with such a heart," the other would often reiterate the same idea in some other form, manifestly supported and confirmed in her strange notion. Urged separately to attend to their salvation, I hoped their error might be corrected. And as I had discovered a greater susceptibility, as I thought, in the younger sister, I determined to commence with her.

Consequently I soon afterwards called upon her, and asked to see her alone. She met me very affectionately. But I had scarcely uttered a single sentence in respect to her duty, before she asked suddenly, and with much animation,—

"Shall I call my sister?"

"Oh, no," said I, "I wish to see you alone. You may say some things which I should not wish your sister to hear."

This reply appeared to give her some little confusion, mingled with sadness; but she made no objections to my proposal, and soon recovered her composure. I urged her to her religious duty as faithfully and affectionately as I could. She listened to me apparently with candour and with some emotion, as, in the language of Scripture, I enjoined upon her repentance, and faith in the Lord Jesus Christ for justification unto life eternal. But the old hindrance was still in her way. The following is a part of our conversation:—

"I suppose you are convinced of the *necessity* of religion?"

"*Oh yes,* sir! I *know* its necessity; but I do not feel it,—I cannot feel it."

"Do you feel that you are a sinner,—without Christ, an *undone* sinner,—and that you have a wicked heart opposed to God?"

"I *know* I am; but I don't feel it as much as I ought."

"What do you mean by saying, 'As much as you ought?'"

"I mean, not enough to be able to seek the Lord, or repent."

"Are you really giving any definite attention to your duty towards God, to your salvation?"

"At times I have thought about it a great deal."

"Are you willing to seek the Lord *now*, in obedience to his word, and as well as you know how?"

"I have felt for a long time that I should like to be a Christian; but it is rather the conviction of my head than the feeling of my heart. My reason teaches me it is wise to make my peace with God; but I suppose such has not been the desire of my heart. My attention has been called to the subject very seriously, and I have felt it deeply at times; but the Spirit has forsaken me, and I have gone further off than ever. Once I could have given my heart to God a great deal easier than I could now," said she, with deep sadness.

"I have no doubt," said I, "that is true, entirely true. It *has* become more difficult for you, and will be more difficult still, the longer you delay. You ought to seek the Lord *now*."

"If I could seek him, sir, with an acceptable heart, I would not neglect it."

"And so, becoming worse and worse, going further and further off, you let your life run on, living without God and without hope,—making no attempt to gain eternal life. My dear girl, this is all wrong. Salvation is to be *sought*,—if there is an item of truth in the Bible, it is to be sought. You may obtain it, if you will. Salvation is offered to you,—it is free,—it is fully within your reach; the gospel calls to you. If you will seek God with all your heart, I know you will not seek in vain. God has said this to you, to induce you to seek him: 'Hear, and your soul shall live'—'I will make an everlasting covenant with you'—'Let the wicked forsake his way, and the unrighteous man his thoughts' (you *think* wrong, remember); 'and let him return unto the Lord, and he will have mercy upon him; and to our God, for he will abundantly pardon.' And all this God says *to you*, and says it just in connection with his command, 'Seek ye the Lord, call ye upon him.' You must seek him. You must turn to him with repentance and prayer. He gives you the fullest encouragement to do so. Let his word sink deep into your heart, my dear girl: 'Then shall ye go and pray unto me, and I will hearken unto you. And ye shall seek me, and find me, when ye shall search for me with all your heart: and I will be found of you.' That is the way which the God of all love calls on you to take in order to be saved; and you do not obey him,—you are not *trying* to obey him!"

"Why, sir, I have been taught that I must *submit to God first*, or he will not hear any prayer I could make. I have heard my *minister* say so."

"I am not teaching you *not* to submit to God, as you call it. He commands you to seek him, and tells you how to do it, and I want you to 'submit' to his command."

"I think," said she, "that praying before submitting to God would only be hypocrisy."

"Then you should do *both*. He certainly commands you to *pray*."

"Not with such a heart as *I* have got," said she, emphatically, and with an air of triumph.

"Yes, he *does*," said I. "Here is his command in the Bible,—it is addressed *to you*, to every sinner on earth,—'Call ye upon him while he is near.' He does, indeed, command you also to repent; but if you choose *not* to repent, that sin does not alter his command to you *to pray*. His command lies on just such a heart as you have at this moment. Your impenitence and unbelief are no excuse for you."

"How can I have any power to pray to him, and seek him rightly?"

"The Bible answers your question: 'To as many as received him, to them gave he power to become the sons of God.' The Bible offers Christ to *you*, a guilty sinner. You are to *receive him* as your own Saviour, in order to have 'power' to become a child of God. You are to 'deny yourself, and take up your cross and follow Christ.'"

"But," said she, with much agitation, "I cannot *ask* God to receive me as *his child*. I cannot plead with my whole heart for his blessing, as I would ask my earthly father for a gift which he could bestow."

"Do you *never* pray?"

"No, I *never prayed*. It seems to me it would be nothing but mockery for me to pray. *I can't pray*."

"You cannot be saved *without* prayer. If you will not ask God's blessing, you cannot have it. 'Ask, and ye shall receive,' is God's direction and promise. You foolishly invert the order, and thus 'handle the word of God deceitfully,' hoping to 'receive' *first*, and then 'ask.' If you would be saved, my dear girl, you must do as God bids you."

"But I *can't ask* with all my heart, and anything short of that would be as bad as sacrilege."

"You are wrong, my child,—all wrong. It is true you ought to seek the Lord with all your heart, as he requires; but it is *not* true, that your praying is worse than neglecting prayer; and it is not *true* that you have any ground to expect his blessing *before* you ask it. You think wrong. 'Let the wicked forsake his THOUGHTS.' You and God do not think alike. Your false notions hinder you from becoming a Christian. God commands you to seek him by prayer. You may think what you will about 'mockery,' still he tells you to pray, in order to your being saved; and while you do *not* pray, you do not take the way which his mercy points out to you."

"I *can't pray*," said she, with an accent of vexation and despair.

"You say you can't pray," said I. "God thinks you can. Just as soon as he has said to you, 'Seek ye the Lord,' he goes on to tell you *how* to seek him,—'Call ye upon him.' *He* thinks you can pray. In that passage he tells you to pray even *before* he tells you to repent. 'Call ye upon him' comes *first:* it stands before the command to repent,—'Let the wicked forsake his way.' God knows that if you do not pray you will not repent. I do not say that you ought to pray with an impenitent heart, but I say you ought to *pray*, be your heart what it may. And what an awfully wicked heart you must have, if you cannot even pray!"

"Oh, I can't *pray*, I have such a heart!"

"You refuse to pray, because you have such an evil heart. That evil heart is the very reason why you have need to pray the more earnestly. Your evil heart, instead of being an argument against prayer, is the strongest of all possible reasons why you *should* pray. You infinitely need God's help, and you should ask for it."

"I *can't* pray! It would be hypocrisy!"

"Perhaps it would; but it is *rebellion* to neglect it."

"Well, hypocrisy is worse, sir."

"I do not know *that*, in such a case as this," said I. "If you pray with such a heart as you have now, you will at least *try* to obey God in the form; but if you do not pray at all, you are a rebel both in heart and outward conduct. Which is the worse—to try and come short, or to stand here before God and say you will not try at all?"

With vexation of spirit she replied, "I *can't* pray; my heart is all wrong."

"How do you expect to get a better one?"

"I know God must give me a new heart, if I ever have it."

"Do you want him to give you a new heart?"

"Oh, sir, I *wish* he *would*," said she, weeping.

"Why, then, don't you tell him so, in earnest prayer?"

"I *can't* pray; it would be insincere."

'Are you insincere to *me*, when you tell me, with so much emotion, you 'wish God *would* give you a new heart?' Do you tell me what is not true?"

"*Oh no, sir!*" said she earnestly, "I hope you don't think I would utter a falsehood to you?"

"Not at all, my friend; but if you spoke the truth, you do sincerely wish God would give you a new heart. Where, then, would be the insincerity of telling *him* so; of *asking* him for what you sincerely desire?"

She paused a long time, pondering this question, apparently with mingled thoughtfulness and vexation; at length she replied,—

"I can't *pray;* I have not the right motives."

"How do you expect to get the right motives?"

"I never *shall* have, if God does not put them into my heart!"

"Do you *want* him to put them into your heart?"

"Yes, *I do,* above all things," said she, earnestly.

"Why, then, don't you ask him? If you are sincere in wanting him to do so, you can sincerely ask him to do so."

"But I *can't* pray, sir; the prayers of the wicked are an abomination to the Lord."

"So *you* say," said I.

"Does not the *Bible* say so, sir?"

"No, my child, nowhere."

"Why, sir, I thought it did."

"It does not. It says, 'The sacrifice of the wicked is an abomination to the Lord;' but the meaning of that is, that when the wicked offer sacrifice, and at the same time do not intend to abandon their wickedness, it is an abomination."

"Well, sir, the Bible requires good motives."

"Certainly it does; and it requires you to pray to God, 'Create in me a clean heart, and renew a right spirit within me.' You need good motives, and for that very reason you should pray."

"But I *can't* pray. It is *not* prayer, such as the Bible demands, if I should ask God for another heart."

Said I, "The *common* complaint of the Bible against sinners is, not that they pray with bad motives, but that they do not pray at all. It censures the wicked, because they 'cast off fear, and restrain prayer,' as you do; while it makes promises to those who seek God by prayer."

"I *never* prayed," said she, with manifest fear and vexation of spirit. "*I can't pray*, till I have the right feelings."

"You must pray, my dear girl, in order to *get* the right feelings. So the Bible teaches you, and you pervert it. You say you must have the right feelings *first*. The Bible tells you to pray for them, if you would ever have them. In Jeremiah xxix. 12, 13, God says, 'Then shall ye call upon me, and ye shall go and pray unto me, and I will hearken unto you. And ye shall seek me and find me, when ye shall search for me with all your heart: and I will be found of you, saith the Lord.' The praying, the seeking, is *first*. The finding comes afterwards. 'Ask, and ye shall receive,' says God. 'Give to me, and then I will ask,' is your answer."

"But, sir, I certainly have no heart to pray. I *can't* pray! God would frown on any prayer I could offer."

"So *you* say, but he has not said so. He will frown upon your *refusing* to pray. It seems to me perfectly clear that God is far more kind to you than you think him,—more kind than you are to yourself. He says to you, in your weakness and all your want, 'In me is thy help.' You demand of your poor heart to be holy first, *before* it can have any encouragement at all, even to pray for help. Your cold heart does him an injustice. He is more kind than that. He encourages you to come to him, and call upon him, with just such a needy and imperfect heart, as you have this moment; to come to him by Christ in all your unworthiness and fear, and tell him your wants, and beg for mercy and divine assistance. He stands ready to hear you, to forgive and love you, and bestow upon you that better heart you long for, if you will ask. And you abuse his kindness by your unbelief. He is far better than you think him. He invites you to come to him in Christ Jesus, and ask him what you will. You demand of your poor heart more, in one sense, than God demands of it. You demand of it faith and holiness *aside* from any divine help, and without prayer; while he *offers* you help, to aid you to holiness and faith. I do not understand him as inviting you to Christ only *after* you have a good heart, but as inviting you *now*, just as you are."

"Oh!" said she, quite overcome with her emotions, "I wish I had a right to come."

"What do you mean, my dear girl? You talk inconsistently, absurdly. You want a right heart *first*, and then you will consent to pray for a right heart."

"I know, sir, my mind is wrong; but it does seem to me I *cannot* pray with such a heart."

"That is only a deceitful *excuse*. If you do not *love* to have such a heart, you will pray God to give you a better one."

"Oh, I am such a sinner! How can such a creature pray?"

"Others just like you *have* prayed, and God has answered them. You can do the same thing, if you will."

"But my very heart is too wicked!"

"You do not more than half believe what you say. If you really believed you had such a wicked heart, you would cry for mercy with all your might."

"I *would pray*," said she, "if I had such motives that God would hear me."

"That is the very essence of self-righteousness," said I. "You expect to be answered, not because you shall have cried, 'God be merciful to me a sinner;' but because you shall have gone to God with such good motives, with a heart so much better, that he will hear and answer you *on that account.* You wish to be able to stand up and offer the Pharisee's prayer, 'God, I thank thee that I am not as other men are.' You are unwilling to be the poor publican,—to smite on your breast, despairing of your wicked heart, and cry, 'God, be merciful to me a sinner.' You won't consent to be a beggar. Your heart is too full of pride and self-righteousness to consent to let you be an infinite debtor to divine mercy, as an undone and helpless sinner."

"Why, sir," said she with amazement, "do you think I am self-righteous?"

"I *know* you are. You have shown it in almost every sentence you have uttered for the last half hour. You justify yourself. You justify your prayerlessness, even. You think to pray with such good motives, some time or other, as to meet acceptance. Rejecting Christ, you rely on the good motives you hope to have, as the ground of your acceptance. And that is all self-righteousness."

After a solemn pause she asked,—

"What *shall* I do? I am undone!"

"Seek the Lord," said I; "call upon him; fly to Christ as you are—remember, *as you are.*"

"*Will* he *hear* me?"

"Yes; he *says* he will. 'Ask, and ye shall receive.' Believe his promise of the 'Holy Spirit to them that ask him.' You have no need to be hindered, my dear child, for an hour. Give God your heart as it is. Go to him as you are, a poor, undone sinner, and beg for mercy; and *believe* he will not cast you off. God loves you, and waits to save you. He offers you all the benefits of the blood of atonement and of the aids of the Holy Spirit—'the Holy Spirit to *them that ask him*,' remember. And what more can your wicked heart need?"

She seemed to be melted into tenderness.

"And now, my dear girl, *will* you *pray?* Will you begin this night?"

"I *ought*," said she trembling.

"Then, *will* you?"

"Yes, sir, *I will*," said she emphatically.

"Good-bye," said I, and instantly left her.

During this interview she became greatly troubled. Evidently she was tossed with conflicting emotions. She began to perceive that her excuse of a wicked heart would not answer her purpose; and at times I thought her affectionate disposition on the very point of yielding to the kindness of God.

I now had some hope that she would seek the Lord. She had promised to *pray*, and thus had yielded the very point in which all her opposition practically centred. But on considering the whole matter more carefully that evening at home, I came to the conclusion that she would not pray as she had promised; but that when she was alone, the influence of her old difficulty would return upon her and overthrow the urgency of all that I had said.

Early the next morning, therefore, I called upon her. She was taken by surprise. Said I,—

"Did you *pray* last night, my dear girl?"

Her eyes filled with tears. She was silent. She told me some days afterwards, "I felt my very heart sick within me, the moment you asked me if I had prayed." I repeated the question,—

"My child, did you keep your promise—did you pray last night?"

Her whole frame was agitated. The question seemed to pierce her heart.

"No, sir, I did not!" said she faintly, and covered her face in her handkerchief, in convulsive agony.

"And why not—why didn't you pray? You make my very heart sorry, when you tell me you neglected it!"

"I did try," said she, weeping,—"I did try. I kneeled down, but I could not open my lips to utter one word! My heart was so cold and wicked, I did not dare to speak one word to my heavenly Father."

"Your heart is far more wicked than you think; and if you wait to make it better, you will wait for ever! But God is a thousand-fold more merciful and kind than you think. Give yourself to him. Just trust to Christ, bad as your heart is."

"Oh, sir, it is hard to learn to *trust!* I have tried to trust myself in Christ's hands. How *can* I trust?"

"Suppose," said I, "you were here on this island, and you knew the island was going to sink under you, and you must get off or sink with it, and you could do nothing at all to save yourself, and then a boat should come to save you, and you had every reason to believe it would keep you from sinking and take you off safely, and land you where you wanted to go,—would it be 'hard to trust' to it? No, no; you would instantly go on board and stay there, and take care not to fall off. You would trust it willingly, fully, joyfully. Just so commit yourself, a helpless sinner, to Christ, and not sink into perdition. He will take you, and land you safe in heaven, if you will ask him and trust him."

"I am afraid I have not such a sense of my sin as to seek God *earnestly*."

"What, then, will you do?"

"I don't know, unless I wait for it."

"And will you get it by waiting?"

"I suppose," said she, "a just sense of sin is the gift of the Holy Spirit."

"I suppose so, too; and therefore you must pray for the Holy Spirit. He is promised as a gift to them that ask. You are not to *wait*. 'Behold, now is the day of salvation.' Give your bad heart to God."

I left her more solemn and docile than ever before. Her stout heart trembled.

The next day but one, I called upon her. She was in her class. I sent for her to meet me in a private room. I asked her,—

"Have you trusted yourself to Christ yet?"

She shook her head. Her eyes filled with tears.

"What have you been waiting for?"

"Oh, my dear friend, I don't know. It seems as if I *cannot* offer myself to God in such a manner that he will accept me. I try with all my power. But my thoughts wander when I try to pray. My heart is *all* unbelief and sin!"

"You must pray for God's help, and *trust* him to help you."

"Oh, sir, if I go to God I am afraid he will not accept me. There *never was* such a sinner."

"You need not fear an item, my dear friend. He has *promised* to accept you. Go to him by faith in his Son for all you want. His very throne shall crumble, sooner than you shall be cast off."

I left her in tears, apparently in a subdued and tender agitation.

Four days afterwards I saw her again. She met me with a smile of gladness.

"Oh, I am glad you have come! I have wanted to see you very much." Grasping my hand, she began to speak to me of her feelings,—"I want to tell you a great many things about myself," but her emotions choked her utterance. I asked her,—

"Can you pray *now*, my dear girl?"

"*Oh yes, I can pray now with my whole heart.* But, sir, it seems to me I do not come fully to Christ, though I *know* I want to do so."

"Do you still love sin and the world too much to give them up for Christ?"

"No, sir, I think not," said she, solemnly.

"There may be some darling sin you do not renounce. Perhaps you love the world too much. Weigh the matter well. Count the cost. 'Choose this day whom you will serve.' If you choose the world, it will cheat you. If you choose the God of love, he will save you."

"I do want to be a Christian," said she, tenderly. "I pray my God for this with all my heart."

"And what has made you so much more earnest?"

"I have felt so ever since I heard your sermons on the text, 'Go thy way for this time.' I was afraid I was like Felix, to tremble and yet delay."

"Do you intend to delay?"

"No, sir, indeed, I do not *intend* to do that," said she, the tears gushing from her eyes.

The next morning I found her in deep solemnity. Her weeping eyes told of her agitated heart. I asked,—

"Are you willing now to give up all and follow Christ?"

"Oh, sir," said she, with the utmost earnestness, "*I do not think there is any other desire in my heart*, except that I may be a Christian."

"Do you now love God?"

With some thoughtful hesitation she replied,—

"I am afraid, sir, to venture an answer to that question."

"You need not answer it. I will not embarrass you. But see to it, that you trust all to the sovereign mercy of God, offered to you in his Son. I can say no more than I have said already. I have told you all. My work is finished. I leave you with God. See to it, that you make an entire surrender of yourself, for time and eternity, to your Lord and Redeemer."

On the evening of the next day I had a long interview with her. It was delightful to hear her expressions. Among other things she said to me,—

"*I feel* that I am now *at peace.* I *trust* my God. I *love* to trust him. The Saviour is everything to me. I know he will fulfil all his promises. Oh, my dear friend, I have had a dreadful struggle! but I have had strength given me to persevere. Now the love of God is very precious to my soul. I never expected this happiness."

"Do you love to pray?"

"*Oh yes;* prayer is sweet to me now. I can *tell all my wants to my heavenly Father.*"

After some further conversation, I said to her,—

"You seem to have come into a different state of mind within a few days. You do not talk as you did. How have you brought yourself to this—to feel so differently?"

"Oh, sir! it is nothing that *I* have done! I *just prayed to God with all my heart and in full faith; and he did everything for me.*"

She appeared to be a very happy Christian. Her joy was full. Her life was prayer.

The elder sister, who so much resembled the younger in her difficulty about prayer, I visited generally at the same times and as often as the younger. I had almost precisely the same things to say to her; and a few days afterwards she also entertained "just a little hope," as she expressed it.

These sisters were deeply interested for each other. Each would say to me frequently, "I want you to see my sister." Their anxiety for one another was beneficial to them, and their thoughts of their absent mother, whom they often mentioned, appeared to me to constrain them to more earnest endeavours to lay hold on eternal life. They both have hope in Christ, and I trust will both have heaven. I first saw them in the month of May, and on the seventh day of the following September, having returned to their distant home, their native place, they both went for the first time to the table of the Lord, happy Christians in the dew of their youth.

I have given this sketch in this extended form, as illustrating the propriety of continued solicitation at the door of a sinner's heart. Here were two young ladies without any special seriousness, worldly, presenting no hopeful appearance, but presenting a cold discouragement, calculated to damp every hope and stop every effort to do them good, and coming out so sadly in the words, "I never prayed in my life."

But one conversation was followed up by another; they were scarcely left a day to themselves and the influences of the world; their strange hindrance of speculative error was assailed in every form, and overthrown again and again by declarations of Scripture and arguments of reason; and their whole history shows that vigorous and persevering attempts to convert sinners, have as much prospect of success as any well-directed attempts in any ordinary matter. Not that man can reach sinners' hearts, but that God may be expected to reach them, when a minister or any other man shall diligently knock at their door with the voice of God's urgent and affectionate truth.

The reluctance of these young women to pray may have been fostered—I suppose it was—by the fogs of a metaphysical theology, in which they had been educated, and which they probably misunderstood. But it *originated* in a consciousness of a home-bred depravity. "I can't *ask* God to make me his child," said one of them, "I *know* my heart does not want it." But there was a propriety in urging them to prayer, because God commands men to pray, and because I expected they would be rendered more sensible of their opposition to God, and their need of his aid, when they should attempt its performance. And so it turned out. Their conviction, which *had* been superficial and speculative only, became more deep, more practical. While superficial and speculative, their depravity was an excuse to them. When rendered deep and thorough by a sincere attempt to pray, it became experimental, it was no longer an excuse, but only made them cry for mercy with all their might, "I prayed to God in full faith, and with all my heart, and he did everything for me." A just conviction of sin makes no excuse, but it will pray.

I might have avoided this girl's excuse by urging her to repentance and faith; I chose to meet it by urging her to prayer. It was her inability to pray in any manner to meet her own approval, which had contributed more than anything else to convince her of her deep-seated depravity and alienation from God; and I did not wish to diminish this conviction, by leading her thoughts from the thing that caused it. It would have been dangerous to turn her thoughts into a new channel. I aimed to conspire with the Holy Spirit. It was important that she should realize the necessity of the direct help of the Divine Spirit, *personally*, *practically*, and therefore more deeply, than by her speculation she ever could; and she was more likely to *have* such a realization through endeavours to pray rightly than by any other means. In her speculation she *thought* she knew full well her wickedness and helplessness, but these were the very things she did *not* know. She found them out just when she endeavoured to pray. Then a full sense of her undone and helpless condition burst upon her. She could do nothing but cry, "I just prayed to God with all my heart, and in full faith." And then, as she expressed it, "*he* did everything for me." "Go thou and do likewise."

XIV.

I Can't Feel.

FROM early spring down to the autumn of the year, a very sedate and contemplative man had been accustomed to call upon me, in respect to his religious thoughts and anxieties. At first he seemed to have *thoughts* only, but they ripened by degrees into anxieties. He began by asking about theories, or doctrines, apparently without any idea of making an application of the truth to himself. He had points of difficulty which he wished to have explained, and then he found *other* points; and these gradually changed in character from abstract questions to those of the application of the truth. From the first I tried to lead him on to the personal application; but months passed away before he appeared to have much sense of his sin, or much anxiety about himself.

But he came to this, and after quite a struggle of mind, as it appeared to me, to lead himself to believe in salvation by personal merit, he gave that up. He said to me, "I have become convinced that sinners are saved, not by their own goodness, but because they are pardoned on account of Jesus Christ. Faith in him is the only way for them."

After this I conversed with him several times, when he appeared to me to be not far from the kingdom of God; but I was as often disappointed, for he would come back to me again in as much trouble and unbelief as before. Again and again I had answered all his inquiries, teaching him out of the Scriptures; had brought up to his mind all the doctrines of truth, the divine promises and directions, sin and salvation; but all in vain. He had become very solemn, and seemed to be entirely candid and really in earnest. His Bible had become his constant study; he was a man of prayer; he attended upon all our religious services with manifest interest; he appeared to have a deep sense of his sin and danger; but he had no hope in Christ.

I finally said to him one evening,—

"I do not know, my dear sir, what more can be said to you. I have told you all that I know. Your state as a sinner lost, exposed to the righteous penalty of God's law, and having a heart alienated from God; and the free offer of redemption by Christ; and your instant duty to repent of sin, and give up the world, and give God your heart; and the source of your help, through the power of the Holy Spirit assured to you, if you will 'receive' Christ;—all these things have become as familiar to you as household words. What more can I say? I know not what more there is to *be* said. I cannot read your heart. God can, and *you* can by his aid. Some things you have said almost made me think you a Christian, and others again have destroyed that hope. I now put it to your own heart—if you are not a Christian, what hinders you?"

He thought a moment; said he,—

"I can't *feel!*"

"Why didn't you tell me this before?"

"I never thought of it before, sir."

"How do you *know* this hinders you?"

"I can think of nothing else. But I am sure I shall never be converted to God, if I have no more feeling than I have now. But *that* is my own fault. I know *you* cannot help me."

"No, sir, I cannot; nor can you help yourself. Your heart will not feel at your bidding."

"What then *can* I do?" said he, with much anxiety.

"Come to Christ *now*. Trust him. Give up your darling world. 'Repent, so iniquity shall not be your ruin.'"

He seemed perplexed, annoyed, vexed; and with an accent

of impatience, such as I had never witnessed in him before, he replied,—

"That is *impossible.* I want the feeling to *bring* me to that, and I *can't* feel!"

"Hear me, sir," said I; "and heed well what I say. I have several points:—

"1. The Bible never tells you that you must *feel*, but that you must *repent* and *believe.*

"2. Your complaint that you '*can't feel*' is just *an excuse* by which your wicked heart would justify you for not coming to Christ *now.*

"3. This complaint that you '*can't feel*' is the complaint of a *self-righteous spirit.*"

"How is it?" said he.

"Because you look to the desired *feeling* to *commend* you to God, or to make you fit to come, or to enable you to come."

"Yes, to *enable* me," said he.

"Well, *that* is *self-righteousness*, in the shape of self-justification for *not* coming; or in the shape of self-reliance if you *attempt* to come. That is all *legalism*, and not the acceptance of a gracious Christianity. You cannot be saved by the *law.*

"4. Your complaint is the language of the most *profound ignorance. To feel* would do you no good. Devils feel—lost spirits feel.

"5. Your complaint that you '*can't feel*' tends to lead you to a *false religion*—a religion of mere self-righteous feeling. Religion is *duty.*"

"But, sir," said he, "there is *feeling* in religion."

"But, sir," said I, "there is *duty* in religion; and which shall come *first?* You *ought* to feel; you ought to *love* God, and *grieve* that you are such a senseless sinner."

"I know I am a sinner, but I can't feel any *confidence* to turn to God, to *draw* me to him."

"You are like the prodigal in the fifteenth of Luke, when he thought of saying to his father, 'Make me as one of the hired servants.' Poor fool! Say *that to his father!* Why, the very idea is a libel on his father's heart. But he didn't think so. Poor fool! he knew no better. And you are a greater fool than he. He went *home.* And where he met his father he found his heart. He could '*feel*' when he found his father's arms around him, and felt the strong beatings of his father's heart. Do as he did. Go home, and you will feel, if you never felt before. You will *starve* where you are; your 'husks' will not save you."

As I was uttering this he hung his head, cast his eyes upon the floor, and stood like a statue of stone. I let him think. There he stood for some minutes; then turning suddenly to me, reaching to me his hand, he said,—

"I am very much obliged to you. Good night."

I let him go.

About a month afterwards I met him riding alone in his waggon, and he insisted upon my taking a seat with him, for he had "something to say" to me, and he would "drive wherever I wanted to go." I was no sooner seated in the waggon than he said to me,—

"The human heart is the greatest mystery in the world,—inexplicable, contradictory to itself; it is *absurd.* The sinner says, as I said to you that last night, 'I *can't* feel,' as an excuse for holding on to the world. I found as soon as I was *willing* to 'go home,' as you called it, the *road* was plain enough."

"Were you hindered *long* with that want of feeling?"

"No; I never thought of it till that night. It came upon me like a flash; and then, just as I was thinking it was a good reason in my favour, you dashed it all into shivers."

"And can you 'feel' now?"

"Oh yes; I have no trouble about that. I find if a poor creature will turn to God, in the name of Jesus, he will learn to *feel* as he never felt before."

Sinners not willing to give up the world, and wanting an excuse for their irreligion, exclaim, "*I can't feel.*"

XV

Willing to be Lost.

I RECEIVED a letter from an individual in a neighbouring state, an entire stranger to me. Omitting some names and dates, I here give some liberal extracts from it. It appears to me that the religious experience which the letter describes, is one of the best possible refutations of the strange theological opinion to which it refers; and perhaps desponding affections in other people may receive some solace by knowing something of the experience of my correspondent, as recorded in the letter:—

"SIR,—I am troubled and perplexed in reference to my spiritual state. Will you allow me to throw off all restraint, forgetting for the time that I am a stranger? With a grateful heart, I tell you my dear parents were very godly persons, and we, their children, were educated most religiously. My blessed father, now gone to heaven, was a great admirer of Dr. Hopkins and Dr. Emmons. The great doctrines they inculcated were among the first lessons I learned on religious subjects; but truly, sir, I could not comprehend them, and the views they gave me of God were truly undesirable. As I knew nothing about the filial love which glowed in the breast of my father, the ideas I entertained of my Creator filled me with dread, and I grew up *afraid* of this holy Sovereign. After my marriage I attended upon the ministry of one who called himself a Hopkinsian; but surely Dr. Hopkins would never have acknowledged him as a disciple. He used to tell me I must be willing to 'be led into sin, if the glory of God required it;' that I must 'go down to the potter's house,' and there become *willing* to see God *form* me into a 'vessel of wrath,' if he saw it most for his glory to do so. Well, as such doctrines were furnished me as 'the sincere milk of the word,' I need not tell you I could not 'grow thereby.'

"In the year 18—, I indulged a faint hope that my heart was renewed; but so weak was my faith, that my days were divided between hope and *fear*. I really loved the society of devout, heavenly-minded

Christians. I saw myself a vile sinner, despaired of making myself any better, and was brought to see that all I could do was to give my whole self to Jesus in all my *sinfulness*. This I did over and over again; but to you I confess I never, never felt *willing* to go to perdition, though I saw God would be *just* in sending me there. But oh, sir! I shrunk from justice, and cried for mercy, mercy! Well, from that time to the present (more than twenty years), I have known nothing like the 'assurance of hope.' Though I am as certain that I love the prosperity of the Redeemer's kingdom as I am of my own existence, yet *fear* so predominates in my heart, that I am at times ready to give up all hope of my adoption. Let me give you a single instance out of a thousand. If seated in the house of God, listening with delight and rapt attention to the preached word, joining with all my heart in the prayers and praises of that sacred place, and feeling in my very soul that to go—

"'Where congregations ne'er break up,
And Sabbaths never end,'

is the heaven I desire; if my ear catches the sound of distant *thunder*, all is over with me; my mind is filled with painful forebodings, and lines like the following are darted through it:—

"'Quite weary is my patience grown,
And bids my fury go;
Swift as the lightning it shall pass,
And be as fatal too.'

Trembling, sick, unable to sit up—vomiting generally follows. Now the dreadful question comes, Is not 'my house founded on the sand?' It is not *dying* that I fear so much, but the thought of dying *unprepared*. I feel no heart-rising against God, his love or his government, but *heart-sinking* fear.

"Now, do we not read, 'Great peace have they who love thy law.' —'Perfect love casteth out fear—'The Lord will keep him in perfect peace, whose mind is stayed on him?' Here now is my trouble. *Afraid* of a holy, *righteous* God—sensible I deserve his anger, I sink beneath the *fear* of it. The other day I was meditating on my strange state of mind, and I thought I would go again, as the hymn says,—

"'I'll go to Jesus, though my sins
Have like a mountain rose;
I know his courts, I'll enter in,
Whatever may oppose.'

When I came to the verse,—

"'Perhaps he will admit my plea,
Perhaps will hear my prayer,'—

the word '*perhaps*' troubled me. I consulted a book in which the author has explained that '*perhaps.*' He says, 'There is no perhaps in the matter. God says there is none. "Hear, and your soul shall live."' He says, 'the *hymn* is right, because it represents what a sinner feels when he is resolving to go to Christ. But let him fling his '*perhaps*' to the winds; the sceptre of Emmanuel shall be shivered into pieces, the throne of the Redeemer Jehovah shall sink, sooner than such a sinner perish. This was enough for my poor heart. All I could do was to weep, and read, and weep again. It seemed to me that if I had ten thousand souls to save, and each as sinful as I felt mine to be, I would lay them all into the arms of Jesus, and not doubt about their acceptance. I thought I could never feel depressed again with fear. Those blessed words were so precious, my heart rested on the ability and *willingness* of Jesus to save me.

"But alas! sir, we have been visited with a tempest since that time, and again my poor house has fallen. O tell me, if I cannot bear a *little storm*, how am I to view the terrors of the last great day? In all the simplicity of a child I ask you, dear sir, what shall I do? I cannot go to the world of despair. But if, after all, I must receive the merited reward of my sins, I will have *nothing* to do with the wicked men in that dreadful place, nor can I ever blaspheme the name of Jehovah Jesus. . . . . . .

"'The lines have fallen unto me in pleasant places; I have a goodly heritage.' God has given me a good, kind, faithful shepherd, whose ministrations I have enjoyed seven years. He is an excellent man. We all love him much. But for some reason he will not let me tell him of my fears; or, at least, he is pleased to treat them so lightly that I do not often say much to him on the subject. He is a man of great energy, was never afraid of anything, and appears ever prepared for death, however sudden it may come. But his views on some points are very different from those of Dr. Emmons." . . . . . .

Such was the letter. I thought it furnished melancholy proof of the unnecessary perplexity and torment of spirit which false theological principles will sometimes produce. This person, evidently, had been annoyed, plagued, tormented for years, by the influence of an extravagant doctrine. The same has happened to others. An eminent clergymen, to whom I read that letter in my study, said to me, "Change the names and the dates, and that case is precisely my own!"

The minister who taught the doctrine, and insisted upon it

with so much plainness and strength, probably went far beyond anything which Hopkins or Emmons would have said, though he deemed himself one of their disciples in theology. This is common to all *followers of men;* the scholar becomes worse than the master.

It is often difficult, indeed, to know how to deal with the troubles of mind which result from strange doctrines. The doctrine *will* come up before the heart which it has once tormented, and will stand as a wall of adamant, to keep from the heart that hope which otherwise the gospel would infuse into it. Or, if the strange doctrine is of an opposite character, and has led to a false hope, it will be very apt to come back again to do its old mischief, after the delusive hope has once been dissipated by the truth. And in the case of such doctrines and despondencies as this letter mentions, it is not easy for us to determine whether we shall reason or ridicule. A woman, who for a long time had been serious, perplexed, and distressed, but who never had attained any hope in Christ, once went to her minister, the Rev. Dr. S——, of H——, and told him that she now believed she had become a Christian.

"What makes you think so, madam?"

"Because," said she, "I am now willing to be damned. I have tried a long time to come to such a state of mind, and never have succeeded; but *now* I am willing to be damned, if God pleases to cast me off."

"Well, madam," said the doctor, coolly, "if *you* are willing to be damned, and *God* is willing you should be, I don't know that I ought to have any objections."

Probably this ridicule was quite as effective to correct a strange notion as any didactic instruction could have been. However this may have been, to the above letter I returned the following answer:—

"My Dear Friend,—It is rather an awkward business to write a letter, when you do not know whether it is a man or a woman to whom you are writing. But I am placed just in that position. Your initials do not indicate your sex.

"The only thing, beyond the ordinary range of strictly religious matter, which (as I judge from your letter) you have any special need that I should write to you, is a few words to call your attention to *the influences of physical condition upon religious sensibilities.* Thunder will sometimes kill goslings, turn milk sour, and spoil the tanner's calf-skins, when they are at a particular point in the process of being manufactured into leather; and it is not a miracle, if thunder sometimes makes you sick. Though it may be a very humiliating idea to us, that we are sometimes under the influence of external physical causes in the sacred sensibilities of our religion, yet it is true. The east wind has shaken many a religious hope. We have not yet 'spiritual bodies,' superior to the power of matter's contact, and we are greatly liable to have our comforts and griefs of mind swayed by the elements, especially when a timid or peculiarly sensitive soul is connected with a body not made of iron. The outward things of nature, such as storms, and thunder, and waters, which you mention (or even our imagination at work upon them), may have upon us a more powerful effect than our intellectual or spiritual pride is willing to confess. Women more than men are liable to this,—and from your hand-writing I *suppose* you to be a woman.

"So far as your religious impressions have been moulded by Hopkins or Emmons, you may be unfortunate; but I see nothing in your case which is very uncommon, or which need greatly perplex you. . . .

"It seems you have resort to Hopkins and Emmons, and to another book which you mention. All this may be very well, but you are quite too much *affected* by a *speculative spirit.* Be a child; not a philosopher, but a child; not a servant, but a child; not an angel, but a child, —just a *humble child.*

"Let me lift the curtain a little, and give you a glimpse of what lies within. When I say that *speculation* never humbles *spiritual pride,* you are startled. I do not wonder at it, though the words are not *thunder.* But you may be sure there is in the suggestion more truth than poetry or politeness.

"I hope you are a Christian; but a little more simplicity would not hurt you, and a little less pride would do you good." . . . . .

———.

Not many days had elapsed before I received from my unknown correspondent the following letter:—

". . . . . You have taught me a lesson I shall not soon forget. Oh, sir, you *have* 'lifted the curtain.' I did not know what manner of spirit I was of. You have read me rightly,—'a little more simplicity would not harm you, a little less pride would do you good.' Here is truth condensed. I really think I feel the force of it as keenly as you *meant* I should. The night I received your most welcome letter I had little to do with sleep, and the only prayer I could utter was, 'God be merciful to me a sinner.' Sir, I *thank* you, *sincerely* thank you for turning my eyes in the *right* direction. Why did I not know my heart better? 'Who can understand his errors? Cleanse thou me from secret faults.'

"'Show me my sins, and how to mourn
My guilt before thy face.'

"In regard to my leaving you in the dark in respect to myself, I am much mortified, and can only say it was inexcusable carelessness. As I sat down to write, I felt as though I was talking to one whom I knew personally. . . . . . I beg you to forgive me, and be assured I shall be more careful in future. I feel so much obliged to you for writing, and especially for your *faithfulness*, that I am not sorry for obtruding my unworthy self upon your notice, however much mortification it has occasioned me. . . . . . Oh, sir, you *have done me good.*"

To this I returned the following answer:—

"MY DEAR MADAM,—I have just received your last letter, and seize a moment to respond to it. I am greatly rejoiced if my letter afforded you profit or satisfaction; but I am quite sorry it kept you awake. That condition of nervous excitability which forbids your sleeping, or forbids your loving thunder, is not to be fostered or indulged. It will do your religion, if you have any, no good; and it certainly will not lead you to it, if you are still an unbeliever. Perhaps you have not sufficiently considered that *nerves* are poor counsellors. You would do well not to ask their advice. You had better ask Paul, or David, or Jeremiah even, if you must have the liberty to utter 'Lamentations.' And more: I am not willing to speak evil of anybody, but I can assure you, that these same creatures, called *nerves*, are the greatest liars in the country. Do not believe them when they tell you that you are a Christian, or when they tell you that you are a reprobate. They will tell lies on both sides, and they don't care which. I did hope that you would be able to perceive their mischief by what I said to you about the goslings, and sour milk, and calf-skins. But you have not mentioned it in your letter. What I mean is simply this: that thunder has an inexplicable effect upon some such things, with which religion has nothing to do; and if it has an inexplicable effect upon *you*, you need not link that effect with your religion: your sickness is caused by the thunder, not by your depravity.

Thunder, winds, storms, waters, may assail your timid nerves, and set them again at their old work of lies; but your *religion* has nothing at all to do with the matter. If old Elijah were alive he could tell you something about this.

"You speak of seeing me, but you 'fear the water.' I should be happy to see you, madam; but I am in duty bound to tell you that you would be greatly disappointed. You might be benefited, indeed, but the *way* of the benefit would be very different from your anticipation. I know a man who once travelled more than a thousand miles for the purpose of seeing a minister, whom he believed to be able to give him some light on the subject of personal religion; and all the good he received from him was just nothing at all;—and yet this was the best possible good, for the experiment *convinced him fully that his help was not in man.*

"Let me lift the curtain a little further. Faith, you know, is the way of salvation,—is an essential in every part of religion. Sometimes we are *drawn* to faith, and sometimes our miserable hearts must be *driven* to it. Now, though I believe you are an amiable woman (but not *too* amiable, after all, *at times*), yet somehow or other you are not easy to be drawn,—you must be driven. And your temptations, and fears, and plans, and efforts, every one of them, just tend to draw you away from the exercise of a naked, simple faith in God,—even many a one of your prayers has had the same effect, because you trusted the *praying* to do you good, instead of trusting God's answer to do you good. And for the proof of this, I call upon your own recollections, extending over years of fear and hope.

"One thing more. There is an *order* in the snares and temptations of the devil. He has three classes of temptations. You have got beyond the first, and perhaps the second; but you are not safe from the third,—yea, you are very much exposed to it, and the more so, probably, because you do not know or even suspect what it is.

"*First,* Satan employs *the world,*—just aims to keep sinners satisfied to love earthly things, and pursue them. If he cannot do that,—if they cannot be made to live on without any kind of religion, hunting for riches, honour, pleasure, ease, or some such thing, then,—

"*Second,* Satan aims to lead them into a *false religion,* into deception, into some delusion, which shall lull them into a false peace to their ruin. (You have been quite sufficiently aware of this,—indeed, you have feared it too much.) But if he cannot do this,—if they have too much knowledge of the Bible, and too much of the influences of the Holy Spirit to be led into a false hope,—then the old liar shifts his ground; and,—

"*Third,* Aims to drive them *to despair.* This is his last effort, and, I do believe, the most devilish one of all. It is most like him, for it is at once the *most false* and *most miserable.*

"But I must stop. 'Satan hath desired to have you, that he may sift you as wheat;' but I trust the Master hath 'prayed for you, that your faith fail not.'

"I want you to think of these three classes of temptations, and to oppose *faith* to each one of them. Just fling your faith into the face of the devil, however he may come to you. Especially, my dear friend, think of this third and last device of the adversary, which you have commonly too much overlooked, and let faith triumph over despair." . . . .

The following is her reply:—

"How shall I sufficiently thank you, dear sir, for your last kind letter? I cannot make you know how deeply your condescension is felt and appreciated. You will allow me now to tell you all my heart —I mean the little part of it that I know.

"You say 'nerves are poor counsellors,' and that 'they are the greatest liars in the country.' Now it has been *my* way to set down all the mischief you ascribe to *nerves*, to a *wicked heart.* Here I have found much trouble; but you have in a measure convinced me that I have got to learn *how* to use the shield of faith. Oh, sir, my eyes are open. Now I see that 'simple, naked faith in God' is what I need; and, if I am not wholly deceived, my resolution is taken. I will give Satan the lie, and believe God. He has said, 'Come unto me;' and, 'Whosoever cometh I will in no wise cast out.' Now I will not be driven from a firm, practical belief of this *blessed, faithful* promise. This doubting, half dead, half alive way of living, is to be abandoned at once and for ever. Not in my own strength may I attempt this; but lifting a tearful, trusting eye to Jesus, I will strive to maintain a 'cheerful courage,' and God helping me, I need never yield to one of either 'class of temptations,' employed by the great adversary. But if my sinful heart will sink in fear and dismay, amidst all the great and precious promises made by Him who is unchanging truth, then I will just bring this wicked heart the sooner to Jesus, that he may renew and sanctify it.

"How well I know what you mean when you tell me that 'all my plans and efforts, every one of them, just tend to drive me away from the exercise of a naked, simple faith in God—even many a one of your prayers has had the same effect.' Oh, I plead guilty. . . . .

"I do not know how it is, but you seem to know me at this distance better than I know myself. . . . . When I read in your last letter, 'But not too amiable, after all, at times,' I laughed and cried both. . . .

"The last time I wrote you, my heart was too full to say what I wanted to. Indeed I did not quite know what you meant by saying what you did in regard to the effect of thunder on goslings, milk, and the tanner's work. The fact is, I was so taken up, or rather, 'cast down,' by the closing part of your letter, that I did not think much about this. Yes, dear sir, I was truly 'cast down, but not destroyed.' You did not intend I should be; but now I will just tell you the whole truth of the matter. I felt distressed, and the question I wanted you to answer was this: Can there be any filial love in the heart that is so *full* of *slavish fear?* Well, I did cherish a secret hope that you would, in your kindness, send me a little soothing *salve,*—but behold a *probe!* Oh, you pierced the festering wound, and I bless the Lord for all you said. Your words, as you say, were not thunder; no, no; they were something very different from mere *sound.* You have been so faithful to me, I want words to tell you how much I thank you for it." . . . . .

This letter was answered, and I afterwards received the following reply:—

". . . . . But now let me tell you how much good you have done my poor soul. For *long years* my time was spent betwixt hope and fear,—fear greatly predominating. When I united with the Church, instead of feeling joyful, I was just able to stand on this precious promise, 'My grace is sufficient for thee.' Often I was led to see my sinfulness in such a light as to *hide* the Saviour from my view. Sometimes I was afraid to pray, lest I should be struck dead in the act. Sometimes I could look only at the *power* and the *justice* of God, and could see in him only the stern lawgiver; and, feeling a deep sense of my *guilt,* I have *trembled* where I ought to have *loved.* But since I read . . . . . and your letters, especially the *second,* I have been made to see that 'faith is,' indeed, 'everything.' Now I can look to Jesus; and I feel so happy in realizing that he is *all* I need. I am so sinful, but he is so holy,—he is *worthy,* he has made *all* the sacrifice the broken, righteous law demanded; and now, as I am a *sinner lost,* I am the one for whom he died,—the one he came to seek and to save. All I *can* do is just to *believe.*

"Hitherto I have read the Bible, especially the promises, for somebody else. I could apply the *greatest* of them in a most comfortable manner to Christians about me, but feared to apply one of them fully to myself, lest I should be lost at last! But now I find much enjoyment often in studying the character of God the Father in the face of Jesus Christ. Did he not say, '*He* that hath seen *me* hath seen the Father?' Now I do so love to look at God in Christ my Redeemer. Oh, why did I so long refuse to trust *alone* in Jesus? I have indeed been a 'fool, and slow of heart to believe.' Nor do I yet know much about it, though I do feel encouraged to persevere in withstanding every temptation to despair. For now I say to Satan, If I am a sinner, utterly lost, and have no hope of making my heart any better, then I must go to an Almighty Saviour, even to him 'who is able to save to the *uttermost.*' Think of this word '*uttermost.*' I will believe God. I will love the Saviour, whom I would embrace in the arms of *faith.* He is all my hope. For a little while at a time, I can *let go* every cord of self-dependence, and just *fall* into the arms, the strong arms of Jesus; and there would I ever lie. Sometimes I do so want to go to heaven, that I may at once feel just as sorry for sin as I want to feel, and love the Saviour as much as I ought. And will a whole *eternity* be long enough to praise him? to tell the saints and angels how *much* I owe to Him who washed me in his own blood? Sometimes I love to look forward to the time when all the redeemed will be gathered *home,* and hope to meet you there, and will tell you, as we sit on some 'green and flowery mount,' all the Saviour hath done for my sinful soul. . . . .

"I will not close this letter without telling you the last thunder shower we had I did not feel *half* so much afraid as usual. I kept thinking all the time, I will give my body and my soul to Jesus. I will 'put that *cloud,*' *all* of it 'into *his hand.*' He can *hold* the *lightning,* and he can and will 'direct it under the whole heaven.' But now you have put *another* comfort into my heart; you say, 'Learn to hear in the thunder the voice of your own Father—a voice not threatening to *you,* but to your *foes.*'" . . . . .

I answered this letter also, and in a few days I was gratified with the reception of the following sentences in her answer:—

' . . . . . I applied to you for aid in reference to *reconciliation* to God. And now, the way of salvation, by *faith in Jesus Christ,* looks so much plainer than it *ever* did before, I feel sometimes as if I could never let go the thought that Christ *alone* is the way. 'I am the way.' Oh, my Saviour, take me!

"You do not know how sinful a heart I have yet. *I* do not know. But Jesus knows just how much I need his pardoning love,—how much grace I need to keep me from falling into sin and destruction. I look back, and try to think what I have been doing to please *Satan* and grieve my Redeemer, while in the dark and cold speculations arising from the perusal of such sermons as Dr. Emmons' 'Pharaoh' sermon, 'For in very deed for this cause have I raised thee up.'

"But I turn away now, and just try to 'be a *child;* not a servant, but a child; not a philosopher, but a child,—just a humble child." . . . .

Extravagant theological opinions are apt to be adopted by those very persons to whom they are most inappropriate and most misguiding. This woman was an example. She was the last woman in the world to have any need of the stern theology of Dr. Hopkins and Dr. Emmons, whom she perhaps misunderstood. By natural disposition she was greatly inclined to fear; and being of delicate sensibilities, nervous, imaginative, poetical, and peculiarly affectionate, the severities of her adopted theology were the last things to profit her. They made her miserable only. They did not reach her heart. The "kindness and love" of the gospel were the very things for her. Her heart, her affectionate heart, was, if I may say so, precisely adapted to them. This was her experience afterwards. She yielded to *love* what she never yielded to *terror*,—she was *drawn* where she could not be *driven*,—*faith* accomplished for her what *fear* could not accomplish,—she found simplicity better than speculation ; and she then exchanged perplexity and despondency for the calmness of trust and the sunshine of hope. The *law* was before her mind when she tried to be "willing to be lost." No wonder that she despaired. She received relief, not by directing her eye downward into that abyss of midnight, her own dark heart ; but by being brought to look away to Christ and his glorious grace. Christ is light. Faith is the eye that sees him. Christ would have sinners willing to be saved. False theology, despondency, and the devil, would have them willing to be damned.

XVI.

The Bird of Paradise.

AMONG my parishioners there was a poor woman who had once seen better days. She had moved in the most respectable society, the wife of a man of wealth, who formerly held an important official station in the state, but who was now reduced to poverty; and, trembling with the weight of threescore years and ten, had greatly lost the powers of his mind. She was many years younger than her husband. Neither of them was a follower of Christ. Indeed, after their early years, they had never paid anything more than a formal and fashionable attention to even the outward duties of religion. For years after their marriage they lived in splendour; and when his extravagance had squandered his fortune, they were under the necessity of occupying the crazy old house where I first became acquainted with them. Through the benevolence of some wealthy relations, who were very kind to them, their temporal necessities were so provided for that they did not suffer.

Earnestly I strove to interest their minds in the subject of religion. The old man appeared to me to be as stupid as any sinner can be; and he remained so, I believe, to the day of his death,—a victim, as I thought, of the foolish love of mere earthly ostentation and pleasure. Not so his far younger wife. She listened to me with attention and apparent interest, as I spread the subject of religion before her mind, on my first visit to her house; and when I called upon her again, a month afterwards, I found she had commenced reading her Bible with evident anxiety and prayer. The questions she asked me, and her tearful attention to my answers, clearly indicated the interest she felt in this great subject, which, she said, was "almost new" to her thoughts; for she had "scarcely given a thought to it in twenty years." Said she, "Pleasure occupied my mind at first, and after my husband's failure, it was all I could think of to contrive how we should live."

She bore her reverses with commendable fortitude,—laboured hard to support herself and her husband, kept her little old cottage a pattern of neatness, and, on the whole, she won the respect of the few neighbours that knew her. There was nothing about her, as a woman or as an inquiring sinner, which appeared to me uncommon or peculiar. There was, indeed, as I thought, some little manifestation of a nervous excitability, when she mentioned to me her wicked heart, her struggles in prayer, and her despondency about "ever gaining the forgiveness of God;" but this I never should have thought of again, had it not been for what occurred afterwards.

About a week after I had seen and conversed with her at her house, not for the first or second time, and when I began to hope that she was "not far from the kingdom of God," she called upon me. She came to tell me of her hope in Christ, and how happy she was now, in the belief that God had forgiven and accepted her. She trusted, as she said, that God had "heard her prayers, and had sent her an answer in peace."

By way of examining her state of mind, in order to know what to say to her, I asked her a few questions, which she answered in a manner quite satisfactory to me. I found in her nothing to make me distrust her,—indeed, nothing but the contrary, till I asked her,—

"How long have you had this hope and 'this delightful happiness,' which you mention?"

"Since last Thursday night," was her reply. It was now Tuesday.

"What *then* led you to believe that God had 'heard your prayer, and sent you an answer of peace?"

"It was what I saw," said she, with some little hesitation, as if reluctant to answer.

"What did you see?"

"It was," said she, hesitating,—"it was a great light;" and she spake it solemnly, and with evident sincerity, but with some excitement.

"Indeed!" said I. "And where did you see it?"

"In my room."

"What was it?—what caused it?"

"I don't know what it was, but it was *wonderful!* I shall never forget it."

"Did it frighten you?"

"Oh no, not at all."

"What did it look like?"

"It was very wonderful,—the sweetest light I ever saw. It was brighter than any sunshine; but it was so mild and soft that it did not dazzle the eyes. It was *perfectly* beautiful—most enchanting."

"Well now, Mrs. L——, just tell me all about it; I want to know how that was, the time, and all about it."

Seeming to arrange her thoughts, she replied,—

"I had been sitting up a long time after Mr. L—— went to bed, reading my Bible and trying to pray, and I almost despaired of mercy, because my heart was so wicked and obstinate. I felt as if I *could not* go to bed that night without some proof that God would have mercy upon me. I was terrified with the thought of his wrath; but I felt that I deserved it all. Finally, I went to bed. I had been lying in bed about half an hour, thinking of my condition and all at once, the most beautiful light I ever saw shined all over the room. It was a strange kind of light,—brighter than day, brighter than any sunshine; but a great deal more beautiful and sweet. It was mild, and so soothing, it filled me with perfect peace,—a kind of sweet ecstasy, like a delightful dream. Then, in an instant, as I was thinking how delightful it was, there appeared the most beautiful creature that I ever saw.

I was perfectly enchanted and carried away with the beauty of it, its colours were so sweet and mingled, and its form so graceful. It was a bird. He had a rainbow in his bill, and a crown of glittering, soft-shining gold upon his head ; he was resting on a globe of the softest blue, the most enchanting colour that ever was. I never before conceived of anything so beautiful. His colour, and his figure, and the crown of shining gold upon his head; the rainbow he held in his bill, and the blue globe he stood on, and the bright sweet light which filled the room, were all of them more beautiful and lovely than anything I ever thought of before. I was amazed and perfectly happy. '*What is it?*' said I, 'what *is* it?' 'Why, it is the bird of Paradise,' said I. 'My gracious Father has sent it to me from heaven ; I will not despair any longer.' Then I thought, 'How happy I am! God has heard me and had mercy upon me.' I have been perfectly happy ever since."

She appeared to be in an ecstasy of delight.

"What makes you so happy?"

"Because I think God has forgiven me, and because *now* I love him and trust him."

"How do you feel about *sin?*"

"Oh, I hate it. It displeases God, and separates me from him."

"What do you think of Christ?"

"He is a precious Saviour. I love him and trust in him."

"For *what* do you trust him?"

"For everything—for pardon, and peace, and heaven."

"Do you think you are holy now?"

"No ; I know that I sin every hour. But God is gracious to me and fills me with joy."

"Do you rejoice because you are so good?"

"No ; I rejoice because God has been so good to me."

"What have you done to gain his favour?"

"*I* have done *nothing*—only turned to him."

"Did you turn to him of yourself?"

"No ; I *tried*, but my heart would not yield, and I prayed for the Holy Spirit."

"How do you expect to be saved?"

"By the *mercy of God*, through my Saviour."

"How do you know he is *your* Saviour?"

"Because I trust in him, and he has promised to save all that come unto him."

"Have you any *doubt* about your forgiveness?"

"No, sir, not much,—none that troubles me. I know my heart is deceitful; but I trust only in Christ, and then I am safe."

"Do you think the appearance which you saw on Thursday night was something sent by God?"

"Yes, I suppose it was."

"For what purpose do you think he sent it?"

"To give me peace."

"What *reason* have you to think it was sent to assure you of God's favour?"

"I don't know what reason I have to think so,—only I was made so happy."

"Does the Bible teach you that God gives such visions as an evidence of his favour?"

"I think not."

"Do you think it was a miracle?"

"I don't know. I thought God sent it."

"Now, Mrs. L——, do you feel sure all that was not *a dream?*"

"It was no dream," said she, seriously. "I was awake. Don't you think *I saw* that light, sir?" said she with an imploring look.

"No, madam; I don't believe you saw any such thing. I believe *you think* you saw it; but I believe it was all in your own imagination, and nowhere else."

She shook her head very emphatically, as if fixed in the opposite opinion.

"Mrs. L——," said I, "are you a nervous woman?"

"At times I think I am."

"Were you nervous that night?"

"I was not sensible of being so. I was weary, and I felt very *sad.* I was quite excited at times before I went to bed, thinking of eternity to come."

"Mrs. L——, can you remember particularly what you were thinking about that evening, just before you retired to rest? See if you can recollect, and tell me exactly what was in your thoughts just before you lay down."

After a considerable pause, she replied,—

"I had been thinking and praying a long time, about my sins and my wicked, miserable heart; and I tried to give up all into the hands of Christ, as you had so often told me I must. I thought I did, and then I wondered that God did not give me peace. And afterwards I thought how happy I should be if God would give me a new heart; and then I wondered how I should know it if he did."

"You thought," said I, "how *happy* you should be if God would give you a new heart; and then you *wondered* how you should know it if he did. But you did not think of seeing a bird, or a rainbow?"

She opened her lips as if to answer, but cast her eyes downward, and said nothing. A slight flush came over her cheek, but her look was that of sorrow, not of resentment.

Said I, "Mrs. L——, I am sorry to trouble you with so many questions, and I do not wish to afflict you. Many things you say to me would almost convince me that you really have peace with God, if these things were not so mixed up with that vision which seems to have been the origin of your joy, and which *I know* was only a dream, or the work of your own imagination, while you were half asleep and half awake. If you rely in the least upon that vision, that miracle, as an evidence of your pardon, you rely on a mere fancy, a mere nothing. It is no evidence at all. It is just as much a proof that you will be lost as that you will be saved. At best your vision was nothing but a fancy, an imagination, coming from your nervousness, induced by the weariness of your brain when you lay down. I can account for your vision. You have just given me the clue. You had just been thinking 'how happy you should be' if God accepted you, and you had been 'wondering how you should know it.' With these two ideas you went to bed—one idea of great *happiness*, and the other of some wonderful thing, you knew not what, to lead you to that happiness. Then, in a state betwixt sleeping and waking, when the imagination is most busy, and the reason and will lie most still, your imagination just wrought out the *expected wonder* (to teach you something, or convince you), and the *expected happiness* which you so eagerly longed for. This accounts for all you *thought* you beheld. Your eyes saw nothing. As soon as your astonishment and ecstasy had so fully waked you up that the spell of your imagination was broken, and your eyes really began *to see*, your vision vanished. This is the truth of the whole matter, probably.

"Now, Mrs. L——, I have only one thing more to ask you, but I am not certain that I can make myself understood. I will try. You know we speak of *remembering* things. We *remember*, because something made an impression on our mind some time before—a thing capable of being remembered. We recollect the impression—that is remembering. Realities make an impression, and dreams make an impression also. And we remember *both*. But when we remember things that really took place, we have to recall the impression left on our mind *by facts*,—and when we remember dreams, we recall the impression left on our mind by *imaginations* only. Now, there is a difference betwixt the impression left on our mind by real occurrences and the impression left on our mind by imaginations only, or by a dream; such a difference, that we are not very apt to mistake a dream for something that really took place. We can remember both, but they are not just alike. The impression of *a dream* is not exactly like the impression made by something when we were *awake*, though it may be very plain and deep. But there is a difference betwixt the impressions, and also betwixt the rememberings. Don't you think so?"

"Yes, I know there is."

"Very well. Now I want you to *remember* very carefully what you saw on Thursday night, and tell me whether the impression left on your mind then is like the impression left by a dream, or like the impression left by something when you were awake. And tell me whether your act of remembering resembles the act of remembering a dream, or resembles the act of remembering what took place when you were awake. Do you understand me?"

"Yes, sir, perfectly."

"Very well. Now, carefully consider the thing. Take time to think of it. Recollect what you saw on Thursday night, and tell me whether your impression and recollection of it most resemble the impression and recollection of a dream, or something *not* a dream."

She sat in silence for two or three minutes, closed her eyes as if absorbed in thought, then rose and looked studiously out at the window, then sat down and closed her eyes for some two or three minutes more.

"Indeed, sir," said she, "I am at a loss. That *does seem* more like a dream than like a real thing. But I was awake. My eyes were open. I don't remember waking up."

Said I, "I don't wish you to *reason*, or *argue*, or *decide* anything about it, whether you were asleep or awake. I only wish you to tell me, as you remember that night, whether your impression resembles the impression of a dream, or an impression made when you were awake."

After a pause she replied slowly and thoughtfully,—

"It is just like a dream; but I was awake, for my eyes were open."

"Very well, madam, I will not trouble you any more. If you want to know what *religion* is, ask your Bible, don't ask night birds, or night rainbows."

I saw this woman afterwards and conversed with her often. Had it not been for her vision, and the use she made of it, she would have appeared to me to be a humble child of God. But I had no confidence in her conversion.

Some few months after this she proposed to unite with the Church. I discouraged her. But after she had lived about a year as a pious woman, so far as I could discover, she was, with much hesitation, received as a communicant; and I knew her for some years afterwards, presenting satisfactory evidence of being a true Christian. In one of the last interviews I had with her, she told me she had become convinced that "the strange sights she saw on that Thursday night existed only in her own fancy." When I asked what had convinced her, she replied, "I have been sick since then two or three times; and when I was sick and very nervous, I had some other strange sights which I know were fancies, though they seemed as *real* as that one did."

"Perhaps they were *not* fancies."

"Yes, they were, sir."

"How do you know?"

"Because, as soon as I went to examine into them, they were gone. When I got up from the bed there was nothing there."

"Were you always in bed when you saw them?"

"Yes."

"What made you get up to examine?"

"Because I remembered what you said about the bird of Paradise, as I called it, and I was determined to know what these things were."

"But you could not catch them."

"No; as soon as I stirred and got out of bed the charm was broken."

"What were these things you call a charm?"

"Various things, such as splendid colours, beautiful animals, ladies dressed with great taste, and in very rich, gay dresses, and moving like angels."

"Are you asleep when these things appear to you?"

"No, not at all; I am awake and thinking."

"What do you think they are?"

"I think they are nothing. But when I have been agitated,

and become nervous and tired, after I get a little calmed down, and feel quiet and happy, these beautiful things seem to be before my eyes."

"Do you see them when your eyes are open?"

"Yes, sometimes, when the room is dark."

"Very well, madam, you have got right now."

"I wish," said she, "you would not say anything about that bird of Paradise and the blue globe I told you about at first. I was deceived. I know they had nothing to do with religion, and I do not rely upon them at all as any witness that God has given me a new heart."

The religious treatment of persons of strong imagination and weak nerves is one of the most delicate and difficult duties. The imagination has an extent of power over both the intellect and the body itself, of which few persons are suitably aware. The voices which are said to be heard by those religiously affected, the sights which are seen, the instances of falling down speechless and without power to move, the sudden cures of infirmity said to be effected by the prayer of faith, the deaths which have occurred just as the persons themselves foretold, and for which they made all their temporal arrangements,—all such things are to be attributed to the power of the imagination and excited nerves. Religion has nothing to do with them. Superstition and fanaticism transform them into miracles, but there is no miracle about them. Much less is there any religion in them. Religion is taught in the Bible. Ignorance and nerves should not attempt to add to it. The east wind is not a good gospel minister. Many of its *doctrines* are very incorrect.

In the case of this woman, the proper influences of divine truth were mingled up with the workings of an excited imagination and weak nerves, and her superstitious notions did not discriminate betwixt the two. She at first supposed, with solemn and grateful sincerity, that God had sent this vision to her as an assurance that she was forgiven. And it is not likely that all I said to her would entirely have corrected her erroneous idea, had not her subsequent experience lent its aid. But when she came to have other visions which resembled it, and on examination found them to be fancies only, her common sense led her to the conclusion that nothing but fancy created that beautiful light, that rainbow, that globe of blue, and bird of Paradise. There can be no security against the worst and wildest of errors, but by a close and exclusive adherence to the word of God, to teach us what religion is.

XVII.

Superstition.

I WAS sent for by a woman who was in great distress in respect to her preparation for death. She was fully convinced that she should not live long, though now able to ride out daily, and seldom confined to her bed by her infirmity. She was a member of a neighbouring Church; but she said, "I have no peace of mind, and no witness that God has given me a new heart."

I had not been acquainted with her before. She appeared to be an unimaginative, amiable woman, who loved her husband and her children; but she had not a very discriminating mind. Her wealthy, moral, but irreligious parents had done little for her, except to indulge her, and train her in the love of money and the enjoyments it can furnish.

I strove to instruct her in the way of life. I visited her almost every week for a long time. She gained little or nothing in hope. There was something strange about her, which I could not understand. Her mind would be drawn off from the very things which I was most anxious to fasten upon it. One day she mentioned to me what a "bright witness," as she called it one of her acquaintances had. She told me what it was. "It was a great light that appeared to her, and filled all the room where she was." The silly girl who told her this silly story some years before, had sometimes induced her to attend religious meetings with her, among a class of people more apt to see such visions, and more fond of them than I am; and now, the poor woman's mind was constantly on the look-out for some such "great light." She said, "I want some witness to myself." With this expectation her mind was occupied; it was called off from the truth, and bewildered and confused by this superstition. Again and again I explained to her the unscriptural nature of all such notions, and taught her that such "great lights" existed only in the imaginations of people very nervous or very silly, or both. I thought I had succeeded in dissipating her superstitious notions, and for some months, during the lapse of which I often saw her, I had hoped that she was led to put faith before fancy, and look to Christ, and not to visions, for comfort and salvation. But after all this, being in trouble she sent for me. I went. She brought up the same story of a "great light," and asked me,—

"Why *don't I* see some such witness?"

"For three reasons," said I: "*first*, you are not *nervous* enough; *second*, you are not *imaginative* enough; *third*, you are not *quite fool* enough."

Then I went over all the explanations of Bible religion again, and all the arguments to demonstrate the superstition of such notions as she had about some external witness, and expel it from her mind. She appeared to be convinced, *said* she was, and for some weeks seemed to enjoy a rational hope in Christ. I had a hope of her.

A few days before her death she sent for me again. She was in deep distress,—in despair. She asked me if I thought she should "not have some such bright witness before she died." She died without it.

Superstition is mischievous. It hinders the exercise of faith, where faith exists; it prevents faith where it does not exist. Superstitious people are silly. The sights they see, the strange sounds they hear, the voices whispering some words or some texts of Scripture in their ears, are nothing but fancies, not facts; and if they were facts, they would be no evidence at all that these persons had become the children of God. Bible evidences of religion are entirely different.

XVIII.

The Whistling Thinker.

"THERE are some instances of religious experience which can never be reconciled to a theological system." The expression of the old gentleman startled me. I was closeted with the Rev. Dr. P——, a man turned of seventy—a divine of a good deal of celebrity in that part of the country. Forty years at least his junior, I had sought opportunity to consult him in respect to some difficulties and peculiarities which troubled the hearts of two or three of my acquaintances. I wished to *learn;* and I thought, from his years and his high reputation, that he could instruct me.

I had just stated to him the case of an indivividual, and he made the remark which surprised me. As he did not add any explanation, and as I thought from his silence that he intended to leave me to digest the remark as best I could, while he whistled and looked out carelessly upon the sky, I repeated his words after him, "There are some instances of religious experience which can never be reconciled to a theological system," and then I added,—"It appears to me, sir, if that declaration is *true*, then the religious experience of which you speak must be *false*, spurious; or else the theological *system* must be false."

"*Why?*" said he, gruffly.

"Because, sir, if the experience and the system are both *true*, surely they will not quarrel. Lies quarrel sometimes; truths never do. Things that agree with truth agree with each other. If a religious experience agrees with truth (as certainly it *must*, as far as it *is* religious), and a theological system agrees with truth, then they are alike; they need no reconciling. 'Things equal to the same are equal to one another.'"

'EUCLID!" said the queer old man; and then he began to whistle again, and look out at the window. In a few minutes he turned to me,—

"All you say is true," said he, in a careless manner; "but if you live to preach many years, and become much acquainted with people, you will find some Christians whose experience will not square with your theology."

"Then," said I, "my theology must be *false*."

The old man whistled again. I waited some time for him to finish his tune, doubtful whether he was thinking of me at all, or whether he whistled as a *means* of thinking. At last he ceased from his music; and, turning his clear, keen eyes upon me, he sat for some time in silence, as if he would read my very soul. I thought he was taking the dimensions of my understanding, and concluded, therefore, to wait in silence until he should get his measure fixed. After a while, he spoke,—

"My son, don't you think I can defend the proposition I laid down, and convince you of its truth?"

"No, sir, not if I understand the proposition rightly."

"Whew,—why can't I? Whew, whew."

"Because the proposition is not true."

"Perhaps it is not," said he; "but suppose you should meet with a person presenting every possible evidence of true religion in his views, and feelings, and conduct, year after year, and yet that same person had never been awakened, never had any change in his views and feelings respecting religion, as converts have, and was not in the least sensible of having been brought out of darkness into light at any time, how would you reconcile that experience with your theology about human depravity, and about regeneration? What would you say of such a person, after a sermon on original sin, or on conversion? How could you say he was 'born unholy and unclean,' as the Psalm Book has it, but had turned to God?"

"I would say, sir, that God had led him in a way that I knew not of, perhaps in a way that *he* knew not of, perhaps had renewed his heart in his infancy,—perhaps had sanctified him *before* he was born, as he sanctified John and Jeremiah. But I would not admit that his experience in religion could not be reconciled with my theological system."

After whistling a while, the old gentleman looked up,—

"Who taught *you* to interpret Scripture? I don't believe Jeremiah, and John, and Paul, were sanctified before they were born. God certainly could have sanctified them then, and I believe he *does* sanctify and save infants,—some that never *are* born; but the Scriptures do not prove that Jeremiah and John were sanctified before they came into the world. What God says to the prophet, 'Before thou camest forth out of the womb, I sanctified thee, and ordained thee a prophet,' no more proves that Jeremiah was *regenerated* before he was born, than it proves that he was 'ordained a prophet,' and preached before he was born. The expression has reference only to God's predetermination, or election. The same is the case in respect to John. As to the rest which you said, I agree with all *that*. One may be truly born again, even in infancy."

"Well, then," said I, "how can your first declaration be true, that some Christian experiences cannot be reconciled with a system of theology?"

Again he whistled for a long time; then suddenly turning to me as if he had whistled himself up into a thought,—

"It is *not* true. I supposed that you was a Seminary man, who had got a system of theology with one leg and one crutch, not able to jump over a stump, and that, therefore, you could not reconcile *your* system with the facts you met; and I only wished you to understand that divine realities go beyond human systematizing, and if men will confine themselves to their narrow systems, the Holy Spirit will go beyond them. The Church has been greatly injured by such men at times. At one period nothing but *doctrines* will do, and so doctrines are preached, and prayed, and sung, till metaphysics have frozen piety to death. At another time, nothing but *practice* will do; and then religion soon degenerated into a lifeless form, an outward show, with no great doctrines to put life into the soul. At one period, nothing but revivals will do, and revival religion; and then, in the midst of that spirit of fanaticism, diffused by some noisy men all over the Churches, a humble, faithful Christian will be looked upon with contempt, because he was not converted in a revival; and a minister will lose caste, if he does not preach '*Revival*, *revival*,' all the time. I have seen this again and again. The Church that needs a minister will cry out, 'We want a *revival* man,—nothing but a *revival* man will do for *us;*' and so they choose for a minister some proud boaster, who can talk of 'revival' more than of Christ. And another result of this proud spirit is, that when it prevails in our Churches, our people by-and-by come to undervalue the common means of grace, and they become *periodical* Christians; and then they undervalue the faithful Christian education of their children; they forget that the God of Abraham is still *alive*, and on the throne, a covenant-keeping God; they do not *expect* religious education in the family to be an effectual means of conversion,—they rely upon revivals. And it soon comes to pass that the revivals are scenes of mere excitement, delusion, and spiritual pride,—'Stand aside; I am holier than thou.' At another period the opposite error prevails. Revivals are looked upon with suspicion. They are not desired and prayed for. All excitement is feared. And then religion will run down into formality, and people will join the Church when they get old enough, or when they get to have a family. There are many truly pious people who have become such under the influence of example and instruction in the family, and under the ordinary Sabbath-preaching, who never could give you any *special* account,—certainly not a *revival* account of their conversion. These would not suit a revival Christian. And revival converts would not suit *them*. But all such things are wrong. They are the results of narrow systems."

Then he whistled again. But before I could collect my

thoughts for any reply, he broke off from his tune in the middle of a bar,—

"*A theological system*, sir, *every minister of sense will have.* He cannot get along without it. A man can no more do without *a system*, than he can do without *a head.* But what I was after, is *this:* there are men of narrow views, linked to their system, and thinking their system contains all that religion contains; and they would not let anybody cast out *devils* any more than the disciples would, unless he would do it by *their* rule. These men love their system, and preach their system, and live in it, like a worm in a nut, and never get out of it, till, like such a worm, they get wings to fly beyond it. When death gives them wings to fly to heaven, they are out of their jail, and not before. In my opinion, Dr. Woods is such a man as Dr. Porter was before him. Dr. Taylor is such a man—almost as much fettered as the rest of them. Dr. Alexander, one of the ripest saints, is such a man. Dr. Dwight was such a man. And if you want an instance of such a man, whose fetters everybody can see, and hear them jingle, too, at every step he takes, look at Dr. Emmons,—poor fellow! These are system men. Examine Dwight's Hymn Book. How narrow its range is! How lean! It is worse than one of Pharaoh's lean heifers! It has just a few subjects; and passes over more than half the region of song, without a single note. I never could be confined to it. I would as soon consent to be confined to four tunes. Mear, Old Hundred, St. Martin's, and Durham, would do as well for all our music, as Dwight's Hymn Book for all our poetry.

"Now, my son, never get into a strait-jacket. You will find it pinch. It will make your bones ache. Many a minister becomes more familiar with his theological system than he is with his Bible; and not only so, but his system stands *first,* and when he gets hold of a text, he interprets it to square with his system, instead of paring and whitling off his system to make it agree with the text; and among his pastoral duties, he sticks to his Calvinism more than he sticks to Christ; and he would *pray* his system, too, if the Holy Spirit didn't make his prayers for him. And in this way he systems his Bible into a corner, and his own soul into a nutshell. Never do *that*, in the pulpit or among the people. 'Preach the word'—the *word*, my son—THE WORD! Are you a Calvinist?" said he, gently, after speaking in a voice of thunder.

"Yes, sir," said I.

"Then don't be afraid of an Arminian text; don't dodge when you come across one. *Out with it;* it is *God's* text, and he doesn't want you to mince it. Are you a Seminary boy?"

"No, sir."

"*Down on your knees*, and thank God for it."

"I *have* thanked him, sir, a hundred times."

"You'll thank him ten thousand, if you live to my age."

"Are you opposed to what is called Calvinism?" I asked.

"*By no means.* I am a Calvinist. But I let the Bible make my Calvinism, instead of bringing Calvinism to make my Bible; and I claim the liberty of going along with my Bible, into a thousand corners beyond the limits of the system."

"You mentioned Dr. Taylor, with a sort of doubtful compliment about his being fettered; some ministers in my neighbourhood have talked to me a great deal about Dr. Taylor. Let me ask whether you regard him as heretical?"

"No! *I* don't. But Dr. Taylor has committed *the Connecticut sin!* He is guilty of *thinking*, sir, of *thinking;* and for that reason, some people over in Jersey and Pennsylvania, and some in York State, count him a half heretic. But he only *thinks*, sir, that's all; and *thinking* is his original sin, and actual transgression too. Now, don't join in and cry '*mad dog*' about Dr. Taylor. *Wait* till you are *sure you see the froth.* His *boys* don't understand him. Dr. *Taylor* isn't a *Taylorite.* Far from it, sir. His *boys* are Taylorites, but *he* isn't. I have had long talks with a whole score of ministers educated under him, and I KNOW that *not one Taylorite among them understands* Dr Taylor's scheme."

"What *is* his scheme, sir?"

"His scheme of *doctrine* is John Calvin's, or John Howe's, or Edwards', substantially; his scheme of *philosophy* is his *own*—and no honour to him. Why, sir, he believes in original sin, and in the special influences of the Holy Spirit (whether his boys do or not), as much as you or I do. He wouldn't use my *lingo*, or, as he would express it, 'TER-MI-NOL-O-GY,' because he must have a word as long as *Yale College* to suit 'the appropriate circumstances of his being;' but he preaches the same doctrines that I do. He is sound at the core. I don't like his *philosophy*. But you get into a *fight*, and Dr. Taylor will be one of the best *backers* you could have. He *thinks*."

"You mentioned several men, sir," said I, "whose praise is in all the Churches; but I do not exactly understand in what rank you mean to place them. Do you mean to speak of Dwight, and Taylor, and Alexander, and Emmons, as men of little mind?"

"Not *little*, my son, not *little;* but *limited*, *narrow*. Every one of them is more or less entangled with a system. Dr. Taylor came nearer to be a *free* man than any of the rest of them, when he was young. He flung off the system fetters nobly; but, like a *goose*, he went to work and hammered out a pair of his own, and they have galled him worse than the old ones would. The old ones had been used and got smooth—the *rust* worn off. These men are *great* men, *very* great men. They are *good* men, —men of truth, and faith, and devoted godliness. They are *safe* men, *to teach* you on all the fundamental points. I should count you a heretic, and would not ask you to preach for me, if you did not agree with them on all the *fundamentals;* not because you disagreed with *them*, but because, disagreeing with them, I should know you disagreed with the Bible. My complaint about them is twofold: *first*, they let their system limit their scope and range; and *second*, they put their system *foremost* in all religion."

"Well, sir, do you object to theological systems, catechisms, and confessions of faith?"

"*No, no!*" said he, impatiently. "I *thought* you could *understand* me! I am no opponent of confessions of faith. If a man tells you he will have no creed or confession to stick to, 'nothing but the Bible,' set him down for a heretic or an idiot, or both. He *has* a creed, if he is a Christian at all; and he will stick to it, if he walks in the Spirit, whether he is in the pulpit or in society. Yes, sir, he has a creed, if he is not a *downright fool!* Indeed, my young friend, our greatest danger at the present moment, throughout the whole of New England, lies just *here;* we have too much shortened our creeds, and forgotten our confessions, and ceased to preach the *great doctrines.* The doctrines are the great things, after all. One of our prominent men, now preaching in the capital of our state, courts popularity by an occasional sneer at 'old, dead orthodoxy,' as he calls it. He is doing injury to the cause of truth. The seeds of error which he is sowing will spring up by-and-by. If he does not become a heretic himself, his admirers and followers will. He does not believe the Westminster Confession of Faith, in my opinion; and, if that were a standard now among our Churches and ministers, as it was once, when the Catechism was taught in all our schools, we should not have so many *creedless* ministers among us, ignorantly working to undermine the great principles of the Reformation, by sneering at 'old, dead orthodoxy,' like the Rev. Dr. ——. They hate the *doctrines,* sir. So you see I am not against systems and creeds; but I want a minister to have a *creed,* and a *heart* too. I want him to have a system; and then I want him to know that his system does not contain *everything,* and that he himself does not *know* everything. The Bible has a depth, and a richness, and an extent too, in its meaning, which no human system can express. Preach your *text,* my boy, your TEXT, *right out,* and not your system."

The old man had waxed quite warm. He forgot to whistle or look out at the window. I liked to hear him talk, and I was not disposed to have him think me quite such a novice as his manner towards me, though he was kind, seemed to indicate that he did. So I replied,—

"Perhaps I do understand you, sir, more fully than you give me credit for. But when you say, 'If I live to preach many years, and become much acquainted with people, I shall find some Christians whose experience cannot be reconciled with a theological system,' I must still beg leave to say I do not believe it."

"*I took that back*," said he, instantly. "I said that on the supposition that you were a *Seminary* man, cut to the length of the bedstead, and foolishly making your system everything."

"But, sir, you supposed a case of inexplicable conversion, and asked me how I could reconcile it with my theological system."

"So I did; but I thought *then* you were a revivalist, and I wanted to trip up your heels, so that you might pick yourself up and plant yourself on firm ground, and not think that all religion must work exactly according to your revival mode. I *told* you that I agreed to all you said about that supposed case."

"Perhaps you did, sir; but you afterwards said 'the Holy Ghost will go beyond systems;' while I maintain, that as far as my system is *true*, human experience in religion will neither contradict my system nor go beyond it."

"I meant to take that back, my son—I take it back now—if you are not a Seminary man or a revivalist, or mounted on some other limping hobby. I only employed an expression to set you thinking. Mark me; I am not opposed to theological seminaries or to revivals, I am only opposed to the injuries and abuses that grow out of them. If ministers and their people come to think that nothing but revival will do, or nothing but a seminary system will do, true religion will soon be eclipsed, either by fanaticism or bigotry,—and I want you to think about it. If theological seminaries would learn their place, and learn to keep it, they would do good. They may be good *servants* of the Church, but they will be very bad *masters* of it. They want to be masters. Such is human nature. The Church would do well to watch them. Cambridge is a beacon in *my* eye. The seeds of heresy and fanaticism are now sown thick, by those men who seek popularity by crying out, '*Revival, revival,*' and 'Seminary, seminary.' I am disgusted with their pride and their popularity-hunting."

The old man turned to the window again, and struck up another tune, in a sort of low, whispering whistle. But before I had mustered my thoughts enough to know what to reply, he suddenly turned to me, solemnly,—

"Now we have come here to preach in a revival. The revival is God's work, and I rejoice in it. The converts *here* will appear very much alike; but let us not think that all other true converts must appear just so too, in their awakening, and repentance, and hope. There are many persons (especially those who have had a careful Christian education, and have always been under the influences of Christian truth and example,) who come to be true Christians, and nobody can tell when they were converted,—they can't tell themselves. The Holy Spirit has led them gently and softly along. We can judge of them by their fruits,—by their attachment to the great doctrines of truth, and their life of faith. We must not judge of them by the *way* in which they were converted. In all the substantial parts of religion, all true converts will be much alike. Their faith will be the same, their repentance the same, their reliance on Christ the same; and they will all hold substantially the same great doctrines,—in their *hearts*, whether they do in their *heads* or not; because it is by these doctrines, law to condemn, and grace to deliver, that the Holy Spirit moulds hearts. He moulds them alike. And for that reason I say that the *doctrines*, sir, the *doctrines* are our *tools* first, and our *tests* afterward. The doctrines are the best revival sermons, —mind, *the best.* Nettleton always preaches them. But we must not expect all our people who are converted to feel them alike suddenly, or alike deeply:—

God moves in a mysterious way.
His wonders to perform.'

But it *is* God who performs the wonders; and he performs them through his own *truth*. I am willing that he should use the truth suddenly or slowly, and convert a man as he converted Paul, or as he converted John."

"That is a part of my theological system, sir," said I.

"Then you and I agree," said he, with a smile. "You are not hood-winked or trammelled with a seminary system or a revival system. I perceive you *think;* and that makes me like you."

Turning again to the window, he struck up another tune, as his eye wandered over the valleys and the distant mountains of blue. Whistling seemed to be as natural to him as breathing. He appeared to whistle up his thoughts. And again, before I had time to contrive what to say, he turned to me,—

"Generations have their fashions, their foibles, as much as women about their dress. Seminaries and revivals are the *fashion* of our age and country. These things have their advantages; but they have their disadvantages also. The two great dangers of the Church in *our* day are these:—the Church must have no ministers but seminary ministers, and no religion but revival religion. Both these exclusive preferences are *wrong*, foolish, and short-sighted. They do, indeed, partly balance each other; and so our seminary ministers do not become altogether *book* ministers,—theorizing, speculative, and heartless as metaphysics; and our revival ministers do not *all* become fanatics, with a bad heart and *no* head. But the time will come, if God has good things in store for us, when the Church will again welcome ministers who have never *seen* a public seminary, and will welcome converts who do not tell a *stereotyped story* about their revival conversion. These two hobbies of the age will get old and worn out by-and by; and then the Church will be wiser than she is now. These hobbies *have* worked well; but the seminary hobby is very stiff in the *joints*, and the revival hobby has had his *wind* injured."

"To hear you talk," said I, "one would think you believed in a gradual regeneration."

"I believe," said he, "in *instantaneous* regeneration in *all* cases. But I do not, on that account, maintain that every regenerated sinner must be able to tell *when* he was regenerated. He may not *know* when, and *never* know till the day of judgment. But, in my opinion, he *will* know *who* regenerated him. I have very much ceased to *ask* persons whom I examine for reception into the Church *when* they became religious, or *how* their minds were affected. Principles are a far better test than mere emotions. They are more *reliable*, and more ascertainable too. My way *now* is, to inquire about their views of *doctrine*, of *truth*, and about some of their religious feelings *at the present time*. In my opinion, many a true child of God is afraid to come to God's table, and is kept away simply because he cannot tell such an experience as he has heard of in others, and as he has been led to think universal with all true converts. He has had none of that *blazing* experience (which I call *comet religion*, because nobody can tell where it comes from, or where it goes to, or what it is good for), because he has been led gently to Christ, following the still, small voice, and does not know *when* or *how* he began to trust him,—*only* that God has led him, as he never would have gone of himself. He has had principle, and conscience, and purpose, and faith, but not tumultuous and whirlwind emotion. And, as I said before, in my opinion, there are many true Christians, who have been well taught from their youth, that never *can* tell *when* they turned to God; and if they attempt to fix on the day of the month, they will fix it *wrong*,—some too soon, and many too late."

"You spoke a little while since of mere excitements, fanaticism, and heresy, sir. I have a special reason for asking you what is the fit mode of counteracting such evils!"

Instantly he replied, with slow and measured words,—

"Preach *on the character of God;* then, *on the depravity of man;* then, *on the nature of holiness;* then, *on secret prayer!* All fanatics have got a new god! My boy, I want you to take notice (put an N.B. to it in your memory) how the Bible, in order to tear up error by the roots, brings up GOD HIMSELF, and tells what HE is. The old prophets do it, all through: 'Thus saith the LORD GOD, Besides ME there is none else: *I* change not'—'Holy, holy, holy, is the Lord.' The apostles do it. Paul is full of it. He employed it on Mars' Hill, to convert the Athenian philosophers; he used it to knock over those who doubted about the resurrection. '*Thou fool*,' says he, 'GOD giveth it a body.' Peter used it: 'One day with the Lord is as a thousand years.' All the divine writers have it. It is their familiar thunder and lightning; and I advise you to borrow a little of it. It will purify the atmosphere all around you."*

In very much this strain, my aged counsellor went on for an hour, relieved only by a whistling interlude; and sometimes, after a pause, roused again to utter some great truth, by some question which I ventured to ask him. He was full of thought. I have never listened to a man of more independent mind, or whose conversation was more rich in suggestions. He thought deeply and carefully, though perhaps many wise men would be slow to adopt all his opinions about men or about things.

My interview with him was of great use to me. He put me to *thinking;* which, he said, was "all that he aimed at."

Years afterwards I was forcibly reminded of him by a case which I am about to relate, and which I have here, in the following sketch, denominated *Unconscious Conversion.*

* When the Rev. Mr. Backus was ordained successor to Dr. Bellamy, in 1791, there was an aged, pious negro belonging to the Church. Soon after Mr. Backus' ordination some one asked this negro how he liked Mr. Backus,—whether he thought him equal to Dr. Bellamy. His reply was, "Like Master Backus very much; great man—good minister, but not equal to Master Bellamy Master Backus make God big, but Master Bellamy make God bigger."

XIX.

Unconscious Conversion.

IN the discharge of pastoral duty, I have never been more deeply interested or more perplexed than I was in the case of a very affectionate and intelligent woman, whom I knew intimately for several years. She was a married woman before I became acquainted with her. She was young in life,—I suppose not more than twenty-five; and her husband was probably about thirty, —not a religious man. I visited her as her pastor, soon after she had removed from another part of the country, and taken up her residence in the place where I lived. I was much pleased with her. She was a woman of refined manners, of excellent sense, of trained mind, of gentle and affectionate disposition; but withal of unusual firmness, having a mind and a heart of her own. Few women, I believe, have ever adorned their station more than she adorned hers. As a wife, mother, friend, as a neighbour, as a daughter (for I became acquainted with her parents, and knew her demeanour towards them), she was a pattern of propriety. A stranger to her might have deemed her manner somewhat reserved and cold, as indeed it was to strangers, for there was no forwardness about her. She was modest, unassuming, unobtrusive. But her reserve wore off by acquaintance; and though she never became imprudent, and never lost a just sense of a woman's dignity, she became peculiarly confiding and companionable. However, she was rather taciturn than talkative. Like a woman of sense, she took care whom she trusted, and what she said.

But there was a shade of melancholy which seemed to hang around her, quite noticeable to a keen observer, and yet not so distinct as to be visible, perhaps, to most of her acquaintance. Her half pensive look gave an additional interest to her intelligent countenance, which had no small claims to be denominated beautiful; and indeed there seemed to be a cast of sadness thrown over the very movements of her tall and graceful figure.

When I first became acquainted with her, I noticed this tender melancholy, which hung around her like the shadow of a cloud; and I supposed that the twilight of some affliction still lingered around her heart, or that some secret grief was buried deep in her own bosom. After a more intimate acquaintance with her, I came to the conclusion that she had some trial of which she never spoke, but which preyed in secret upon her heart. I thought her appearance indicative of a concealed grief, which, like a worm in the bud, was preying upon her life.

On account of this opinion, I aimed to mention the subject of religion to her in the most delicate and affectionate manner possible. I called upon her for that purpose. I found her alone. After a few moments of conversation I said to her,—

"I have several times mentioned the subject of religion to you, Mrs. C——, but you have been quite reserved; and I have called to-day to converse with you upon that subject, if you will allow me such a favour."

"I am glad to see you, sir."

"Allow me to ask you whether you are a member of the Church?"

"No, sir, I am not."

"And do you think you are still living in unbelief, after all your opportunities?"

"I suppose, sir, I have no reason to think I am a Christian," said she, with a look of mingled solemnity and sorrow.

"Is it wise for you to neglect your salvation?"

"I know it is not wise, sir. My own heart condemns me," said she, with much emotion.

"Then, madam, do not neglect it any longer. The favour of God is within your reach. He calls to you in his gracious kindness, and invites you to turn to him for pardon and peace, freely offered to you through the great Redeemer of sinners. But how comes it about, Mrs. C——, that you have neglected salvation so long?"

"I do not know, indeed, sir. I suppose I have been too worldly, and too much led away by my own heart, though I have thought about religion a great deal all my life."

"I suppose so too. And I *know* you ought, instantly, to 'deny yourself, and take up your cross and follow Jesus Christ,' and not suffer your heart to lead you away any longer."

She was much affected. I asked her some questions which she did not answer, because, as I then supposed, of a conflict in her own mind, betwixt a sense of duty and the love of the world. I therefore urged her, as solemnly and affectionately as I could, to give her attention to religion without delay, and left her.

Again I called to see her. I inquired,—

"Have you been giving your attention to religion since I saw you?"

"I have thought of it very often, sir."

"And have you prayed about it very often?"

"I have *tried* to pray," said she sadly; "but I do not know that it was true prayer."

"Do you feel your *need* of God's blessing, as an undone sinner, condemned by the law of God, and having a wicked heart?"

"Sometimes I *think* I feel it; but I suppose I do not feel it as much as I ought."

"Do you feel that you need Christ to save you?"

"I *know* it, sir; but I am afraid I do not feel it. My heart seems hard, very hard. I wonder at myself, my stupid self."

"It must be a very senseless or stupid heart, my dear friend, if it cannot feel the most solemn matter, save one, in all the universe. Nothing short of perdition itself can be a more affecting and solemn thing, than to be an undone sinner without Christ to save you!"

"I am very sensible of my stupidity. I have often wondered at myself. I have tried to feel, but—"

She was overcome by this thought, and could not finish the sentence. She wept bitterly, though she evidently strove hard to control her emotions. "Pardon my infirmity, sir," said she. "I do not know why it is, but I cannot restrain my feelings. I hope you will not think me *quite* a child."

I assured her of my entire respect for her, and my attachment to her as a friend; that I was unwilling to say one word to make her unhappy, but that I wanted her attention to a happiness unequalled and everlasting.

"I know it, sir, I know it; and I thank you for all your kindness to me," said she with tears.

I besought her to come freely, and affectionately, and fully to Christ, without any distrust and without any delay, because *salvation* is by *free grace.*

Afterwards I had several interviews with her, in all of which she was solemn and much affected, but ordinarily her *words* were few. I told her from time to time the same truths, which I was accustomed to urge upon the attention of other anxious inquirers. I referred her to the same texts, the same promises, the same cautions and directions. Months passed on in this way, and still she found no peace of mind, no hope. She did not come out of her darkness into the light of faith, as I had so long and so confidently expected; nor did she become any less solemn or less studious or less tender in feeling, as latterly I had so much feared. Indeed, at almost every interview I had with her, she would be melted into tears in spite of all her efforts; and then she would beg me to "pardon her weakness," as she called it, and apologizing for her emotions, she would say, "I would not afflict you with these tears if I could help it. I know it must be painful to you to see me affected in this manner, after all you have done for me; and I feel that my state of mind is but a poor return for your kindness. But I assure you, my dear pastor, I am not ungrateful to you, if I am unhappy."

I soothed and comforted her to the utmost of my power, with the promises of God, and encouragements to trust in him. I reasoned with her, and aimed to reach her conscience, and win her heart to the love of Christ. Again and again I taught her all God's truth which I thought adapted to her state of mind. She heard it all attentively, kindly, and, as I sometimes thought, gladly. She never uttered an objection, complaint, or excuse. I confidently believed, as she continued to seek the Lord so assiduously, she would soon find peace, or be left to return to indifference. But it was not so with her. Through many months she continued, so far as *I* could see, in the same state,—solemn, tender, prayerful ordinarily, but uncomforted.

Her condition perplexed me, and very much grieved me. I had become greatly attached to her as a friend; and I believe she respected and loved me as her minister; and I could feel no reconciliation to the idea that she should continue in this unhappy condition. I blamed *myself* very much; for I supposed I must have failed to instruct her appropriately, even though she was desirous to be taught,—perhaps had not sufficiently explained the way of salvation, by insisting upon those great doctrines of truth through which the Holy Spirit leads sinners to repentance. Consequently I called upon her again, resolved to probe her heart, and, after some little conversation, inquired of her,—

"Have you yet found your heart at peace with God?"

"No sir, I am not at peace,—I am far from it."

"Do you still remain in the same state of mind that you have been in so long?"

"I am sorry to say, sir, that I can tell you nothing new about myself,—nothing different from what I have told you before."

"And certainly, madam, I can tell *you* nothing new,—can preach no new gospel, can tell you nothing different from what I have told *you* before. If you do not obey the gospel, nothing can save you. The gospel will not change. *You* must change. The gospel offers Christ to you, to enlighten you, to atone for you, to defend you from every danger. And since this offer is so free, and so kind, and so appropriate, and is made in the infinite sincerity of God, what hinders you that you do not accept it, and trust your Saviour humbly, penitently, gladly?"

"I wish, sir, I could tell what hinders," said she, sadly.

"My dear friend," said I, "have you ever really felt, and do you feel *now*, that you are an *undone sinner*, and have infinite need of Christ to save you!"

"Yes, sir, I think I do. I never have had any doubt of that. I *know* I am undone, and I know I need Christ; but perhaps I do not feel it as I should."

"Do you *want* to feel it?"

"Yes, I know *I do*," said she, with some difficulty, and burst into tears. "I have prayed a great many times to be enabled to feel it more, if that is what I lack."

"Allow me to ask you if you have ever been fully convinced that you have by nature an evil heart, depraved, 'deceitful above all things, and desperately wicked'?"

"Yes, sir, I know I have. I cannot conceive how anybody can doubt that, after examining himself at all. Perhaps I am worse than I suppose, or I should not continue in this sad state. I am fully sensible there is nothing in myself but sin."

"And do you think you can make your heart any better?"

"I am sure I can do nothing for myself. Certainly I ought to be convinced of that by this time."

"Are you fully sensible that nothing but the Holy Spirit can meet the necessities of your poor heart, and bring you to Christ?"

"Yes, I have long felt it. I am sure I ought to know that, for I have tried often enough of myself to turn to God, and my heart is still the same."

"Why don't you give that heart to God, and *trust him* to renew it and control it, since you find all your own efforts vain?"

"I have often *tried* to do so, but it seems to be all useless."

"Do you constantly pray for divine assistance?"

"I have always been accustomed to pray, in my poor way. At times I have neglected prayer for a little while, when I thought it did no good, and was afraid I should rely too much upon the mere act of praying, and when I have thought God would not accept such prayers as mine. But I do not often neglect daily prayer."

"Do you seek the Lord with all your heart?"

"I suppose not, sir; for if I did I should not remain in this miserable condition. I *try*, but it seems I fail."

"Do you rely upon any righteousness of your own to save you, or commend you to Christ?"

"I have no righteousness. I know very well there is nothing in me but sin and misery."

"Do you try to *make* a righteousness out of repentance, or humiliation, or faith, and thus expect your *religion* to commend you to the Saviour? Sinners sometimes seek *religion*, and think they must; but the Bible never tells them to seek *religion*—it tells them to 'seek *the Lord*.' And when they seek *religion*, in order to have their religion render them acceptable to God, all that is nothing but an operation of a self-righteous spirit. Do you think of being accepted in this way, instead of expecting God to receive you as you are, a sinner to be saved?"

"Perhaps it may be so, through the deceitfulness of my heart; but I am not conscious of it. I have thought of that point very often, since you explained to me the difference betwixt trusting to the righteousness of Christ and aiming to establish a righteousness of our own."

"Don't you love the world too well?"

"The love of the world *tempts* me, I am afraid, sometimes; but I feel that I am willing to forsake all for Christ."

"Are you willing *now* to give up yourself into the hands of Christ to save you, denying yourself in order to serve him?"

"It seems to me that I am; but I suppose it cannot be so, for if I were I should not feel as I do."

"Christ offers to receive you *freely*, *now*,—*just as you are*. He invites you to trust him. Why do you refuse?"

"I *do* try—I have tried—I have tried for a long time; but I —"

Her voice faltered, she could say no more. I waited a little time for her to become composed, and then inquired,—

"Let me ask you, my dear friend, with all respect and affection, don't you indulge in some sin—sin of enmity, or envy, or discontent, or something else; some sin that keeps you from peace of conscience and peace with God?"

"No, sir, I am not conscious of any such sin. I know I sin very frequently; but I struggle against it, and I do not *indulge* myself in any sin that I know of. If there is any such thing that keeps me from my Saviour, I should be glad to know what it is."

I recited to her some of the divine promises and directions as I had often done before, prayed with her, and left her.

Such conversations with her were repeated. She continued still the same. It was evident, as I thought, that I had not been able to profit her at all. In order to have a more perfect knowledge of her, if possible, I sometimes called upon her without saying a word upon the subject of religion. Her manner was cordial, and her conversation cheerful; but the old shade of pensiveness that hung around her, like a mysterious spirit, cast a sort of tender and touching melancholy over her whole appearance.

Several years had now passed away since my acquaintance with her commenced. She had been called to pass through some severe trials, in which I had sympathized with her and aimed to lead her to improve them rightly. She appeared to repose in me the most perfect confidence, told me her sorrows, consulted me in her difficulties, but continued without hope.

At one time I had great expectation that she would soon turn to her Lord in faith. She had a daughter, a young girl of sixteen perhaps, who became interested about religion, and was led to hope in the mercy of God through Jesus Christ. For this lovely daughter she was most intensely anxious and prayerful. I strove to make use of this solicitude for her child, and of God's mercy to her, now in the bloom of her youth and beauty, as a means of leading the pensive-hearted mother to the same fountain of life. All *this* failed.

On one occasion, when I called to see her, I asked,—

"Have you made any progress towards religion?" With trembling voice she answered,—

"I do not know that I can say anything to you, sir, on that subject, which I have not often said to you before. I am sorry to be obliged to tell you so. It must be very discouraging and unpleasant to you, after all your kindness and attempts to do me good. I do feel grateful to you for your attentions to me and to my child; but I make you a poor return when I am always compelled to tell you the same thing about myself, and meet you with these tears. I know it must be unpleasant to you. I wonder you have not been discouraged with me and left me long ago."

"My dear lady, don't think of *me*. It is *God*, whose kindness ought to affect you, and attract you instantly to his arms. I am sorry for you—my heart bleeds for you. I cannot give you up. I do believe God has mercy in store for you."

"I am sure my heart requites your kindness, my dear pastor; I am not ungrateful for it."

"And will you be grateful to *God*, to *Christ Jesus*, your suffering Lord, who bore the curse for you, who grappled with death and the devil *for you*, and opened your way into heaven?"

"I hope I am *not* ungrateful to him," said she, sobbing aloud.

"Do you *trust* in him, as a friend to save you?"

"Oh! I am afraid not."

"You *may*—a thousand times, *you may*. 'Come, for all things are ready.'"

I could only exhort her, and pray for her.

I called on her again, and our interview was much the same as usual. I did not know but I was making her unhappy by my constant solicitations, and perhaps doing her harm; so I said to her,—

"My dear child, I will not press this subject upon your attention any more, if it is unpleasant to you to have me mention it. I have loved you, and aimed to do you good; but I have failed. I do not wish to make you unhappy. I will leave you hereafter entirely to yourself, if you desire it, and never say a word more to you on the subject of your religion."

Covering her face again with her handkerchief, she wept convulsively, as I went on to say,—

"I will do just as you desire; I will continue to offer you Christ and his salvation, or be silent on the whole subject, just as is most agreeable to—"

"*Oh, sir,*" interrupting me, "I do *not* wish you to leave me. I wonder your patience has not been exhausted, and I am sensible it must pain you to see me always in this tearful condition. I am sorry to make you unhappy; but I hope you will never think me pained by your visits. I am *not*, I assure you. Almost my only hope is—"

She could say no more, and I could utter no reply. I prayed with her, and promised to see her again. She *demanded* a promise.

On a future occasion, as I was conversing with her, I asked her,—

"Is it not strange that you do not *love* such a God?"

Greatly to my surprise, she answered,—

"I think I do love God, sir."

"How long do you think you have loved him?"

"Ever since I was a little child. I cannot remember the time when I did *not* love him. It has always seemed to me, so far as I know my own heart, that I did love God."

With amazement, I inquired,—

"Why did you never tell me this before?"

"I was afraid you would think me better than I am."

"And do you hate sin?"

"I have always hated it, if I can judge of my own feelings, ever since I can remember."

"*Why* do you hate sin?"

"Because it offends God, it is wrong, and because it makes me unhappy."

"Do you desire to be free from it?"

"Yes, I do, if I know anything at all of my own desires."

"Do you love to pray?"

"Yes, I love to pray,—it is my most precious comfort. Sometimes I feel it a task, I am afraid; when I fear that I am not sincere, and that my prayers are an offence."

"Is prayer a relief to you in trouble?"

"Sometimes it is. At other times a burden lies on my heart, which I cannot leave with God; indeed, commonly I have a burden left, because I am afraid I am not right with God."

"Do you *rely* on Christ to save you?"

"I have nothing else to rely upon; but I am afraid I do not rely upon him as much as I ought."

"Do you *wish* to rely upon him?"

"Yes, I do. It is my constant prayer that I may be able to do so. I know he is able and willing to save even me, unworthy as I am. I have never doubted that."

"Are you willing to *trust him* to save you?"

"I certainly *wish* to trust him."

"Do you receive him as *your* Saviour?"

"I hope so; I *try* to do it."

"Do you feel grateful for what he has done for you?"

"Yes, sir, I am sure I do."

"Are you *glad* to be in God's hands, and in his world, and willing to let him do with you as he will? You know he *wills*, but are you *glad* of it?"

"Yes, I am. I would not desire to be anywhere else than in his hands. It is pleasant to me to think that he reigns over me and over all."

"Then are you not *reconciled* to God?"

"I don't know. If I were really reconciled to him, I have always thought I should have more assurance of his favour. I am afraid to think I am reconciled."

"Do you love God's people?"

"Yes, sir; their society has always been more pleasant to me than any other. I enjoy it."

"Don't you think that these feelings, which you have now expressed, are evidences of true religion?"

"I *should* think so, perhaps, if I had not always had them. But I have never been sensible of any particular change. I have *always* felt so since I was a little child, as far back as I can remember."

I was utterly amazed! Here I had been for years aiming to make conviction of sin more deep, instead of binding up the broken heart! I had been aiming to lead a sinner to Christ, instead of showing her that she was not a stranger and an outcast! I was ashamed of myself! I had often talked to this precious woman as if she had been an alien from God, and an enemy; and now it appeared as if all the while she had been one of his most affectionate children, her very anguish consisting in this,—that she loved him no more, and could not get assurance of *his* love towards her. It was true she had never told me these things before; but that did not satisfy me. I ought to have *learnt* them before. I went out and wept bitterly! I felt as if I had been pouring anguish into the crushed heart of the publican, as he cried, "God be merciful to me a sinner!"

On my way home, I thought of what my old friend that whistled had said to me years before, and I was convinced that I had *practically* run into the error against which his wisdom aimed to guard me. Over the recollection of the tears of anguish which I had so often caused this noble woman, in secret I poured out my own.

Afterwards I aimed repeatedly to show her what *were* and what were *not* evidences of saving faith; and she said to me more than once,—

"I should think myself a Christian if it were not for one thing,—that I have had these feelings ever since I can remember. I have never been sensible of any such change as other people experience, and as the gospel mentions. I could not tell the time when I became a Christian, and I am afraid to think I am a child of God."

So she felt; and she continued after this for months downcast and burdened, with only an occasional gleam of sunshine to gladden her heart. I deem it not improbable that that secret grief which preyed upon her heart, and cast such a shade of melancholy over all her appearance, may have damped her religious joy and hope all along. I may not here record what it was. Gradually I discovered it, and it was cause enough, I am sure, to excuse all the melancholy which so long held possession of one of the noblest hearts that ever beat.

This woman had a *pious mother.* That mother taught her from her infancy, in a most faithful and affectionate manner; and it is probable that the gentle influences of the Holy Spirit renewed her heart in her early life, so that she "could not remember the time when she did *not* love God."

She finally came to a calm but feeble and timorous hope that she was indeed a Christian. She hoped hesitatingly and humbly; as she said to me, "It is almost hope against hope." She removed to another part of the country; and *there* she and her daughter came (on the same Sabbath, I believe) for the first time to the communion table of their Lord. I have occasionally seen them since. They have sometimes done me the favour to write to me. They are still my precious friends; and I have reason to hope they are both on their way to heaven. When she arrives there, she may know what she will never know here,—*the time of her conversion.*

We are apt to have too limited views of God. We think we understand him; but he constantly goes beyond us, and shames us. It is well for us to have wisdom enough to *be ashamed.* The man or minister who thinks he can trace all the operations of God's Spirit upon the souls of men, or thinks that God's Spirit will be confined to the ways of his wisdom or modes of his imagining, knows very little of God. God sanctifies souls through the truth. *That* is about all that we know. If we think we have got beyond this in knowledge, and so understand the "different operations" of the Holy Spirit, that all true conversions will come within the scope of our favourite patterns, we have much yet to learn. That is a very common error with our revivalists.

Many persons who have had a religious education, who have never thrown off the restraints of religious influence, and with whom the power of conscience and just principle has been felt, become truly the children of God without any such sudden and sensible change in their feelings as we often behold in others. I have learnt not to distrust the religion of such persons. They *wear* well. *Feeling* is not the only evidence of religion. Just principles, an effective conscience, and proper habits of life, are evidences of it also.

The Rev. Dr. A——, now gone to his rest and reward, once the distinguished and very useful pastor of a large Church in the State of New York, said to me, more than twenty years since,— "After I was settled over my Church, for about fifteen years we used to receive into the Church on their profession of faith, from twelve to twenty persons every year. But we had no revival. Then, there was a great revival among us, and we received in six months more than all we had received before in three years. After that we had no more gradual admissions, or only a very few, for six or seven years. And so it has been ever since for a period of twenty years. Every few years we have a revival, and after it a dearth, and then another revival. And now, if anybody should ask me which system I prefer, the revival system or the old one, I should have no hesitation in saying the old one. I know it is not for me to choose—God is a Sovereign, and sends his Spirit as he chooses; but I am sure our prosperity, on the whole, was greater, and our converts were better, under the old system."

XX.

Ceasing to Pray.

AT the earnest solicitation of a friend, very dear to me, who had herself just come to a happy tranquillity of mind, I sought an interview with her sister—an accomplished young woman, of about seventeen years of age. I found that the attention of my new acquaintance had been directed to religion some few months previous to this; but though her mind was still very tenderly affected, yet she had ceased to pray. She appeared very much discouraged and very miserable.

"I have given up trying to seek God," said she; "it does me no good. I would give anything to be a Christian; but I never shall be!"

"You ought not to say *that*, my child," said I. "You do not *know* that. *I* know you may be a Christian if you will; for God has never said, 'Seek ye my face in vain.'"

"Well, sir, it seems to *me* that I can never be a Christian. I have that feeling; it comes over me every time I think about religion."

"And is that the reason why you have ceased to pray?"

"Yes, sir. My prayers will do me no good!"

"How do you know they will do you no good?"

"Because I don't pray with a right heart."

"And do you expect to get a right heart *without* prayer?"

"I don't expect to get a right heart at all, sir."

"Well, if you *could* get a right heart, would you get it without prayer?"

"I suppose not. But all my praying is only an abomination in the sight of God!"

"Does not God command you to pray, to seek him by prayer; to seek his aid and favour?"

"Yes, sir; I know he does."

"Then is it not a greater abomination in his sight when you *neglect* prayer, than when you pray as well as you can?"

"Perhaps it may be," said she, sadly, "I don't know; but 'if I regard iniquity in my heart, the Lord will not hear.'"

"Then you had better not 'regard iniquity in your heart.' You ought to give God your heart; you ought to repent; you ought to 'cease to do evil,' and 'learn to do well.'"

I then took up her Bible, which was lying upon the table, and read and explained to her Prov. ii. I–5, Isaiah lv. 1–10, and Jer. xxix. 12, 13. Then I appealed to her,—

"Is it not plain that God requires you to pray? and is it not just as plain that he connects encouragements and promises with that requirement?"

"Yes, sir, I suppose it is."

"Then, will you obey him?"

"I would, sir," said she, "if I had any heart to pray;" and she burst into tears.

"Do you *want* to have a heart to pray?"

"Oh, sir, I do wish I *had* one!"

"Then, cannot you ask God *to give* you such a heart? Cannot you go to Christ, and give up your heart to him, and beg him to accept you, since he loves to save sinners; and *trust* him to put a right spirit within you, as he has promised to do?"

In this way I reasoned with her out of the Scriptures for a long time. It appeared to me that she was deeply sensible of her sins. She was evidently very miserable. She longed to be a Christian. But she was prevented from every attempt to seek the Lord, by the discouraging idea that her prayers would be useless, and were an offence to God. I had no expectation that she would gain any blessing without prayer, and, therefore, I requested her to listen to me, as calmly as she could, for she had become much agitated, while I should mention to her some things which I wanted her to remember. She tried to repress her emotions; and drying her tears, lifted her face from her handkerchief,—

"I will hear you, sir, very willingly; but you don't know what a wicked heart I have."

I proceeded,—

"The *first* thing I would have you remember is this, that your God *commands you to pray*. This is your duty. Nothing can excuse you from it. Wicked heart as you may have, God commands you to pray.

"The *second* thing is, that *God connects his promises with these commands.* You have no right to separate them. The promise and the command stand together.

"The *third* thing is, that when you do thus separate them, saying the promises are not for such wicked hearts as yours, and therefore refuse to pray, you *are not taking God's way*, but your own. You are teaching *him*, instead of suffering him to teach *you.* Your duty is to take *his* way. His thoughts are not your thoughts.

"The *fourth* thing, therefore, is,—you are *never to despair*. Despair never yet made a human being any better; it has made many a devil worse. Hope in God, by *believing* what he says. You need not have any hope in yourself; but you may have hope in God, and you may *pray* in hope. Never despair.

"The *fifth* thing is, that your wicked heart, instead of being a reason why you should *not* pray, is the *very reason why you should* pray most earnestly. It is the strongest of all reasons. Pray just because you *have* a wicked heart. Such a heart needs God's help.

"The *sixth* thing is, that a great many persons have thought, and felt, and talked about prayer just as you do; and afterwards *have found out that they were mistaken*, have prayed, and have become true and happy Christians. I could name to you, this moment, at least a dozen, whom I have known and have talked to just as I do now to you. They have been persuaded to pray, and they are now happy in hope. If you will go with me, I will introduce you to some of them, and they will tell you their own story. Remember this: others just like you have found out their error. You may find out yours.

"The *seventh* thing is, that your impression about prayer *is a temptation of the devil*, it is a falsehood, a deception, a lie designed to keep you in sin and misery. Not that you think your *heart* worse than it is; but that you do *not* think God so gracious and merciful as he is, to hear the prayers of even such a heart. 'Resist the devil and he will flee from you.'

"The *eighth* thing is, that this idea of yours, about not praying with such a heart, is just an *idea of self-righteousness*. You are 'going about to establish a righteousness of your own, and have not submitted yourself to the righteousness of God. Christ is the end of the law for righteousness.' You wish to pray with such *a good heart*, that God will hear you on that account. This is pride, wicked, foolish pride, a spirit of self-righteousness, self-justification, and self-reliance. It is *this* which keeps you from prayer.

"Do you understand me?"

"Yes sir, I think I do."

"And are not all these things true?"

"I don't know but they are, sir."

"Then will you pray? Will you begin *now*, to-day?"

"Yes, sir, *I will* try."

For a time she faithfully kept her promise. Several times after this I conversed with her, and though she did not appear to me to become more unhappy, yet she did appear to me to become more truly convicted. Her *conscience* seemed to be more awakened. Her mind seemed to be more influenced by the principles of truth, and I fondly expected that she would soon find "peace in believing." But she did not. She yielded to the old temptation. She neglected prayer; and, in a few weeks, divine truths ceased to affect her!

I strove to bring her back to her closet duty, but in vain! Years have passed,—she is still without hope!

XXI.

Continuing to Pray.

HAVING noticed from the pulpit, for several Sabbaths, the very fixed attention of a young friend to all that I uttered in my sermons, I called upon her at her residence. She had been a gay girl; and her social disposition, the pleasantness of her manners, her taste, and the almost unequalled kindness of her heart, while they made her a favourite everywhere, exposed her, as I thought, to be drawn into temptations to volatility and the vanities of the world. As I spoke to her of religion, her eyes filled with tears, and she frankly told me, that, for several weeks, she had been thinking very much upon that subject, and had been "very unhappy" in finding herself "so far from God,—just as you described in your sermon," said she "'*without God and without hope.*' That sermon told me my heart, and I have had no peace since. I am astonished at my sinfulness, and I am more astonished at my stupidity and hardness of heart." I conversed with her, and counselled her, as well as I could, and we kneeled together in prayer.

After this I saw her three or four times within the space of a fortnight. She studied the way of salvation most assiduously, and, as I thought, with a most docile disposition; and she prayed for pardon, and for the aid of the Holy Spirit, with most intense earnestness. "I do want to love my heavenly Father," said she; "I do pray for the Holy Spirit to show my poor heart the way to the Saviour."

Calling upon her a few days after, I found that her appearance was very much altered. She was less frank than I had ever found her before; and though not less solemn, perhaps, it was a different sort of solemnity. She appeared to be more downcast than ever, though not so much agitated; not affected to tears, but having now the appearance of fixed, pensive thought. The impression came over my mind, that she had been led to yield up the world, and that the peculiarity which I noticed in her manner and conversation was the mute humility of a broken-hearted penitent, now musing over the world she had sacrificed, more than rejoicing over the Christ she had found. But after a little further interrogation, I found it was not that: she was as far from peace as ever.

But I could not understand her. Her heart did not seem to me the same as formerly. She had no tears to shed now; her manner was cold, and unlike herself; her words were measured and few; her misery, which seemed deeper than before, had put on an aspect almost of sullenness.

It was somewhat difficult for me to ascertain her state of mind; but after a few minutes, yielding to my urgency to tell me her feelings as a friend, she said to me, with a fixed look of despair,—

"I am entirely discouraged! I never shall be a Christian! My heart is so wicked, that it is wrong for me to pray at all, and for the last three days I have not tried! I have given up all hope of ever being saved!" She thanked me for my kindness and good intentions; but gave me to understand, that she did not wish to have the subject of religion urged upon her attention any more.

I encouraged her to persevere in her attempts to gain salvation. Especially I enjoined upon her the duty of prayer, and said to her almost *precisely the same things* which I had said before to another friend, and which are recorded in the sketch preceding this, as eight things to be remembered.

As I was speaking to her in the way of encouragement, her look appeared to alter, her bosom heaved, she burst into tears, and sobbed aloud. Referring to this some weeks afterwards, she said to me, "When you encouraged me so kindly, that day, my whole heart melted; I would have done anything you told me. I thought, if God is so kind, I *must* love him,—I *will* love him." She promised to resume prayer again. She kept her promise. And about a week after that, light broke in upon her darkness; she was one of the most bright and joyous creatures, and, I am sure, one of the most lovely ones, that ever consecrated to God the dew of her youth. She has continued to be so. Her days are all sunshine. Her heart is all happiness, and humility, and love. "My dear pastor," said she to me, when I asked what particular *truth or means* it was that led her to Christ, "I never *should* have found my Saviour, if you had not encouraged me so kindly, and led me back to prayer. Prayer is *everything*,—for God answers it."

These young persons (mentioned in this, and in the preceding sketch) were very much alike in conviction, in despondency, in temptation—they had the same means, the same ministry—the same truths were urged upon them in the same manner. Surely God is the hearer of prayer. If that other young woman could have been "led back to prayer," as this happy one expressed it, who can doubt that she would have been happy too, in "the kindness of her youth, and the love of her espousals?" If this page ever meets her eye may it lead her back to prayer.

XXII.

Human Ability.

A MEMBER of my Church called upon me, with manifest solicitude, in respect to a friend of his, whom he desired me to visit,—a young woman, who was a stranger to me. She was a member of the Church—but not of mine; though she was a resident in the place where I lived, she did not attend upon my ministry. I had reason to believe that she had tried it, but soon left the congregation, because she disliked the preaching. She attended worship with another congregation, whose minister, as I suppose, preached many doctrines not only *different* from those which I preached, but *contrary* to them; and I had little doubt that he would talk to inquiring sinners very differently from myself.

To visit this young woman under such circumstances was not pleasant to me. I should have to encounter her prejudices, and very likely should be obliged to contradict many things which had been taught to her; and, in such a case, it seemed to me almost beyond hope that I should be the instrument of any good. However, she had consented to meet me, and it would be ungracious, if not unchristian, for me to refuse. I understood that a deep and painful anxiety respecting her salvation had troubled her for many months; and when her friend desired her to converse with me, she had consented *reluctantly*, I had no doubt. She told him she was "willing to converse with *anybody;*" an expression indicative, as I thought, of no great confidence in myself, but yet it manifested an anxiety of mind.

I immediately called upon her. She was an intelligent young woman; her manners refined, her education excellent, her well-trained mind evidently accustomed to deep and extensive study. I am confident she has few equals in intellectual excellence.

She was in deep trouble. She had been a professor of religion for more than ten years, having united with the Church in a distant part of the country, but for several years past she had been convinced that she was an unconverted sinner still.

Besides possessing a mind of great strength, she appeared to me to have much firmness of character, great power of discrimination, much pride of reason, and an independence which bordered hard upon obstinacy. But I thought she was of an amiable disposition. Her frankness pleased me, and I discovered in her such a tenderness and depth of sensibility as are not common. On the whole, I was much pleased with her—I esteemed her; but I feared that her firmness and her pride of reason would not easily yield to Christ, as prophet, priest, and king. She had much philosophy and no faith.

"For years," she said to me, "I have been fully convinced that there is *something* in religion which I know nothing about, and know not where to find it." And as I endeavoured to point out to her, as clearly and simply as I could, the way of salvation, explaining to her the great truths of Christianity, I soon found that her opinions came into conflict with the truths which I presented to her; and she seemed wedded to her opinions with intense fondness, firmness, and confidence.

She evidently disliked, and very *greatly* disliked, the whole system of truth which I urged upon her attention and her acceptance; but those truths to which she seemed most opposed, and which she was ready to call in question, combat, or explain away, were such as have respect to human depravity, the dependence of a sinner on the special influences of the Holy Spirit, and justification by faith in Jesus Christ, as making atonement for our sins, delivering us from the curse of the law, and securing to us the full favour of God. But she did not appear to be so *much* opposed to the atonement as to the divine sovereignty and a sinner's dependence. She fully believed in "*human ability.*" She had not a doubt that a sinner possesses full power to come to Christ,—to repent and turn to God. The idea that a sinner can do nothing of himself, which will have any saving efficacy, she could not endure. The doctrine of helpless dependence was unutterably odious to her. She said to me, as I was urging upon her heart some of the practical truths of God, "I believe as Mr. F—— believes." We had some little argumentation upon the points whereon we differed; but I soon perceived she was so much attached to her false system, had defended it so long, and had so much pride and false philosophy embarked for its support, that no direct demonstrations addressed to the intellect would probably avail to batter it down.

But *her system had not saved her*. That was her weak point. It had not led her to peace. It had not satisfied her heart,—a heart still wanting something, and roaming, like Noah's dove on weary wing, over a world of waters,—no rock to rest upon. So I waived all disputation, avoided theological points (as much as I *could*, while still uttering the truths appropriate to her), and left her own wanting heart to convince her of the truth, by the pains of its own experience. I kindly assured her that there was salvation for her,—a peace and a repose to which she was now a stranger; and encouraged her to seek the Lord with all her heart, under the direction of the Bible, and to pray for the help of the Holy Spirit; for I was fully convinced that nothing but *the experience* of her own soul would correct the errors of her understanding, and lead her to believe the truths of God. If her "ability" was sufficient to repent without the aids of the Holy Spirit, I thought she had better try.

After several interviews with her, I was compelled to leave home, and I saw her no more for nearly a month. As I took my leave of her, I had little hope in her case. Evidently she was prejudiced against me, against my principles, and against all my preaching. Personally, therefore, it seemed impossible for me to have any influence over her. Her mind was filled with a system, in all its spirit, and in all its influences upon personal experience in religion, entirely contrary to my religious views. She constantly heard preaching, which I thought, by her account of it, to be directly contrary to the truth which I was most desirous to impress upon her heart. I could not talk to her of seeking God, or explain to her the way of salvation, without coming into conflict with some of her darling opinions; and hence I could not expect that all I had said to her would be of much avail. Much as I esteemed her, I was half sorry that I had ever seen her at all.

On my return home, about a month afterwards, I called upon her, as she had politely requested. I found her in a very different state of mind. She was most solemn, but full of peace. Her mind was all light, her heart all joy. As she talked to me, every one of her thoughts was clear as a sunbeam. She related to me her religious exercises with so much precision, clearness, and graphic power of description, and in such sweet humility and loveliness of spirit, that I was utterly astonished: I thought I had never heard anything equal to it. On that account I asked of her the favour to write down the account she had given me,—her own religious history. She yielded to my solicitation, and a few days afterwards I received from her the following account, which I think one of the most instructive and graphic descriptions I have ever seen. I am sure the reader will join me in thanking her for allowing it to take a place in this volume.

"Dr. Spencer,

"Dear Sir,—In compliance with your request, I transmit to you the following sketch of my religious history:—

"Almost eleven years have elapsed since I made a profession of religion. I thought then that I was a Christian; but I made a mistake. I found out my mistake gradually. One thing was enough to teach it to me. As weeks and months passed on, I found my path, instead of being like that of the just, 'shining more and more unto the perfect day,' only grew darker and darker; so that I finally feared its end must be in utter darkness.

"The time, when I first thought I had begun the Christian course, was during a revival. The teaching I then continually heard, was, 'Give yourselves to God, and go right about serving him,' as if doing *that* would of itself make one a Christian. I finally concluded that must be all; the importunities of friends were pressing me, and I at last expressed my determination and readiness to begin then the service of God, believing, as I was told, that we must not wait for light, we should find it in the discharge of duty. And herein I see now how the mistake of my life was made; my religion was one of works, and not of faith. I knew nothing about faith.

"As time passed on, I became fully convinced that there was no Christian principle at work in my heart. What then could I do? I always had a great repugnance to saying anything about my personal feelings; and if I should say I was not a Christian, and ask advice, I should only be told what I already knew, and what I heard preached every Sabbath-day. I believed I might make my professed religion a religion of the heart, and there was no need of any publicity about it: as I was already a professor, why, it would make no great change in me. And I have tried to do so again and again, and wondered as often, why it was that religion was a thing so utterly unattainable for *me*. This always made me miserable, except when I forgot it. And though I have sometimes almost forgotten it for weeks and months, still it has ever been a shadow in my heart, a secret blight upon everything.

"A few years since I spent a season in the State of Michigan, where I was under the influence and preaching of the 'Oberlin Doctrines.' My prejudices were against them, supposing some mysterious evil, I scarcely knew what, was lurking among them. But when I began to understand those views on depravity, ability, imputation, the atonement, &c., they pleased me exceedingly. They addressed themselves to my *reason* as I thought, and commended themselves to my heart. I found something tangible to work upon; and ever since, religion as a speculative matter, has been to me the most interesting of all things. I adopted the views of Mr. F—— with my whole heart and soul, and have ever since been openly committed to that faith, and everywhere its avowed and ready advocate.

"For some two years past I have taken very special interest in theological discussions. I resided in W——, Pennsylvania, where every one belonged to the genuine 'Old School.' The superintendent of the seminary, in which I was engaged as a teacher, was a clergyman of the Associate Reformed Church, and a large portion of the community were of that denomination. I was alone in my opinions, but openly committed to them. Last summer, the pastor of the Presbyterian church which I attended formed a class among his young people, to study the 'Confession of Faith.' I despised the book with my whole heart; but I joined the class and entered upon the work, all ready for a contest. A great deal of interest was soon awakened, not only among the members of the class, but among others also. To me, finding myself alone as I was, it was a matter of most intense interest and excitement. I possessed myself of all possible aids, studied carefully, and if I found a point that baffled me, I sent it to a reverend friend of mine, who was a disciple of Mr. F——, and in whose logic I had the utmost confidence. He allowed me to ask him as many questions as I chose, replied very fully to them all, and was ready to procure me all the means of information I desired.

"In the midst of this I was called away, all unexpectedly, suddenly, wonderfully; and I regretted it, because it put an end to my discussions, which were in prospect for the winter. I came here into a new world to me, and with work enough to occupy all my thoughts and all my time. Then I thought to myself, 'How shall I ever become a Christian now?' It seemed as if the most hopeful time had just passed, and now it was entirely out of the question; and I felt sad, as I thought 'perhaps God has given me to the world to take all my portion.' And during the first part of the winter I had little disposition as well as little time for serious thought.

"I had great difficulty in deciding what place of worship to attend. There were several things which might have induced me to attend upon your preaching, but then I thought, 'Dr. Spencer, with his blue Calvinistic notions, I shall quarrel with him every Sabbath.' No, I would not go there. I finally found preaching elsewhere much more congenial to my taste, and took a seat in that congregation.

"Some weeks since I heard a sermon one Sabbath morning on human responsibility, which the clergyman brought out by dwelling very much on the god-like faculties with which we are endowed, and the obligations we are under to develop them. It pleased me exceedingly, for that had always been one of my favourite topics; and it tended to make me feel self-reliant and strong. In the afternoon, it so happened that I attended your church, where I heard a sermon on humility. Such a *contrast of sermons* really startled me! They actually came in conflict. If the thing could have been possible, I should readily have believed that the sermon of the afternoon was *meant* for a reply to that of the morning. I rebelled against it with all my heart. Yet I could not help thinking that humility, after all, was most truly Christian-like, and the most eminent Christians had always expressed just such humiliating views of themselves. It would be easy to be a Christian if I only felt so; but I could *not* feel so, for I did not *believe* we were such 'weak miserable worms,' and altogether, between the impressions of the two sermons I was exceedingly troubled.

"About that time the things of religion were continually presenting themselves to my thoughts with an unusual power. I realized as never before how utterly unsatisfying everything earthly proved. In all the past there had been nothing substantial or enduring: the future could promise nothing, but to repeat the emptiness of the past; and the present brought only the consciousness that I was sowing the wind and feeding on ashes! That higher and worthier life I almost despaired of ever attaining; for what more could I do than I had done! any other attempt would be but a repetition of struggles, that had been just as determined as they were unavailing. Yet there remained those fearful certainties—an eternity before me, and a soul in constant peril!

"Every Sabbath-day these thoughts would possess me with such a fearful power that I would be led to form resolutions and purposes, immediately and with my whole heart, to make one more trial to find peace with God. Yet, in the daily duties of the week, such thoughts would in a measure be dissipated, and such purposes forgotten. On one of those solemn Sabbaths, a few weeks since, notice was given by the clergyman that during the week evening services would be held in the church, and that Mr. F—— would preach. That seemed like a message to *me*. It brought me to a point where I felt compelled to consider if this was not the time for the final decision. I found no interest or pleasure in the present, that need allure away my thoughts; I knew no better time could come in the future. More than all this, all unexpectedly my old prophet had appeared! I certainly should have no disposition to quarrel with *him*: all my combativeness would be laid at rest. I could receive whatever *he* would say. Not an excuse was left me. God had certainly met me half way. I dared not defer the work. I felt it must be done now or never.

"I resolved to attend these meetings. I went simply to learn what I should do. Though not very much prepossessed with his manner, yet in his matter I recognised the same Mr. F——, with whom I was already so well acquainted through his writings. His sermons were very much like those revival sermons of his, which were published some years ago. His philosophy came out occasionally in an incidental way, awakening most pleasing responses in my heart. I heard him with the greatest pleasure and satisfaction. Because I dared not then neglect any means that seemed to lie in my way, I went into the inquiry meetings. It cost my pride a struggle, yet I dared not excuse myself. At the close of a conversation I had there one night with Mr. F——, he said to me, in his peculiar manner, just as he was leaving me,—'Give your heart to God to-night. Won't you? Give your heart to God, before you go to bed: promise me.'

"'I have no faith in my promises,' said I.

"'*What?*'

"I repeated the answer, 'I have no faith in my promises.'

"'Well, make a promise,' said he, 'and stick to it.'

"But I did not then think how unwittingly I was confessing, in my answer, an inability I would have denied. God was then beginning to teach me the hardest lesson I had to learn.

"I came home from that meeting in a perfect sea of troubles. I was utterly amazed to find how much my pride had suffered, in putting myself in such a new attitude. I felt mortified, humbled, broken, in the desperate conflict. And I thought within myself, 'If I am so proud as this, perhaps it is only the beginning of what I must come to.'

"Then, not knowing what else to do, I resolved to visit a friend of mine, who was a professor of religion, confess to him I was no Christian, and hear what he would say to me. This resolve was just reversing my previous determination, and cost me another severe struggle. But after I had seen him, and all the thoughts of my soul had found utterance, it relieved me. Yet still my heart almost fainted, as I found how the committal had forced me on, shutting up all retreat against me.

"That night was with me a serious counting of the cost. I had begun somewhat to realize how my pride and will must suffer; and I brought into full consideration what more I might have to do. The idea of telling my friends about my personal religious feelings was most repugnant to me: I had always felt it an insurmountable difficulty. I *never could* do it; and I had often feared this would prove a fatal hindrance. Every thought of this kind came up before me; and then I balanced all with my eternal interests. The question was settled decisively, finally.

"My friend had expressed a very earnest wish that I should see you, sir. Well, I was in such deep waters, I told him 'I would talk with *anybody*.' The next day you came to see me; and after hearing my account of myself, you told me I had been 'going about to establish a righteousness of my own,' and therefore I had failed to find what I needed. You told me that my reliance always had been, and still was, upon my own powers and will to work out my salvation, without God to work in me. You said I 'could not do it; I could do nothing of myself.' That was the hardest of all things for me to receive. I could not understand it. I did not believe it. I told you I *knew* I had got something to do. And afterwards, when I saw you, that was the point you continually endeavoured to impress upon me,*—that I could do

* This representation is true, but defective. I did not fail to impress upon her attention her *obligation* to repent, her *duty* to be a Christian, and the truth, that she had *much to do*, which she must do freely, voluntarily. But I insisted upon it, that her *help* was in God,—that she was an undone and dependent sinner, to be saved, if saved at all, by grace through Jesus Christ. I did "continually endeavour to impress upon her that she could do nothing of herself." It was needful to do so. That was a truth which she neither felt nor believed. I taught her that she had "lost all ability of will to any spiritual good accompanying salvation," and that she needed the Holy Spirit to "enable her freely to will and to do that which is spiritually good." She speaks of her "favourite doctrine of ability." It was a favourite falsehood with her; and I "continually endeavoured" to undeceive her.

nothing of myself. It seemed to me the darkest mystery in the universe. Anything on earth I would *do,* but here my understanding was hopelessly baffled. Yet when, two or three days after, you sailed for Savannah, I felt exceedingly disappointed. I heard it with the greatest regret, for your kindness to me, and interest in me, had won my most sincere gratitude and affection.

"I had endeavoured to avoid touching upon theological points. I did not wish to think of them. I felt that now it was another question with me. My theology was safe, and safely put away. I had not a suspicion that it was to be interfered with. I knew well enough the wide difference of opinion betwixt you and myself, and to enter upon any discussion would be most unprofitable and vain. Besides, you seemed no more inclined to treat upon theological points than I did. So I did not happen to think until afterwards, the bow you had drawn at a venture had sent its shaft with a tremendous thrust right upon my favourite doctrine of ability. It struck the doctrine as much as it struck me. Indeed, it could not hit me without hitting the doctrine, for the doctrine was directly betwixt me and the arrow of truth. But you were gone, and I was left to think of it.

"Nothing yet seemed bringing me nearer to the light. I became almost discouraged. Human helps failed me, and I found that I failed myself. *It was so.* My utmost efforts of *will* were wholly ineffectual. I *did thoroughly prove them.* Anything on earth I was willing to do. As I had told you, 'I would die ten thousand deaths.' And my own multiplied endeavours,—my own experiences, did finally convince me that it *was not of myself to turn to God.* And then, with some sense that I was lost for ever unless he did help me, I tried to look to him for help.

"But then came my difficulty,—*I could not find him!* The heavens were dark, my heart was dark, and the only God I could think of was a cold abstraction of my own forming! For a long time I struggled with that difficulty,—I *could* not find him. Finally, the thought flashed upon me, 'There *is* a God.' (And then I recognised a familiar principle,—when knowing the solution of a question *does exist,* we are patient to follow through all dark ways to find it.) 'It is *true,* though I have not yet found him, there *is* a God,—God is.' It was like finding one spot on which I could rest. Wherever he was, *he* was the God I wanted. The idea of his *power* then possessed me. That was my first *realization* of any attribute of God. And it seems to me to show the wisdom of divine teaching, that when I had been full of miserable self-reliances, and vainly seeking in myself the strength to turn to God, the first attribute of his that I realized was *his power.* It came upon me with such force and vividness, that it seemed as if I had never before really believed there *was* a God. And then I remembered that he is '*mighty* to save.' That idea came so upon me that it seemed to fill my whole being. Such a great and glorious Saviour then he was, that human pride might well be set aside for most humble thankfulness. *Such* an one I could worship for ever. So different he seemed from what had been my own miserable conceptions of a Saviour, that I would find myself questioning if there *could* be *such* a Saviour. But yet it was most true,—I *felt* it to be true, and wanted to tell it to everybody in the house; besides, the whole Bible told of One just so mighty to save.'

"And then came new views—clearer views of the atonement. I saw and felt how God himself had paid the ransom for us; he had himself borne the penalty; on him was laid the iniquity of us all; it was all *done,* so that now there was nothing to *be* done—only to trust in him to save us. It seemed such an *infinite* atonement—so full and so free; so that *every one* that thirsteth may come—whosoever will, may take freely. It was infinite *love* that, when extended to those so lost and guilty--became infinite mercy. There every sin might be covered and lost.

"That night I read 'My goodness, my fortress,' &c.; and the thought struck me, 'Is it so, then, that even a Christian has not his own goodness?—is his goodness Christ?' Yes, it was so. In him was all fulness—and *such* a fulness, then, there must be; whatever the sinner needed, whatever the sinner had not, was all found in him. And it was such a new idea, that the principle of holiness was not, after all, to be found in our own heart, but it was all in Christ—Christ was the 'end of the law for righteousness.' He was our goodness, our righteousness, our sanctification, our redemption—he alone our salvation. And when that idea fully broke upon me, I was lost in it. The *forms* in which I had always brought God to my mind had dropped away, and a new God, a Saviour, seemed to have appeared out of heaven, and filled every place around me. It was an *uncreated* glory and purity all about me—and *such* a purity, and *such* a glory! my only expression for it was, '*Such a glorious Saviour!*' The intensity and vividness of that feeling and conception—which was the most glorious of anything that ever entered my soul—passed away after a time; but I was still happy in thinking there was just such a Saviour, until I attempted to express something of my idea to my friend who first directed me to you, and then it seemed to amount to nothing more than what I had known before—what everybody knew, that there was a God and a Saviour.

"But it was a day or two after that before I happened to think that here was another of my favourite doctrines torn up, root and branch—that against imputation. But so it was; I felt it was gone. I knew in my very heart that Christ's righteousness was the only ground of acceptance. That expression, 'making mention of his righteousness, struck me with peculiar force. And it came to me again and again, so full of meaning! But I did not feel a regret that my own former speculations were swept away; for the plan, as I now saw it, seemed so infinitely more glorious, that I could only rejoice in it. Not only had he paid our debt, but he had clothed us also in his own robe of righteousness; so that we need not depend on ourselves, or look for righteousness in ourselves, but find all in Christ. That was truly a glorious redemption.

"The vividness of these conceptions gradually dimmed; but still the *truth* remained. I *believed* everything that I had now learned; for *it was my heart's experience.* And because I found these impressions lost their vividness, and I did not feel them moving me, but felt how great a work was to be done in my heart, I could not, dared not think my heart was really changed; and I was continually fearful of falling again upon a false hope.

"About that time, in a prayer-meeting, I heard the minister to whose congregation I belonged make the remark, as he was giving some directions to inquirers, 'Now, we are not going to pray God to *enable* you to consecrate yourselves to him; there is not a soul here but is able to do that.' He said it was 'just as easy as giving away a book' he held in his hand—'all an act of the will.' That startled me. I *had just learned better!* I had found in my own soul that 'it is *not* of him that willeth, nor of him that runneth, but of God that showeth mercy.' I did believe he was 'the Author and Finisher of our faith' —even the *Author*. This boasted power of the human will I found to be the very rock on which I had split before, so that that minister's teaching would not do for me. He had invited any who wished to see him, to meet him the next evening, and I had proposed to go; but now I would not venture.

"In the preaching of Mr. F—— hitherto, his peculiar doctrines had only come out incidentally; but a few nights after this, I heard a sermon from him almost entirely devoted to his peculiar views. He went on to speak of the fall, and that 'when man had changed his heart one way, he could as well do it the other;'—to speak also of an 'imputed righteousness,' which he seemed to think was 'the same as an imputed heaven' would be;—to speak of the power of example being the strongest moral force that could be brought to bear upon the mind, and this we had in Christ. He said that motives presented would work out their effects. These were the same things that I continually dwelt upon last summer. They now swept over me like a torrent; not *convincingly,* however, for *my own heart disproved them,* but with a strange power. It was like reviving what I had just buried. Those old speculations (which my own experience had *proved* to be *false*) all woke up fresh, and my mind was filled with them. It was true that sermon touched a chord that was dear to me, and I was compelled to have all the struggle over again. Clouds and darkness closed over me, and I could not see my way out. But I did not go to hear Mr. F.—— any more.

"By this time I began to look at my theology in earnest, to see if anything therein was keeping me back from the light; and I finally acknowledged that whatever the Bible said, whatever God taught, however it might come into conflict with my prejudice, *I must receive it*—I must take it, and learn it, and believe it as a little child, my own prejudice and *reason* out of the question. If Adam's sin had anything to do with us—why, I must submit. And more than all else, if God did even ordain to leave some to everlasting punishment, I had nothing to say—it was his right. That ninth chapter of the Romans, which I had quarrelled with more than any other chapter in the Bible, and had been determined not to receive, unless it could all be explained away—why, if God had really said so, I must take it, I must take it just as it reads, for, 'who art thou that repliest against God?' And I could see now that, if it were so, it did more fully manifest the riches of his glory on the 'vessels of mercy.' His plans and purposes were none of my business. God would reign, and all I had to do was to be willing to be saved in the only way he had provided.

"But even after all this, I found myself in trouble. For some days I seemed to have come to a stopping-place. I could not go back. I knew not how to go forward. All was dark, and God was far away. I knew not what hindered me, or why I was in darkness. I could think of nothing which I was not willing to give up—nothing that I was not willing God should do with me; and yet it seemed as if something must be wanting. Unquestionably the fault was in me; my deceitful heart had hidden away a part of the price, and I could not find it.

"I was remarking this difficulty to my friend, when he suggested that I seemed to be looking to my past experiences, fearful of being again deceived; and added, that never before in my life had I had such a course of thought. That remark struck me, and when I was alone that evening, it induced a long train of reflections. I had never had such a course of thought before—*that was most true.* Never in my life, not at all before, when I expressed the hope that I was a Christian, had I experienced anything like this. Never before had eternal things come to me with such reality and power, concentrating my whole soul upon one intense, absorbing thought. And now I bethought myself of all the various processes through which my mind within a few days had passed. My very power of thinking surprised me. I thought, that while ever before I had found it difficult to fix my mind for any length of time upon my own eternal interests, now my soul's salvation had been the one thing continually before me. Engaged in my usual occupations, there was a constant under-current of thought; and when at leisure, my mind was filled with one intense, absorbing interest. Here certainly was one thing unlike what I had ever known before. In this respect I found myself a new creature. I reflected, also, that I had always revolted from telling my friends that I was not a Christian, or from expressing to them any religious concern; but now it was very different with me. I had actually surprised myself several times in thinking, with a sort of pleasure, how I would *tell* all my friends what wonderful things God had done for me. And it occurred to me now, how *unlike me* that was—how totally different from what I had always felt before. I was astonished, and said to myself, 'What has wrought this change?'

"Again, I reflected that night I had been fully grounded and settled in a system of theology; it had been a matter of exceeding interest to me. I had believed it as fully and firmly as *reason* fully persuaded *can* believe. Neither had it been a mere prejudice of education. The prejudices of education, and the influences under which I had always been (except at one time for a few months), would all have led me far enough the other way; but it was a theological belief, brought about by the power of my own reason. I honestly believed when I rested on that system, and I believe now that no force of argument in the world could have changed me. If I had not succeeded in sustaining my system, I should have felt that the *truth* of it remained untouched—I had only failed in the way of showing it. I had repeatedly heard all the strongest arguments that could be adduced against me, and they never moved me. The first sermon I heard after I came to this place was a sermon from Dr. Skinner, on 'Depravity.' It was a master-piece. As an effort of intellect, and for its logic, I admired it with all my heart. But I said, 'A man equally logical could answer him on the other side, and do even better *there*.' Besides, my pride was concerned; for I had been so openly and everywhere committed to my faith, I had contended for it so often and with so many, that this *alone* might make it a hard matter for me to retract,—almost impossible. And besides all this, when I began to think about being a Christian now, theology had been left out of my thoughts. I felt it was another thing that interested me. I did not wish to bring it up, and it never entered into my mind that it would be meddled with, much less that I should renounce one point. The idea of doing so I knew would have astonished me. Indeed, my attention had not been at all called to my theology, until arrested by finding it breaking away under me. But now, *understandingly, willingly*, I found I had given it all to the winds. *Human* agency seemed to have had nothing to do about it. Even you, sir, had to be called away, so I could not say your persuasion or influence had done it; and on the other hand, Mr. F—— was here to prompt me; nevertheless it was all gone. I had been almost entirely shut in to myself and my Bible, and there had been no form of argument or reason; the change had come about almost unconsciously to myself—like the wind blowing where it listeth. And now, what had done this? No person else had done it, and I felt that it *was not at all* like *me* to do it,—it was the most unlike me of anything on earth; and then I felt convinced it must be some higher Power—some divine agency. *It must be so.* And you cannot imagine with what tremendous power that conviction forced itself upon me,—how it startled my very being! —unless you know that my old speculations had led me to the conclusion that there was no such thing as the *special* influence of the Holy Spirit. I never could understand that doctrine of *special* divine influence. I thought it was irreconcilable with free moral agency, and so I concluded it was a delusion, or a mere figure of speech. But now I found God himself had taught it to me. The conviction forced itself upon me that here was a work of God's Holy Spirit.

"And as I tried to account for all that I had experienced in any other way (aiming to guard against being deceived again into a false hope), that passage came very strikingly to my mind, where the Jews, when they could not deny that devils were really gone out, said, 'He casteth out devils by Beelzebub;' and Christ answered, 'A house divided against itself cannot stand; if Satan cast out Satan, he is divided against himself.' That might be a crafty suggestion, I thought; but it was not like Satan to do for me what I had experienced; nor was it like my own wicked heart to do it. It must be *God,* who was leading me by his Spirit, 'in a way that I knew not.'

"Then, in that night of reflection, I thought also of other things, many lesser things, in which, as it seemed, in spite of myself, I had been completely turned around. It did seem like turning the rivers of water. They were flowing backward against their current.

"Well *then,* I thought, if God's Spirit has done such wonderful things in me (and I could not now doubt it),—if he has already done things which I never before believed *could* have been done,—then *he can do all things* else; and he would, I did believe he would, I could trust him that he would,—he would work in me to will and to do what I could never do myself. He would continue the work that he had begun, and finish it in righteousness. There I could rest; there the promises seemed to meet me. God's word was pledged, sure as his everlasting throne; he was faithful; the word witnessed with the Spirit; and what he had promised, he was also able to perform. This was my light, my hope, and joy.

"And as I thus looked back, and saw how I *had* been led, I felt assured I might account that the long-suffering of God was salvation,—

that he had purposes of mercy for me; and now, if he had met me, it had truly been when I 'was a great way off;' and he had received me in such a wonderful way, that he would have all the glory. I thought, too, it was because he was a covenant-keeping God; and as he kept his covenant with faithful Abraham, because 'he *believed* God, and it was accounted unto him for righteousness,' so now he does keep his covenant with believing parents. And such faith as my father and mother exercised when they gave me to God would be remembered and accepted. This seemed to me like another added to the multiplied assurances of his faithfulness,—that he *is* a God keeping covenant and showing mercy; and, therefore, he kept me from an utter destruction, and followed me with purposes of mercy, to make me 'willing in the day of his power.' I did feel in my soul that *he* had done everything for me that had been done; so I could truly say, '*He* sent from above, *he* took me, *he* drew me out of many waters.' Whatever I had learned, he had taught me; and I did believe that same Spirit of truth would yet lead me into all truth. And I rejoiced that our salvation did not depend any more upon our own will, or our own power of enduring unto the end;—if it did, I felt it would be a yoke harder than that which the Jews were not able to bear. It was wonderful to think how the whole work was of God. He paid the debt; he clothed us in his own righteousness; his Spirit made us willing, and then continues to work in us, keeping us by the *power of God* through faith unto salvation. Such contemplations and experiences as these assured my heart, —I felt that God was with me. The darkness is past; the true light now shineth.

"It seems to me now, that one of my greatest errors has been, making my *reason* the test for everything,—bringing every principle to the court of *reason* for trial. Starting in that way, it is not wonderful that I fell into error. I see now that *faith* is infinitely higher,—just faith in God and his word. Reason gets blinded, dizzy, lost, where faith is clear, calm, steady, and in a region of light. Reason *cannot* understand the things of the Spirit of God: not that they are contrary to it, but beyond it,—seen only by faith. And this is one of the most wonderful things that I have learned,—the beauty and power of faith. I never could understand it before. It has perplexed me a great deal. If it meant anything more than a mere intellectual belief, I could not at all apprehend it. I believe I finally concluded it did not. But *now* I see it is everything. The Bible is full of it. And to think that is all,—just to *believe* God is able and willing to do it all, and let him do it,—it is wonderful *that* should be such a stone of stumbling! Yet as I think of it, it seems to me I cannot conceive of any such other sublime act of the mind as that *faith in things invisible,* which the Christian exercises; and to think, too, that any one, the very lowest orders of intellect, can and do exercise it strongly,—it must be the work of the Spirit of God. Really to believe in God, in a Saviour, in the power of the Holy Spirit, and to feel that the things of the soul and eternity are *realities*, seems to me like a new and wonderful thing. Even the thought that *there is a God*, as it happens to flash across my mind, *thrills* through my very soul. All these things,—it seems to me as if I had just been taught them.

"If I had been a Christian when I took hold of those theological matters, it might have been different with me; but as it was, they pleased my unregenerate heart as well as my reason, and it startles me to think to what conclusions I was arriving. *I know* those doctrines well-nigh made shipwreck with me.

"The doctrine of election seems to me *now*, naturally and necessarily to grow out of God's sovereignty. I rebelled against it, because I rebelled against him. And now nothing melts me like it. To hear him say, 'Ye have not chosen me, but I have chosen you;' and then to think there was not a shadow of merit or claim in me, but it was all his own sovereign, absolute will and pleasure,—I can only say, 'Not unto us, not unto us, but unto thy name be all the glory.' That he should have '*predestinated* us unto the adoption of children, according to the good pleasure of his will,' is certainly in keeping with everything else that I have learned,—that it is all of God. 'Esaias is very bold,' but I begin to see how he may still be *right*, when he says, 'I was found of them that sought me not, I was made manifest unto them that asked not after me.'

"I know and feel that there is yet a great deal to be done in my heart; but I believe I do feel more and more as if I could follow on through darkness and shadowy light, trusting that God will at length lead me out into perfect day. I cannot but think that my old rebellion is gone. I do feel willing that he should reign, and I rejoice that he does. And if I have any desire in my soul, it is for God, for the living God, the God that reigns, and reigns in grace by Jesus Christ. While heaven once seemed desirable only as a place of security from eternal death, or at most, of intellectual pleasure, now what makes my heart go out toward it is, that there I 'shall be like him, for I shall see him as he is.'

"And now it is my heart's desire to live 'as seeing Him who is invisible.' And whatever it costs me, I would be a humble, decided, constant follower of Christ, feeling in my own soul the power of that faith, that 'worketh by love, and purifieth the heart,'—living the life which I now live, 'by the faith of the Son of God, who loved me, and gave himself for me.'"

Conversion to God is conversion to truth.

XXIII.

The Faults of Christians.

AMONG my parishioners, at one time, there was a very industrious and respectable man, a mechanic, for whom I entertained a high esteem. I thought him a man of talent, and of much good feeling. He was about thirty years of age, was married, and his wife had recently become a child of God, as she believed, and had made a public profession of her faith in Christ. I had now the more hope of being useful to him, on account of his wife's experience of grace, and the uniformly happy state of her mind. He had also some other relatives who were members of my Church, and were exemplary Christians. He was himself a constant and attentive hearer of the gospel every Sabbath-day, and whenever I met him (which was very often), he spoke freely of religion, and confessed his obligation and his anxiety to be a Christian. I had no small hope in his case. I had noticed the increasing depth of his seriousness. Besides, I knew him to be a personal friend to myself, very much attached to me; and on that account I had the more expectation of being able to influence his mind upon the subject, which now occupied, as he said, "all his thoughts."

After his wife had become a pious woman and a member of the Church, he appeared to become more deeply impressed than ever. The day on which she was baptized, and came for the first time to the Lord's table, was a most solemn day to him. He afterwards said to me, "When I saw my wife go forward before all the congregation to be baptized, I could not hold up my head, I was forced into tears, and I solemnly resolved to put off my salvation no longer. And I mean to keep that resolution."

After this I took some pains to see him several times, for the purpose of personal conversation. He was thoughtful, serious, prayerful ; and, as I thought, was "not far from the kingdom of heaven." But as the weeks passed on, I was surprised and sorry to find that his religious impressions appeared to have come to a stand. They did not vanish,—I could not say they had diminished ; but they evidently had not become more deep and influential. He used to say to me, "I am *trying*, and I hope I shall yet be a Christian." I cautioned him against delay, and against any reliance upon the mere fact that he *continued* his attempts, while he did not flee to Christ.

In this manner several months passed on. He uniformly appeared solemn, often avowed his conviction of his lost condition as a sinner, acknowledged his need of a Saviour, and lamented the wickedness and hardness of his heart. But finding him, as I thought, very much stationary, I feared that his perceptions of divine truth were not correct and clear, or that his impressions were only superficial or occasional; and therefore I aimed to deal the more plainly with him, and tried, in every way I could contrive, to bring the gospel truths more clearly before his mind, and impress them more deeply upon his conscience and his heart. With the law of God on the one hand, and the gospel on the other, his conscience to condemn him, and Christ to invite him, I hoped his heart would be brought to surrender in faith.

It was in one of these conversations, which I was accustomed to have with him, that he surprised me by expressing a thought, which I had never heard from him before. I had just asked him,—

"What *hinders* you, my dear sir, from being a Christian indeed, since all the grace of the gospel is so free, and since you are so sensible that you need it?" His answer was,—

"I think a great many more of us would be Christians, if *professors of religion were different from what they are.*"

"That may be," said I; "but you know, each one 'shall give

account of *himself* unto God.' *You* are not accountable for professors of religion; and *they* are not accountable for your irreligion."

"I know that," said he. "But how can we believe in the reality of religion, when members of the Church, and the elders too, are dishonest—will lie and cheat, and make hard bargains, a great deal worse than other people?"

"Have you any doubt of the reality of religion?"

"Oh no, I believe in the reality of religion. I believe in a change of heart as much as you do."

"Then," said I, "*you* can believe in the reality of religion, somehow or other. In that respect *you* have not been misled by our 'dishonest elders and Church members,' who drive such 'hard bargains, a great deal worse than other people.' As to the accusation, that our elders and Church-members are such dishonest and hard men, I deny it: the accusation is not true. There may be some bad men in the Church. There was a Judas among Christ's disciples. One of the chosen twelve was *a thief.* But that was no good reason why other people should reject Christ. The *general* character of our Church-members is not such as you have mentioned. You ought not to condemn Matthew and the other disciples because Judas was a villain.

"Well," said he, with some hesitation, "I know some Church-members who are no better than other people,—not a bit better than a great many of us who make no profession."

"Perhaps you do. But what of that? Will their imperfections do *you* any good? Will their sins save *you,* or excuse you?"

"Why," hesitatingly, "they ought to set us a better example."

"No doubt of that. And allow me to say, you ought to set *them* a better example. You are under as much obligation to set *me* a good example, as I am to set you a good example. You and I are under the same law. God commands *you* to be holy as he commands *me.* It is quite likely that those Church-members of whom you complain would be better men, if it were not for such persons as *you,*—persons who set them no holy example."

"Well, I believe many members of the Church are great stumbling-blocks; I know they are."

Said I, "I believe many, who are *not* members of the Church, are great stumbling-blocks; I know they are. You are one of them. You are a stumbling-block and a hindrance to many impenitent sinners, to your partner in business, to your neighbours, to your sisters, and other acquaintances. I am sorry for it, but so it is. If you would become a truly pious man, these persons would feel your influence constraining them to seek the Lord, and your example would be a stumbling-block to them no longer."

"I make no *profession* of religion," said he.

"That is the very thing," I replied. "You stand aloof from religion entirely, as if you disbelieved it; and your example just encourages others to neglect it as you do. You once told me yourself how greatly it affected you, when you saw your wife come out to be baptized in the presence of the great congregation. If you would set such an example, it would probably affect others."

"*My wife* is a good woman; she lives as a Christian ought to live."

"Then you have at least *one* good example."

"If all professors of religion were like her, I should not find fault with them."

"And if *you* were like her, other people would not find fault with *you*. Your example would commend religion."

"Well, the example of a great many professors does not commend it to *me*."

"Why do you look at the *bad* examples? Look nearer home. Look at your wife's example. You are very unwise to let your thoughts dwell upon the faults of Christians at all; and when you do so, you hunt up a few professors of religion, who are not by any means a fair specimen of our Church-members, and you take *them* as samples of all the rest. That is unfair. I am sorry you have run into this way of thinking. It will only lead you into error, and call off your attention from the eternal interests of your own soul. The faults of others cannot save *you*. I beg of you to think less about other people's sins, and more about your own."

"Well, I will. I know I have had my mind turned away from religion many a time, by thinking of the conduct of professors."

A few days after this I met my friend in the street, and asked him if he thought he had gained the "one thing needful?" He replied,—

"No, I don't think I have. But I believe I am as good a man as a great many who took the sacrament yesterday in your church."

"I am sorry to hear you talk of others again," said I. "You promised me that you would think of your own sins, and let the sins of other people alone; and now the very first sentence you utter is a reflection upon some who were at the Lord's table yesterday. I am surprised at this. Your hard thoughts about other people will lead you, I am afraid, further and further off from religion."

"Very likely," said he, "but *I* can't help it. The members of the Church set such examples, that my mind is turned away from religion by them many a time."

"Yes," said I, "the old prophet knew how that was: 'They eat up the sin of my people, and set their heart upon iniquity; they have left off to take heed to the Lord.' You are one of that stamp. You seize upon 'the sin of God's people,' as if it were bread to you; and then you forget to pray—you have 'left off to take heed to the Lord.' After you have eagerly fed yourself upon the 'sin of God's people' for a while, then you have no inclination 'to take heed' to anything God says to you. I advise you to eat some other sort of food. 'The sin of God's people' is a bad breakfast. It is very indigestible. The wicked seize upon it, as if it were bread to the hungry; and the worst of it all is, that after they have eaten such a breakfast they have no family prayer; they do not 'take heed to the Lord.' That is your case precisely; you complain of Christians, instead of praying for yourself. You *never* pray, after finding fault with members of the Church for half an hour."

"How do *you* know I don't pray?"

"I know by the text which I just quoted. You '*eat up the sin of God's people;'* and for that reason, I know that the other part of the text belongs to you. You '*have left off to take heed to the Lord.*' Is it not so? Have you not left off, ceased to pray, since you began to find fault with Christians?"

"*Yes*, I own it. I am not going to deny it."

Said I, "I am very sorry you take such a course. You yield to a temptation of the devil. The best Christians are imperfect, very imperfect. They do not profess to be sinless. You may see their faults, but you cannot see their penitence, and tears, and agony of spirit, when in secret they mourn over their many imperfections, and beg forgiveness of God, and grace to be more faithful. If *you* felt so, if *you* had done wrong in public through thoughtlessness, or through some temptation, and then in secret should mourn bitterly over your fault—would you think it generous, would think your disposition well treated, or even that any kind of justice had been done to it, if your neighbour should be going around complaining of your faults, as if you were a bad man?"

"No, I should not think I deserved that."

"Very well. These imperfect Christians have such secret mournings. And if you will go to them, and kindly tell them their faults, you will hear things from them which will alter your feelings about them; you will have a better opinion of their hearts than you have now, and a more just opinion too. Did you ever mention to these people the things you complain of?"

"No, I never did."

"I think you ought to do it. Certainly you ought to do it, or cease to make complaints about them to others. Jesus Christ has taught us our duty in such a case. 'If thy brother trespass against thee, go to him, and tell him his fault betwixt him and thee alone.'"

"That applies to Christians."

"It applies to *you*. You ought to be a Christian. And your neglect of one duty cannot excuse your neglect of another. You must not plead one sin as an excuse for another. If one of your neighbours had a bad opinion of you, surely you would much rather he should come and tell you what he had against you, and hear your explanation, than that he should tell it to other people."

"Yes, I should. But I have given nobody's name."

"I know it; and I complain of that. Instead of pointing out the guilty individuals, you complain of Christians in general; and thus you make the innocent suffer with the guilty. You make *religion* suffer (at least in your estimation) by the faults of a few, who profess to be religious people. How would *you* like it, if I should speak of the men of your trade as you speak of Christians, and say, 'Blacksmiths are villains, dishonest men?"

"I should want you to name the men."

"And I want *you* to name the men. Come, tell me who they are, and what they have done; and I promise you I will have their conduct investigated. They shall be tried before the proper tribunal. You shall be a witness against them. And if they are found guilty, they shall be turned out of the Church; and then they will be complained of by you no longer, and the good name of religion will no more be dishonoured by them."

"Oh, *I* can't be *a witness* against anybody."

"Why not? Can't you tell the truth? Will you make religion suffer, rather than bring bad men to justice? Will you injure the good name of all of us, 'Church-members and elders too,' as you say, instead of lending your assistance to purify the Church from unworthy members? Will you let this thing go on, and let it hinder, as you say it does, a great many of you from being Christians?"

"It is not *my* business to bear witness against Church-members."

"Why do you *do it*, then? You *have* been doing it, every time I have met you, for the last three months. And though I have tried to persuade you to cease, you still keep on, bearing witness against 'Church-members and elders,' every time I meet you."

"Well, I don't mean to *injure* anybody."

"No, sir, I don't think you do. The only one you injure is *yourself*. The general imputations which you so often fling out against professors of religion are *slanders.* They are *not true.* You may *think* them true, but they are *not* true. I affirm them to be utterly unfounded and false. There may be, indeed, a few persons in the Church who are as bad as you declare them to be; but your general accusations are falsehoods. But suppose all you say, or even suspect, were true,—suppose half of our Church-members to be bad men; in the name of all that is common sense, I ask you, what has that to do with your religion? If half the money that is in circulation is counterfeit, does that make the good money in your pocket valueless? or will it lead you to refuse to take *all* money?"

"I don't want to have *counterfeit* money!"

"And I don't want you to have a counterfeit religion. The very fact that you complain of counterfeit money, is full proof that you believe there is such a thing as good money somewhere; and your complaint of counterfeit religion is full proof that you believe there is such a thing as good religion."

"Yes, I believe all that."

"And you believe that you have not attained it."

"I suppose I haven't."

"And are you striving to attain it, or are you as anxious and prayerful about it as you were a few weeks since?"

"No, I don't think I am."

"Will you answer me one more question? Has not your seriousness diminished, and your prayerfulness ceased, very much in proportion as you have had hard thoughts, and made hard speeches about the faults of Christians?"

"I can't say *no* to that question."

"Then I wish you very seriously to consider whether your fault-finding has not provoked God to withdraw from you the influences of the Holy Spirit! You *do know,* that your regard for religion and your attempts after salvation have never been promoted by your complaining about Christian people. Thinking of their sins, you forget your own, as I have told you before. You foster in your own heart a spirit of self-righteousness by your miserable and foolish way. I have warned you against it before, and I will now warn you again, if you will permit me. If you will go on in this way, God will leave you to your deceptions and your impenitence; you will live without religion, and you will die without it! I beseech you, therefore, as a friend, as a neighbour, as a minister, dismiss your thoughts about the faults of a *few*, for they are only a few, professors of religion, and seek from God the forgiveness of your own sins, and the salvation you so much need."

I left him. But he never sought me again. Fifteen years have since passed away, and he is still as far from God as ever. Often when I have met him, I have endeavoured to draw him into some conversation upon religion; but he avoids the subject. and commonly shuns me.

The Holy Spirit would lead us to think much about our own sins. It is a dangerous thing for us to dwell upon the imperfections of others. There are many in our congregations who 'quench the Spirit' by complainings and hard speeches about communicants of the Church. The natural effect of this is just to dispel conviction of sin. "I am as good as many who belong to the Church." If that declaration is true, it is utterly deceptive to the man that makes it. It leads him to think his sin and danger less than they are; it blinds his conscience. I never have heard of any mortal, on the bed of death, apologizing for his irreligion by mentioning the faults of Christians.

XXIV.

Trying to Find God in the Wrong.

THE young woman who wrote the following letter had been known to me for years. I had often conversed with her upon religion, and she made it very much a matter of speculation merely, as I believed. The state of her mind now when she writes, very different from anything I had ever known of her before, may be judged of by the following extracts from her letter:—

"For years I have not been indifferent to my personal religion; but the incubus that formerly held me within its thrall still distresses me. Dreadful thoughts, that I dare not utter, against the goodness and justice of God interrupt my efforts to do right, and so mingle with my petitions that I have sometimes arisen from prayer in a sort of desperation—afraid *not* to pray, but afraid *to* pray; and I indulge in such fearful imaginations against the God of heaven, even while in the act of asking his blessing

"I have often tried, sometimes successfully, to lay this matter entirely aside, to give it up, hoping that in the course of time some event in the providence of God would occur which would satisfy my mind and heart, and bring me to an involuntary decision. But I find that time and waiting do me no good, and shed no light upon my path.

"I have endeavoured prayerfully to study my heart and analyse my feelings; and I can see no reason to hope that I have experienced a change of heart. I realize that I am deeply sinful; but when I try to feel grateful to God that he has provided for me an atonement, and to the Saviour that he is that atonement, my spirit returns no response of tenderness and love—'a mail defends my untouched heart,' that seems impenetrable to any appeal. Still, it is my desire to live hereafter entirely to the glory of God.

"Christ is to me 'as a root out of a dry ground.' I see no beauty in him 'that I should desire him.' I feel no mournful sorrow for my sins; and my mind and heart seem constantly rising in dreadful questioning of every attribute of the character of God.

"I do not ask, as formerly, *why* these things are so? *why* I was created sinful? *why* I inherit the body of this death? My appeal to you is no longer to answer to me what God has never revealed; but it is that you will pray for me, that I be not utterly rejected of God,—that he will hear my prayer and give me repentance and *faith in Christ.* Oh, that I could feel that God is my Father, that Jesus Christ is my Saviour! Oh, that I could *love* God,—that Christ were precious to me!

"For many months I have wished for counsel on this great subject, and I have endeavoured to come to a decision through prayer and study of the Bible. I have wished to visit you, but have feared that I was not sufficiently in earnest thus to commit myself. But I can stay away no longer. And *may* I come to you? And may I ask that you will respond to my letter? . . . . It is my sincere prayer that you may be instrumental in shedding some light upon the cold and callous heart that prompts these lines." ———.

Such was her letter. The next day I sent her the following answer:—

"Your state of mind has nothing in it new or uncommon. The same perplexities, the same discouragements, despondencies, and 'desperations,' the same fitfulness and vain hopes of some undefined and undefinable good, which have so long affected you, have as much affected others. If your heart refuses to love God and trust in Christ, and in the strength of its rebellion not only refuses to obey your will, but also entertains feelings, and leads to thoughts about God, which you dare not utter;' the same thing has afflicted thousands before you, so that you have no grounds for religious 'desperation' on this account.

"But on this point I have two things to say to you:—

"*First*, It is well, perhaps, that you see so much of your heart's sinfulness. It *may* be well now and for ever, if you *obey* the knowledge which truth and the Holy Spirit have given you. This *sense* of not 'loving God,' of finding 'no beauty in Christ,' of perplexity and fitful 'desperation,' constitutes a part of conviction of sin, and it proves the presence of the Holy Spirit striving with your soul.

"*Second*, After all you have learnt of the depravity of your heart, you have yet seen but a very little of it. It is a far more corrupt and abominable heart in the sight of God, than in your darkest or lightest moments you have ever imagined. You have conviction, but evidently your conviction is but partial or superficial. You know only a small part of your depravity and danger.

"And this leads me to say, that your failure to see appropriateness and goodness in Christ, and to feel an unbounded gratitude to him, and to the love of the Father which gave him, arises just from your lack of feeling your undone condition and your lack of a heart right with God. If you knew well your lost estate, you would at least 'receive the word with gladness,' that there *is* such a thing as redemption for sinners; you would rejoice that one gleam of hope remains,—that there is provision and possibility of salvation. And then you would *see clearly* that the best thing you could do, and the *first* you *ought* to do, is just to flee to Christ, an undone sinner, and fall into his arms,—'Lord, save me, or I perish.' But even after *seeing that clearly*, and determining to *do* that sincerely, another and a worse affliction would meet you, because you would find your obstinate heart refuse. And thus the very *amount of conviction* which you sometimes aim after would not do for you what you are wont to suppose. Conviction is not the Holy Spirit. You need the infinite aid of the Holy Ghost. If you ever know your own heart well, you will know that you need it, and must have it, or die an alienated, unconverted sinner! And *then*, prayer will be a reality with you,—the cry of want, the voice of despair in self, the voice of hope in God, and in God only. And then, if your resistance of the Holy Ghost does not provoke him to depart from you, your seeking the Lord will be with your *whole* heart, and not as it hitherto has been, with only half of it. I refer you to Jer. xxix. 12–14; to Prov. ii. 1–5; to Isa. lv. 6–13. Your grounds of hope to bring you to faith in Christ must be the Bible and the Holy Spirit.

"Your reference to the high and mysterious things of God brings up a matter which I think may easily be disposed of:—

"1. Whoever believes in a God at all, believes in an *infinite mystery;* and if the *existence* of God is such an infinite mystery, we can very well expect and afford to have many of his *ways* mysterious to us,—yea, our reason demands it. Why? how? wherefore? often demand things which not only lie beyond man to explain, but beyond man to *comprehend*, even if they were revealed by the tongue of an angel, or the lips of Jehovah himself!

"2. There are no more mysteries in religion than there are in nature,—no more dark and inexplicable things. Our life is a mystery, and so is every tree and every flower. The power of our will over our muscles is a mystery. The same line of demarcation which separates knowledge from ignorance in natural things, separates knowledge from ignorance in religious things. The case is this, in general,—we know *facts;* the *modes* of them, the *why*, the *how*, we do *not* know. In natural things we have no hesitancy in acting on the facts, though ignorant of the reason of them; for example, we breathe, though ignorant of the reason *why* breathing keeps us alive. And if we would act upon the facts of religion in the same manner, we should be Christians indeed. . . . . .

"You say you do not love God. You *ought* to love him. Be ashamed of your heart (what a heart!), if you do *not* love him. You have been, are, ashamed of it. And yet, when you try to make it feel, it will not feel at your bidding,—'a mail defends your untouched heart.' Do you not then feel your helplessness? Have you not an *experience*, which ought to make you both glad and grateful that God has said to you, '*In me is thy help?*' Fly to him, fly now,—fly just *as you are*, poor, vile, guilty, *lost*. Do you not know that Jesus Christ 'came to seek and to *save* that which was lost?' Delay has done you no good. It never can do you any. You wait in vain for 'some event of Providence to bring you to an involuntary decision.' Such a decision is an absurdity,—no decision at all. And were it not so, it would be inacceptable to God, as it is contrary to the Bible. 'Choose ye this day whom ye will serve.' The choice must be your own.

"What hinders that you should be a child of God? Is not salvation free? Is not the invitation to it flung out to you on every page of the New Testament? Is not Christ offered to you in all his offices? and are you not welcome to all his benefits if you want them? Is not the Holy Spirit promised 'to them that ask him?' 'What more could have been done to my vineyard?'

"You say you want to be a Christian. What hinders you, then? God the Father wants you to be a Christian. God the Son wants you to be a Christian. God the Holy Ghost wants you to be a Christian. Nothing can hinder you from being a Christian, but your own worldly, selfish, proud, obstinate, unworthy, and self-righteous heart."

———.

The following expressions are taken from her reply:—

"And is it *my* fault that I cannot feel? I thought that I had done all I could, and that God was withholding from me his Spirit.

"My heart aches and is very sad. Do not let me deceive you; it does not *feel*, but it aches because it cannot. The heavens and the earth seem very dark."

I wrote to her in a second letter,—

"It seems to me your note requires from me the following remarks—

"1. Your hesitancy and backwardness to speak of your feelings, to send your letter, &c., are things not uncommon with awakened sinners. Such sinners are often ashamed of Christ. You see, my dear girl, that if you would be his disciple, you must 'deny yourself, take up your cross and follow' him. I respect the shrinking modesty of your feelings, but I suspect that the *shame of sin* has also an influence upon you. If you shrink from Christ you cannot be his.

"2. The complaint that you 'cannot feel,' is an almost universal one with sinners whom God's Spirit alarms. It is one of the strongest of all proofs that the Holy Spirit is striving with the soul. Tread softly, my dear girl. 'Quench not the Spirit.' 'Grieve not the Holy Spirit of God.' Remember, 'My Spirit shall not always strive with man.' 'To-day, if ye will hear his voice.'

"3. Evidently you *try* to make your heart *feel*. I do not wonder at you. I do not blame you. But it will not feel for you. You cannot make it feel. Only one hope remains for you,—give it to God, and he will make it feel,—to God as it is, hard, senseless, stupid,—to God in Christ, promising to be your Father and your Friend.

"When you aim to make your heart feel, you are making (ignorantly) an effort of self-righteousness. You wish it to feel, because you think there would be some worthiness in its emotions. It is too hard for you. Give it to God *as it is*,—you cannot make it any better.

"4. You 'thought you had done all you could.' I suppose you have 'done all you could' to *save yourself*. And yet you have accomplished nothing. You cannot. Fly, then, to Christ,—to Christ, just *as you are*, just as unfeeling, just as unworthy,—to Christ *now*, 'while it is called *to-day*.' Be assured you are welcome to all his benefits.

"Finally, you are 'sad.' You ought to be joyful. You *may* be, if you will trust your Saviour. 'Rejoice in the Lord' is the Bible exhortation,—a *precept*. Obey it. *Why* are you sad? Because you look into your dark heart, instead of looking *to Christ*, who died to redeem you. Look *up*, if you would have your eye catch the sunbeam that shall gladden you."

Her reply contained the following expressions :—

"How *can* I dare to ask or expect that Christ will accept of such a cold, strange, unloving, unfeeling heart, and not only *love* me, but allow me to ask of him such vast favours? Surely there is no analogy to such a case in nature or reason. It seems to me as if (pardon me) you don't understand *me*. If God ever softens my heart, I suppose it will follow as a matter of course that I shall love Christ, and then I can dare to venture to go to him. . . . . . I spoke of my *heart*, but I used a wrong expression. It seems to me as if, in regard to God, Christ, repentance, I am but senseless matter; *heart* I have none, and even my brain seems stupified upon this great subject. . . . . . Oh, that I could 'look up and see the bright sunbeam that should gladden me!' The thought brings tears to my eyes,—would that it could thaw my very heart!"

So she wrote. I sent the following answer :—

"Your present hindrance appears to me to be very much this: you aim to do for yourself what the Holy Spirit must do for you. 'In me is thy help,' says God; and he would have you believe it. All along you have been aiming to work yourself up into a state of affection, which should bring you relief. But, my dear child, it is *God* that must bring you relief. You are to trust *him*, rely on *him*, leave all with *him*. You cannot help *yourself*. You can no more put your heart right than you can pardon your own sins. Your heart has been too mighty for all your efforts, and will remain so. But it is not too mighty for God. There is help for you in him; and you will find it if you will fling down the weapons of your rebellion, and submit to him *in Christ*. . . . . . Would to God that you knew your utterly helpless condition, and would fall into the arms of the Saviour, who loves you and invites you to his arms. Go to your God and Saviour, my child, just as the prodigal went to his father (Luke xv.), and you shall be accepted as he was. If you do *not* go, you must find your grave in some far-off land! Go now. Go just as you are." ———.

She afterwards referred to this letter. Said she,—"Until I received that letter, I *never had* the idea that some other Power must help me. That letter first gave me the idea that I must go somewhere else than to myself. Not till then had I understood at all your former letters, directing me to the Saviour."

After this I had frequent conversations with her. Evidently she was perfectly sincere, and deeply anxious. But she could not perceive that her failure to gain peace with God was owing to anything in herself; nor could she believe that she was powerless in herself, in respect to putting her heart right, aside from God's help. Often she said to me,—"I am very miserable. I do desire to love God. Above all things I wish to be a Christian. What is the reason I do not get some light?" I constantly presented to her the same truths which I had written, assured her of the fulness and free grace of Christ, and that it was her self-reliance and self-seeking alone which hindered her salvation.

One evening she left me in a most anxious and downcast state of mind. The next day, she said to me, "I have called, you will think, very soon. But I have come to tell you that I am as happy to-day as I was miserable yesterday. I found I could *do nothing*. I was helpless. I had exhausted all my powers, and still was just the same. All I could do was to pray, and depend on God. I am nothing. Never before have I had such a sense of my sinfulness, and it is now sweet to think I may rely upon God." I asked her,—

"What hindered you so long?"

"All my life," said she, "I have stopped at the same place. I have read the Bible, and prayed, but my mind would find some difficulty, and stop there. *All my days I have been trying to find God in the wrong.*"

"Wherein were *you* wrong yourself?"

"I was not willing to trust God. I thought, or *tried* to think, it was not *my* fault that I was not a Christian. Your letter astonished me. How could I have been so ignorant of God? I did not know till I got your letter that a sinner *may* come to Christ just as he is. It seems to me that people do not understand that. I never understood it before. I want you to preach that, so that people may know it. It was all new to me! At first I did not believe it. How could you know how I should be affected all along; and that, after I *should* see the sinfulness of my heart, and be determined to obey God, a 'worse difficulty would meet' me,—my heart 'would refuse to trust?' I see it now. Before, I did not think it was *my* fault that I was not a Christian. I tried all the time to *find God in the wrong.*"

Because this young woman had asked me to preach the same things to others which had so much surprised and profited her, I requested her to make for me a written statement of her religious experience. A short time afterwards she gave me the following:—

"Ever since I had given up the study of religious truth as a mere intellectual speculation, I had for years tried to pursue it with and for my heart. Distressed with doubts and darkness, but hoping that God would some time or other take them from me, I studied the Bible with prayer, and endeavoured to be governed by its teachings, and enjoyed and appreciated spiritual things to such a degree that my state seemed often very strange to me; for I realized that I did not love God, and felt no interest in Christ, and knew that without this there was no true religion. Still I felt no alarm, thinking it evidence that I was not vitally in error, because I was so desirous to be right. I thought I was *all but entirely* religious; but as these were fundamental wants, and as I was sincerely desirous to come to a decision upon this subject, I determined to attain them. But in this I could not succeed. I tried very hard, laboriously, but could not make myself love God. My mind in its efforts invariably at a certain point came to a stop. I perceived that there was an obstacle there that always overthrew me, but could not tell what it was. I felt no pain at this, because I thought I had done all I could, when God withheld from me his Spirit, and (can I express the dreadful thought!) that the fault was God's, and not mine! But as others did succeed, it must be that I could; and, afraid to die as I was, I persisted in using every faculty to gain my object; but it was of no use.

"I became convinced that all my trying and all my searching were in vain; and, tired of wearying myself longer in fruitless efforts, I determined to make a statement of my feelings to you, not doubting that you could soon enlighten me; and thinking that, as soon as I discovered the point that was now hidden from me, I should love God, and that then a knowledge of and interest in the Saviour would follow as a matter of course.

"I can give you no idea of the FAR OFF distance with which I had always regarded Christ. It is with difficulty that I can suppress the comments that my heart instinctively responded to every sentence of your letters, as I read them. But I will only say, that my mind, heart, and senses, were in a maze, when I perceived their contents so contrary to my expectations.

"That my '*heart* REFUSED *to love God and trust in Christ,*'—that '*the Holy Spirit was striving with me,*'—that '*I knew only a small part of my depravity and danger,*'—that 'my failure to feel an unbounded gratitude to the Saviour, and to the love of the Father who gave him, arose from my lack of feeling my *undone condition*, and my lack of a heart right with God,'—that 'I had been seeking God with *only half my heart,*'—were positions totally inadmissible to my belief, so strong was the impression on my mind that I was *nearly, entirely* right; and I was between laughing and displeasure at the denunciations you pronounced upon my heart throughout, and especially at the close of your first letter.

"At first I concluded that you had not in the least understood or appreciated me; and next, that you were unnecessarily severe; but by degrees the conviction began to steal over me, with a feeling that I cannot describe—*Is it so? Am I all wrong?* Is it *my* fault that I do not love God? *Has the Holy Spirit been striving with my heart?* when I thought I had been breasting the tide alone so long, and God had looked so coldly on my struggles?

"But a greater surprise awaited me,—your remedy for my difficulties, when you directed me to 'fly to Christ *just as I was.*' 'When you aim to make your heart feel, you are making (ignorantly) an effort of self-righteousness.' . . . . 'It is too hard for you. Give it to God *as it is;* you cannot make it better. . . . . You thought you had done all you could. I suppose you have done all you could *to save yourself,* and yet you have accomplished nothing. You cannot. Fly then to *Christ*—to Christ, *just as you are*—just as unfeeling, just as unworthy; to Christ *now.*' So you wrote to me.

"Here my heart fails me to express my emotions. I require another medium than words to tell what I felt. *Fly to Christ? just as I am?* to Christ *now?* Give *him* my heart, *just as it is?* I have never thought anything about Christ. He has always been *last* in my thoughts; and fly to him *first?* fly to him *now?* stop trying, and let him do all? Impossible! You did not understand me! My powers seemed stunned. I tried not to think about it; and after some days of perturbation I went to see you, hoping you would say to me something different—something on which I could act; but your remarks were all the same. I was very much disappointed, and listened in respectful silence—though thinking while you were speaking that you had little idea of their subsequent use to me. I came home without the slightest idea of doing as you had said, certain that you were not aware of what you had told me to do. But that I was *all wrong*—that I had not a single right feeling—that I was so far, far from God, when I thought I was all right, but in one item (which would necessarily come right after I loved God), was very distressing to me. What could I do? It seemed to me that I had a mightier effort to make now than ever before, and I was afraid I should die before I should have time to accomplish it. Oh, the troubled sea that tossed within my poor heart!—I cannot bear to think of it! But do something I must. I tried to pray; but it seemed as if the heavens and earth were brass above and beneath me. I examined the Bible, and all the references to the texts to which you referred me, and found that it substantiated your every word, and I began to feel that all you had said was true. And then I wondered that *you had never told me so before! I was sure that I had never heard it in any of the years of your sermons, to which I had so interestedly listened; and I could not remember that you had ever told it to me in any of the previous conversations* that you had had with me. I was not conscious that I had ever before seen it in the Bible. *If* I had, I had *never comprehended it with even an ordinary amount of common intelligence;* it was an *entirely new truth.*

"Oh, how can I describe my ineffectual efforts to grope and *feel after Christ,* through the *thick darkness!* I could not find him. I could only cry, 'Jesus, Master, have *mercy* upon me;' and ask him to *take* my heart, for I could not give it to him." ———.

XXV.

Delay;

OR, THE ACCEPTED TIME.

A YOUNG man called upon me one Sabbath evening, and as soon as we were seated, he said to me,—

"I have accepted the invitation that you have so often given from the pulpit, to any who are willing to converse with you upon the subject of religion."

"I am glad to see you," said I.

"I don't know," he replied, "that I have anything to say, such as I ought to have; but I am convinced that I have neglected religion long *enough*, and I am determined to put it off no longer."

"That is a good determination," said I, "'Behold, now is the accepted time; behold, now is the day of salvation.'"

"Well, I don't know that that text is for me, because—"

"Yes, it *is* for you," said I, interrupting him.

"I was going to say, sir, I don't suppose I have got so far as that yet, so that salvation is for me *now*."

"You *told* me that you was 'determined to put off religion no longer;' and therefore I say, 'Now is the accepted time, now is the day of salvation.'"

"But I don't wish to be in a hurry, sir."

"You *ought* to be in haste. David was. He says, 'I thought on my ways and turned my feet to thy testimonies. I made haste and delayed not to keep thy commandments.' God now commandeth all men, everywhere, to repent, and you are one of them.

And if you are like David, you will 'make haste and delay not to keep God's commandments."

"I don't suppose I am in such a state of mind as to be prepared to become a Christian *now.*"

"Will disobeying God put you in a *better* state of mind, do you think?"

"Why, I don't know; but I have not much deep conviction. I know that I am a sinner against God, and I wish to turn to him, and live a different life."

"Then turn to him. 'Now is the accepted time.'"

"But I find my heart is full of sin; I am all wrong; I feel an opposition to God such as I never felt before."

"Then repent and turn to God instantly, while it is called to-day."

"But I don't suppose I can be ready to come to religion so *quickly?*"

"You *said* you was determined to put it off no longer, and I told you 'Now is the accepted time.'"

"But I never began to think seriously about my religion till last Sunday."

"And so you want to put it off a little longer?"

"Why I want to get *ready.*"

"And are you getting ready? You have tried it for a week."

"No, sir," said he, in a sad manner, "I don't think I am any nearer to it than I was at first."

"I don't think you are. And I suppose the reason is, that you don't believe 'now is the accepted time.'"

"Oh, yes, I do; for the Bible says so."

"Then don't wait for any other time. Repent *now.* Flee to Christ *now*, in the 'accepted time.'"

"I have not conviction enough yet."

"Then it cannot be the 'accepted time' yet."

"But I have not faith enough."

"Then it cannot be 'the accepted time.'"

"Well, sir I—I—I am not ready *now.*"

"Then it cannot be 'the accepted time' *now*."

"But it seems to me it is too *quick*," said he earnestly.

"Then it cannot be 'the accepted time,' and the Bible has made a mistake."

"But, sir, my heart is not *prepared*."

"Then it is not 'the accepted time.'"

With much embarrassment in his manner, he replied,—

"What *shall* I do?"

"Repent and turn to God, with faith in Christ to save you as a lost, unworthy sinner, *now* in 'the accepted time.'"

He appeared to be in a great strait. He sat in silence with very manifest uneasiness for a few moments, and then asked,—

"Is it possible that *any one* should repent, and give up the world, and turn to God *so soon*, when I began to think about it only last Sunday?"

"'Now is the accepted time,'" said I.

Again he sat in thoughtful silence, and after a time he asked me,—

"Is *salvation* offered to sinners *now?*"

"Yes, *now*. 'Now is the day of salvation.'"

"But it seems to me I am not *prepared* now to give up the world."

"That very thing is your difficulty. *You* are not prepared; but 'now is the accepted time.' You wish to put off your repentance and conversion to Christ till some *other* time; but 'now is the accepted time.' You and your Bible disagree. And if nothing else kept you from salvation, this would be enough. I beseech you, my dear friend, delay no longer. Now is God's time. 'Deny yourself, and take up your cross, and follow Jesus Christ.' You told me you was determined to put off religion no longer. I suspected you did not know your own heart, and therefore said to you, 'Now is the accepted time.' And now it has become manifest that you meant to put off religion till some other time all the while."

"It seems hard to shut up a man just to the present time," said he, in an imploring accent.

"If you were a dying man, and had only an hour to live, you would not say so. You would be glad to have the Bible say to you, 'Now is the accepted time,' instead of telling you you needed a month or a week to flee to Christ. It is *mercy* in God to say to you, 'Behold now is the day of salvation,' when you do not know that you will live till to-morrow morning."

"Will you pray with me?" said he.

I prayed with him, and we separated. The last words I uttered to him as he left the door were, "Now is the accepted time."

Just one week afterwards he called upon me, "to give an account of himself," as he said,—

"I have got out of my trouble," said he. "Now, I trust in Christ, and I am reconciled to God, or at least I think so. I thought you were very hard upon me last Sunday night, when you *hammered* me, and *hammered* me with that text, 'Now is the accepted time.' But I couldn't get away from it. It followed me everywhere. I would think of one thing, and then that would come up, 'Now is the accepted time.' Then I would begin to think of something else, and it would come up again, 'Now is the accepted time.' So I went on for three days. I tried to *forget* that text, but I *could not.* I said to myself, 'There is something else in the Bible except that;' but wherever I read, that *would* come to my mind. It annoyed me, and *tormented* me. Finally, I began to question myself, *why it was* that this plagued me so much? And I found it was because I was *not willing to be saved by Christ.* I was trying to do something for myself, and I wanted more time. But it was not done. Everything failed me. And then I thought, if 'now *is* the accepted time,' I may go to Christ now, wicked as I am. So I just prayed for *mercy*, and gave up all to him."

The idea of this young man was new to me. It had never entered my mind, that when one wants more time, it is "*because he is not willing to be saved by Christ.*" I suppose that is true. A delaying sinner is a legalist. Self-righteousness delays. How little the procrastinating know about their own hearts!

XXVI.

Physical Influence.

A MEMBER of my Church, the mother of a family, was sick, and I visited her. In conversation with her I discovered that her mind was shrouded in darkness and gloom. I prolonged the conversation, hoping to be able so to present divine truth to her mind, that she should see some light, and gain some comfort from the promises; or if I failed in that, hoping to discover the cause of her religious darkness. But it was all in vain. I left her as dark as ever, without discovering the cause of her gloom.

I soon visited her again. She was the same as before. "Dark! dark! *all* dark!" said she, in answer to my inquiry. "I have not long to live, and I am sure I am not fit to die." She wept in agony. I pointed her to Christ, and recited to her the promises. I explained justification by faith in Christ Jesus, the undone condition of sinners, salvation by free grace, the offer and operations of the Holy Spirit, and the readiness of Christ to accept *all* that come unto him. She only wept and groaned.

With much the same result I conversed with her many times. I could but imperfectly discover what had been the character of her religious exercises while she was in health; but she despised them all, and counted them only as deception. When I treated her as a backslider, and referred her to what the sacred Scriptures address to such persons, inviting them to return unto their God, the very freeness and friendliness of the invitations appeared to distress her. When I treated her as a believer under a cloud, a child of God, from whom our heavenly Father takes away the light of his countenance, for some reason which we cannot explain,—perhaps to manifest his sovereignty, perhaps to teach us our spiritual dependence, perhaps to arouse our efforts to draw nearer to him, perhaps to teach us deeper lessons about religion, and give us richer experiences as he leads us, for a time, " in a way we know not,"—all these ideas appeared to increase her distress. If I treated her as an impenitent sinner, it was the same thing. Gloom, distress, despair, had taken possession of her soul!

After I had known her to be in this condition for several months, I called upon her, and to my surprise found that her mind was calm; her despair and distress had given place to hope and gladness of spirit. She could trust in God; she could submit to his will, rejoicing to be in his hands; she could rest upon the sufficiency of her Saviour;—" Jesus Christ is mine," said she; " and I am glad to be his."

Three days after this, when I saw her again her light had departed, and all her former darkness and despair had returned. A few days afterwards, I found she had become calm and hopeful again; and then again in a few days I found her as gloomy as ever. Thus for months she alternated from gloom to gladness, and from gladness to gloom. I could not understand it. I studied her case, and tried, in every mode I could think of, to find out why she should thus be tossed about betwixt hope and fear. But I studied in vain.

After a while, as I was conversing with her one morning, when she was in one of her happy frames, I recollected that she had always been so whenever I had seen her in the morning, and had always been in darkness whenever I had seen her in the afternoon. I mentioned this fact to her, and asked her to account for it. She acknowledged the fact, but made no attempt to explain it. I explained it to her as the result of her physical condition. Every morning she awoke free from pain, and then her views were clear and her mind comfortable. She continued in this comfortable frame till nearly noon, when, as her pain in the head returned, all her peace of mind vanished. This experience was uniform with her, week after week; and when I now called her attention to it, and explained her religious gloom as the result of her physical state, she was satisfied that the explanation was just. But a week afterwards, when I saw her in the afternoon, her mind was as dark as ever ; and then she rejected the explanation,—she could not be made to believe that her darkness was owing to her disease. So it was with her, week after week. She had a comfortable hope every morning; she was in despair every afternoon. In the morning she would *believe* that her afternoon despair was caused by her bodily infirmity; but in the afternoon, she would entirely *dis*believe it. Thus she continued.

A few weeks before her death, and when her bodily condition had become different, all her darkness was gone, her mind continued light through the whole twenty-four hours; and she finally died in peace, with the full hope of a blessed immortality through our Lord Jesus Christ.

Despondency does not always arise from the same cause. It is difficult to deal with it; but there is one great principle, which has been of much use to myself, and which has some illustration in the following sketch.

XXVII.

Treatment of the Desponding.

IN making visits to the sick, I became acquainted with a woman belonging to my congregation, with whom I had very little acquaintance before. She was in a very distressful state of mind. "I am a sinner," said she; "I am the vilest of sinners! I must soon meet my God, and I have *no preparation* to meet him! I see before me nothing but his wrath, his dreadful wrath for ever! Indeed I feel it this moment within my soul! It drinks up my spirit! God curses me now; and oh! how can I bear his eternal curse, when he shall cast me off for ever!"

"God is *merciful*, madam," said I.

"I know he is merciful, sir; but I have despised his mercy, and now the thought of it torments my soul! If he had *no* mercy, I could meet him: I could take the curse of the law, and it would not be the half of the hell which now awaits me! But oh, I *cannot bear*,—I *cannot* bear the curse of the *law* and the *gospel* both! I must account to the Lord Jesus Christ for having slighted his offers! I have turned a deaf ear to all his kind invitations! I have trampled under foot the blood of the covenant! and I am soon to appear before him,—my *feet* wet with his blood, instead of having it sprinkled on my heart!" (She wept and wailed as if on the borders of the pit.)

"Madam, there is *no need* that you should appear *thus* before him. The *same* offers of mercy are still made to you which have been made to you before. The same throne of grace still stands in heaven; the same God is seated upon it; the same Christ reigns as Mediator; and the same Spirit is still promised 'to them that ask him.' The invitation of God is as broad as the wants of sinners: 'Whosoever will, let him take the water of life freely.'"

"I know it, sir; I know all that. And this is the burden of my anguish—the offer is so free, and I have no heart to accept it! If the offer were accompanied by any difficult conditions, I might think myself partly excusable for not accepting it. But it is all so free, and, *fool* that I am, I have all my days shut up my heart against it; and even now, I am rebellious and unbelieving. Oh! my heart is senseless as a brute's! it cannot feel! it is harder than the nether millstone!"

"I am glad you are sensible of that; because it prepares you to understand the promise, '*I* will take away the stony heart out of your flesh, and *I* will give you a heart of flesh, and *I* will put my Spirit within you.' *God* says this; and you perceive he makes his promise for just such hearts as yours."

"Oh, I wish I could believe it! My heart won't believe. It disbelieves God! It makes him a liar, because it believes not the testimony which God gave of his Son!"

"Madam, think a moment; if you did *not* believe that testimony, you could not be distressed on account of your *unbelief*. If you were hungry, and you did not believe there was any food upon the earth, you could not be distressed because you did not *believe* there was food enough. You might be distressed because there was no food, but you could not be distressed because you did not *believe* there was any; you would not wish to believe in a falsehood, or in what you deem a falsehood."

"I have not any doubt of the *truth* of God's word, sir; but my heart does not *trust* in it. It *will* not trust. I have no faith."

"You have sometimes thought you had faith?"

"Yes, I *did* think so; but I was deceived. I have made a false profession. I have profaned the Lord's table! When I was a young woman, in Scotland, I first came forward, and I have attended on the ordinance of the table ever since, whenever

I could. But I see now that I have been only a mere professor—one of the foolish virgins. For forty years I have been a communicant; and now, when my days are nearly done, the Lord frowns upon me for my sin. I feel it; I feel it. His wrath lies heavy on my soul! He knows I am an empty hypocrite, and he frowns upon me in his awful displeasure!"

"How long is it since you found out that you had no true faith?"

"I have suspected it a great many times, but I was never fully convinced of it till confined to the house with this sickness."

"Before you was sick did you enjoy a comfortable hope in Christ?"

"I *thought* I did, almost always after my first sacrament. That was a very solemn day to me. It was before I was married. I was nearly twenty, and my parents and the minister had often enjoined my duty upon me; and after a long struggle with my wicked heart, and after much prayer, I thought I was prepared. But I deceived my own soul! I have been deceived ever since till now; and now God fills me with terror! I shall soon meet him, and he will cast me off?" She wept piteously.

"Have you lived a prayerful life since you came to the communion first?"

"Yes, I have prayed night and morning; but I see now that I never prayed acceptably."

"Are you penitent for your sins? Do you mourn over them?"

"Yes, I mourn; but I have 'only a fearful looking for of judgment and fiery indignation.' My soul is in torment! God will cast me off! I shall be lost for ever!—*lost! lost!*"

"It is a faithful saying and worthy of ALL acceptation, that Jesus Christ came into the world to *save* sinners."

"I believe it, sir. He is a great and glorious Saviour."

"*Your* Saviour, madam, if you want him to be."

"*No, sir; no,* not *mine,*—not mine." Again bursting into tears.

"*Yes,* madam,—*yours,* if you want him;—yours in welcome;

—yours now, on the spot;—*yours*, if you will 'receive and rest upon him, as he is offered in the gospel;'—*yours*, if you have never received him before;—*yours* still, even if you have profaned his covenant, as you say, for forty years. You have only to believe in him with penitence and humility. Christ is greater than your sin."

As I was uttering these words she continued to repeat the word, "*No, no, no, no*," weeping most distressfully. Said I,—

"Madam, suffer me to beg of you to hear me calmly."

"I will try, sir."

"I utter to you *God's own truth*, madam. I tell you Jesus Christ *is* for you. He is *offered to* you by the God of heaven. He proposes to be your Prophet, Priest, and King, to do for you all you need as a sinner to be saved. He is an all-sufficient Saviour. And in the presence of his merits, *I defy your despair*. Salvation is of grace—of *God's* grace,—of grace operating in the infinite love of God, and by the infinite humiliation of his Son. Here is fulness, the fulness of God. 'Christ is the end of the law for righteousness.' Jesus Christ did not fail in his attempt, when he undertook to redeem sinners. He did his work well. His love brought him from heaven, and took him through all the path of his humiliation, from the cradle to the grave. *He* bore the curse, and sinners may go free. He reigns in heaven, the King of glory, and sinners may meet him there."

"Indeed, sir, he is a wonderful Lord. He hath done all things well. I am glad he is on the throne. When I can catch a glimpse of his glory my heart rejoices."

"And his glory lies in grace, madam; *such* grace that he invites you to cast all your cares upon him, for *he careth* for you."

"I praise him for it; I will praise him for ever. I rejoice that Christ *is* Lord over all."

She appeared to have lost her trouble. She had become calm; and she continued to speak of the love of God, and the adorable condescension of Jesus Christ, for some minutes. She asked me to pray with her, and praise God for his wondrous grace. After prayer I left her, supposing that her despondency had been but for a few minutes, and would not return.

The next week I saw her again, as she had requested me to do; and I found her in the same deep despondency as before. She continued to speak of herself; and all I said to her gave no alleviation to her anguish.

Several times I visited her. Uniformly I found her depressed, and sometimes left her rejoicing, and sometimes sad. I could not account for it.

At length it occurred to me, as I was thinking of the different conversations I had had with her, that her mind had uniformly become composed, if not happy, whenever I had led her thoughts *away* from herself, to fix on such subjects as God, Christ, Redeeming love, the covenant of grace, the sufferings of the Redeemer, the divine attributes, or the glory of God. Afterwards I tried the experiment with her frequently, and the result was always so. I finally stated to her that fact.

"Oh yes, sir," said she, "*I know that very well.* It has always been so with me ever since about the time of my first sacrament. If I can get my mind fixed on my covenant God and Saviour, then I can rest. But how can I rest when I have no faith?"

"But, madam, can you not *remember*, in your dark hours, what it was that made you have light ones? and can you not then recur to the same things which made them light, and thus get light again?"

"Oh, sir, I *cannot see the Sun through the thick clouds.* God hides himself, and I cannot find him; and then I mourn. I know it is Satan that would drive me to despair. He shoots out his 'fiery darts' at me; and my poor soul trembles in anguish. I cannot help trembling, even when I *know* it is Satan. I have such awful doubts, such horrible temptations darting through my mind, and such blasphemous thoughts, that I feel sure God will cast me off."

This woman never recovered from her sickness; but the last ten weeks of her life were all sunshine. She had not a doubt not a fear; all was peace and joy. Alluding to this, she said,—

"God does not suffer the adversary to buffet me any more. Christ has vanquished him for me, and I find the blessed promises are the supports of my soul. I fly to them. I fly to Christ, and hide myself in him. I expect soon he will 'come again and receive me to himself,' that I may be with him 'where he is.' I shall behold his glory, and Satan shall never torment me any more."

She died in perfect peace.

There is a difference betwixt the despondency of a believer and the despondency of an unbeliever. A desponding believer still has faith. It only needs to be brought into lively exercise, and his despondency will melt away. He becomes desponding because he has lost sight of the objects of faith, and has fixed his thoughts upon himself and his sins. Let the matters of faith be brought up before his mind, and they are *realities* to him,—unquestionable realities. He only needs to keep his eye upon them.

The despondency of an unbeliever is different. He does not despond because he has lost sight of the objects of faith, for he never *had* any faith; and there is, therefore, no preparation in his heart to welcome the doctrines of grace, of free forgiveness, of redemption through the blood of Christ, of eternal life for sinners. These things are not *realities* to him. His faith never embraced them. When, therefore, in his despondency, whether he looks at his own wickedness or looks at God, he sees only darkness. Especially the love and mercy of God, the death of Christ for sinners, *all* redemption, are things as dark to him as his own soul. He does not realize them as facts; much less does he embrace them for himself. In the self-righteousness of his spirit he desponds, because he thinks himself too guilty to be forgiven. He is a mere legalist; he sees only the *law*,—not Christ.

But there is only one way of relief for believer and unbeliever in their despondency. They must look to Christ, and to Christ *alone*, all-sufficient and free. A believer has a sort of preparation to do this; an unbeliever has an obstinate reluctance. He thinks only of himself and his sins. Nothing can magnify equal to melancholy, and nothing is so monotonous. A melancholy man left to himself and the sway of his melancholy, will not have a new thought once in a month. His thoughts will move round and round in the same dark circle. This will do him no good. He ought to get out of it.

Despondency originates from physical causes more than from all other causes. Disordered nerves are the origin of much religious despair, when the individual does not suspect it; and then the body and mind have a reciprocal influence upon each other, and it is difficult to tell which influences the other most. The physician is often blamed, when the fault lies in the minister. Depression never benefits body or soul. "We are saved by hope."

XXVIII.

Unknown Presence of the Spirit.

AS I was passing along the street one morning, I saw a lady, a member of my Church, just leaving her house, and I supposed she would probably be absent half an hour or more,—long enough for me to accomplish what I had often desired. There was a young woman, a member of her family, who was very beautiful, and reputed to be quite gay, to whom I had sometimes spoken on the subject of religion, but I had never found any opportunity to speak to her *alone.* I had thought that she was embarrassed and somewhat confused by the presence of this lady, whenever I had mentioned the subject of religion to her, and therefore I was glad to seize this opportunity to see her alone,—such an opportunity as I thought the lady indisposed to furnish me.

I rang the bell, and the young woman soon met me in the parlour. I then felt some little embarrassment myself; for I had rushed into this enterprise through an unexpected occurrence, and without much premeditation of the manner in which it would be most wise for me to proceed. I expected a cold reception, if not a repulse. I deemed her a very careless, volatile girl. I thought she would be unwilling to have me urge the claims of religion upon her; and the idea that much depended upon the manner in which I should commence, embarrassed me for a moment. But I soon came to the conclusion that I owed it to honesty and truth, to my own reputation for frankness, and to my young friend herself, to tell her plainly what was my intention in then calling to see her. I did so in the most direct manner possible.

"I am *very* glad to see you," said she. "I have wanted to see you for a good while; for I want to tell you my feelings. I thank you for thinking of me, and being so kind as to come and see me. I should have gone to your house many a time, when you have so often invited persons like me; but when the hour came, my courage always failed me, for I did not know what to say to you. I am in trouble, and know not what to do; I am *very* glad of this opportunity." She opened to me her whole heart in the most frank and confiding manner. Among other things she said,—

"I know I have been a thoughtless girl," while her voice trembled, and tears dimmed her eyes; "I have been gay, and have done many things you would condemn, I suppose; but, my dear minister, *I have been urged into gaiety*, when my *heart* was *not there*. I do not believe I am such a girl as they think I am, —may I say, as *you* think I am? I know I have a wicked heart, and have too much forgotten God; but I have often wondered *what there is about me* that makes my religious friends think that I care for nothing but —." She sprang from her seat, put her hands upon her face, and hurried out of the room, sobbing aloud.

In a few moments she returned. "I know you will pardon me for this," said she, the tears coursing down her cheeks. "I do not wish to make any excuse for my sins, nor do I wish to blame *any one* for supposing me thoughtless; but I am sure *I want* to be led in the right way. *I am ready* to do all you tell me. I hope I can be saved yet."

"*Certainly* you can be, my child."

"Then tell me, sir, what to do."

I did tell her, and left her one of the most grateful and affectionate creatures that have ever lived.

As I took my leave of her and found myself again in the street, I commenced my old business of street meditation. My first emotion was gladness, the second shame; for I was ashamed of myself, that I had just been thinking of that young girl so differently from what she deserved, and that I should have gone into her presence, and opened my lips to her with no more faith in God. The next reflection was, how much more common than we think, are the influences of the Holy Spirit. God does often what we never give him credit for doing. The influences of the Holy Spirit are more common than our unbelief allows us to think.

The inquiry then came into my mind, May there not be others of my congregation who would welcome me also? I stopped in my track, and looked around me for another house to enter. I saw one; I rang the bell, and asked for the elder of two sisters,—a girl of about nineteen, I suppose, and reputed to be very fond of gaiety. She soon met me, and I immediately told her why I had come.

"And I *thank* you for coming," said she. "I am glad you have spoken to me about religion. Why did you not do it before? I *could not* go to your house. I know it is my duty to seek Christ, and I *do want* to be a Christian."

After some conversation with her, in the whole of which she was very frank, and in the course of which she became very solemn, I asked for her sister.

"Yes, sir, I will call her. I was going to ask you to see her; but *don't tell her* anything about *me*."

Her sister came; and as the elder one was about to leave the room, I begged the younger one's permission for her to remain, stating to her at the same time why I had asked to see her. She consented, and the elder sister remained, I thought, gladly.

I then stated to the younger sister my message, and having explained her condition to her as a sinner, and explained the mercy of God through Jesus Christ, I was urging her to accept the profferred salvation, when she became much affected; she turned pale, covered her face with her hands,—"I *will try* to seek God," said she, sobbing aloud. The elder sister, who had delicately taken her seat behind her, so as not to be seen by her, clasped her hands together, overcome with her emotions, and lifted her eyes to heaven, while the tears of gladness coursed down her beautiful cheeks, as she sat in silence and listened to us.

I prayed with them, and soon found myself again in the street. I immediately entered another house, in like manner, and for the same reason as before; and another unconverted sinner met me with the same mingled gladness and anxiety, manifesting the same readiness to seek the Lord.

By this time I had given up all thought of finishing a sermon which was to have been completed that day; for if I could find, among my unconverted parishioners, such instances of readiness and desire to see me, I thought my duty called me to leave my study and my sermons to take care of themselves, and to trust in God for the preparation I should be able to make for the pulpit on the coming Lord's day. I therefore went to another house, and inquired for another acquaintance, who was not a member of the Church. I did not find her. But in the next house after *that*, which I entered, I found another of my young friends, who told me she never *had* paid any particular attention to the demands and offers of the gospel, but that she would "neglect it *no longer*;"—"*I will*, sir, attend to my salvation," said she, "as well as I know how."

Here, then, I had found five young persons, in the course of a few hours, all of whom were "almost persuaded to be Christians." They all afterwards become the hopeful subjects of grace; and within six months of that morning were received as members of the Church. I knew them all intimately for years, prayerful, happy Christians.

The strivings of the Holy Spirit are more common than we think. If unconverted sinners would improve these secret calls, none of them would be lost. These persons had been awakened before. Probably at this time, as formerly, they would have gone back again to indifference, had not their seriousness been discovered and confirmed. It is important to "watch for souls."

XXIX.

A Revival is Coming.

AN aged woman, a member of my Church, whom I frequently met, always appeared to me to have a more than common interest in the prosperity of religion; and whenever I saw her she had something to say in respect to the success of the gospel. Her heart appeared to be bound up in the welfare of the Church. She would often inquire, "Are any of our young people coming to Christ?"

One day as I was passing her house she called me in. Said she, "I have asked you to come in here because I wanted to tell you a revival is coming."

"How do you know *that?*" said I.

"We shall have a revival here," said she, "before another year is past."

"How do you know that?" said I.

"Dear me," said she, "now don't think me one of that sort of folks who think themselves particular favourites of the Lord, as if they were inspired; I'm none of that sort, by a great deal. But I have got faith, and I have got eyes and ears, and I believe in prayer. Perhaps you may think me too certain, but I tell you a revival *is coming;* and I don't know it by any miracle either, or because I am any better than other people, or nearer to God. But, for this good while, every day when I have been out in my garden, I have heard that old deacon," pointing to his house, "at prayer up in his chamber, where he thinks nobody hears him. The window is open just a little way off from my garden, and I hear him praying there every day. He is not able to leave his house much, you know, because he has got only one leg; but if he can't work he can pray; and his prayers will be answered. I am sure a revival is coming, and I should not be surprised if some of his children should be converted. I am not so foolish as to think I am a prophet, or to think I know the secrets of the Lord. I am not a fanatic either. But remember, I tell you a revival is coming. God answers prayer. You will see."

A revival did come. Before a year from that time more than a hundred persons in that congregation were led to indulge the hope that they had been "born of the Spirit." Among them were a son and a daughter of that old man of prayer, and a grandson of this woman who "believed in prayer."

There was no miracle or inspiration in this aged woman's confidence. She employed only faith, and her own careful observation. "God answers prayer," said she; and she had noticed that earnest prayer was offered, such as had prevailed before.

She was not so singular as she supposed. Others expressed the same confidence, and about the same time, and for a similar reason. One of them said to me, "I notice *how they pray*, at the prayer-meeting in the school-house up Bridge Street, every Tuesday night." God does answer prayer.

XXX.

The Broken Resolution.

AS I was one day in familiar conversation with a man who was a member of my Church, and, as we all thought, one of the most faithful and happy Christians among us, he surprised me by a half desponding expression about himself. On my inquiring what he meant, he frankly told me what had been his experience, in respect to his comforts of hope.

He said that he entertained a hope in Christ, and united with the Church, when he was a young man. He was now about fifty years of age, and still retained his hope. "I believe I am a Christian," said he; "but I am not the *happy* Christian that I once was." He then went on to tell me more particularly the history of his heart. He said, that for some time after he made a public profession of religion, his faith became more and more established, and his hope more fixed and clear; till he finally arrived at a full assurance of his gracious state, and lived for some years in perfect peace, and commonly in the sweetest joy and delight. As these happy years glided by he never was troubled with a single doubt about his piety; he had no dark days, no discouragements,—not an hour's interruption of his precious communion with God.

Several years had passed away in this happy manner, when a melancholy change came over him. He recollected well the time, and remembered it with deep distress. He said, that he and several others members of the Church, after some conversation about the state and prospects of religion in the congregation, agreed to hold a meeting for conference and prayer, in a familiar way

They held it. "It was a precious meeting," said he; "at least it was so to me. My faith was strengthened, my joy was great."

Just at this time, filled with gratitude and love on account of God's gracious goodness to him, he resolved most solemnly that he "would be more faithful." "But," said he, with the deepest solemnity and sadness, "*I did not keep that resolution.* And since that time, I have never been able to get back my former assurance and peace with God! I have a hope, a strong hope; but my former *peace* is gone! I have prayed, and repented, and laboured to get near to God; but I have never been able to rejoice in such happiness as I used to have!"

In answer to my question, he replied,—

"No, I am not conscious of any *indulgence* in sin, though I sin every hour; nor do I know that I was unfaithful in any one thing in particular. I do not know why God frowns upon me so long; but I know I did not keep my resolution, and my *enjoyment* in religion is very much gone!"

"Perhaps," said I, "you have sought enjoyment too much."

"I thought of that years ago," said he, "and left off *seeking* for it, in any other way than in serving God."

"Perhaps you think too much of your service," said I, "and too little of the free grace of Christ."

"I think not," he replied. "I never put *my* duties into the place of Christ, betwixt me and God."

"Do you *receive* Christ as your *own* Saviour?"

"I think so; if I did *not*, I should despair. I have *hope* in Christ; but I live on, with a saddened heart. And now, whenever I find Christians rejoicing, I always want to caution them not to be unfaithful, as I have been."

"Do you doubt the reality of your conversion to Christ?"

"No, I have not that trouble; but I have not such delights of peace and joy as I had once."

"Do you expect ever to attain your former happiness?"

"I trust,—I *hope* I shall not *die* without it. I could not die in any peace as I am now!"

"Is not all this darkness your own fault? Do you believe it is God's will that you should go mourning all your days?"

"I know it is my *own fault*,—the result of unfaithfulness and broken resolutions; but I do *not* know that I can now overcome the evil. I have tried for years, but *God* keeps me in this state."

I aimed to convince him that *God* did not "*keep* him" in it, but that he kept *himself* in it. Before I had finished what I intended to say to him, we were interrupted; and at that time, as well as on several future occasions, he avoided saying anything to me about himself in the presence of other people. I afterwards asked him privately why he avoided the subject. He said he was afraid he should bring others into darkness, and injure the cause of religion, if he spoke of his trouble. I had several conversations and arguments with him, but they seemed to be useless; he would reply, "God keeps me in this darkness." I proved to him, both by Scripture and by argument, that God did *not* keep him in it,—that he kept himself in it. It might tire the reader if I should record here the half of the conversations I held with him. Let the last one suffice. He replied to what I had just said to him,—

"I think I *have* faith; and why do you say *unbelief* keeps me in darkness?"

"I believe, too, that you have faith; but I believe you fail to exercise it on a particular point, on which you have special need to exercise it."

"What point do you mean?"

"Last Tuesday evening," I replied, "you attended the prayer-meeting in Bridge Street. You offered the last prayer. I heard you. After I left another prayer-meeting I came across that way, intending to make some brief remarks in your meeting, as I had just done in the other; but when I got to the door I heard your voice in prayer, for the door was open, and I did not go in. Just at the close of your prayer, I walked silently away in the dark. I wished to avoid saying anything to *any one* who heard that prayer. I believed that anything I could say would do more harm than good. Do you recollect how you prayed?"

"No, not particularly."

"Well, I will tell you. You prayed that the Lord would convince unconverted sinners that he is infinitely kind and gracious, willing and waiting to save them; constantly calling to them, 'Turn ye, turn ye, for why will ye die?' You prayed that they might be led to *believe* in God's willingness to accept them, to adopt them as his own children, and make them blessed in his love. You prayed that the Holy Ghost would lead them to a right understanding of the invitations and promises of his word, so that they *might know* that 'a way and a highway' is opened to them into his full love and everlasting favour. You prayed that they might see and know, that if they were not happy in God's love, and in the hope of dwelling with him for ever in heaven, it was their own fault, because they would not *believe* in our blessed Lord and Saviour Jesus Christ, and turn to him. You prayed that anxious sinners might hear Jesus Christ saying unto them, 'Come unto me, all ye that labour and are heavy laden, and I will give you rest.' In this manner you prayed, and I have repeated some of your expressions exactly as you made them."

"I recollect it now," said he.

"Very well. Now what *I* mean by your not exercising faith on an important point is precisely what *you* meant in that prayer. You meant, that what God was waiting to give, they were not willing to receive; that they did not *believe* in his mercy to sinners through Christ, and did not come and accept it freely, and without hesitation or fear. *You* meant that they might be happy and safe if they would flee to Christ and trust him; and what *I* mean is, that you prayed exactly right, and that you yourself ought to exercise the same faith and same freedom in coming to Christ which you prayed that *they* might exercise. Precisely the same peace and joy in God which your prayer implied as offered to them, is now positively offered to you, and in precisely the same way. You ought to *believe* this. You ought to *act* upon it. And I am surprised that while you can see 'the way, and a highway open' for them, you cannot with the same eyes see it open for you."

"But," said he, "I am not like them. They have never sinned in the way I did. They have never known peace with God, and such enjoyments as I had once."

"That may be true," said I; "but you make a distinction which God has *not* made. Nowhere in his word has he said anything to imply an unwillingness to be reconciled to backsliders, and to restore unto them the joys of his salvation; or to imply that he is *less* willing and ready to fill them with peace than he is to give peace to unconverted sinners who turn to him.

"But it seems to me," he replied, "a greater sin to forsake him after having once experienced his gracious love."

"Let it seem so, then. I do not say it is not. But when you hesitate to believe in his readiness to forgive you, and smile on you as he used to do, I say that you 'limit the Holy One of Israel,' as he has not limited himself."

"I know he freely invites unconverted sinners to come to him."

"And do you *not* know he invites backsliders just *as* freely? How often he called upon the Israelites who had offended; and when they turned to him he restored to them his favour. Just so he treated David and Peter. Just so he has treated at times almost every Christian on earth. He performs what he has threatened and promised: 'If they break my statutes and keep not my commandments, then will I visit their transgression with the rod, and their iniquity with stripes; nevertheless, my loving kindness will I not utterly take from him, nor suffer my faithfulness to fail. My covenant will I not break, nor alter the thing that is gone out of my lips.' 'Turn, O backsliding children, for I am married unto you.'"

"I know it is so in general," he answered; "but are there not some sins that are exceptions?"

"*No;* what business have *you to make exceptions* when God

has made none? Suppose Sarah Parker had said to you, just after your prayer, 'Mr. H——, I know the way is open for sinners in general, but are there not some sins that are exceptions?' what would you have said to her?"

"I should have assured her that Christ gives a universal invitation to all sinners, without exception."

"Well, give the same assurance to *yourself.* Will you direct others in a way in which you yourself have no confidence to proceed?"

"Others are not like me."

"Are you better or worse?"

"It seems to me I am a great deal worse."

"What if Sarah Parker should say to you, 'It seems to me that I am a great deal worse?' Her 'seems to me' would be as much in place as your 'seems to me.' Neither of them proves anything. The question is not how 'it seems to you,' but how it seems to God—what *he* has said, and we are to believe,—what provision is made for us in Christ."

"I wish I could see it as you do; but, somehow or other, I cannot get out of my darkness, and don't know that I ever shall."

"Perhaps not," said I; "but I assure you the spirit and efforts of self-righteousness will never help you out.'

"Do you think it is *self-righteousness* that keeps me in the dark?"

"*Unquestionably,*" said I.

"Then I should be glad if you would explain it to me, for I cannot see *how.*"

"Precisely as the self-righteousness of a convicted sinner keeps *him* in the dark, when he is 'going about to establish a righteousness of his own, and has not submitted himself to the righteousness of Christ.' He does not 'receive Christ, and rest upon him alone for salvation, as he is offered in the gospel.' He tries to save himself. He tries to be righteous enough to be saved; and if he cannot think himself to be so, he desponds and wanders in the dark, *because* he does not trust Jesus Christ. And though you trust Jesus Christ for eternal life, yet you limit your faith, so that you do not trust him to make peace for you *now;* to be your light, and hope, and joy, in reference to your unfaithfulness and broken resolution. *That sin* you make an exception. You do it in the spirit of self-righteousness; and the evidence of this is found in the fact that you think *God keeps* you in the dark, because your transgression was *so bad.* It is the darkness, then, of self-righteousness. On that one point you have a self-righteous spirit, a spirit of *legalism,* to think of the *extent* of sin, and weigh it and measure it by *law,* instead of exercising full faith in Christ, to be your peace with God."

"It may be so," said he; "but if it is, I am not sensible of it. It appears to me that I am *not* looking for any righteousness in myself, to furnish ground for any confidence and peace with God."

"You think so. But at the same time you mention your offence as a very bad one, and your case as 'an exception;' which shows that you turn, on that point, from the *gospel* to the *law,* in the spirit of a self-righteous legalism. You do not, indeed, *exult* in self-righteousness, but you *despond* in self-righteousness. You do not *appropriate* Christ to yourself on that one point, and accept of peace through him, and take confidence and comfort to your heart. But, on the contrary, just like an entire unbeliever, and in his spirit of legalism (which is always self-righteousness), you think of the magnitude of your offence, and thus fall into darkness and gloom. Instead of this, you ought to think of the magnitude of Christ, and accept *him* alone as *all* and *enough.*

All I could say to him furnished him no relief. He continued in much the same state as long as I knew him, one of the most faithful of believers, and yet one of the most sad. A pensive gloom, a deep, and settled, and heavy sadness, hung almost constantly over his soul, which all his faith and all his hope could not dispel! His hope had lost its brightness, his faith its buoyancy; indeed, both faith and hope seemed to have retired in a great measure from his *heart,* and lingered only around his *mind*

Melancholy state! "God appears to me now," said he, "a great way off! I pray to him from a distant land; but he does not allow me to come near! Still I am always happy at the prayer-meeting."

I found it impossible to persuade him to feel that he might come near, if he would,—just as any other sinner might. He would reply, "My *mind* is convinced, but my *heart* has not any of its old feelings of freedom and nearness to God. But I mourn in silence. I don't wish others to know how I feel, lest it should injure the cause of religion."

This good man may have been mistaken in reference to the primary cause of his loss of peace; but the probability is that he thought rightly. And it is probable, too, that many Christians have the distressful feelings of outcast, and distant, and disinherited children, by reason of their unfaithfulness, after their God and Father had given them peace. It is dangerous for a child of God to let his heart wander from home. Bitter, bitter are the tears of unfaithfulness.

XXXI.

What can I Do?

IN a pleasant interview with a young woman of my congregation, who had recently been led to a hope in Christ, she particularly desired me to see her brother. She had had some little conversation with him, and thought he would be glad of an opportunity to speak with me, for he had some difficulties which she thought troubled him. I immediately requested the favour of seeing him, and in a few moments he came to me. Said I,—

"I asked to see you, sir, because I wished to speak with you on the subject of religion. Have you been considering that subject much?"

"Yes, sir, a good deal, lately."

"And have you prayed about it much?"

"I have prayed sometimes."

"And have you renounced sin, and accepted the salvation which God offers you through Christ?"

"No, I don't think I have."

"Don't you think you *ought?*"

"Yes, if it were not for one thing I would."

"What thing is that?"

"The doctrine of election."

"How does that doctrine hinder you?"

"Why, if that doctrine is true, I can do nothing."

"What can you do if it is *not* true?"

"Why, I don't know," said he hesitatingly. "But what have *I* to do! *I* can do nothing. It is not my business to interfere with God's determinations; if he 'has foreordained whatsoever comes to pass,' as the Catechism says he has."

"Well, do you think he *has?*"

"*Yes!*" said he, with an accent of much impatience.

I then tried very carefully to explain to him our duty, our freedom of will, our accountability, God's gracious offers of both pardon and assistance; and that God's secret foreordination is no rule of duty to us, and can be no *hindrance* to our duty or salvation. As I thus went on in the mildest and most persuasive manner I could, his countenance changed, he appeared vexed and angry, and finally, in the most impudent and passionate manner, exclaimed,—

"I don't want to hear any such stuff as that! If God has foreordained whatsoever comes to pass, what have I to do?"

"Just what he tells you to do," said I.

"I can do *nothing*," he replied furiously.

"Did you eat your breakfast this morning, sir?"

"Yes, to be sure I did!"

"How could you do it if God has foreordained whatsoever comes to pass? *you* can do nothing. Did you eat your dinner to-day?"

"Yes, to be sure; I don't go without my dinner."

"Why did you eat your dinner, if God has foreordained whatsoever comes to pass, as you say he has? What have you to do? You can do nothing. Do you mean to go to bed to-night?"

"Yes; I shall try."

"Why will you '*try?*' What have *you* to do? You can do nothing. If God foreordains whatsoever comes to pass, it is not your business to interfere with God's determinations. Will you answer me one question more?"

"Yes."

"Why do you say 'yes?' What have you to do? You can do nothing. God has foreordained whatsoever comes to pass, and you have no business to interfere with his determinations."

He appeared to be confused, if not convinced; and after a few more words, I asked him if he could tell me plainly what he himself meant when he said he could do nothing.

"*No*," said he, "I don't know *what* I mean."

"Can you explain to me how, in your view, the foreordination of God makes you incapable of doing anything, or hinders you?"

He hesitated for some moments, and then answered,—

"No, *I* am not able to tell anything about it."

I then carefully explained to him his duty, his freedom of will, his accountability to God, and earnestly strove to persuade him to dismiss his cavillings and come to immediate repentance, as God requires, and as a rebel against God ought to do, while mercy solicits him to salvation. He seemed to be somewhat affected; and when I explained to him more fully that the foreordination of God did not take away his liberty, power, or accountability, he appeared to be convinced. I invited him to come to me, if he ever found any more trouble or hindrance, or difficulty of mind, and tell me what it was. But he never came. He frequently muttered some objection to his sister, on the ground of predestination, but he never afterwards introduced that subject in conversation with me. Yet I was not able to persuade him to be a Christian; and now, after fifteen years more of his life have passed away, he still remains in his sins; entirely neglecting all public worship,—manifestly a hardened sinner.

It is not safe for a sinner to trifle with divine truth. The falsehood, insincerely uttered as an excuse, comes to be believed as a truth. Sad state,—given over to believe a lie!

XXXII.

Religion and Rum.

A MAN about forty years of age, with whom I had previously had but a slight acquaintance, called upon me one evening, in the greatest anxiety of mind. Seldom have I seen a man more agitated. He had become suddenly alarmed on account of his condition as a sinner. His feelings quite overcame him. He wept much. I answered his questions, and urged him to repent and flee to Christ, now in the "accepted time."

He was an intelligent, well-educated man, who had seen much of the world, and evidently had moved in good society. He conversed with much fluency and correctness, evidently possessing a quick and ready mind. His parents, as he told me, were communicants in a neighbouring Church, and until about three weeks before he came to my house, he had been accustomed to attend Church with them. He had a good degree of intellectual knowledge on the subject of religion. He was evidently a man of sound understanding.

He continued to call upon me frequently for some months; but he attained no peace of mind,—no hope in Christ. I was surprised at this. He appeared, from the first, so sincere, so earnest, attended all our religious services so punctually, and in all respects manifested so much determination, that I had confidently expected he would become a Christian indeed. And as he continued in much the same state of mind, I aimed to teach him the truth more carefully, and examine into his views, and feelings, and habits, in order to ascertain, if possible, and remove the obstacles, whatever they might be, which kept him from yielding to the

Holy Spirit. But I could not even conjecture why a man who appeared to know the truths of the gospel so well and feel them so deeply, should not make some progress in his religious attempts. I noticed nothing peculiar or remarkable in him, unless it was some degree of fitfulness, and the ease and frequency of his tears. He wept more than I had been accustomed to see men of his years weep.

I mentioned his case to one of the office-bearers of the Church, with whom I knew he was acquainted, and requested him to converse with him. He complied with this request. He had several conversations with him ; but he was disappointed and perplexed as much as I had been. "He weeps," said he, "and that is pretty much all that I can say about him."

A few weeks after this, and while his tearful seriousness continued, I saw him one day in such company, that the thought was suggested to my mind, whether he did not indulge himself in the use of intoxicating drink. I made inquiry about this, and found it was so. The next time he called upon me, I told him, as plainly as words could possibly express it, that I had not a doubt but his drinking was a device of the great adversary to keep him from salvation. He appeared to be surprised—did not deny drinking, but positively denied that he ever drank to any excess. I aimed to convince him that any drinking at all of stimulating liquors was an excess *for him.* Again and again I urged him to quit. He promised he would; but he did not. On one occasion, he confessed to me that he had resorted to brandy, in order "to sustain himself," as he expressed it, at times when his "mind was burdened and cast down with the thoughts of another world." I explained to him the folly, the danger, and wickedness of dealing with his serious impressions in that way. He promised to do it no more. But he kept on,—he lost all regard for religion,—he forsook the church, and now he is ten years nearer death,—an irreligious man, and probably an intemperate man.

Mr. Nettleton once said to me, "If a hard-drinking man gets a hope, it will be likely to be a false hope."

XXXIII.

The Word of a Companion.

SEVERAL years ago, on a Monday following the administration of the sacrament of the Lord's supper, a young man of my congregation called upon me in great agitation of mind. He said he felt that he was "a great sinner;" that he could "not bear to live in the condition he was in;" that his "attention had been anxiously turned to the subject of salvation several times before, but he soon forgot it again," and he "was afraid it would be so now." Said he, "I have wanted to come and see you a good many times, but I never *could* make up my mind to do it till yesterday."

I was not surprised to see him. The exercises of the communion Sabbath had been more solemn and joyful for the people of God than any such exercises that I have ever witnessed; and as similar occasions of communion had often before been times of awakening for those who were not communicants, I had *expected* that the same things would be experienced *now*. I told him this, and aimed to make him realize the solemnity of the fact, that the Holy Spirit was striving with him. I noticed in him two things which particularly characterized his state of mind,—the depth of his convictions, and his fixed determination to turn unto God.

As I was to leave home that day, and should not see him again for several weeks, I took the more care to teach him the gospel truths, and to impress them upon his mind. And because his attention had been arrested before, and he had gone back to indifference, I aimed to convince him that his danger lay on that very spot, and his only security was to be found in a full and instant determination to 'deny himself, and take up his cross and follow Jesus Christ.'

He left me, and such was my impression of his fixed *purpose*, that I had little doubt or fear about the result.

On my return home a few weeks afterwards, he immediately called on me, to tell of his happy "hope in God through Jesus Christ, *my Saviour*," as he emphatically expressed it.

Some months afterwards he united with the Church. But in making, at that time, a statement of the exercises of his mind at the period when he first came to see me, he mentioned one thing which astonished, instructed, and humbled me. After mentioning his anxieties, his sense of sin, and his interveiw with myself, he added, "That day one of my *companions* spoke to me on the subject of religion. *That determined me!*"

This was the turning point, therefore. *I* thought he was "determined" before; he thought so; he appeared to be. Indeed I had never witnessed the appearance of a more full and fixed determination in any anxious inquirer save one; and it was the very thing which gave me such a confident expectation of his conversion. But I was greatly mistaken. His heart wavered, and hesitated, and hung round the world, till one of his "companions spoke to him." That young companion was the successful preacher, after all. Suppose that "companion" had *not* spoken to him, what would this young man have done? We cannot tell; but there is a high degree of probability that he would have done just what he had so often done before,—would have quenched the Spirit and gone back to the world. Such companions are greatly needed.

Salvation ought to be urged upon the *will*, the *choice*, the "*determination*" of sinners, up to the very point of their "receiving Christ, and resting upon him alone for salvation, as he is offered in the gospel." Such an urgency is never out of place. The *will* is wanting, the determination is wanting, in every unconverted sinner, whether he believes it or not. The Bible has it right,—"*Choose* ye this day whom ye will serve."

XXXIV.

God Reigns;

OR, DESPAIR.

I DO not deem it a departure from the purpose or the title-page of this publication when I insert the following sketch of experience, which I copy from a paper which lies before me. The author of it, a clergyman, is still living, and still exercises the functions of his pastoral office. He here writes a little sketch of his own sad experience, which I am permitted to copy from his own hand-writing, though it was not designed for publication, being in a letter to a friend. As he has here explained how it was that he rose out of the dark and turbid waters of despair, the explanation may be of some service to others,—as I know it has been to his friend. Despair is opposed to faith, and every sinner on earth has the right to oppose faith to despair.

The following is a part of the letter :—

"My Dear Friend,—You say I am always happy, but you know little about me. I am not accustomed to obtrude my griefs upon others, for awakening a painful and useless sympathy; and I have sadly learnt that there may be griefs utterly beyond the power of others to understand, and which, therefore, their sympathies cannot reach. But I have seasons (and they are not unfrequent), when my soul is cast down within me. I am sure *I* can sympathize with any and every trouble of your darkest hours. . . . . .

"It is not a year since I found myself involved in all the horrors of darkness. I had hoped that such a season would never again return upon me ; but it did. I had formerly learnt that ill health, or rather nervousness in any state of health, has a great influence in bringing on depressed feelings; and at the period to which I now allude I was fully conscious of my nervous condition, and I recollected and reflected upo its influence. But this did not help me out of my trouble. Day by day the darkness settled down upon my soul, deeper and deeper. I could see *no* light! I was no Christian! The Bible was a sealed book to me; Christ was as a fiction, and salvation as a dream. Prayer was not so much of a mockery as *a lie*, for I felt that I did not *believe* what my lips uttered, when they said they called upon God. I did not believe in God. I was a dark sceptic. I could realize *nothing* but my own wretchedness; and in the depth of that wretchedness, I cursed the day in which I was born! Many and many a time I wished I never *had* been born, or had died when I first saw the light. Many and many a time I wished myself a dog, a horse, a stone,—*anything* but myself. I could realize nothing, rest on nothing, believe nothing.

"No pen can describe the horrors I endured. They were of every sort. I can only give you a few hints of them.

"Blasphemous thoughts, not lawful to utter even here,—temptations which I may not name,—things that would freeze your blood,—yea, things which made me feel that hell itself could be no worse,—would be darted through the mind, without volition or control! My poor soul was their sport. She had no power over them, not an item. She was tossed about, like a leaf in the storm, helpless, hopeless. At times things would flash over my mind like the flashes of the pit, as I thought; for I could not account for them in any other way. It was as if Satan spoke to me, to jeer at me, and taunt me, and triumph over me in his malignity,—'Where is your God *now?* What do you think of prayer *now?*' These ideas would come with such suddenness and vividness,—so involuntary were they, so surprising to myself, that I could not believe them the production of my own mind;—it must be that Satan was permitted to buffet me, and expend all his malice upon me, giving me a foretaste of hell.

"In my agony I used to roll upon the floor of my study, hour after hour, in despair, thinking it a sin, a shame, an impossibility for me to make another sermon. I knew I was not fit to preach. I thought I should be only acting a part, only playing the hypocrite *knowingly*. I would have relinquished the ministry if I could. But what could I do? I *must* preach. And after I had put it off as long as I could, and had scarcely time enough left to prepare for the Sabbath, I used to get my texts, and enter upon the composition of my sermons, feeling that I was the most miserable and most unworthy being on this side of the pit, and that I should soon be in it. When I got engaged over my sermons, I used to forget *myself;* and then, as my thoughts were occupied with the truth of God, I would become interested in the study, and get along pretty well till Sunday was over. I would preach like an apostle, and go home in despair! I tried every device, but no relief came.

"I went to a distinguished clergyman, and told him my case. He was kind to me. He said some wise things to me. But he began to say to me that God was disciplining me, to prepare me for some greater usefulness: 'Stop, sir!' said I. 'I cannot receive that!—I *can't!* I *can't!* It does not belong to me. I thought of that, but my conscience rejected it as a snare of the devil, to keep me at peace in my sins.' I told him I *knew* better; I was afraid, and had good reason to be afraid that I had never had any religion;—I could not live so, and certainly I could not die so. I told him that I could comfort others, and lift them out of such troubles as *seemed* to resemble mine,—*had* done it,—was skilled in doing it,—if nothing else, I could *beguile* them out of their despair, without their knowing how I did it; but I could not comfort myself,—my case was different, and I could not receive the same truths I preached to *them*. The ideas and promises which cheered them could not cheer me. I told him I had often thought myself like the man of gloom who applied in his despair to some friend (perhaps minister), and his friend said to him, 'Divert your thoughts,—take exercise, amusement,—go to hear Carlini play' (a famous harlequin, attracting crowds at the time). 'Alas! sir,' said he, in despair, '*I* am Carlini myself!' And so was I. I went home in despair, weeping along the street as I went.

"While I was in just this state, perplexed, agitated, tormented night and day, fearing and half expecting I should become a maniac, I had occasion to take a woman to the madhouse. (She would go with *me*,—her friends could not manage her.) As I rode along with her in the carriage, and conversed with her, I felt in my soul that *I* was more fit for the madhouse than she! I left her there. As I came out, I looked around upon the grounds, the trees, the sky, and knew nothing, and doubted everything, and thought of *myself*,—my torment of soul became intolerable! It was with difficulty that I could restrain myself from screaming out in my agony! I got into the carriage to go home. The young man who was with me made some attempts at conversation, but I could not attend to him; and finding my answers incoherent, I suppose, or finding me mute, he looked at me with astonishment, and afterwards left me to myself.

"We rode on. I could realize nothing—believe nothing. I did not believe there was a God! I felt that I was sinking down into the madness of despair! a forlorn, hopeless, eternal wreck! a wretch too wicked to live, and not fit to die!

"By-and-by my mind began to question and reason. *I am*—that is certain. These are *trees*—that is a *river*—yonder is the *sun*. All these things are certain. But where did they come from? They did not make *themselves*. *I* did not make myself. There is *dependence* here. They do not *govern* themselves. There is *order* here. The sun keeps his place, and is now hiding himself in his west in due time. '*There is a God!* Yes, there *is* a God!' That was the first gleam of light. I held on to that idea,—'*There is a God! there is a God! there is a God!*' I kept affirming it in my mind. I felt I had got hold of *one certainty*, and I would not let it go. I could believe *one* thing.

"In a moment, for these ideas flashed through my mind like flashes of lightning, I got hold of another idea, another *certainty*, and then linked the two certainties together. It was *order*—dominion. God *has* dominion. Yes, *he* rules. '*God reigns!*' said I. It was an ocean of light to me! It flooded the universe! '*God reigns! God reigns! God reigns!*' I kept repeating these two words mentally, '*God reigns! God reigns!*' It was triumph to me. It was glory. I almost leaped from the carriage. I groaned aloud under the burden of my joy. The young man started up and gazed at me. I did not notice him. I held on to the idea. '*God reigns!*' said I. I dared not let it go,—'*God reigns!*' I dared not let any other idea enter my mind, —'*God reigns! God reigns! God reigns!*' said my exulting soul.

"Then came a contest within me,—a conflict like the clash between thousands of opposing sabres! I felt the full power of my idea, if I could but hold it; but the assaults that were made upon it came like the shock of battle! One thought after another seemed to heave over my soul, like the waves, to dash me from my rock! You are a lost sinner; vile—a wretch! '*God reigns!*' said my soul. You are a hypocrite! '*God reigns!*' said my soul. You are a fool! '*God reigns!*' You are a madman! '*God reigns!*' You *are* mad, for no sane mind ever acted in this way! '*God reigns!*' I am certain of *that*—'*God reigns!*' Woe to you if he does! '*God reigns!*' What do you know about God? '*God reigns!*' You are a sceptic—an infidel! '*God reigns!*' God has abandoned *you!* '*God reigns!*' You are moved this moment by the power of the devil! '*God reigns!*' said my exulting soul.

"Thus one temptation after another dashed upon me, and all I could do was to hold on to my rock—'*God reigns!*' At one moment I trembled as an onset was made upon me; the next moment I triumphed, as the onset was hurled back by the power of the *one certainty* I wielded. I was sinking, amid the dark surges that dashed over me. In an instant I was above them all—governed them all—and could have governed a thousand such oceans, because '*God reigns!*' I opposed that shield to every wave of midnight—to every shock of scepticism—to every 'fiery dart' that Satan hurled at me. I held it up and defied despair and the devil. I turned it in every direction, upon every foe, every fear, every doubt,—'GOD REIGNS!' and I wished to *know* nothing else.

"I came home holding these two words over my poor soul, now settled, soothed down to perfect peace—calm, happy. I did not want to think anything, know anything, care for anything,—'*God reigns!*' and that is enough.

"Gradually I got hold of other truths, and employed them, I hope, in faith; but for many days I needed nothing to fill my soul with delight, but that glorious idea,—'*God reigns!*' '*God reigns!*' It saved me from being a maniac.

"This is but a very imperfect glance at one of my dark seasons. It can give you only a partial idea of them. No pen can ever describe them, and no imagination conceive of their horrors, unless the positive experiences of despair have been such as to make imagination ashamed of its feebleness.

"I do not wish the return of such seasons. They may, indeed, have been of some use to me, as my wiser friend suggested; but I do not like such discipline; I do not wish to learn the power of faith by being scorched by the blaze of hell.

"Never can I even recollect those dark trials without being overcome with emotion. I wish I could forget them. But they are burnt upon my memory, and I have not been able to write this without many tears. God grant you may not be able to understand me now, or at any time hereafter. But if you ever should come into such depths, I know of but one way to get out,—FAITH, FAITH, FAITH. You must not *try* to get out. You must let *God take* you out. You can do nothing for yourself. You might as well breast the dash of the ocean, or brave the thunder of heaven. You must let God 'hide you in the cleft of the rock, and cover you with his hand!' You must just exercise *a passive faith*,—much more difficult than an active one. At least *I* have found no other way. *Reason* with such feelings?—reason with a whirlwind as soon!—with a tempest!—with the maddened ocean! You *cannot* reason with them. They will take you up, and dash you about like the veriest mite in the universe. Look;—do nothing but look. God reigns! Jesus Christ is King! Leave ALL to HIM,—it is Faith."

It was a bright doctrine to which this minister clung in the time of his trouble. It is a great truth, "God reigns;" and, therefore, "grace reigns through righteousness unto eternal life, by Jesus Christ our Lord:" and, therefore, no sinner on earth need ever despair.

XXXV.

The Last Hour.

ONE of the most distressing instances of religious darkness and despondency, that I have ever been called to witness, was that of a poor girl, whom I first knew when I was called upon to visit her in her last sickness. She was not twenty years old, her health had departed,—she seemed to be doomed to an early grave. A seated pulmonary affection deprived her of all hope of recovery, and she had no hope in God. From her earliest childhood she had had excellent religious instruction. Her parents were pious people; and though they were poor, they had carefully educated her. She had been a scholar in the Sabbath school from her childhood, under the weekly instructions of a teacher who loved her, and who had taught her with assiduity, kindness, and skill. But though she had been long the subject of religious impressions, and had carefully studied her Bible, and earnestly prayed to be directed into the path of life, she had never found peace with God.

When I first knew her, none but herself had any special fears that her life was near its end. She was then able to go about the house, and sometimes, in pleasant weather, to walk out into the fields. But she had given up all expectation that she should recover, and she now addressed herself to the work of preparation for death, to which she looked forward with an indescribable anguish. She regarded it as the commencement of eternal woe.

At first I felt no peculiar discouragement on account of her religious depression. I regarded her fearful distress of mind as only the natural accompaniment of a just conviction of sin, and confidently expected that she would soon be led to hope and peace in believing. But it was far otherwise with her. She attained no peace. As week passed after week, she continued in the same despondency, receiving no light, no hope, no comfort. She read, she examined, she wept, she prayed in vain. And as her health declined more and more, her mind became wrought up to an intensity of anguish most distressful to witness. It was enough to melt any one's heart, to hear her cries for mercy. Never did a sinner plead more earnestly to be delivered from going down to perdition. She cried for mercy, as if standing in the very sight of hell! She had not a single gleam of light. Her soul was dark as a double midnight, and seemed plunged into an ocean of horrors. No one, I am sure, could have listened to her dreadful wailings without feeling a sympathy with her which would have wrung the heart with anguish.

I visited her often, conversed with her many times, taught her most carefully all the truths of the Bible which I supposed could possibly have any tendency to awaken her faith in Christ, and prepare her to meet him; but I never had the slightest evidence, to the last, that anything I ever said to her was the means of any benefit.

I wondered at her continued despair. It seemed to be the more remarkable, on account of the clear views which she appeared to have of the character of God, of his holy law, of her condemnation by it, of her wicked heart, of redemption by Christ, and of the faithfulness of God to fulfil all his promises. I often examined her thoughts and feelings on all such points as well as I could, in order to detect any error into which she might have fallen, and which might be a hindrance to her faith and peace, and in order to persuade her to trust all her eternal interests to the grace of the great Redeemer. She had not a doubt about any of these truths. She knew and bewailed her guiltiness and depravity; she fully believed in the love of God towards sinners, and the willingness of Christ to save her, unworthy as she was; —she said she hated sin with all her heart; she longed to be holy;

she did not believe that she hated God, though she would not say that she loved him; she admired "the kindness and love of God our Saviour" towards sinners; and wanted, above all things, to have an interest in his redemption, and to be *sure* that he had accepted her.

Months before her death I believed that she was a child of God. I thought I could discover every evidence of it, except hope, and peace, and the spirit of adoption. She had now come to believe that she had some love to God; "but," said she, "I am afraid God does not love *me*, and will cast me off for ever, as I deserve."

I strove, in every possible manner, and time after time, to lead her to the peace of faith. By holding directly before her mind the character of God, the redeeming kindness and work of Christ, and especially God's free invitations and firm promises, I strove to lead her to an appropriating faith, which should beguile her into a half-forgetfulness of herself, by causing her to delight in God. By teaching her according to the Scriptures what are the evidences of a new heart, and then by taking her own declarations to demonstrate to her that her own exercises of mind and heart were precisely these evidences, I laboured hard to induce her mind to rest upon the "witness within,"—a witness really there as I believed, if she would only hear and heed its voice. I explained to her what I honestly supposed to be the cause of her darkness, namely, her bodily condition, which prevented her seeing things as they were, by throwing a deceptive and dismal cloud over everything that pertained to herself. At times, when she appeared to me to be coming out of her gloom, and to be standing on the very borders of a light which she could not but see, a single recurring idea about herself would fling her back into all her darkness, and she would weep and wail in despair.

I had been describing heaven to her, and referring to its song of redemption, "Unto Him that loved us, and washed us from our sins in his own blood,"—

"Others will be in heaven," said she, "but *I* shall be cast out! From the distant region of my doom I shall behold my companions by the river of life, happy, happy spirits,—perhaps I shall hear their song; but no such home *for me!*"

"How came they there?" said I. "They were not saved by their goodness. They were no better than you. Jesus Christ saved them by his blood; and he offers to save you."

"He passes *me* by, sir. He called them, and they obeyed the call in due time; but he does not call *me!*"

"*He does*, my child, he *does*. He calls you *now*,—'Come unto ME.'"

"If he does, sir, I have no heart to hear him! My day is past! My day is past! I shall be cast off, as I deserve! Oh, I wish I had never been born!"

"Your day is *not* past. 'Now is the day of salvation.'"

Her only answer was tears and groans.

Such was her melancholy condition, as she declined more and more. Her strength was now almost gone. She evidently had but few weeks to live, if indeed a few days even remained to be measured by the falling sands of her life.

One day, some weeks before her death, after I had been stating to her the evidences of a regenerate state, and she had clearly described to me her own views and feelings, which seemed to me to accord with these evidences in one particular after another, almost throughout the entire chapter, I said to her, with some earnestness,—

"Mary-Ann, what do you want more, to convince you that you are a child of God? What do you expect? If these things do not convince you, what could? What evidence more do you *want?* Do you want an angel to come down from heaven here to your bedside, to tell you that you are a Christian, and shall go to heaven as soon as you die?"

"Oh, yes," said she, in a transport of emotion, clasping her death-pale hands, "*that is just what I want—just what I want!*"

"That is just what you cannot have," said I: "God is not going to give you any such kind of evidence"

I then explained to her how she must rest upon spiritual evidences, as all Christians do, and not on any evidence of the senses, or supernatural occurrences outside of her own heart.

As she approached fast to her end, and evidently could not survive much longer; I was greatly disappointed and saddened that her mind continued in the same unbroken gloom. I had not expected it. I had looked for a different experience. But it now seemed that her sun must go down in clouds!

One Sabbath morning, just before the time of public service, I was sent for to "see her die." She could still speak, in a very clear and intelligible manner,—better than for weeks before. Her reason was continued to her, all her faculties appeared as unimpaired and bright as ever. All that I could discover of any alteration in her mind, appeared to me to consist simply in this,—she now thought of *herself* less, and of her God and Saviour more. I told her, as I was requested to do, that she was now very soon to die. The bell was tolling for me to go to the pulpit, and having prayed with her, commending her to her God, I gave her my hand to bid her farewell. "Will you come to see me at noon?" says she.

"My dear child, you cannot live till noon. The doctor says you cannot live half an hour. I will come here as soon as I leave the church."

I went to the church and preached; and as soon as the service closed, I went immediately to her house. She was still alive. One of her friends met me at the door, and hastily told me that soon after I left the house, an hour and a half before, she avowed her perfect trust in Christ, and her firm confidence that he would "take her home to heaven." "I am full of peace," says she, "I can trust my God. This is enough. I am happy, happy. I die happy." A little while after, she said she wanted to see me "once more." She was told I was in church, and that she could not live till the sermon was closed. "*I shall live!*" said she firmly. She seemed to refuse to die. She inquired what time the service would close, and being told, she often afterwards inquired what time it was. She watched the hands of the clock, frequently turning her eyes upon them, in the intervals between her prayers and praises and rapturous thanksgivings. As I entered the room she turned her eyes upon me; "Oh," said she, "I am glad you have come,—I have been waiting for you. I wanted to see you once more, and tell you how happy I am. I have found out that a poor sinner has *nothing* to do—only to believe. I am not afraid of death now. I am willing to die. God has forgiven me, and I die happy,—I am very happy. I wanted to tell you this. I thought I should live long enough to tell you. I thought God would not let me die till I had seen you, and told you of my joy, so as not to have you discouraged when you meet with other persons who have such dark minds as mine was. Tell them to *seek* the Saviour. Light will come some time,—it may be at the last hour. I prayed God to let me see you once more. He has granted my last prayer; and now—now I am ready."

Her voice faltered,—she could say no more. I prayed some two or three minutes by her bedside; we rose from our knees, and in less than five minutes more she "fell asleep." "Blessed are the dead that die in the Lord."

It was pleasant to hear this dying girl affirm her faith, and to witness her joy at the moment of death. But I do not know that this joy amounted to any more real evidence of her effectual calling to Christ by the Holy Spirit than she had presented before. Faith is one thing, and feeling is another. It is the faith that saves; it is the feeling that comforts. But the faith may exist where the feeling is wanting. The principle may exist where its action is wanting.

If this poor girl had died in all her darkness and fears, I should not have despaired of her. Amid all her glooms of guilt, I thought she exhibited proofs of faith. It seemed to me that it was faith which made her attend to the truths of the Bible, with such careful scrutiny and enduring perseverance, at the very moment when she saw no light in it for *her*:—that it was faith which made her pray so fervently and without faltering, month after month, at the very time when she did not suppose she received any answer; —that it was faith which kept her, in her most gloomy times, perfectly free from any besetting doubt that there *is* salvation for sinners in Jesus Christ, freely offered to them in the love of God; —that it was faith which made her so perfectly assured that peace with God is attainable, and made her long for it as the only thing she cared for ;—yea, that it was faith which gave to her very glooms their most terrible aspect, creating such a confident and continued conviction that if Christ was not found everything was lost. Her grief was not that of an alien and an enemy, but that of an affectionate, but disinherited child. The very point of her anguish consisted in this, namely, that she believed Christ to be a full and free Saviour, and yet could find no evidence in her heart that she trusted in him. The promises were precious things in her heart's estimation; but they seemed to her to be precious things which she did not embrace. She distrusted herself, but not God. She was afraid to believe that she was a believer. She was so tremblingly afraid of getting wrong, that she dared not think she could possibly be right. On this ground, I was led to believe that Mary-Ann was a child of God long before that memorable light shone on her soul in the hour of death. She was in darkness, not because she had no faith, but because she did not believe she had any. She had a title to heaven without having eyes to read it.

Her mother, father, and physician (who was a pious man), all her friends, as I suppose, regarded this bright close of her earthly experience very differently from myself. They appeared to look upon it as the commencement of her faith, thinking that God had first appeared for her in that time of her first triumph and joy. Such an idea in similar cases, I suppose, to be common; and I suppose it to be an error, and a very misleading one, especially to many unconverted sinners. Such unconverted sinners hear of instances like this and therefore *hope* that it may be just so with themselves when they shall be called to die. On the ground of this hope, they speak a deceitful peace to their own hearts, without any definite, determined, and prayerful efforts to prepare for death,—just leaving it to that coming hour itself to bring along with it the preparation they need. Their secret thought is,—"Such a one, who always *lived* without religion, died in peace at last, and why should not I?" Delusive thought, and often fatal! These persons never stop to inquire what had been the previous heart-history, the struggles, and prayers of those whose peaceful death they mention. They themselves are not *living such a life* as their now departed acquaintance did, who died in peace; and therefore they have no good reason to think they shall *die such a death.* Too hastily they say of such a one, "He lived all his life without religion." They say what they do *not* know, and what probably is *false.* If any one would hope to *die* like Mary-Ann, let him *live* like Mary-Ann. Her supreme aim, and her agonizing prayer for months, sought the favour of God. To gain this, she omitted nothing which she deemed a duty,—she deferred nothing to a future hour. To gain this was all her desire, and no discouragement could make her falter, or turn her aside. "Go thou and do likewise," if thou wouldst *die* like Mary-Ann.

XXXVI.

The Dawn of Heaven.

SIXTEEN years after the death of Mary-Ann (mentioned in the preceding sketch), I was summoned to the sick-bed of her sister. She was a younger sister, whom I had never seen since she was a mere child, and of whose religious character I had no knowledge. She had married; and after many trying changes, she was now in the city of New York. A kind lady, one of my own friends who resided in that city, and who had formerly known something of her family in another State, had accidentally heard of her illness, had called upon her, and now did me the favour to bring me the sick woman's request, that I "would go and see her." She told me I should find her in a very destitute condition, very much unbefriended and alone, though she had herself done something for her, to make her a little more comfortable. I received this message in the evening, and early the next morning I made my way to the house to which she had directed me.

I found the sick woman in a boarding-house, among strangers, where nobody knew her except her husband, and manifestly nobody cared for her. She was in the garret, in a little room close under the roof of the house. The scanty furniture, and the whole appearance of the room, showed me at a glance how unenviable was her condition. There was but one chair in the room, and this was used for the table, the only one she had, on which were placed some vials of medicine, a tea-cup and a saucer; which constituted all the furniture of the room, except her humble bed. But all was neat and clean. If there was scantiness, there was decency.

As I entered the room, I perceived at once her hopeless condition. She was emaciated, pale, tormented with a hollow cough, unable to speak but in a whisper, and her cheek was flushed with that round spot of peculiar red, with which I had become too familiar to mistake it for anything else than the fatal signal. I approached the bed on which she was lying, told her who I was, and offered her my hand.

"I am *very* happy—to see you," said she, speaking with effort and only in a whisper, and compelled to pause at almost every word. "I did not suppose—you would remember me—at all;—and for a long time—I could not have courage—to send—for you,—or—let you know—that I was here. But I remembered—you visited—my sister,—Mary-Ann,—when *she* died,—and I had—a great desire to—see you."

"I am very glad," said I, "to be able to see you; but I am sorry to find you so ill. I wish I had known that you were here, sooner."

"You are—very kind, sir;—but I was—afraid to trouble you. I have—not seen you—before,—since I was—a little child;—and I supposed—you had—forgotten that—there was such a person. I am very thankful to you—for being so kind—as to come—to see me."

"Have you been sick long?"

"Yes, sir,—a good many—months. I have lately—been growing—much worse,—and I want now—to get home—to my mother,—this week,—if I can. I think—I should be better there—for a little while,—though I cannot tell."

"Do you think you are well enough to go home?"

"I hope—I could go—in the boat,—and live to get there. The hottest—of the summer—is coming on soon,—and our place here—is very uncomfortable; but—most of all,—I want to see—my *mother,—once* more,—before I die." And the big tears rolled fast over her fevered cheeks.

"I hope," said I, "you may be able to see her; but you do not seem to have much strength just now."

"Indeed, sir,—my strength—is—all gone. I cannot—stand or my feet—any longer. Before I became—so weak—I used to work with my needle—and help my husband—to earn something; —and then, we had—a more comfortable place. But I can do nothing—now,—and so we came—to this—garret—to save rent."

"Have you much pain?"

"Yes sir,—I am in—great pain now,—the most—of the time."

"Do you expect ever to get well?"

"Oh no, sir,—I shall—never get well. I know I am—to die —before long;—consumption—is—a hopeless disease. This painful cough—will soon end—my days."

"Are you afraid to die?"

"Oh no, sir," said she with a smile; "Jesus—is my hope. He—*will* save me."

"Trust him," said I; "you trust the eternal Rock. He has promised,—"

Interrupting me, she replied,—

"What *can*—anybody want—more than the *promises?* It seems to me—the promises—are enough—for everybody;—*so sweet*—they are so *full*. Why, God—has promised—to make—an everlasting covenant—with us—poor sinners!" And tears of joy coursed down her smiling face.

I conversed with her as long as I thought it good for her. All her conversation was in the same happy strain. She appeared very much exhausted, and I had little hope that her desire to "see her *mother once* more" would ever be gratified. Indeed, I did not think she would live till sun-set. I prayed with her, and promising to call again in the afternoon, I left her.

Some little arrangements were made for her comfort, and in the afternoon I called there again. She was evidently worse, but her joy was full.

Said she, "I bless my God—for all my pain,—for the disappointments—of my past life,—and the strange—strange way—in which—he has—led me on. I have had trials—many trials. My husband—did not prosper—as—he hoped—to do,—and sometimes

—we have been—in distress. But—my trials have—done me good. Now we have few wants. You know I cannot—eat anything now,—and I hope—his wages—will keep him—from suffering. I came—to this—little room—when I—could not work—any longer,—on purpose to relieve him. The rent—is cheaper—here—in this—little garret,—and I want to be—as little burdensome—to him—as possible. I used to think—when I first made a profession—of religion—trials would—overcome me,—but God makes me happy—in them. I find—if one—is not worldly—trials are easy—to bear;—and if—we look towards God—and heaven—they are—nothing at all—but mercies."

"And does your husband feel as you do? Is he a pious man?"

She turned her languid head upon her pillow, and glanced around the room, to see if the nurse who had been procured for her had left the room; and perceiving she was not there, she said,—

"I suppose—I may speak—freely—to you—about my husband,—since—we are alone. He is not—religious,—and that is the trouble—of my heart."

She could say no more; she wept and sobbed aloud. After a little time, becoming more composed, evidently struggling to suppress her emotions, she continued,—

"I must leave that—I can't—speak—of *him*. Oh, it seems to me—as if the careless, who neglect—salvation,—have never—read—God's promises. If they had,—and knew—what they meant,—they could not—help trusting—them. I am happier now—than ever—I was before. It is sweet to—suffer—this pain—when Christ—puts such delights—into my soul."

She was now stronger than I had expected to find her. I prayed with her, and promising to see her again the next day, I left her.

I was prevented from calling to see her next morning, as I had intended; and when I called in the afternoon, I perceived her end was very fast approaching. Her countenance was changed, and her pulse more feeble and fluttering. Her voice was now perfectly restored, and she could speak with strong, clear articulation. She mentioned her recovered voice as an instance of God's goodness to her, and both she and her husband took it as an evidence that she might live to reach her home. To me it was only an evidence to the contrary. She did not appear to be at all aware how near she was to death, and still entertained the hope of starting the next day, "to go home to her mother." I felt very reluctant to crush that hope; but I thought she ought to be made acquainted with the prospect before her. She was still very weak and in some pain, and when I mentioned her sufferings to her, and expressed my sorrow that she had so much to endure, her face lighted up with a glad smile.

Said she, "Oh, it is *pleasant* to suffer when we know it is *our God* that brings us to it. He does not afflict me too much. My poor body is weak and almost gone; but my God fills me with the delights of his love. My heart is full of joy. I am perfectly happy. I shall soon be where Christ is, and love him for ever."

"I suppose," said I, "you are aware that you can now last but a little while, and are prepared to go at any moment when God bids."

"I have no desire, sir, to get well. Why should I have? There is nothing in this world for me. You see we have nothing. I have parted with all my little furniture and my clothes to get bread and pay our debts; and I don't want the world; it is nothing to me now, and I leave it willingly. I am happy. God makes me happy. Christ is enough for me. I love to trust God's promises. I trust him for all I want, and he makes me very happy. Death seems like nothing to me. It is my friend. I welcome it. Dying is only a step, and then I shall be at home,—at home!" and tears of joy coursed down her smiling face. The last word—*home*, which she had uttered, seemed to remind her of her earthly home, and she added,—

"To-morrow I hope to go home to my *mother*, and see her and all my other friends once more;—*perhaps* I may."

"I am afraid not, my dear friend. You are very low, and I wish you to be ready to die at any moment."

Turning her death-glazed eyes upon me, she asked,—

"Shall I die *to-night?* If you think so, *tell me plainly*. Don't weep so for me. I thank you for all your kind sympathy, but I am perfectly happy. God fulfils to me all his promises. I leave all in his hands—gladly, joyfully. But I think I can live to get home. *You* think I shall die to-night. I thank you for letting me know it; and I am *ready*, if God calls. But if I am alive, may I see you in the morning? God will reward you, I know, for all your kindness to me."

"Yes, my child, you may expect me here in the morning; but if you have anything you wish to say to me, you had better say it now."

"I have no more to say but to thank you again. Your kind words have done me great good; and it has been sweet to me, *very* sweet, to join with you in prayer. Help me to praise God for the delights that fill my soul. Don't weep so for me."

I prayed with her, and praised God as she desired, and then bade her *farewell*.

"Do not think I weep because I am sorry," said she; "I weep because I am overcome with joy. Delights fill my happy soul. This is the dawn of heaven. My heaven is begun. Dying is sweet to me. I go to my blessed Lord. I thank you for coming to me. Farewell,—farewell."

Early the next morning I returned to that privileged garret. It was empty! Even her corpse was not there. She had died about four hours after I left her; her body had been placed in its coffin, conveyed on board the vessel, and on the very day in which she expected to see her "*mother once* more," her mother received the lifeless body of her child!

It now lies buried in the grave-yard of her native valley. She and Mary-Ann sleep side by side. And they shall rise together from the dead in that coming day when our Lord Jesus Christ shall be revealed from heaven, "to be glorified in his saints, and to be admired in all them that believe."

If grace is there, how instructive, how glorious is—

THE DEATH-BED OF THE POOR!

"Tread softly—bow the head—
In reverent silence bow;
No passing bell doth toll—
Yet an immortal soul
Is passing now.

Stranger! however great,
With lowly reverence bow;
There's one in that poor shed—
One on that paltry bed—
Greater than thou.

Beneath that beggar's roof,
Lo! Death doth keep his state.
Enter—no crowd attend;
Enter—no guards defend
This palace gate.

That pavement, damp and cold,
No smiling courtiers tread;
One silent woman stands—
Lifting with meagre hands
A dying head.

No mingling voices sound—
An infant wail alone;
A sob suppressed—again
That short, deep gasp, and then
The parting groan.

Oh, change!—oh, wondrous change!—
Burst are the prison bars;
This moment *there*, so low,
So agonized; and now
Beyond the stars.

Oh, change!—stupendous change!
There lies the soulless clod.
The sun eternal breaks—
The new immortal wakes—
Wakes with his God."

XXXVII.

Fasting and Prayer

The sixteenth day of March, in the year 1831, was observed, by the church, in which I was pastor, as a day of fasting and prayer. This appointment was made with special reference to the outpouring of the Holy Spirit; to seek, by united prayer, the revival of God's work in the midst of the congregation. The meetings for prayer were held in the church building, and a large portion of the members were present.

The next week, as I was returning home from a religious meeting late in the evening, and had turned into an unfrequented crossroad, in order to shorten the distance I had to walk; I was startled at the sudden sound of footsteps behind me, which seemed to be those of a man rapidly approaching me in the dark. I did not know but some evil-minded person might intend to do me harm in that obscure place, and under cover of the impenetrable darkness of one of the darkest nights that I ever saw. I did not choose *to run,* for, in that case, I should never know why I was so hotly pursued. I felt glad, that I had some corporeal strength; and though I cannot say that my courage very specially forsook me, yet I had no particular liking for a hostile attack and a tussle in the dark. As the footsteps so rapidly approaching me appeared to be directly in my rear, like a lover of peace I crossed to the other side of the road; and not preferring an attack in the rear, I stopped and faced about. My pursuer espied me, and, without slackening his pace, ran directly towards me across the street, till, coming within ten feet of me, much out of breath, he called my name. "That is my name, sir," said I. He came close up to me, panting for breath, and stopped in silence. After a few heavy and rapid breathing, he spoke. He told me who he was, and why he had run after me. He was a young man of my congregation, to whom I had never before spoken. I did not know him personally. He had just come from the schoolhouse where I had been preaching; and, not willing to be seen by his companions speaking to me, he had waited till they were out of the way, and then run after me, through the obscure street into which he had seen me turn. He wanted to see me, for he felt that he was "a sinner unreconciled to God, and in danger of hell." "What shall I *do?*" said he; "I can't live so another week. Is there any way that such a one as *I* am can be saved?"

I had a long conversation with him standing there in the dark, (for he did not choose to go home with me,) and I found, that his first impressions of any particular seriousness had commenced in the church, on the *Fast-day*, the week before. He was an apprentice in a mechanic's shop, where there were more than a dozen other irreligious young men. The master of the shop (not a professor of religion), told the whole of them, that if they wished to attend church on the Fast-day, they need not work. They accepted his proposal. And as he himself afterwards told me, *that* was the reason why *he* went to church that day himself. He said, he "did not expect the boys would take his offer, but would prefer to stay at home and work;" and if they had done so, he would have done so too; "but when they were all going to church," says he, "I was *ashamed* to stay at home."

That young man, his employer, and almost the entire number of those young men in the shop, became communicants in the church before the close of that year. Thirteen persons were received into the church, whose seriousness commenced *that day, in the church,* while the *people of God were praying* for that *very thing.* 'The Lord is with you while ye be with Him.' 'Before they call I will answer; and while they are yet speaking, I will hear.'

Sixteen Short Sermons

Published by the

American Tract Society

See the chapter "The Neglected Bible"
for the significance of this tract to Spencer's ministry.

Sermon # 1

"What is a man profited,
if he shall gain the whole world, and lose his own soul?
Or what shall a man give in exchange for his soul?
Matthew 16:26

How little attention does this infinitely important subject gain in the world! How few consider the salvation of their precious souls, as the great business of life! You who are reading these lines, did you ever consider it? Did you ever lay it to heart, and are you acting accordingly? If this is the case, the following language will express your heart-felt convictions: "I have a soul as well as a body. My soul must live for ever in happiness or misery. It is capable of pain or pleasure inconceivably greater than my body. It is a matter of comparatively little importance whether I am in abject poverty or the greatest affluence, during the few years I am to continue in the present world; whether I am respected or despised by my fellow mortals; whether my body is sickly or healthy, painful or at ease. These are matters of small consequence; death is certain, is near. 'Ashes to ashes, and dust to dust,' must soon be pronounced over my lifeless body. In a dying moment, if I could call the whole world my own, what good would it do me? What comfort could it afford me? But whether my soul is to be eternally happy or miserable; the companion of angels and saints made perfect around the throne of God, or doomed to weeping, and wailing, and gnashing of teeth, with devils and damned spirits in hell, where the worm never dieth and where the fire never will be quenched; this is the momentous inquiry I ought to make. To escape from the wrath to come, and secure an inheritance among the saints in light, ought to be my great concern. Is it so? Which world is most in my thoughts, this or the next? What am I most anxious about? Am I not often inquiring, what shall I eat, what shall I drink, or wherewithal shall I be clothed? But when did I seriously inquire, 'What shall I do to be saved?' If I have no prevailing concern about my soul, I may be certain my state is bad, and its danger awfully great."

Sermon # 2

"Sin is the transgression of the law."
1 John 3:4

Sinner, did you ever inquire what sin is? Did you ever study the word of God, that you might have proper views of this greatest of all evils? If you have never made the inquiry, your state is bad, dreadfully bad. Your salvation is at stake. Look seriously into the text. Lift up your heart to God, and say, "Lord, give me proper views of sin." *"Sin is the transgression of the law."* What law? The law of the most holy God. Where is this law to be found? It is contained in the ten commandments. Did you ever read them with a trembling heart and a faltering voice, asking, "Have I transgressed this or that part of God's holy law? Did I ever consider that the law may be broken by thought, as well as by word or deed? Did I ever reflect that the law is spiritual, reaching to the thoughts, purposes, and intentions of the heart; that every irregular thought is a transgression of the law; that every unholy desire is sin; that *'for every idle word that men speak, they must give account in the day of judgment,'* (Matt. 12:36) - that awful day, when the heart-searching God shall judge the secrets of our hearts? Alas! How many idle thoughts have passed through my mind, without the proper conviction attending each of them, that this is sin! See Genesis 6:5. How many idle words have I every day spoken, without reflecting, that for every one of these I must give an account! Matthew 12:36. When did the evil of my thoughts and words extort an anxious cry from my heart, *'God be merciful to me a sinner?'* If sin be the transgression of the law; that is, if falling short of the perfection which the law requires, in thought, word, or deed, be sin, as well as doing that which the law forbids; how much have I to answer for, that perhaps I have never before thought of? Yet I have often confessed, 'We have done what we ought not to have done, and have left undone what we ought to have done, and there is no health in us.' Alas! I have mocked God, by confessing with my lips what I did not feel in my heart."

Let my conscience, O Lord, now be awakened to feel what sin is.

Sermon # 3

"All have sinned, and come short of the glory of God."
Romans 3:23

All, and therefore you, my dear Reader, and myself. We have sinned; that is, we have broken God's law; for *'there is none righteous, no, not one'* (Rom. 3:10). There is none that has kept the law of God. We have transgressed *every* precept of his moral law, either in act, word, or evil desire. The charge is heavy, but the verdict is true. Let us consider the case, earnestly entreating God to enlighten our minds. Take the ten commandments into your hand, and read. We have broken the *first* commandment, by trusting in and loving other things more than God. *"Thou shalt love the Lord thy God with all thy heart"* (Matt. 22:37). In this we have come short. The *second* respects the manner in which God is to be worshiped, not with outward form and ceremony, but in spirit and truth. Alas! how deficient have we been in that serious attention, that inward reverence, and that devout affection, which his worship required! God is a jealous God. You say you have never been guilty of profane cursing and swearing, and so think you have kept the *third;* but have you never in prayer, and in reading the sacred Scriptures, suffered the holy name of God to pass through your lips without an awful sense of what you were doing, or even without thought? *"God will not hold him guiltless that taketh his name in vain"* (Ex. 20:7). Have you always employed the whole Sabbath in those religious exercises which the *fourth* commandment enjoins; and performed those exercises in such a devout manner, that the law has nothing to charge you with, in thought, word, or deed? Sinner, lay your hand upon your mouth, and plead guilty. Need I go through the second table? Dost thou love thy neighbor as thyself? Hast thou done unto all men as thou wouldst they should do unto thee? Have you never been guilty of disobedience to your parents? Know ye not that every rising of causeless anger is murder? (Matt. 5:22) that every unchaste desire is adultery? (Matt. 5:28) that every secret fraud and neglect of affording that succour to the poor which is in your power, is theft? That every uncharitable thought is a breach of the *ninth,* and every covetous wish a transgression of the *tenth* commandment? Surely all have sinned, in doing that which the law forbids, and in not doing that which the law commands. What have I then done; and what have I not done? All have sinned. What is my state? A state of sinfulness and misery. Why have I not felt it till now? Because sin hath blinded my eyes against the light of truth.

Sermon # 4

"Cursed is every one that continueth not in all things, that are written in the book of the law, to do them."
Galatians 3:10

What means that awful word, *"Cursed"*? The curse of God is the declaration of his just anger and wrath against sin and the sinner. Who can stand in his sight, if he is angry? Psalm 76:7. But who is cursed? Every one, whether young or old, rich or poor, learned or ignorant, that continueth not throughout the whole period of life, without any intermission, failure, or defect whatever, in all things, in thought, word, and deed, doing perfectly what the law requires, and keeping himself absolutely free from what the law condemns, *'in all things, that are written in the book of the law, to do them;'* the law being understood in its spiritual and most exalted sense and interpretation. And remember that it is further said, (Jas. 2:10) that whosoever shall keep the whole law, and yet offend in one point, he is guilty of all. Now consider, has there been a day, an hour, a moment, in which your state has been such as the law requires? The curse is pronounced on every transgressor for every transgression: not only for profaneness, murder, adultery, and such like gross acts of sin; but for every sinful thought, and for every moment in which you have failed to love the Lord your God with all your heart and with all your soul. O, how many curses, then, has the law denounced against you and me! It has been revealing the wrath of God against us every moment of our lives; for every moment of our lives we have been sinning against God. Are these things so? Can you from Scripture prove them to be false? What! Is every sinner cursed for every sin, and have I been perpetually sinning all my life? Is it true, that I have never, from a sincere regard for God, made conscience of one thought, word, or action; never performed one duty, or abstained from one sin, from a right motive, love to God? Has my whole life been one uninterrupted course of evil? Is my state, then, a state of condemnation? How astonishing it is! What a proof of the darkness of my mind, and the hardness of my heart, that I can live one hour at ease under the curse of God; that I can lie down or rise up without trembling, since the curse of God must plunge the impenitent sinner into hell!

Sermon # 5

"The wages of sin is death."
Romans 6:23

Sin is the transgression of the law (1 John 3:4), that eternal rule of right to rational beings, the moral law of God. It is sin, all sin, every sin, that is here spoken of. Death, whatever that word means, is the just and certain reward of every sin committed in thought, word, or deed. But what is death? The death of the body is its separation from the soul. You are a sinner; and this effect of sin you have begun to feel in all those pains and sicknesses which are bringing your body to the grave. You are now a dying man. The death of the body, or its separation from the soul, will occasion its return to the dust from whence it was taken. But death in the text means vastly more: *the death of the soul.* What is that? It is something as much more dreadful than that of the body, as the soul is of more value than the body. It is the separation of the soul from God, as its life and happiness; hence it becomes a state of unavoidable sin, and first or last, a state of self-tormenting anguish, arising from the forfeiture of the friendship of God, with all its attendant blessings. Spiritual death, or the death of the soul, consists not in the loss of consciousness or feeling, but in the loss of the image and favor of God. For in his favor is life (Psalm 30:5); and in his frown is death. If you, my dear fellow sinner, are not made alive by God's converting grace, this is your state. You are dead in trespasses and sins (Eph. 2:1); and unless you are quickened by God's Spirit, communicated to you before your departure hence, in this unhappy state you must forever continue; for the death spoken of in the text, is opposed to eternal life in the following clause (Rom. 6:23b). And oh, if the effect of this spiritual death be misery, even in this present life (as the experience of every man testifies, if he will own the truth), then what must it be in the world to come? Ah! Who can tell? We read of a worm that never dies, to prey on the tormented conscience; of fire that never can be quenched, to destroy both body and soul in hell; of weeping, and wailing, and gnashing of teeth; and all this is to last forever. But is there not a disproportion between the offence and punishment? Let God be true, and every man a liar. He says the wages, the just reward of sin, is death. God's truth binds him to fulfill his threatenings, as well as his promises. O fly from the wrath to come; for *"who among us can dwell with devouring fire? Who among us can dwell with everlasting burnings?"* (Isaiah 33:14).

Sermon # 6

"What must I do to be saved?"
Acts 16:30

This is the anxious inquiry of an awakened sinner. By an awakened sinner, I mean the man who knows what sin is, and who painfully feels that he is a sinner; and as such, under the curse of God, and in danger of hell fire. Are you an awakened sinner? Alas! all men are naturally asleep, insensible of their danger; and so they continue till they are roused up out of their carnal slumbers by the word and Spirit of God. They cry peace, peace to themselves, when there is no peace; for God hath said, *"There is no peace to the wicked"* (Isa. 48:22). They live on, day after day, keeping death, judgment, and eternity, out of their thoughts; never reading the Bible with a sincere desire to know what their state is, and never praying to God from the bottom of their hearts, *"God be merciful to me a sinner"* (Luke 18:13). If you can live without earnest prayer to God for mercy, habitually neglecting it, you give as full proof that you are alienated from the life of God through the ignorance that is in you, as if you were living in the grossest immoralities. But when it pleases God to fasten conviction on the heart of a man, and to awaken his conscience, then he starts up as one out of sleep. He sees, what he never discovered before, that it is an evil and bitter thing to sin against God. He reads in the word of truth, that the wicked shall be turned into hell, and all the nations that forget God (Psalm 9:17); and he trembles as he reads. He acknowledges, "I have forgotten God and sinned against him;" and being convinced that the wages of sin is death, he asks, "how shall I escape the damnation of hell?" Such a man is deeply in earnest when he makes the inquiry, *"What must I do to be saved?"* He feels that his all for eternity is at stake. The world with all its pleasures, profits, and honors, becomes tasteless and insipid; it cannot give ease to his aching heart, nor heal his wounded conscience. He now begins to pray. His prayer is now the real language of his heart, not the formal, unmeaning service it was before. A sense of his danger drives him to the throne of grace. The word of God he now reads as the decision of eternal truth; and he reads it as having an interest in every line. Sinner, has this inquiry ever been yours, *"What must I do to be saved?"*

Sermon # 7

"Repent ye, and believe the Gospel."
Mark 1:15

These are the words of our blessed Savior, addressed to poor guilty sinners like you and me. But what is repentance? It is a work of the Spirit of God upon the heart, producing such an inward sense of the evil and guilt of sin, as makes a man wonder that he is out of hell; such a hatred of sin as causes a man to forsake it; and such an apprehension of the consequences of sin, as makes a man willing to be saved wholly and solely through what Jesus Christ has done and suffered for lost souls. The penitent sinner is convinced that sin deserves punishment; that he himself, as a sinner, is liable to the wrath of God; that sin must be pardoned or punished; that he can make no amends for the least of his transgressions; and consequently that his salvation must be all of grace. The man thus humbled, is prepared to welcome the news of a Savior who came to seek and to save that which was lost (Matt. 18:11). Such is the Gospel. It is glad tidings to a lost, guilty world. The sum and substance of it is this, that *"Christ Jesus came into the world to save sinners"* (1 Tim. 1:15). He died to make satisfaction for their sins; and being God and man in one Savior, *"He is able to save to the uttermost all that come unto God by him"* (Heb. 7:25). His blood being the blood of God incarnate (Acts 20:28), was infinitely meritorious; and it was shed for this very purpose, to take away sin; so that if your sins, poor self-condemned sinner, are more in number than the hairs of your head, or the sand on the sea shore; if they are great and aggravated, and red like scarlet, yet there is hope. *"The blood of Jesus Christ cleanseth* (hath virtue to cleanse) *from all sin"* (1 John 1:7). But how am I to become interested in this, and get comfort of it? *"Believe the Gospel:"* rely on what the word of God says about Jesus Christ, and his willingness and power to save sinners. But may I without presumption believe that Jesus Christ came to save such a wretch as I am? Yes, *"this is the commandment, that ye believe on the name of his Son Jesus Christ"* (1 John 3:23). There can be no presumption in doing what God has commanded, and taking God at his word.

Sermon # 8

"This is a faithful saying, and worthy of all acceptation,
that Jesus Christ came into the world to save sinners,
of whom I am chief."
1 Timothy 1:15

This is the sum of the Gospel. Jesus Christ is God: he made the world, and all that therein is (Col. 1:16): but we his creatures broke his laws, and rebelled against him. He might justly have cast us all into hell, the lake that burneth with fire and brimstone. But, O wondrous love! *"God was manifest in the flesh"* (1 Tim. 3:16), was born into the world. For what purpose? *To save sinners.* How did he save them? By dying for them upon the cross, *"bearing their sins in his own body upon the tree"* (1 Peter 2:24), and washing them from their sins in his own blood. Did I ever consider this wonderful love of God? I am a sinner, born in sin, and as such liable to eternal punishment. *"Jesus Christ came into the world to save sinners,"* even such as I am. Have I ever earnestly entreated him to save me? Do I believe that I am a miserable sinner? Do I feel it, and lament it? And am I sensible, that unless Christ saves me, I must be a damned soul forever? Alas, how many never go to Jesus Christ to save them! How many are careless and unconcerned about what Jesus Christ has done for sinners! But do I lay it to heart? Are all my hopes built upon this faithful saying, that *"Jesus Christ came into the world to save sinners"?* O what a comfortable saying it is, that though I am a sinner, the chief of sinners, yet I may be saved from the sins I have committed, and the hell I have deserved, if, under a penitential sense of my wickedness, I look up to Jesus Christ, and trust in him! O may the Holy Spirit enable me thus to look unto Jesus. Oh what should I, a poor, wretched, helpless sinner do, if there were no Jesus to save me? How eagerly should I welcome such glad tidings! Surely the message is *"worthy of all acceptation,"* and ought to be received by all, since all have sinned, and stand in need of being saved; and since all who feel their lost estate, may come to HIM who is able to save them.

O Lord, the Holy Ghost, enable me to believe to the saving of my soul.

Sermon # 9

"Him that cometh to me I will in no wise cast out."
John 6:37

How tenderly compassionate is the dear Friend of poor lost sinners! How anxious does he appear to remove every objection out of the way of the inquiring soul, that is made willing to be saved on Gospel terms, *"by grace through faith"* (Eph. 2:8). Lest such should be discouraged, how graciously does he describe their character and feelings, inviting them, with all the eloquence of God-like pity, to come unto him! Hear his words, *"Come unto me all ye that labor and are heavy laden, and I will give you rest"* (Matt. 11:28). Are *you* weary of the slavery of sin, and the bondage of Satan and the world? Are *you* heavy laden with guilt on your conscience, and fear in your heart? Behold, the loving Savior stands with open arms to receive you; and these are the gracious words which proceed out of his mouth, *"Come unto me, and I will give you rest." "He is faithful that hath promised"* (Heb. 10:23), and cannot deceive you. *"He will not alter the thing that is gone out of his lips"* (Psalm 89:34). Make the experiment; come to him. He is able to save, and he is willing to save; wherefore should you doubt?

But you say, "I am a great sinner." Be it known unto you, that Jesus Christ is an Almighty Savior. You say further, "I have continued long in open rebellion against him; I have been many years sinning against him with a high hand." Be it so, you are not out of reach of mercy, nor is your case too desperate for the skill and power of the great Physician. Do you still object, "I am a sinner of no common kind; of sinners I am chief." Even unto *you* is the word of this salvation sent. The blood of Jesus is the blood of God (Acts 20:28), and therefore *"cleanseth from all sin"* (1 John 1:7). The righteousness of Jesus Christ is the righteousness of God (Rom. 3:22), and therefore is sufficient to justify the most ungodly. Do not despair; for thus saith thy Savior, the lover of thy poor lost soul, *"Him that cometh unto me I will in no wise cast out"* (John 6:37). He makes no exceptions: being *"not willing that any should perish, but that all should come to repentance"* (2 Peter 3:9).

But you say, "Must I not mend my heart and reform my life before I venture to approach him?" If you wait till you have effected this in your own strength, you will, after all, die in your sins. This he must do for you; and this he will effectually do for you, when you come to his cross, confessing your sins, and trusting in his blood as your atonement. You must come to him just as you are, a poor, vile sinner, to be washed in his blood, to be clothed in his righteousness, sanctified by his Spirit, and fitted for his glory. Why do you object to receive what he is so ready to give; and that freely, *"without money and without price"* (Isa. 55:1), even pardon, holiness, and heaven? He professedly receiveth sinners (Luke 15:2), that he may save them; and has solemnly declared, *"him that cometh unto me,"* be the person who or what he may, *"I will in no wise cast out."*

Sermon # 10

"Being justified by faith, we have peace with God, through our Lord Jesus Christ."
Romans 5:1

"There is no peace, saith my God, to the wicked!" (Isaiah 48:22). An unpardoned sinner can have no peace with God. While his conscience is unawakened, he may be careless and secure; but as soon as his eyes are opened, and his heart is made to feel, he must be miserable, till God speaks peace to his guilty soul. To be justified, is to be pardoned and accepted of God. Pardon and acceptance are only obtained by faith in Jesus Christ, as having atoned for sin by his precious blood. When it is given me to believe that Jesus Christ hath taken away my sins, there is nothing more to distress my conscience; then I have peace with God. The distress of an awakened soul arises from a guilty conscience, and a sense of his sins. As soon therefore as the poor trembling sinner discovers, that Christ died for such as he is; that Christ, being God, is able to save the chief of sinners; that this was his errand into the world, and that he hath said, *"Him that cometh to me I will in no wise cast out"* (John 6:37): as soon as the poor sinner believes this, he hath peace with God; he can call God his father; he can trust God for everything; he can think of death with comfort, and rejoice in hope of the glory of God. Sinner, is this your state? Do you know that there is no salvation without an interest in Christ? That there is no peace with God but through Jesus Christ? That unless your sins be pardoned, your life must be unhappy, and your death the entrance of eternal misery? If I am looking unto Jesus as the only Savior, and in self-despair have fled to him for refuge, then God is no longer angry with me; my sins, which are many, are forgiven; my person is accepted; and if I die tonight, I shall go to God. O happy state, to have nothing to fear in life or death! To have God for our Father, Christ for our Redeemer, the Holy Ghost for our Comforter, death our friend, heaven our home, and a happy eternity before us of peace and joy. Sinner, is this thy case?

Sermon # 11

"Unto you which believe He is precious."
1 Peter 2:7

The Apostle is speaking of Jesus Christ, the dear dying friend of poor lost sinners, who pitied us when we had no pity on ourselves; and died for us when otherwise we must have been cast into hell. Now, if you believe this, that your sins would have damned you if Christ had not taken them on himself; and that you must have been cursed forever, if Christ had not been made a curse for you: if you feel in your hearts a humble assurance of pardon purchased by his blood; and if you can consider him as saying to you in the Gospel, what he said to the poor sinful woman, *"Go in peace, thy sins are forgiven"* (Luke 7:48,50); then Christ is precious to you; you love him above all things. You love to think of him, you love to hear of him, you love to talk of him; whatever he has commanded, you desire to do; and what he has forbidden, you will not willingly do, to gain the whole world. You are now become a new creature. You cannot live as you once lived. You are born again. Old things are passed away, and all things are become new (2 Cor. 5:17). The things which you once hated, such as prayer, praise, hearing and reading God's word, you now love; and the things you once loved, such as vain, sinful conversation, and trifling amusements, you now hate. You cannot now go to bed at night without thanking your precious and adorable Jesus for the mercies of the day; nor without committing yourself to his protection for the night, and trusting your soul in his hands, that if you die before morning, he may receive you unto himself: and when you rise in the morning, you cannot go out into the world about your lawful business, without begging him to keep you from the snares of the world and the temptations of Satan. Your one object is to please your beloved Savior, and above all things you fear to offend him. You desire, that *"whether you eat or drink, or whatever you do, you may do all to the glory of God"* (1 Cor. 10:31). *"The love of Christ constrains you"* (2 Cor. 5:14).

Sermon # 12

"Follow holiness, without which no man shall see the Lord."
Hebrews 12:14

God is a holy God: Christ is a holy Savior: the Spirit of God is a holy Spirit: heaven is a holy place: the angels are holy angels: and all God's redeemed people are a holy people. Am I a holy person? If I am not, the Scripture assures me, that I shall not (cannot) see God. Holiness is a separation of heart from sin to God. It is not mere decency of conduct; there may be external morality where there is no holiness, though there can be no holiness without morality. If you are a holy person, you not only abstain from sin, but you really hate it. You hate all sin; whatever is not consistent with the will of God, you hate and abhor. Your abhorrence is turned against yourself on account of your remaining sinfulness. You not only discover sin in your life, but in your heart. If you are a sanctified person, you make conscience not only of your actions and words, but of your thoughts. You not only desire to appear good in the eyes of the world, but to approve yourself to God who searcheth the heart. You seek an inward conformity to the mind and will of God. Is this the case? Remember that it is written, *"Without holiness no man shall see the Lord."* Holiness is, in short, the love of God shed abroad in the heart by the Holy Ghost given unto us. This love becomes the *motive* to all holy obedience; the word of God then becomes the *rule* of the whole conduct; and the glory of God is proposed as the *end* of our conversation. Now no man can enter heaven till he is made holy. Do you believe it? And is it the prayer of your heart, "Lord, sanctify me wholly, soul, body, and spirit" ? (see 1 Thess. 5:23). If it be, the Lord hath begun the good work in your heart, and he will perfect it unto the day of Jesus Christ, that you may be presented holy and unblameable before him in love.

Sermon # 13

"Looking for the blessed hope, and glorious appearing of the great God and our Savior Jesus Christ."
Titus 2:13

This is the happy privilege of the believer in Jesus, to be looking for the second appearance of his Lord. Jesus has promised that he will come again; that he will *"come quickly"* (Rev. 22:20). He has declared that his coming will be sudden, like that of *"a thief in the night"* (1 Thess. 5:2). The believer is a man who is expecting it, waiting for it, and preparing to welcome it. He knows that though *"the Lord Jesus shall be revealed from heaven with his mighty angels in flaming fire, taking vengeance on them that know not God and obey not the Gospel of our Lord Jesus Christ, who shall be punished with everlasting destruction from the presence of the Lord and from the glory of his power;"* yet that another end of his coming is, that he may *"be glorified in his saints and admired in all them that believe"* (2 Thess. 1:8,10). Therefore he looks for that blessed hope. He has peace with God through Jesus Christ. Guilt, the cause of fear, is taken away. He believes that the Judge is his friend, therefore he looks forward with a comfortable expectation. He feels that his present state is not his rest; for though the guilt of sin is taken out of his conscience, and the love and power of it out of his heart; he painfully feels that sin yet dwelleth in him; and therefore longs for the coming of Christ, that he may totally destroy it. The hope he has, is a blessed hope, because the things hoped for are inestimable in value, eternal in duration, and certain to the man who looks for them in faith and hope. *"We that are in this tabernacle,* (of flesh and blood) *do groan, being burdened"* (2 Cor. 5:4), with sin, affliction, and temptation; but at the glorious appearing of our Lord Jesus Christ, *"God shall wipe away all tears from our eyes; and there shall be no more death, neither sorrow, nor crying, neither shall there be any more pain; for the former things are passed away"* (Rev. 21:4).

Sermon # 14

"If ye then, being evil, know how to give good gifts unto your children, how much more shall your heavenly Father give the Holy Spirit to them that ask him."
Luke 11:13

In these words, our gracious Father who is in heaven, permits us to decide an important point by the conviction of our own consciences. He appeals to our feelings as parents, in order to encourage our hope, and enliven our confidence. *"If a son asks bread of any of you that is a father, will he give him a stone?"* (Luke 11:11). If a hungry child come to a father, saying, "Father, I am starving for want, give me bread to eat;" would the father (unless he were worse than a brute) give his child a stone, to mock him? *"Or if he ask a fish, will he give him a serpent? Or if he ask an egg, will he give him a scorpion,"* to destroy him? Certainly not. *"How much more then shall your heavenly Father,"* whose affection for his poor sinful children is so infinitely superior to yours for the offspring of your bodies, *"give the Holy Spirit to them that ask him"*?

I am a poor, ignorant sinner. I want to know myself as a sinner before God, and as exposed to his just indignation. I want to know Jesus Christ as a Savior to my poor soul; for to know him is life eternal. But this saving knowledge I can only derive from divine teaching. God has promised his Holy Spirit, to lead the poor ignorant sinner, that feels his ignorance (for that is the point), into all truth necessary for his comfort and salvation. "O Lord, let thy Holy Spirit be my teacher."

I am a poor, *helpless* sinner. I find I have no power to believe on the Son of God. Yet faith in him is essential to salvation. My conscience is distressed on account of my sins. I want to *"know him and the power of his resurrection"* (Phil. 3:10). But I can no more believe, by any mere exertion of my own powers, than I can make a world. God has promised his Holy Spirit, to create faith in the heart of every humble suppliant. "O Lord, help me to believe, to the peace of my conscience, the joy of my heart, the sanctification of my nature, the salvation of my soul, and the eternal glory of thy name."

God giveth his Holy Spirit to them that ask him. We can do no good, we can do nothing but sin, and so destroy ourselves, without his special assistance. Do *you* feel you want it? And do want and absolute necessity drive *you* to a throne of grace for this comprehensive blessing? Do you ask as a hungry child asks his father for bread? Are you sensible of your ignorance, so as earnestly to seek his divine teaching; and of your helpless state, so as to ask help of God? *"Ask, and ye shall receive; seek, and ye shall find; knock, and it shall be opened unto you"* (Matt. 7:7). Consider, God cannot break his word. If you have asked without receiving, it is because you did not ask in earnest. You do not feel your want. Ask of God to give you to feel your wants, and then he will supply them; ask him to teach you to pray. Come to him as a poor, ignorant, helpless child, for *"except ye be converted and become as little children, ye cannot enter into the kingdom of heaven"* (Matt. 18:3). "Lord, give unto us this childlike spirit."

Sermon # 15

"It is appointed unto men once to die,
and after this the judgment."
Hebrews 9:27

You and I are dying creatures. We have seen many of our friends and relatives laid in the grave; many as young as ourselves, and apparently as likely to live. Some we have seen carried off by long and lingering diseases, and some cut down suddenly without warning. God only knows when we are to follow them into the eternal world. *"We know not the day of our death"* (Gen. 27:2). *"Our times are in God's hand"* (Ps. 31:15). It may be tonight. We are certain the moment of death must come. We are certain it can be at no great distance; but we know not how near. Now if these things are true, what madness it is to put off the necessary work of repentance to a future day! We are not certain of seeing tomorrow; and as repentance is *"the gift of God,"* if we neglect to ask for it today, and refuse to hear his warning voice, he may say to us, *"Because I have called, and ye refused; I have stretched out my hand, and no man regarded; but ye have set at nought all my counsel, and would none of my reproof; I also will laugh at your calamity, I will mock when your fear cometh. When your fear cometh as desolation, and your destruction cometh as a whirlwind; when distress and anguish come upon you, then shall they call upon me, but I will not answer; they shall seek me early, but they shall not find me: for that they hated knowledge, and did not choose the fear of the Lord"* (Proverbs 1:24-29).

After death comes the judgment. We must all stand before the judgment seat of Christ, to give account of the things done in the body, whether they be good or bad (2 Cor. 5:10). *Who* must appear there? All, young and old, rich and poor, without distinction or exception. You and I must meet there. But for what purpose? To give an account of what? Of all our secret thoughts, known only to ourselves; of all our secret actions, which no eye saw but the all-seeing eye of the omniscient Judge. He keeps a book of remembrance in which every evil thought, word and work is registered; every one of which will be then brought forth to our eternal confusion, *unless* they are washed away in the precious blood of the Lord Jesus Christ. We read (in Rev. 6:16) that some, in that day, will call to the rocks and the mountains, *"Fall on us and hide us from the face of him that sitteth on the throne, and from the wrath of the Lamb."* God grant it may not be your case, or mine. But in order to avoid this dreadful state, we must *"seek the Lord while he may be found, and call upon him while he is near; the wicked must forsake his way, and the unrighteous man his thoughts, and return unto the Lord, and he will have mercy upon him, and to our God, and he will abundantly pardon"* (Isa. 55:6,7).

This is the day of grace. But it will be too late to seek for mercy when the day of judgment comes. If you die without an interest in Christ, it had been good for you if you had never been born (Mark 14:21); for it would be better to have had no existence at all, than have a miserable existence in hell forever. This must be the portion of every unpardoned, unconverted sinner. God hath said it, who cannot lie.

Sermon # 16

"How shall we escape, if we neglect so great salvation?"
Hebrews 2:3

A salvation great indeed, beyond description, or conception, contrived by the wisdom and love of God for my poor lost soul! A salvation, procured by the death of the only begotten Son of God. How near was I to the brink of hell! How deeply was I fallen! How many and great my sins, to make such a salvation necessary! How dangerous must it be to neglect it! God has no other Son to give. If you are unconcerned about it; if you take no pains to secure it; if you are unaffected with your danger and with the salvation that is proposed to you; *how can you escape?* It is impossible. You reject the only Savior, and therefore commit the greatest sin: you spurn at God's free mercy in Christ. Are you not shocked at such a thought? Be assured that every careless sinner is guilty of this. There is no relief provided for those who finally reject Christ. *"There remaineth no more sacrifice for sin"* (Heb. 10:26). Their ruin is certain, is near, and will be eternal and intolerable. Remember, this is the accepted time, and this is the day of salvation (2 Cor. 6:2). If you die without Christ, you can never see the face of God with comfort. You must hear the Judge pronounce your sentence, *"Depart, ye cursed, into everlasting fire, prepared for the devil and his angels"* (Matt. 25:41). God forbid!

Once more I entreat you, my fellow sinner, before you close the book, stop and think. Nay, go upon your knees, and pray to God to awaken your conscience, and give you the knowledge of Christ. My poor prayers are offered for your salvation. I have no motive in putting this into your hands, but your eternal good. I close with this prayer:

"O God, may this little book be productive of good to the reader's soul, in time and eternity. Follow it with thy blessing, and may the precious truths, therein set forth, be *'the savor of life unto life'* and not *'of death unto death'* (2 Cor. 2:16). Grant it, O Lord, for Jesus Christ's sake. Amen."

Other Ichabod Spencer Titles

In addition to *A Pastor's Sketches* which you now hold in your hand, Solid Ground Christian Books is honored to be able to present the only other three volumes from the pen and heart of Ichabod Spencer:

The Bunyan of Brooklyn: Volume One – *The Life and Practical Sermons of Ichabod Spencer.*

This volume includes a Biographical Sketch of the man known as *The Bunyan of Brooklyn* by his dear friend Rev. J.M. Sherwood, and 20 complete sermons on Practical Subjects such as, *A Devotional Spirit, Sorrow for the Death of Friends, Reasons for Afflictions, Enduring Temptations, Contentment* and many more.

The Bunyan of Brooklyn: Volume Two – *The Doctrinal Sermons of Ichabod Spencer.*

This volume contains 25 complete sermons on Doctrinal Topics such as *The Magnificence of God, On Knowing God, Wisdom of God in Mystery, Election, Atonement, The Mercy of God, Forgiveness, The Depths of Salvation, The Lamb Slain Worshipped in Heaven, Sketch of the Plan of Salvation* and many more.

The Bunyan of Brooklyn: Volume Three – *The Sacramental Sermons of Ichabod Spencer.*

This final volume contains 26 complete sermons that were preached in preparation for partaking of the Lord's Supper. In the words of his close friend Gardiner Spring, *"The old Christian and the young Christian, as well as those who seek the best preparatives for coming to the Table of their Divine Lord for the first time, will be instructed and comforted by these Sacramental Discourses. With such a volume in their hands, they will be furnished with more than the rudiments of Christianity."* Among these sermons are the following: *Christ Precious to Believers, Why Hast Thou Forsaken Me?, Why Weepest Thou?, Christ Our Passover, Behold the Lamb of God!, He Loved Them to the End, Christ Made Perfect by Suffering, Jesus Christ's Parting Address, Faith Without Sight* and many more.

NEW "BURNING ISSUES" SERIES

Solid Ground has always been known for our *"uncovering buried treasure"* from the past and bringing them back before the church and the world. We are now introducing a new series of titles addressing the *Burning Issues* of our day from the hearts of those on fire for the Lord. Our first three titles are as follows:

YEARNING TO BREATHE FREE? ***Thoughts on Immigration, Islam & Freedom*** by David Dykstra

"I have read David Dykstra's book with great interest. His description of the real nature of jihad and its continuing power today is valuable. What he has written is especially important since so many on the upper levels of government continue to claim that Islam is fundamentally a peaceful religion; it is not. Dykstra has made that very clear. I do hope that Dykstra's book is well accepted. Its main message is sorely needed." - Dr. Joel Nederhood

"The kind face of Islam has not fooled David Dykstra about its true nature, and he writes with a passion that would not leave us fooled either. He is not afraid to take on difficult issues currently before our nation and to come to conclusions that are not politically correct. Drawing from Scripture, history, and an obvious love for his country, Dykstra presents his case in a compelling way." – Jon Hueni
Now available!

PULPIT CRIMES: ***The Criminal Mishandling of God's Word*** by James White

James White of Alpha-Omega Ministries is writing what may be his most provocative book yet. White sets out to examine numerous "crimes" being committed in pulpits throughout the land every week, as he seeks to leave no stone unturned. Based firmly upon the bedrock of Holy Scripture, one "crime" after another is laid bare for all to see. In his own words: "The pulpit is to be a place where God speaks from His Word: what has happened to this sacred duty in our day? Let pulpit crimes be exposed by the light of God's Word."
Due November 2006.

TWO MEN FROM MALTA by Joel Nederhood & Joe Serge

One of the men is the Apostle Paul, the other is Joe Serge, a Toronto newspaperman and columnist. In this book Serge describes his odyssey from Roman Catholicism to the faith of the Reformation. Serge invited Joel Nederhood, a theologian and long time radio and television teacher, to join him in examining primary Roman teaching such as "the Mass," "Mary," "the Papacy," and the essence of salvation itself. This is a warm invitation to Roman Catholics to examine their faith. Due Fall 2006.

SGCB Titles for the Young

Truth Made Simple by John Todd is sub-titled *Lectures to Children on the Attributes of God.* His opening *Address to Mothers* is worth the price the book. Todd taught Richard Newton how to teach children.

Feed My Lambs: *Lectures to Children* by John Todd is drawn from actual sermons preached in Philadelphia, PA and Pittsfield, MA to the children of the church, one Sunday each month. A pure gold-mine of instruction.

The College Days of Calvin by William M. Blackburn is the prequel to *Young Calvin in Paris.* It will open the eyes of anyone who takes time to read about the brilliant student who served Christ in College.

Bible Promises: *Sermons for Children on God's Word as our Solid Rock* by Richard Newton. As with all his books light and heat are on every page.

The Child's Book on the Fall by Thomas H. Gallaudet is a simple and practical exposition of the Fall of man into sin, and his only hope of salvation.

Repentance & Faith: *Explained and Illustrated for the Young* by Charles Walker, is a two in one book introducing children to the difference between true and false faith and repentance.

The Child at Home by John S.C. Abbott is the sequel to his popular book *The Mother at Home.* A must read for children and their parents.

My Brother's Keeper: *Letters to a Younger Brother* by J.W. Alexander contains the actual letters Alexander sent to his ten year old brother.

The Scripture Guide by J.W. Alexander is filled with page after page of information on getting the most from our Bibles. Invaluable

Heroes of the Reformation by Richard Newton is a unique volume that introduces children and young people to the leading figures and incidents of the Reformation. Spurgeon called him, *"The Prince of preachers to the young."*

Heroes of the Early Church by Richard Newton is the sequel to the above-named volume. The very last book Newton wrote introduces all the leading figures of the early church with lessons to be learned from each figure.

The King's Highway: *Ten Commandments to the Young* by Richard Newton is a volume of Newton's sermons to children. Highly recommended!

The Life of Jesus Christ for the Young by Richard Newton is a double volume set that traces the Gospel from Genesis 3:15 to the Ascension of our Lord and the outpouring of His Spirit on the Day of Pentecost. Excellent!

The Young Lady's Guide by Harvey Newcomb will speak directly to the heart of the young women who desire to serve Christ with all their being.

The Chief End of Man by John Hall is an exposition and application of the first question of the Westminster Shorter Catechism. Full of rich illustrations.

Printed in the United States
109204LV00002B/181-183/A